"I heartily recommend *Facebuddha*, a wonderfully written, exciting and at times elegiac and rhapsodic presentation of the potentials and difficulties of connecting in relationship – especially in our modern age of technology and as seen through a Buddhist lens. Ravi Chandra is a wonderful storyteller, a psychiatrist, a Buddhist student and teacher, an Asian American, and an able, eloquent writer with the capacity and personal experience to address all the contemporary issues this book brings together. I think *Facebuddha* will be inspiring to many, many people."

Sylvia Boorstein, Ph.D., Buddhist teacher and author
Co-founder Spirit Rock Meditation Center

"*Facebuddha* is both personal journey and social commentary, a good-hearted meander across cultural, artistic and occupational worlds that explores a deep concern for our modern dilemmas with the perspective of a devoted Buddhist."

Jack Kornfield, Ph.D., Buddhist teacher and author
Co-founder Spirit Rock Meditation Center

"*Facebuddha* is magnificent, a breathtakingly personal work that combines memoir, media commentary, Buddhist practicum and depth psychology. Like Martin Luther's theses, these chapters are nailed on the door of the Cathedral of Technology asking us to look beyond our screens by way of reforming contemporary indulgences. As we do so our world moves beneath the surface sheen and towards the interior. Ravi Chandra's effervescent prose locates compassion, in his own soul and in the soul of humanity, in real world relationships endangered by modernity."

F.B. Steele, M.D., psychiatrist and teacher
Former Executive Director, C.G. Jung Institute of San Francisco

"*Facebuddha* mourns the loss of meaningful human connections in the age of social networks and raises the alarm about how apps and devices are changing our social lives and our inner selves. The book is an exhortation to cultivate genuine love, kindness, and compassion, imperiled by a rapidly changing and anxiety-ridden world."

Deann Borshay Liem, documentary filmmaker

"Ravi Chandra has been CAAM's thoughtful and dedicated Superfan for many years. His essays about our film festival combine spiritual and psychological insights with infectious wit and profound social concern. I hope many more people discover his writing through *Facebuddha*, which is ultimately an invitation to depth and personal growth."

Stephen Gong, Executive Director, Center for Asian American Media

"Ravi Chandra's voice as an Asian American psychiatrist in San Francisco grounded in Buddhist practice and the study of Carl Jung fascinated me as he explores in this book how social networks affect our cultivation of compassion and humanity. Thought-provoking, engagingly written, and enriched by memoir and haiku-like stories and vignettes, this book deepens our understanding of our relationship with this new technology and is an inspiration for our own human development. Bravo!"

Francis Lu, MD, Luke & Grace Kim Professor in Cultural Psychiatry, Emeritus, University of California Davis

"Ravi Chandra portrays the importance of truly relating to people, something that so many of us have lost in a world saturated by social media. As he travels to Asia, he connects with history, his own past and with the hearts of those he meets. *Facebuddha* is poetic and poignant and a reminder that the most important landscape is the one where people talk face to face."

Louise Nayer, author, Burned: A Memoir

To Facebook or not to Facebook: that is the 21st century question:

"Whether tis' nobler in the mind to suffer
The slings and arrows of outrageous fortune
Or to bear arms against a sea of troubles
And, by opposing, end them?"

In reading Ravi Chandra's *Facebuddha: Transcendence in the Age of Social Networks*, we're led to think about how we juggle the virtual identity(ies) we have out there in social media, and how we struggle with our human identity in dealing not only with others, but also with our multiple consciousnesses on social networks. We kinda sorta get turned on by all the friend requests, likes, retweets, views, etc.; we yearn for connection as we make "friends"; and we thrill when we are "liked", which we equate to being "loved". This will make us happy. Or so we think.

A psychiatrist and a Buddhist teacher/student, Ravi Chandra allows us to peer into his own self-examination in the social media world. He takes us on his very personal, often funny, warmly intelligent, thoughtful and heartfelt journey (filled with nerdy/cool pop-culture fan stories!) navigating "there and back again" to lovingkindness in an age where we all are searching for relationship, for 'real'ationship with others, and especially, our self, our true self.

Like a pensive Hamlet, Ravi presents observations and experiences of our lives on and off social networks. He bears witness that to find the answer to the question the Shakespearean prince asks of all of us (there is no "I", "me", or "my" in the soliloquy!), we just might have to go through the act (on Facebook) that Hamlet contemplates in this most famous speech. Consciousness of death "does make cowards of us all," but the death of our online profiles could lead us to life. Be courageous, says Ravi. He assures us, with his heart, his mind, and his emotions that we just might find our way back around and beyond through it all. To transcendence.

Tamlyn Tomita, actor

Facebuddha

Transcendence in the Age of Social Networks

RAVI CHANDRA, M.D.

Pacific Heart Books
San Francisco, California

Facebuddha: Transcendence in the Age of Social Networks
Pacific Heart Books
San Francisco, CA
www.facebuddha.co

ISBN: 978-0-9909339-2-2 (Hardcover Edition)
ISBN: 978-0-9909339-3-9 (eBook Edition)

Library of Congress Control Number: 2017909657

Jacket design by Việt Lê
Cover image "Hollywood Buddha" courtesy of the artist, Tenzing Rigdol
Author photo by Bob Hsiang
Composed with Scrivener

Poems and lyrics quoted:

Basho, Matsuo. *Narrow Road to the Interior and Other Writings*. Trans. Sam Hamill. Boston: Shambala Publications, 1998. p. 3. Courtesy of the publisher.

Shantideva. *A Guide to the Bodhisattva's Way of Life*. Trans. Stephen Batchelor. Dharamsala: Library of Tibetan Works and Archives, 1979. Patience, verse 107. Courtesy of the publisher.

Phi, Bao. *Sông I Sing*. Minneapolis: Coffee House Press, 2011. p. 16, excerpt from The Nguyens. Courtesy of Bao Phi.

Some elements of this manuscript have appeared online on Ravi Chandra's Pacific Heart blog on PsychologyToday.com and in *Asian American Anger: It's a Thing!* San Francisco: Pacific Heart Books, 2014, including a version of "The Social Network is an IndigNation."

To my mother:
Your love, strength, wisdom,
acceptance and friendliness
have guided me, all these years.
I am humbled by all that you are.

To young souls, old souls, and souls middling-in-age:
I wrote this with you in mind,
because life is difficult.
May love and hope guide you.

To my work-in-progress Self:
May you be filled with lovingkindness,
May you be well.
May you be peaceful and at ease,
May you be happy.

The moon and sun are eternal travelers. Even the years wander on. Adrift in a boat, or in old age leading a tired horse into the years, every day is a journey, and the journey itself is home.

Matsuo Basho
Narrow Road to the Interior

Contents

Introduction

We are deep in the throes of amped-up relational intensity through social media and an ever-shrinking world. We are all profoundly affected by our new connectedness. We project our opinions, insights and worldviews, and these invariably become areas of resonance and conflict. Social media have become a kind of secondary limbic system, an auxiliary amygdala: quick to respond, vast in influence, and yet lacking the healing, empathic power that only real relationships can offer.* Social media may challenge our actual amygdalae, it may inform and inflame our synapses, but our higher brains need more to fully ripen. Social networks create new forms of suffering that call out for wisdom and connection. The social network cannot be an auxiliary cortex, though it might inform and entertain us. The culture and our mental and relational topography are transforming, and people all over the world are fascinated and overwhelmed by the metamorphosis and desperate for ways to cope. Each of us, just like the Buddha in his day, is born in a time of social, economic, political and psychological challenges. He had the wilderness to wander before coming to enlightenment. We have Facebook. We need, therefore, Facebuddha.

30% of U.S. teens and adults seem uninterested in creating Facebook accounts, and a substantial number of the 72% of adults who do use the site are likely ambivalent, reluctantly putting up with aspects of

---

* The amygdalae, deep within each temporal lobe, are part of the limbic system, which senses threat and triggers the survival brain's fight-or-flight response. It is also responsible for emotional memory, processing social cues, and attention. The limbic system knows how to hold a grudge, shall we say, and is very sensitive to social connection.

social media they don't like to get what they do. I believe that this group comprises a considerable band of seekers who are looking for something more. Relationship grounded in the real world. Conversation. Community. Resolution of our political polarization. Inner peace. And ultimately, I would say, transcendence itself. In a world where we are increasingly connected and aware of our connections, we are tasked to develop perspectives about our interdependence, and moved to generate a deeper compassion capable of holding our diversity and potential, and thus heal our suffering. The opposite of suffering is belonging, and belonging ultimately involves transcending the self: both the problems of the ego and the defensive, self-centered ideologies, attitudes and actions that stand in the way of dialogue, unity and peace. This book proposes to be a means to that end.

Facebook has become deeply ingrained in our lives, surfacing the problem of belonging without solving it. With 1.8 billion users as of 2017, this "most populous country on Earth" presents a fascinating topic that won't just go away. We are insatiably curious about how this newly emerged nation affects us, its citizens and dissidents. Are we to learn how to use it effectively – or is it using and abusing us? Are we on Facebook or is Facebook on us? What exactly is it doing to our minds and hearts, and what do we do about it? What should we aim for? This is a subject of constant ferment in the culture, reflected in many popular articles in major magazines and newspapers, and in conversation after conversation with everyone from teenagers to the elderly. Courses are being taught everywhere from secondary and high schools to colleges and graduate school about navigating social media and understanding its implications for our psychological well being. Despite all those articles, conversations, and courses there is no consensus on the subject, and no defining, widely read book that delivers knowledge and wisdom about Facebook and social networking in a compelling, readable way. Our path to the future – with, without or through Facebook – will best be informed by hard-won insights about relationship and "Love in the Time of Cyberia."

In 2012, I hit a breaking point. I felt, on the one hand, completely enamored of Facebook and immersed in my online experience. I reveled in the way Facebook helped my own Asian American community find a voice, most noticeably around the season of Linsanity in February 2012, but also in the way it helped my writing spread virally through the web. On the other hand, I was extremely dissatisfied with it as well, noticing I spent a lot of time on it and yet emerged unhappy and even disoriented. I had Facebivalence. Facebook was a huge intrusion on my life, and a welcome companion at the same time. Nearly every conversation I had touched on Facebook in some way. I needed to understand its appeal and come to terms with it. I had to grapple with the intruder, and wrest back control. I had an extensive discussion with one of my patients about the annoying comment thread on one of his political posts. I smiled and said, "on Facebook, you need to be Facebuddha." He laughed. "Did you just make that up?"

Actually, I hadn't. I'd been thinking of writing a series of "Facebuddha" posts for my expert blog on *Psychology Today* filled with advice about how to interact on the site. But that project stalled as I realized that most people naturally developed wisdom about the everyday mechanics of using Facebook. Such a simple how-to post would not be very interesting to me, nor did I think it would be compelling to the reading public.

As a psychiatrist, I wanted to make clear what psychologists were discovering about Facebook and social media more generally, so I could better help people navigate the new terrain. And my experience in Buddhism had taught me that the Buddhist lens was invaluable in understanding what happened to the mind and heart as they encountered various stimuli, including Facebook. So the idea for *Facebuddha: Transcendence in the Age of Social Networks* was born. I wanted to explore our addictive, deceptively breezy-and-easy new online environment, and contrast it with the difficult (but necessary and rewarding) relationships of the real world, relationships I specialized in as a psychiatrist and humanist. *Facebuddha* would bring together psychological research, an introduction to Buddhism, a compelling narrative memoir of family, professional and personal relationships, and my unique psychiatric perspective to create an experience of deep engagement with the defining questions of the day:

- What are social networks doing to us, and what are their benefits and dangers?
- Do social networks help or hinder the goal of being more compassionate, connected, and understanding?
- How do we cultivate our humanity and reach for transcendence under the siege of technology? (For me, this answer could be found in Buddhist and relational practices.)

Furthermore, I hoped to be a strong advocate for relationships in the real world through writing that was captivating, urgent, and evocative. I aimed to portray my own relational journey, from infatuation with online relationships, to dissatisfaction, and ultimately to a renewal of relationships in the real world, delivering a vision for social connection that could help us manage our current era of great promise and conflict.

Facebook and other social networks are curios for the exploration of self and identity. Reflecting on our personal and cultural experiences with social media can add to our awareness of human challenges, needs, desires and potentials. What we each choose to do with our awareness is an individual decision. Living consciously in the modern world requires sustained effort; there are many squalls to push our sails off course. I hope this book provides a steady alternative breeze.

Facebuddha is part memoir, part personal analysis of social media, part exploration and consolidation of psychological research done by others, and part introduction to Buddhism. It is presented as a linear tale in time, but some will find the various threads episodic and difficult to follow. If you find yourself bored, just flip to the next chapters until you find the thread you need. Some readers will want to skip parts or all of the chapters dealing with CAAMFest ("Online to Ecstasy") and the doctor-patient-bureaucracy relationship ("An Elegy for Doctorbot;

or The Big Short Circuit"). I think the book as a whole says something about the non-linear, bricolage self, made of interdependent components, sometimes only loosely connected. Narrative emerges as we pay attention to our lives with intention, remaining agreeable, open and conscientious.

Synchronistically, as I prepared my manuscript for publication, I had powerful meditative and spiritual experiences which brought the wisdom of the Buddha closer to home. So my journey through Facebook and the world turn out to be just the beginning of yet another journey. I humbly offer you all these experiences in hopes that they will be helpful to you on your own journey in life.

Ravi Chandra, M.D.
July, 2017
San Francisco, California

Foreword:

The Blowing Wind Is a Scalding, Hot Air

The Zen Master texted his student. "What is the sound of one man chatting?"

There was no reply. The teacher nodded his head in approval. "He's making progress."

It turned out however, that silence wasn't the intended reply. His student was submerged in his Facebook newsfeed at the time.

When he finally got the message, he decided to write this book, a lengthy response to the challenge of his Master's koan.

Facebuddha.

We were sailing into uncharted, but alluring, waters. The sirens sang to us, seeking our attention. Technology had transformed the way we communicate, live and learn. We had an insatiable lust for bright, new, shiny things, and an increasingly high-tech future seemed inevitable and desirable, each day bringing promise of reaching some dazzling pinnacle of human history, or even post-human history. History, we were told, would culminate in a totality, a completion. They called it "the singularity," the point at which technology outstripped human capabilities and took over from lowly, fleshy, fragile mortals. This was gospel amongst the digital illuminati, the technorati, the digerati, and they preached it with verve and with their captivating products.

You didn't have to look far to find wide-eyed proclamations of the grandeurs that awaited, made possible by gadgets, apps, and of course, the Social Network. A Portuguese man I met at an outdoor cafe on a sunny summer day in San Francisco proclaimed "Silicon Valley is the wind blowing the sails of the world!" The Portuguese love their sailing metaphors, of course. It was hard to argue with him. Apple, Google and Facebook were renowned, world-leading brands, and Apple had recently been named the most valuable company in the world, eclipsing automakers and the other industries that employed several orders of magnitude more people, yet whose household names belonged to a clunky, outmoded past. Silicon Valley products, most of them actually made in China, with often questionable human and environmental impact, were ubiquitous throughout the developed world, and high-tech companies eagerly sought inroads to the developing world as well. Or as they called them, developing markets. Apparatuses and apps would change the world. They would change politics. They would change us.

But would this be for the better? Fewer people took on this question. It seemed easier to simply lie down before our conquering tech gods, or even say that their technology was serving only to democratize the world and empower individuals.

Twitter co-founder Biz Stone rhapsodized on Charlie Rose that Twitter would enable us to accelerate the reshaping of the world. What would have taken 100 years would only take 5. A relief for Asimov's Foundation scientists, to be sure. "Humanity will be like a flock of birds, all turning together..." We would become nodes in a common neural net (a harbinger of his new mysterious venture, Jelly, perhaps), all quivering to each other's web-emanations. Our better angels would just naturally take flight on the wings of the Twitter bird. Surely we wouldn't be a mob. We just needed a Desmond Tweetu, a Matweetma Gandhi. If only Dr. King had Twitter. He could have tweet-shamed the South into desegregation. Freedom Summer could have been Facebook Summer, far more efficient and groundbreaking. But now, utopia was just a few tweets away. Tweetopia. Or was this a twuckload? Didn't consciousness require more than the flow of information? Didn't it require real relationship, real presence *in vivo* and *in situ*? Didn't it require real, hard-going-but-rewarding love?

Facebook founder Mark Zuckerberg aimed to bring poor countries into the wired world with internet.org. Critics scoffed that this seemed at least a tad self-interested. Access to the internet meant access to his social network, and access to Facebook meant more ad revenue. The Silicon Valley and Supercapitalist view was that all relationships had to be monetized, after all. (And monetization of human relationships is the first step in the process of turning humans into batteries in the Facetrix, of course.) Was this the accelerated change we wanted, a consumerist cyberdawn, consisting of more of the same, but faster? The few getting rich, while the majority getting used, encouraged even to make utilities of each other, to relate to each other more as things, and less as people? Was this democratization, or concentration of power and wealth, and a loss of privacy to boot?

The utopian dreams of the Social Networks require that their new form of connection is not only desirable, but good, and has some emergent properties which will move us all unstoppably into shimmering, silver, metallic perfection. I, for one, have my doubts. It is a seductive concept, silicon accelerating our union – but no remedy is without side effects, and the side effects are substantial. We must carefully observe what happens to our minds and hearts as we *like* and *ping* and *update*. We must know ourselves, an objective that seems more and more against the stream in a culture that wants to turn us simply into consumers and friends in screen-face only. We know how to use the "Find my iPhone" app. But we really need to "Find my I." Who am I? Where am I? Who do I become when I am in relationship to social networks and devices? Who can I become in deeper relationship to others, and indeed, myself? I think we will find that the Ubuntu proverb "people become people through other people" is indeed wisdom for the ages, and specifically, wisdom for our age. The consciousness of a people depends on their relationship to one another. This consciousness can elevate the Social Network, not the other way around.

Does the Social Network enhance or degrade the relationships of the people? This is a difficult question, and one could cite examples in either direction. Social networks can indeed encourage people to vote, for example. They can also polarize and compartmentalize groups that might change if they would only interact with each other in real life. At the very least, they might see each other as human beings, and not as enemies on a screen. And technology, as virtual-reality-pioneer-cum-philosopher Jaron Lanier has noted, has tended to enthrone a few in wealth and power while impoverishing many, surely a debasement of relationship.

But perhaps it is impossible to speak of the "consciousness of the people" at all. We must speak of individual consciousness, and ask what happens to it under the impact of the Social Network. We must "Find my I." The answers will vary from person to person. This book is, then, a memoir of exploration, of happy engagement and ultimate dissatisfaction with the guiding myth of the Age of Social Networks: that technology is an unalloyed and assured enhancement of human relationship and possibility. As a psychiatrist, I am deeply interested in these. For me, personally, the tools and practices of Buddhist philosophy have been and continue to be particularly helpful in understanding and cultivating the possibilities of relationship, mind and heart. *Facebuddha* is a document of how we fail each other, and a passionate call to fight against failure, in friendship, family, and even in the doctor-patient relationship. Ultimately, we all have the face of Buddha. But to become Buddha, in body, speech, mind and heart, requires deep knowledge of and connection with oneself and others. It requires, as Venerable Thich Nhat Hanh says, interbeing. Interbeing requires awareness of one's vulnerability, and awareness of one's vulnerability and connectedness to all other vulnerable beings is the beginning of kindness and compassion for all those with whom we share the Earth. Can Facebook, or any other social network, help bring us to this state? It's a question that must be asked.

Join me, as I travel worlds, real and virtual, from San Francisco to Hanoi to India and back, with Facebook as my companion, confidante, object of inquiry and burden. Along the way, ask yourself these Zen riddles:

What was your face before your grandparents were born?
What was your face before Mark Zuckerberg was born?
What was your face before Facebook?

In the end, I think you'll find that a three-rupee Buddha, white porcelain figure seated on a humble, cluttered altar, means more than a newsfeed, more than a shiny smartphone, more than luxury goods bought on the future's, and the planet's, credit.

We are woozy with SMF – Social Media Fatigue. It's time we meet each other in the World Wide World.

Hanoi Rooftop

Hanoi. A hot summer night, June, 2007. I am almost at the exact halfway point of my five-month pilgrimage across Asia, tracing the paths of Buddhism, war and peace from India to Japan. I celebrated Buddha's Enlightenment in Bodhgaya, learned about civil wars in Nepal and Sri Lanka, said prayers for peace and democracy in Burma, marked my 40th birthday at a monastery in Thailand, bore witness to the dead in Cambodia, and now am visiting my friend, the Vietnamese American writer and journalist Nguyen Qui Duc, in Hanoi, nearly 40 years after the middle of the war which forced his family to leave Vietnam and take refuge in the United States. He recently returned here with his mother, in hopes of providing better care for her as she ages with Alzheimer's disease. Moving here was an act of extraordinary filial piety; he left home, work and friends in San Francisco to do this. I admire his devotion to his mother, his embodiment of Confucian virtue. It seems like self-denial, but he might say it is fulfillment. His family has been uprooted by war and migrations. He has what my friend, poet Bao Phi, calls a "refugeography." This return is an exercise in completing, or at least continuing, the circle of relationships – to mother, birth country, and perhaps, in time, to his own heart, which bears both loss and hope. Perhaps it is a move towards redemption, renewal and wholeness, not just for himself but for all the people he represents and to whom he is connected. I'm at the middle of my own journeys, across Asia and in life. The movement of the heart, transcending nations and boundaries, appeals to me. I savor this time with him, a dear friend in an unfamiliar land, which he makes familiar to me.

Duc seems to live at the fulcrum of expatriate and artist communities in Hanoi. Tonight, we are going to an expat friend's birthday party. Her apartment is on the top floor, and opens onto a rooftop, where we sit and mingle with expats from around the world, all of them looking for opportunity, adventure or a kind of asylum in Vietnam, far from their native homes. Wine flows, and conversations and laughter echo into a warm, dark night under the stars.

A beautiful young woman, Yasue, introduces herself as she sits down next to me. Soon, we're immersed in each other's stories. She's Japanese, but grew up in England, and could easily be a Japanese Kate Middleton, complete with British accent. Now she calls Vietnam her home-for-now. Yasue tells me of family and relationships, past and present. They've been a challenge, to say the least, especially a boyfriend or two. Her loves have been passionate, intense, and even dangerous, taking her to extraordinary vulnerability, where she'd shown her strength, faced down the threat of violence, and transformed the ones who threatened her. The coin of this queen's realm was coolness under fire. Keep Calm and Relate On. Relationships were messy, but they could be revolutionary. As she discloses difficulties and traumas, my heart opens for her. It seems to be just the two of us here, our friends forgotten in a moonlight spell. It doesn't seem that we've met for the first time, but that we're reunited after lifetimes apart. But even if we didn't know each other before, from some enchanted past life, we're new best friends now, on this Hanoi rooftop, with the stars aligned above us.

After a few hours of listening and sharing, I have to leave. Duc gathers me, shooting me a look of bewilderment and perhaps a twinge of jealousy as he mentally compares our evenings. He seems to think I got a bigger slice of the pie tonight. But he has many Hanoi rooftops ahead of him; this is my first, and possibly last.

Yasue calls out to me as I leave.

"Are you on Facebook?" she asks.

"What's that?" I ask in return.

She says she'll send me an invitation for this Facebook thing, whatever it is.

Tripping the Lin Facetastic

2012. Five years after my fantastic, life-changing voyage across Asia, tracing the route of Buddhism across the continent, facing the history of war and peace, trying to voyage to peace myself. Five years later, and the calendar is an echo of 2007 – the days and dates match 2007 precisely, as if to say "remember." "Renew your commitment to the journey. Complete it." The days have cycled and recycled, spiraling outwards in semi-parallel orbit, in fugue from some forgotten origin or its alternative, beginningless time; spiraling in search of resolution, cessation, and transformation. The journey is unended, and there is only open road ahead; the steps I choose and the steps chosen by the world.

Even the news seems an echo of the past. Myanmar and Daw Aung San Suu Kyi are making tentatively positive headlines this time, as their country takes some promising steps towards democracy. Barack Obama is now President, in actual fulfillment of 2007's dream, about to run for his second term. The war in Iraq has officially ended, but the violence continues, and the war in Afghanistan wrenches gloomily on. Iran and North Korea's nuclear ambitions, strife in the Middle East, starvation in Africa, climate change – are themes as continuous as the Earth's rotation. New themes have emerged, most prominently the state of the national and global economy, but even this is a continuation of questions about relationship: how can humanity get along and get by in this time of limited resources, great need, and disparities of income and opportunity? The clock is ticking, but the hands move in a circle. It always seems like a few minutes to midnight, to me – with both the hope of a new day and the melancholic feeling that our day is ending.

Early in the year, something new happens. It's "only" sports, but it shifts the orbit of millions. Jeremy Lin bursts onto the scene, as unexpected as a visit from an extraterrestrial ambassador. Maybe he is one. Now, I'm not much of a sports fan. I hardly ever watch a basketball game or any other sporting event. But this brings me out of my chair. He's electrifying – and he's Asian American. Heads are turning. Fans in New York go wild, and then the whole nation. An Asian American man is making waves in basketball – that just wasn't supposed to happen. Although there have been Asian Americans in basketball before (Japanese American Wat Misaka was the first person of color on any major team in 1947, also for the Knicks; Filipino American Raymond Townsend and Japanese American Rex Walters each played many seasons in the NBA in the 70s and 90s respectively; Yao Ming was a sensation, but some would consider him Chinese or a Chinese immigrant, and not strictly speaking a Chinese American), none has made this kind of impact on the game, or on the consciousness of Asian America and indeed, all America. Lin has a seven game winning streak, magic number 7 from magic number 17, and he and the Knicks best the Lakers and Kobe Bryant on their home turf. He is finally sidelined by an injury after 25 games, and we fall back into our seats, exhausted and out of breath. We've had a full court press, and the stands are packed.

Asian Americans have faced racism, exclusion and violent oppression from the first Chinese immigrants to the South Asian victims of hate crimes after 9/11. In the 80s, we got saddled with the "model minority" stereotype, which ignored the great socioeconomic disparities of our communities, and the human reality that we weren't simply overachieving robots, useful primarily to bludgeon other disadvantaged minority groups and trigger racial resentment. We're seen as successful, and thus have "no reason to complain." But we're cast as worker drones – emotionless, silent, obsequious laborers or sidekicks who will never play a leading role in the life of the nation. There's a "bamboo ceiling" that limits our potential, be it in the boardroom, the big screen, or the bedroom. Asian men, at least until recently, were not seen as sexy, or even sexual. They would never have an alpha-male winning game. Jeremy Lin changes all of that. His performance and presence upends a limited cultural imagination that had always relegated us to anonymous bit parts, our desires frustrated by a society that wasn't all that interested in us. Sometimes, even we were not sure we were worth anyone's interest, maybe not even our own. We were in a box, aching to bust out. Boom! Out comes Lin! When he comes out, we all come out. Out of our chairs, out of our minds.

We go Linsane.

Linsanity pops our gourd, mutating us a new mother tongue. We all turn into goofy nerdy punsters, feverishly reveling in Asian American pride and the ability to put an Asian name into, well, everything. Our mania wants to own the English language, re-order it, alchemize it, transform it once and for all in the exultation of feeling like we finally belong and are seen. We become silver-tongued with Linness, in expression of how he's transforming our brains, rewiring our synapses into Linapses. He reorganizes our molecules into molincules. It's Lincredible. We raise the Red Lintern. We develop BorderLin Personality Disorder. We are Lindivisible, and we are no longer invisible.

Jeremy Lin dominates the court and my Facebook feed, day after day, with viral blogposts and articles, memed photographs, and status updates that are truly statuses of the Asian American soul. By mid-February, nearly every post I make or see involves Jeremy Lin in some way. One friend writes that she got misty-eyed during the winning streak in the same way she did on the night of Obama's victory in 2008. Another friend adds "he *is* our Obama!" Facebook, I decide, was made for this kind of cultural happening. Facebook was made for Linsanity. While Jeremy Lin was putting on an exhilarating show on the court, there was a historic conversation happening on blue screens all over the country, pulling in viewers from all over the world. And on my block, the conversation was created, curated and expressed by my fellow Asian Americans. Cue second burst of Asian American pride.

I am helpless under the sway of Linfluenza. I read (and share) articles by Jay Caspian Kang, Oliver Wang, Jeff Yang, Jenn Fang, Phil Yu and others. I become friends with people I have never met, all because of Jeremy Lin. I become closer, at least in Facebook terms, to friends I hardly interacted with before Lin. It's all Linteraction now, we're all on the same court. He's like some universal bonding agent, pulling Asian Americans together and into each other's lives – or at least their newsfeeds. It's the glory of a shared new experience, a culmination of our shared history and aspirations. We are brothers and sisters in Lin. We have a cause and reason to connect and celebrate the success of one of our own – in the arena of sports, that bastion of All American delight, typically off-limits to *all* Asian Americans. And in basketball, no less, a truly All American invention. We, Asian Americans, were All American after all.

When my blog post on *Psychology Today* about Lin wouldn't post properly, my friend, poet Bao Phi, quips "Linsanity has broken the internet!" (I was soon able to upload my modestly viral contribution to feed the insatiable frenzy for Lin commentary. It was the Linternet, after all.)

Facebook was made for Linsanity. And Linsanity would hardly exist as it did without Facebook. Of course, there are many documented cases of "contagious hysteria" in communities – but this emotion traveled faster, farther, and in a more sustained way than any emotion I've witnessed in my life. I can't put a number on it, but certainly hundreds of thousands, perhaps millions, of people experienced a dramatic shift in mood, focus and energy over the course of several weeks, at least as I witnessed in my Facebook sample. Facebook couldn't have invented this craze, but it amplified it manifold, flooding and overwhelming the Asian American Pride and B-ball fanboy/fangirl neurons of everyone looking at a screen.

There were some it didn't reach. I casually brought up Jeremy Lin's name to a couple of Asian American male patients, and they were quite unaware. They were also largely untouched by the Facebook phenomenon in general, and perhaps didn't identify strongly with the Asian American community either – all markers of a kind of isolation. I actually felt a little sad for them, thinking that a dose of Linsanity would likely do their depression and self-esteem some good. Jeremy Lin had to be worth at least ten milligrams of Prozac. At least a contact high. Could Facebook have made a difference in their depressions?

For others, Linsanity was practically a full-blown manic episode. "Everything changed," said a usually sober civil rights attorney, dreamily remembering the thrills of February, 2012. From my vantage, it seemed like the whole country dropped acid at the same time. LSD - LinSurgic Diethylamide. I watched a video clip of one Asian mother "giving Lin the power," trying to transmit some kind of supernatural energy through her television to Madison Square Garden. Other Asian mothers became obsessed with trying to get their daughters set up with Lin. A Tumblr titled "My Parents Are Linsane" showed iPhone screens filled with messages spaced minutes apart, all from a certain mother named Anne Fong, all of them about Jeremy Lin. Now, I'm not diagnosing anyone, but these can all be tell-tale signs of bipolar breaks. Well, at the very least, it tells us that manic energy, creativity, impulsivity, obsession, grandiosity, imagination and even psychosis – can be exhibited by otherwise (presumably) non-bipolar people. The Japanese have a word – *oyabaka* – meaning "going nutty over your children" (baka means idiot). Jeremy Lin was the child of Asian America, and we all went Linabaka. His rise shook us to the core of our identities. More than fan fanaticism, this was archetypal alchemy. Lin, and what he meant, reached into our souls, and we all realized we had possibilities that we dared not imagine before. Linsanity was a prison break for the archetypal ideal of our deepest hopes, long denied. Our superpower smashed stereotypes like Hulk smashed insults to his frame, soared like Superman into the air, against a gravity that could never contain him. Being Asian could mean being successful, even esteemed. Loved, even desired. Talented. Strong. Playful. It could mean being on top. It could mean exulting in ourselves, fully, finally. Jeremy Lin was rocket fuel for Asian American identity. Facebook was the rocket.

The craziness of Asian moms during Linsanity showed us we can all relate to having Asian moms. Even non-Asians. Amy Chua was so 2011. This was Tiger Mom stoned. (And not in the way that some of my friends wanted Chua stoned the year before. Just kidding. This is not a threat. I know you're a lawyer.) Children delighted in their parents' sudden – or at least more obvious – loss of reason, and fended off instructions to have someone introduce them to the Linster. More interest in Asian men? I could live with that. Pass some of that Lin Effect my way.

But Lin's rise triggered cultural mistakes and worse. Racism reared its ugly head. This time, thanks to Facebook and social media, the Asian American community and its allies were quick to respond. ESPN put up an offensive headline highlighting Lin's imperfect performance in one game. "Chink in the Armor" pushed Linsane brains into brawl mode. ESPN was quickly flooded by angry comments about the use of the racial slur as a double entendre. The incident made national news, and the headline writer was promptly fired. I write a blogpost about the incident, titled, of course, "There Are Only LINks in Our Armor!" Ben and Jerry's had to reformulate their new "Linsanity" flavor after many objected that making it with fortune cookie pieces was an example of racial stereotyping. (My take: "A Pint of Racism: Ben and Jerry's Scoops up Stereotypes.") Jeremy Lin was more about Now n' Later's (his favorite candy) than fortune cookies. Once again, Asian Americans bonded in my newsfeed in defiance of mainstream media. We were making our own news, finally, and we were making corporations heed our call for respect.

The internet, and Facebook, became a living, breathing organism for me during Linsanity. A viable, vibrant, pulsating expression of our collective consciousness, and a vital way for Asian Americans to assert their identity. And be proud, finally.

Thank you, Jeremy Lin.

Thank you, Mark Zuckerberg and crew.

"This Facebook thing has mojo," I thought to myself.

Surveying Facelandia

Facebook, Facebook, Facebook. It seems like nearly every conversation I've had in the last year or two has involved Facebook in some way. It has become a verb: "I'll Facebook you." A ubiquitous touchstone. "Did you see that article that went around on Facebook?" A taken-for-granted communique of our lives. "Did you see what I did on my vacation on Facebook?" Part of our goodbye. "I'll see you on Facebook!"

My friends and I commonly note and complain about the intrusive and addictive quality of the website. I've taken to calling it Wastebook, for the hours spent scrolling down an endlessly updating newsfeed; another friend calls it FaceCrack, for its drug-like ability to hook us and keep us coming back for more. "I got sucked into the Face-trix last night." We complain, yet by and large, we log in our hours. The average teen spends almost 2 hours a day on the site. Older users spend nearly an hour. And there are a billion and a half active users, a population that would be the largest country in the world if gathered together, a larger congregation than the entire Catholic Church. And we are clustered, in Facelandia, liking, sharing, commenting, and finding a kind of expression, community and connection. We live on a big blue planet, but an overwhelming number of us are navigating the Big Blue Wall that Mark Zuckerberg created.

The Blue Wall is dependent on the Blue Planet, of course, but it can seem like its own world. The Blue Wall can be a lens on the Blue Planet, with an ability to shape what we see, to focus and distort. A mirror, a lens, a blindfold. Some hope that the Wall will shape the planet itself, and point to the role of social media in protests and revolutions, particularly the Arab Spring. I'm sure that employees at Twitter and Facebook take more than their share of credit for creating supply lines for freedom. "Oh, yeah. We did that." Silicon Valley seems to think it steers the world, like it was a video game.

On a less heady note, some do use Facebook as their sole news channel. "If it's not on Facebook, it didn't happen, as far as I know," said one friend. I've resisted that extreme, but on Blue Wall I've been like a pig in mud. It's just plain fun to see what everyone's up to, what's on their minds, what they've been reading. For a single man unlikely ever to have a family of his own, it's a joy to see friends' children. It's a taste of their very full lives, even as I realize that they're only posting smiles, and very few heartaches and difficulties. No one posts pictures of themselves changing diapers at three in the morning. Hardly anyone showcases their frustrations, especially the frustrations of family and intimacy, on a regular basis. The workaday dullness of the daily grind is titrated away, and we're left with mostly jewels, occasional tribulation, a lot of information, lots 'o LOLs, and sporadic sparks of wisdom. Our lives look good on Facebook, most of the time. Facebook is the new happiest place on Earth. Move over, Disneyland. I appreciate the lives of others from thin screen distance, but wonder if that screen is liminal or limiting.

I have come to appreciate some friends even more, as they share their thoughts, opinions, activities and humor. But even so, the sharers don't divulge – they deluge, perhaps more *in toto* than individually. Yet I must seem a deluge as well. I too have enjoyed sharing my thoughts, opinions, activities and humor. I have occasionally misstepped – disagreeing with someone on an issue they care about deeply has consequences in Facelandia – but by and large have held fast to the rule I had to learn for myself: post only what supports the IRL (In Real Life) relationship. That Blue Planet, with its true-blue people, is, after all, more important than my Facepinion. Not everyone plays by this rule though, and this has had consequences as well. Yes, folks, I've defriended as well as been defriended.

Facebook has expanded and perhaps cheapened the meaning of the word "friend" – can anyone really have 5,000 "friends", or even 500? As 19th century journalist Henry Adams said, "one friend in a lifetime is much, two are many, three are hardly possible." "Friendship," he continued, "needs a certain parallelism of life, a community of thought, a rivalry of aim." Is this a hopelessly outmoded viewpoint, or timeless wisdom? Adams' words ring true to my IRL experience, yet some would suggest Facebook is creating or enhancing the parallelism, community, and rivalry of aim that Adams idealized. To my mind, though, Facebook aims to replace the wisdom of the ages, the friendship of the ages, with the expediency of a fast-paced now. More is better. Your relevance and worth are quantifiable, by "friends," likes and shares. There is probably an instinct that urges safety in numbers; but there is also a tyranny in numbers, in the superficiality of the majority of these connections and the nature of the connecting apparatus itself. But still, we explore friendship in the new medium; something must survive, something must out. We friend and defriend; that is our digital frontier.

To "friend" and "defriend," to connect and excommunicate in our little blue church in Facelandia, to welcome to and deport from our page and sovereign domain, are hopeful and tragic sides of the same Facebook coin. We want to be happy, we don't want to be disturbed, distressed or dissatisfied. People have different set points for adding friends – some add friends-of-friends and even strangers at will, striving to enlarge their Face-community. As I said, the more friends the better – whether or not you actually know them. You will get to know them. They will get to know you. Is that important in this medium, or are we just greedy for likes and shares, more interested in ourselves than anyone else?

Some want to widen their reach on the digital plane, to support their work, art, writing, or egos. "Fast friends" might mean something completely different now – perhaps someone you simply friended quickly online. Friending fills some need, even if it's simply the need to not deny a Faceland visa to someone who wants to be your Facebook friend, your ffriend, your potential supplier of likes. We want friend-ship, most of us, and satisfaction. There are other needs. Having more ffriends, maintaining IRL relationships through internet tendrils, hav-ing a global water cooler to share our moods, to participate in some bigger picture as it lands on our consciousnesses and newsfeeds – this soothes us, helps us feel a little less alone. The party is always on at Facebook, and we're always invited.

Defriending fills a need as well. It is also a reminder of just how superficial and fragile the online connection is. If someone is consis-tently objectionable to you – why maintain an interweb connection? Well, perhaps you can tolerate objectionable behavior – but what if the person targets you personally – and YOUR WALL, for Zuck's sake – with their rants? It's irritating to have someone constantly arguing with you online. It's not good netiquette, and it amounts to harassment. I defriended a man for this reason. Disappointingly, but not surprisingly, this action was met with hostility and the loss or hibernation of the IRL relationship. And once, a woman (a somewhat distant acquaintance) defriended me after I disagreed with her. More importantly, I disagreed with her about something she was angry about. She dumped me, very quickly. We made up in private message, and I telegraphed my apolo-gies – but the damage was done. Though she admitted she had been "quick on the defriend trigger," and very kind in her reminiscence of our real life meeting, I was too respectful of her to request a refriend. I was disappointed, and fantasized about seeing her again, being good to her, and her liking me, and I don't just mean pressing "like." My INL (Internet Life) had impacted IRL, and I was left with a wistful longing for it all to be okay. Lesson learned. Empathy and harmony beat discord, IRL or INL. But discord becomes dissolution all too easily, especially online.

Some people defriend because their ffriend has offended them IRL. In the old days, friends could disagree, even vociferously, and they might part company for a while, or even a lifetime. Our real world connections sometimes silently go cold. Now we have Facebook, where you can formalize your outrage and sever the tie in the dust of atomized silicon particles. Defriending is the equivalent of divorce papers for the age of social networks. One man I know called it "the most accepted antisocial act of the internet age." But the last thing you want is to be reminded of the unfriend's existence, especially their happy existence. And should they try to check up on you, they should get a notice that they're no longer in your online mind or anywhere near your good graces. We "defriend to keep us safe in here," I wrote in a poem about Facebook. "It is safer in here, so fortunately, we can keep making the world scarier." We make the world scarier by nurturing our grudges and animosities, leaving no room for reconciliation.

It's true. The world is a strange, glorious, and all-too-often scary place. Facebook is good at giving us a virtual hug sometimes, a glimmer of the real thing. It is a social network, a largely pro-social network, at least within each suburb of the Facelandic Empire. The suburbs themselves may be antagonistic to each other, and the common spaces may be a platform for trolls (see the comments on President Barack Obama's Facebook updates, for example), but my own suburb, my network of hundreds, my groups – are largely a very respectful community. I'm sure that most others say the same of their online neighborhoods.

But as pro-social as Facebook can be, it reflects and contains the seeds of the larger society, including the anti-social elements. These anti-social elements are not simply certain people who disagree with us, annoy us, or make our lives difficult; these anti-social elements are within us as well. It may be a stretch to call the commonplace vices of human nature – to dislike, to grow disaffected, to harbor animosity – "anti-social," but there you have it. Buddhists call greed, hatred and delusion the "three poisons" of mental life. Nirvana is defined as the extinction of these poisons within our minds. As I engage with Facebook, as I "play Facebook," I notice what my mind does. Sometimes I feel like Facebuddha – all is one, all is peace, all is joy and union. And other times, peace is nowhere to be found, there is only online trouble, and a disaffected mind. Facebook has activated me, not all for the better. But in the activation, there are lessons, and a treasure of difficulty I must own. That is, own up to. Shantideva writes, in *The Way of the Bodhisattva,*

> "Therefore, just like treasure appearing in my house
> Without any effort on my part to obtain it,
> I should be happy to have an enemy
> For he assists me in my conduct of Awakening."

Facebook is that treasure appearing on my laptop, without any effort on my part to obtain it. And it is, sometimes, an enemy. My relationship to it, I'm convinced, is important in my own, personal awakening. And maybe, just maybe, Facebook can assist us all in a bigger, wider awakening. That is the potential of a social network, where ideas, relationship and influence can reverberate through and reorder synapses that stubbornly insist on their separateness. The delusion of separateness, or self-centeredness, is at the root of suffering and those irksome three poisons.

Sometimes, though, I like being at least a little separate. I'm not always sure of how social and connected I want to be, especially on Facebook. Sometimes being a little separate helps me make sense of myself, helps me get to peace. That little bit of separation makes the connection all the better. The signal-to-noise ratio improves substantially with a tincture of being aloof and apart. My internal and external gains do better with a smidge of reflective space.

But we have a lot more than a smidge. A lot more than we're comfortable with. We're all ultimately alone in our skins, silently pining, sometimes screaming, our existential panic into the void. We could find freedom here, or wisdom, but much of the time we avoid or dread being alone with ourselves. We crave distractions from our anxious, lonely reality. We don't want to look.

> We upload our loneliness,
> Let it gust from the Cloud.
> Chill wind blows from forlorn screens;
> We pull close our technological shroud.

If Facebook didn't exist, it would have to be invented. Facebook, or its successor social network, is likely here to stay. Unless, of course, we outgrow our need for social networks and become, instead, a full-fledged, IRL Beloved Community. Until then, Facebook will placate the empty nooks of our communal longing, our desperate wish to not be alone, our wish to be seen, our wish to see, our wish to be heard, our wish to hear, our need to stay in touch, somehow, someway.

Online to Ecstasy

The second week of March always brings the exciting highpoint of my year: the San Francisco International Asian American Film Festival (SFIAAFF) put on by the Center for Asian American Media (CAAM).* In eleven days, over a hundred features and shorts are shown highlighting the Asian and Asian American experience. From sober documentaries about the aftermath of war and dislocation, to serious and zany films about family, relationships, and identity, this festival has had my heart for well over a decade. SFIAAFF has been called "the Cannes of the Asian American Film Festival Circuit." OK, I think I called it that. It's the biggest, and arguably the best, of its kind. Organizers from every other Asian American film festival in North America are regularly in attendance. It's supercharged, high-quality fun, and extraordinarily educational all at once. Nowhere else have I found this density of insight into all aspects of the Asian American identity and adventure. It's a trip across time, continents, and perspectives, and invariably fits and fills a place in me that craves completion and wholeness, a place that has often been achingly empty. This festival undoes and remakes me, year after year.

For years, I've taken the festival week off from work, and plunged full time into movie-watching mode. Between previewing films and actual screenings at the festival, I take in well over 60 hours of cinema every year. In 2006, Festival organizers asked me to write about the festival. We launched "Memoirs of a Superfan." I, of course, was Superfan.

---

*   In 2013, the festival changed its name to CAAMFest, and in 2018, CAAMFest will move to May.

My writing always brought out the best in relatedness – to the festival, to the Asian American community, and to myself. This year is Volume 7, lucky number 7.[†]

In 2012, my blogging began just after the high point of Linsanity, and after the "backlash" – the ESPN headline that declared Lin had a "Chink in the Armor", and the Ben and Jerry's "Linsanity" flavor that was made of fortune cookie pieces.

Memoirs of a Superfan, Volume 7.1: CAAMily Reunion
February 27, 2012

I get comfortable. Too comfortable. I am connected to colleagues and friends, feeling effective at my job and in my social life. Just like most Asian Americans and other Americans, I get overjoyed, buoyant, ebullient when Jeremy Lin makes his mark on the court and on the world stage. I catch the Linsanity. I literally felt about 3 inches taller. But then ESPN happens, and Ben and Jerry's happens, and it takes me back, back to a place where I once felt alone and angry about a world that seems so out of touch with good sense and respect, a world that often seems unconsciously ignorant, or consciously and malevolently racist. I morph into an Angry Asian Man – but since Phil Yu owns that trademark, and I'm now a psychiatrist, I morph into what my friend calls "reasonably and analytically offended South Asian man. Nope, doesn't have the same ring to it."

It's the stinging realization that despite the progress we've made, and the fact that there is a lot more media sensitivity than there was even just a few years ago – we still have a long way to go. I get a reminder with every comment on my blog post at

---

† This chapter aims to give a firsthand account of the transformative interplay between social networks, blogging and real world experience. However, if you are not interested in film and the Asian American experience, you can safely read simply the beginning and end of this chapter, and move ahead.

Psychology Today. On Facebook, I had an initial reaction about a Jeremy Lin meme by poet Bao Phi and Huynh Que-Lam that declared "Hey girl/guy/gender non-conforming, I'm getting tired of these microaggressions, wherein whites fail to realize the power they have to define racial realities for people of color and deny their own prejudice." I thought to myself – "wait, I define my reality. No one else can tell me what my reality is."

Guess what? Reality is a co-creation. And some individuals and institutions have enormous power to perpetuate delusion, ignorance and racism. And the result is that communities of color have a far greater share of unemployment, disease, war, death and suffering. So we're not done yet. Not by a long shot.

SFIAAFF has been home for me and many of us in the Asian American community for 30 years. CAAM's mission is to show-case the stories of the Asian and Asian American communities and to be an institution that not only combats ignorance but also is a force for enlightenment. I am deeply grateful to what every person at CAAM has done over the years – bringing conscious-ness to big and small screens and helping to create community and dialogue.

Not to mention, making it all fun!

I look forward to seeing you all at SFIAAFF 30. Let's have a great CAAMily Reunion!

CAAM. Making Asians taller since 1980.

I continued, writing previews for films that would screen during the festival week.

Memoirs of a Superfan, Volume 7.2: CAAMsanity!
March 7, 2012

Are you excited?! Are you ready?! Full court press! SFIAAFF is the champion point guard for the Asian American experience! I've already screened a few films – here is a sampling, by no means complete. In the paint this week – journeys, pilgrimages, and other genres.

SURROGATE VALENTINE, last year's closing night film, introduced me to the "mumblecore" or "bedhead" genre of films. (Thanks to G. Allen Smith of the Chronicle for writing about those terms last year!) This year we have SURROGATE VALENTINE 2, likely also in that genre (unless Goh Nakamura reveals his true identity as a superhero, puts on a cape and starts jumping over buildings). I previewed SALAD DAYS (Directors/ Writers Hiram Chan, Jeff Mizushima and Emily Yoshida) and THE CRUMBLES (Director/Writer Akira Boch), which I really enjoyed, and which (I think) also fit in this genre. These are all low-key films about real life – there are no heroes or villains, just people, stumbling and mumbling through life. There is, in these films, a quality of "just being with" the experience of life. There isn't a huge narrative arc, much dramatic tension, or an amazing monologue to speak of. Yet there is a display of life's subtle but insistent demands: relationship, ambition, popularity....the undercurrent of ego which pulls the characters out to sea, where they drift, and look for rafts. To me, that's a very touching kind of film, very true to a-certain-kind of 20-something life, and I congratulate the filmmakers on their wonderful work.

These films could also be seen as a display of an empty, shallow, and superficial "modernity." If you're looking to see reality with a different lens, I would recommend THE SUN BEATEN PATH and ABU, SON OF ADAM. In each film, faith and culture resonate in the lives of men, whose deep emotions are lived out in broad gesture. In the first film, a Tibetan man, Nyma, accidentally kills a relative. For Tibetans, whose religion and culture focus on compassion, who are known to move earthworms out of the paths of construction cranes, this is a profound and deeply scarring event which motivates a cross-country pilgrimage, a wandering that stretches a lost soul over the barren landscape of the Tibetan plateau. The kindness of a stranger, an older man, breaks Nyma's isolation briefly, acting as a seed of relatedness in the setting of trauma to inner and outer relationships.

ABU, SON OF ADAM is about the preparation for a voyage, a pilgrimage to Mecca by a poor Indian Muslim man and his wife. We see life in a small Kerala village, where everyone knows everyone, and faith runs deep. Abu sets his sights on purity first, trying to mend his relationships and clear his conscience even as he sells many belongings in an attempt to gather enough money to make the trip. He is a man who makes many personal sacrifices to hone his virtue; I was left with both an abiding respect for his choices, the power of human bonds, and also a sense of how much Abu's piety – perhaps moral rigidity – has cost him.

IN THE FAMILY also shows us the sun-beaten path of grief and loss, and the path of connection and relatedness which makes us whole, and keeps making us whole, time and time again. This is a must-see, amazing film by first-time director Patrick Wang, who also stars in the film as Joey, a father who loses his partner, Cody, leading to a custody battle over their son, Chip. What emerges in this nearly 3-hour long epic of the heart is a humble, certain humanity, and a love that assuredly erodes the walls which keep a family apart – and which redefines, in understated but poetic ways, the meaning of family itself. IN THE FAMILY reminded me of Ozu masterpieces, in its long takes, restrained pacing, focus on relationships and barely spoken but deeply felt emotion. Wang shows us the power of low-key, evocative film-making at its best.

A LOT LIKE YOU features journeys as well, inner and outer. I hope to feature a Q and A with director Eli Kimaro later during the fest. Her documentary is powerful and heart-warming, telling several stories at once, and all of them well: the story of her Tanzanian father's leaving his Chagga tribal roots, coming to America and marrying her Korean mother; a story from Tanzanian Independence; the story of her parents' amazing lives together; the story of her father's family, particularly his sisters, and the difficulties they endured; and her own long-secret story of abuse which led her to become a trauma counselor. All these stories are finally woven together in a womb-like, circular Chagga hut, a replica of her father's family home that he has rebuilt in honor of family and memory. There is only one way in and out of this womb – one feels it is the path of relating, remembering and holding memory across the generations, a thread and tie made secure by the active work of the director, and now passed to us, the audience, in the womb of a darkened theater.

Other journey films include RETURN TO BURMA, where the constant search for a job contrasts with red-robed monks' daily alms rounds and the spaciousness of the natural world. I loved TIBET IN SONG when I saw it last year – my review is available online.

We keep emerging to light, this week; we enter the darkness, see visions on walls – the dreams of others – then emerge again, back to our own life-dreams, now an altered state. There's plenty to contemplate this week – to CAAMtemplate (had to do it, sorry). This week, you'll find ample provisions for your own voyage in life.

SFIAAFF is more than our point guard – it's the passage to our Asian American frontier.

Even when I wasn't greatly thrilled by a film, I found something of value. At least these were Asian American stories being told by Asian Americans.

Memoirs of a Superfan Volume 7.3: CAAMmy the Love Bug
March 9, 2012

A relatively balmy San Francisco March day blessed Opening Night 2012 with sunshine, and the warmth of revelers made up for any chill in the air. We chillaxed in the Castro Theater instead, ready for a WHITE FROG – sans fog – adventure. It was a full moon night, and we took our chances, inviting at least two once-and-future werewolves to take the stage. Booboo Stewart (TWILIGHT: BREAKING DAWN) and Tyler Posey (TEEN WOLF) joined veteran actors Joan Chen and BD Wong, award-winning playwright, screenwriter, script-advisor, executive producer and actor David Henry Hwang, director (and SFIAAFF regular) Quentin Lee, actor Gregg Sulkin and producer/writer Ellie Wen for a charming Q and A after their movie screened.

Ellie Wen wrote WHITE FROG with her mother, Fabienne Wen, inspired by families whose children they knew or suspected had Asperger's Syndrome – a condition similar to autism, except the difficulties are primarily with social interactions and repetitive behaviors, and not with language capability. People with this disorder can differ widely from one another, as Booboo Stewart (who plays Nick, the son with Asperger's) pointed out. He researched the role by watching YouTube Vlogs of "Aspies," as they sometimes call themselves. Bill Gates is regularly diagnosed in the press with Asperger's – the stereotype is the detail-obsessed person who lacks social graces and is unable to interpret social cues. It can be notoriously difficult to diagnose and treat. Some afflicted individuals do extremely well, in technical professions, for example – but others run into trouble with relationships and "fitting in." But that, ultimately, was the point of WHITE FROG: "we're all different," as Nick says at the end, and should be celebrated and loved as individuals. I don't think I would be reading too far between the lines of the script to presume that the tragic back-story of the film is that too many young people end their lives because of non-acceptance. WHITE FROG celebrates many kinds of diversity. Charles, the idealized older son, and Randy, his best friend and lover, are gay; nearly everyone involved with the film, in front of and behind the camera, is Asian American, a powerful testament to under-recognized and under-utilized community capability and talent; and perhaps with Nick's story, the film celebrates neurodiversity, the sometimes controversial concept that atypical neurological development is just part of the spectrum of normal human variance.

Whoa, am I a shrink or what?! Seriously, I was glad to see a film that portrayed mental health issues in a sensitive and helpful manner. Three cheers for the filmmakers! And for once, we even got a likable psychiatrist on the silver screen in Amy Hill! (But I've got to say for the record that while I've done a lot of things in therapy, I've never flossed my teeth in session. Just in case anyone wonders what I do at work. I have been known to crack a joke or two, though. Who knew, right?! Laughing at life is always therapeutic, and Amy Hill has that down.) It was nice to see a film take a stab at spirituality as well, with themes of rebirth and Christianity popping up here and there, as well as David Henry Hwang doing a nice job with a eulogy as well as pastoral counseling. Of course, I couldn't help but think that the story was really about Booboo Stewart ultimately donning an orange shirt – read robe – and becoming a Buddhist monk. But that's just where my mind goes. I'm looking forward to seeing Stewart replace Keanu Reeves in the remake of LITTLE BUDDHA. Wait a minute… Buddha WAS enlightened on the full moon…kinda like a were-wolf….Booboo, Buddha….hmmmm……The Four Noble Truths become The Four Noble Tooths (canines)….this has possibilities. Hey Quentin, how about a SHOPPING FOR FANGS remake?

Other highlights from the Q and A included BD Wong (LAW AND ORDER) saying it was "rare to be cast in a role where I actually have a relationship with somebody, and to have the line 'all gay people think everyone is gay!'" And with everyone talking about how good the food on the set was, I was surprised they weren't burping in every scene. Panda Express had a cameo, anyway.

Joan Chen said she enjoyed this film for several reasons, including the fact that it was one film of hers she could actually show her under-age children. She plays the mother in the film, and said "family life and motherhood is the most important thing I do. Love is the hardest thing. This movie is about love." When she said "everything we do is a preparation for love," we knew it was time to head to the Asian Art Museum, to howl the night away and, uhh, prepare. It's all about homework, people! We are Asian American, after all!

This is an assignment we can all have fun with – and Asians and Asian Americans have plenty of libido on display this week. (And every week. There's a reason why there are so many of us, after all.) From the erotic homage to soft-core in TOUCH, to the rush-only NICE GIRLS CREW, to the centerpiece YES, WE'RE OPEN – SFIAAFF turns into a giant Love Shack. Make sure you choose your seatmates wisely for the open-relationship-themed OPEN, because...you never know... OK, that sounds a little creepy. Mom, I'm joking.

...The Museum welcomed us...Sapporo and sushi kept primal urges at bay – but who knows what happened at the afterparty...

See you at the movies!

One of my favorite parts of being the Festival blogger was the ability to get interviews with my favorite directors. Every year, I looked forward to my "date" with an amazing individual whose work really expanded my reality. Coincidentally – or maybe not so coincidentally – these had almost always been women. The festival was my number one relationship of the week, and she was usually represented by a talented woman. This year was no different, as I interviewed Eli Kimaro, director of the documentary A LOT LIKE YOU, which went on to win Best Documentary at our festival and many others.

Memoirs of a Superfan, Volume 7.4:
Six Questions with Eli Kimaro
March 12, 2012

I had the great pleasure of viewing Eliaichi Kimaro's wonderful documentary A LOT LIKE YOU. The film will screen again on Tuesday, March 13th at 9:20 pm, and I highly recommend it. As I wrote about it last week,

"Her documentary is powerful and heart-warming, telling several stories at once, and all of them well: the story of her Tanzanian father's leaving his Chagga tribal roots, coming to America and marrying her Korean mother; a story from Tanzanian Independence; the story of her parents' amazing lives together; the story of her father's family, particularly his sisters, and the difficulties they endured; and her own long-secret story of abuse which led her to become a trauma counselor. All these stories are finally woven together in a womb-like, circular Chagga hut, a replica of her father's family home that he has rebuilt in honor of family and memory. There is only one way in and out of this womb – one feels it is the path of relating, remembering and holding memory across the generations, a thread and tie made secure by the active work of the director, and now passed to us, the audience, in the womb of a darkened theater."

From her press kit: "Independent Director and Producer Eliaichi Kimaro is a mixed race, first-generation American who worked for 15 years as a professional crisis counselor for survivors of rape and domestic violence before becoming a filmmaker.

"Her company, 9elephants productions (www.9elephants. org), uses video as a means to address social justice issues, bringing stories of struggle, resistance and survival to a broader audience. Eliaichi produces videos for non-profits working within underserved communities to address social and economic justice issues.

"Eliaichi brings a lifetime of personal and professional experience dealing with race, gender, domestic and sexual violence to her directorial debut, the autobiographical film, A Lot Like You, which won Best Documentary at the 2011 Montreal International Film Festival, and won the Top 10 Audience Choice Award when it premiered at the 2011 Seattle International Film Festival."

Eli Kimaro was kind enough to answer a few questions by email.

1. A LOT LIKE YOU reminded me of other documentaries where people look for their roots. Were you inspired by any documentaries in particular?

Before leaving for Tanzania, my partner Tom and I immersed ourselves in personal documentaries. This was my schooling – learning from what others have done, what worked, what rubbed me the wrong way. Some docs that stood out for me during this period were First Person Plural, My Architect, Tell Them Who You Are, Tongues Untied.

But the film that stuck with me the most while filming in our village on Mt Kilimanjaro was Daughter from Danang. Heidi's struggle with her racial identity and issues of belonging, the challenging dynamics of both her American and her Vietnamese families -- it was so familiar, the discomfort so visceral, it was hard for me to watch. And I was really struck by the power of the camera to command your attention, almost forcing you to attend to a situation when you would rather look away.

2. Whom do you think you're "A lot like"?

Our title definitely leaves a lot to interpretation...

For me personally, over the course of making this film, I've come to understand that I am like my Chagga aunts in ways I never could have imagined. And that I'm a lot more like my father than I realized.

And then, there's this way that people, after seeing our film, often make the mistake of calling it "A Lot Like Me." That slip up makes me smile, and I never correct it. Because it speaks to how strongly this story resonates with anyone—regardless of race, culture, age, gender, class—who's curious about exploring their family or their culture to better understand who they are and where they come from. So then our title also refers to the surprising connection that viewers sometimes feel to my family and this journey that unfolds on the screen.

3. Indeed, you found resonances with your father's sisters, and even your father. It was very touching to see your daughter watching your aunties sing on the television, a thread of history that she carries with her as well, through your work. That seemed to be the most unexpected resonance. Maybe you can talk a little bit about what you were expecting or hoping to find when you started this project.

This project was born out of that slightly panicked realization that, if my partner and I were to have kids, their understanding about what it means for them to be Korean or Chagga would have to come from me. The mere thought of that responsibility was terrifying. Because what the hell did I know?!

So when we came up with the idea to make this film, I felt a huge sense of relief. Never mind that we had zero skills or equipment or know-how...I felt like I had finally figured out a way to preserve our cultural heritage and family stories – not only for our (future) kids, but also for me.

But I was surprised to discover that this film project was of benefit to my Dad as well. My cultural exploration was helping him reconnect with his Chagga roots. Because despite having been born and raised in Tanzania, after living in the US for 40 years, my Dad had become a cultural insider/outsider like me – just to a different degree.

When we landed in Tanzania, my original intent was to make a film about the challenges my Dad was facing as he tried to fit back in with the family and culture that he'd left behind 40 years earlier (our working title then, "Worlds Apart"). We showed up with all the hubris of novice American filmmakers raised on a healthy diet of National Geographic specials. And the "brand" of Chagga culture I was hoping to capture was robust and colorful, complete with songs, dance, folklore, spirituality, traditional healing practices, systems of governance and discipline and justice...

So for months, we went on this wild goose chase as we tried to capture what we thought of as Chagga culture. It wasn't until we stopped chasing down some non-existent ideal, and just opened ourselves up to what was right in front of us – my family's stories – that we came to a deeper understanding of what culture is really about.

4. Did the making of the film change your relationship with your parents? I think all the audience will wonder what happened when your parents saw the film, and found out what had happened to you – do you want to reveal any of that?

I appreciate that it can be hard to sit with ambiguity. Our film definitely captures that moment when you know exactly *what* you need to do to make something right...but the thought of doing it fills you with dread. That tension is perfectly preserved in this film, because on the day we locked picture and I recorded those final lines of narration, that is *precisely* where I was in my process – sitting with the uncertainty of not knowing how the story was going to unfold from here.

And you're right. After every screening, when the lights come up, people are curious about what happened next. I'm amazed at how invested they are in the story, wanting to know how my parents responded when they saw the film. And I'm always happy to reflect on this question in person after a screening, when the entirety of our story is still fresh in people's minds.

But answering this question, in writing, in advance of people seeing the film, is a tricky balance. So I will keep this answer brief:

My parents saw the film on their own, in their home in Tanzania. And it wasn't until 2 years later that I saw my Dad in person. When asked how he felt about what was shared in the film, his response was "the conversations this film is opening up for all of us has been nothing short of liberating, and can only make us stronger as a family."

5. How did your exploration bring up issues that perhaps were never discussed openly between your parents? I am thinking of their disagreement/different points of view about your aunties.

While I can't speak specifically to the impact of my journey on my parents, what I have come to realize is that, at its core, this film explores how our own hidden truths filter the stories that get passed down. In three separate instances – first with my Aunts, then my Dad, then me – we each arrive at that moment where we must choose whether to be complicit in the shaming silence or to finally break through it...

We witness the transformation that takes place in my Aunts as they find the words to finally speak their truth. It's the Power of their story that compels us to deeply consider the hidden truths in our own lives. And it invites us to reach out and connect with each other from this vulnerable, humble place.

At the end of our interview, my Aunts asked me, "Now that we've shared our stories with you...what are you going to do about it?" It really was more of a commandment, a call to action, than a question. But their courage in speaking up inspired me (albeit years later) to do the same in my storytelling. And now, it's amazing to see how many lives are being transformed by this small ripple that was set in motion 9 years ago when my Aunts opened up and shared their truth with me in a hut on a mountain halfway around the world.

6. How did the doc fit into and change your life?

I am still involved in sexual and domestic violence work, just not in the crisis counseling and support capacity of my earlier years. In 2003, when we returned from our 9-month shoot on Mt Kilimanjaro, I realized that I now had a skill set that is relevant and greatly needed in our activist communities. So I founded my own video production company, 9elephants Productions. And for the past eight years, I have been producing videos for local and national non-profits working within traditionally marginalized and underserved communities to address social/ economic justice issues. I love helping people, who are passionate and relentless in their commitment to justice, find creative ways to bring their stories, their mission, their vision, to the screen.

The festival offered opportunities for insight, a way to challenge any rigidities of thought that I'd acquired, as well as affirm my deepest values. The spotlight was on Joan Chen this week; I admired her greatly, but I had also been troubled by an opinion piece she'd written for the Washington Post during the uprisings in Tibet. She had given a very unempathic appraisal of the protestors, saving her empathy for those of Chinese ethnicity who had been tragically killed. So I carried both respect for Ms. Chen and a bit of skepticism. I attended a press conference which featured her and others involved in the ground-breaking debut feature from 2006, SAVING FACE. The festival's P.R. person, Karen Larsen, urged me to ask a question, any question – perhaps fearful that there wouldn't be enough to talk about. I obliged, and produced this the next day – a plea for artistic freedom, ostensibly in support of Ms. Chen, but surreptitiously making a plea for all dissenters, including Tibetans.

Memoirs of a Superfan Volume 7.5: A Mala of Movies
March 13, 2012

Festival week is my movie retreat. I love to lose myself, and find myself, in a mala of films – and indeed, SFIAAFF usually offers about 108 films, identical to the number of beads on a mala, a Buddhist prayer rosary. Film is entertaining, of course, but also contemplative, deconstructive and creative. It can affirm identity, and also question, subvert and transform it.

I was reminded of the power of film at the press conference for the SAVING FACE reunion. Director Alice Wu, Actor/Director/Honoree Joan Chen, and Actors Lynn Chen and Michelle Krusiec reminisced on how joyous it was to work on the film. More than a few audience members have been moved to tears by the movie, then and now. It's won many awards, including Taiwan's Golden Horse, and been "bootlegged all over" China and Asia. I imagine all those viewers getting a dose of solace and hope, laughter and tears. "You created family," I told Wu later. Family and Church, really – I'll always remember the Castro Theater in 2006, when SAVING FACE premiered, as being a Temple of Heart. "It was a special experience," Krusiec said. "It was an opportunity that can never be repeated or topped. Alice really allowed me to explore and grow. It's very moving to think about it."

Joan Chen spoke on Friday and Monday about her films, particularly XIU XIU and SAVING FACE. "It's gratifying to see XIU XIU on the big screen again," she said. Movies fit a certain time. The Cultural Revolution "now would be seen through different lenses – a dark comedy rather than tragedy."

For myself, I'm not quite sure we're done with tragedy, though dark comedy can help us get through. XIU XIU still plays extremely well, the power of an extraordinary film. But one of the tragedies of the courageous act of making the film was that Chen got on the wrong side of the Chinese government by shooting without the proper permissions. She says that now "there is no tension. I did something wrong (and paid for it)." I like to think that paying the fine was a way for both parties to "save face": the Chinese government surely didn't want to ban the illustrious and beloved Joan Chen forever, and Joan Chen surely didn't want to be viewed adversarially by the Chinese government. Money is paid, the point is made, and everyone is happy.

It's really hard to keep a government happy, though; one would hope that all governments would try to keep their people happy, including the artists. To remix Jesus, "rules were made for people, not people for rules." And artists like rules even less than most people who get caught on the tenterhooks of unjust judgments. Being creative is nearly always a transgressive act – the artist must break free of their own "inner critic" and the stultifying mold of past experience to reach something new. This occurs whether the artist is telling their own story or seeing deeply into someone else's. Being a person means not only understanding the rules of society, the rules that help us live with and respect one another, but also knowing the deepest rules and demands of the human heart.

I heard a variation on this theme at the PRESENT/FUTURE SUMMIT on Sunday, when Gary Chou spoke of the growing influence of individuals and networks of individuals, most prominently in social media, displacing the power of hierarchies. He quoted someone as saying "the battle between hierarchies and networks will be bigger than the battles between religions." I really hope that religions will come to learn from each other, and not simply battle; similarly, I hope that the discourse between hierarchies and networks will turn out to be far less bloody than what's happening in Syria, for example. I hope that our Constitution will affirm our "constitution," what composes us, our composition, to speak artistically. Our very being is a composition, a network, a symphony of neurons and synapses; and the ones that fire the fastest are the ones that usually get us into trouble. I hope that the slow network of our global cell – the one that honors the waves, the breeze, the earth, the migrations of birds – the eco-ego, if you will – I hope this network spreads its pulse before it's too late.

We must all be artists to heed this call of life; to save the face of our planet. If I were the director of the big picture, this is what I'd be looking at. And I wouldn't want it to be a dark comedy or tragedy.

I'm glad to have directors like Briar March (THERE ONCE WAS AN ISLAND, about how climate change and the rising sea are threatening island-dwellers) and Lucy Walker (THE TSUNAMI AND THE CHERRY BLOSSOM, playing again in San Jose this weekend) to keep this mala in motion.

But that's just where my mind goes, on film.

The festival was always a peak experience, but this year blew the lid on all past peaks, just like you'd expect from a Hawaiian volcano. This year featured a documentary about, and performance by, Jake Shimabukuro, ukulele-wielding Orpheus on an odyssey of Aloha. I met a Jake Superfan, and became a Jake fan myself, having only known him from YouTube before. It was an ideal evening, topped off by a late night dinner with friends, as we tried to carry the heartfelt spirit of the concert outwards in all directions. The next morning, I wrote what would be my most popular blog post of the week, and indeed all time up to that point, garnering over 400 likes in short order.

Memoirs of a Superfan, Volume 7.6: The Jake Edition
March 15, 2012

The torch was passed and a fire lit Wednesday night in the Castro Theater. Yes, we saw an extraordinary film about and performance by the incomparable Jake Shimabukuro; but we also witnessed a ritual uncommon in this cynical age – a gathering of families to bless the young, and in turn to receive musical and cinematic blessings from the new bearers of hope.

Like President Obama, Jake was named a *Keiki O' Ka 'Aina*, a child of the island, and he brought his aloha spirit like a ukelele hero, a humble Hawai'ian Superman with a tender heart of gold, quicksilver hands and a ready smile. Japanese American, child of immigrants to the island, yet part of Hawai'i and one of its chief musical messengers, Jake also embodies what Supervisor Jane Kim called "San Francisco values." Kim highlighted "the role that arts and artists play in building and advocating for community." She said Jake exemplified the artist "who cares and has a conscience," who shows his love through free shows for youth and seniors, including those devastated by the 2011 earthquake and tsunami in Japan. He seems the ideal "Mu Artist," named for my friends at Mu Performing Arts in Minneapolis – "mu" (pronounced "moo") being the Korean pronunciation of the Chinese character for the shaman/artist/warrior who connects heaven and earth through the tree of life. (Mu is also translated as "the space that exists between all things," the space that connects and contains, or the quality of interdependence.) Through his Music is Good Medicine program (jakeshimabukuro.com/migm) he is a doctor as well, one that could put guys like me out of business. Music can heal and connect hearts; Tad Nakamura's film and Jake's music could become a gateway to aloha-world, the world where the values of the Pacific Heart beat through us all.

The Director of Pacific Islanders in Communication, Ruth Bolan, reminded us of those values as well, saying the ocean between us connects and doesn't divide us, just as our differences "unite us and make us stronger." (Also as good a definition of Mu as any.)

I can only imagine the joy and pride of the parents in the Theater – Bob Nakamura and Karen Ishizuka, pioneers and founding heroes of Asian American film and parents of Tad; and Carol Shimabukuro, mother of Jake and Bruce, who raised them as a single mom working two jobs. She says in the film that Jake, watching her shake tip money out of her purse night after night, said "someday, Mom, I'm going to take care of you." "That's so sweet, so touching – but I never thought it was gonna come true!" From the parents' hands come gifts of love, history, music, and film – and from the children's hands those gifts come to all of us, amplified and resonant. Individual achievement and hard work become pillars of community and beacons for hard times.

I was captured immediately by the artistry of Tad Nakamura's film. We move from Jake practicing ukelele in a dressing room, to his performing to a packed theater, and then to playing in front of children – perfectly encapsulating the way that his music comes from a personal to public and neighborhood spaces. The film was born in a personal way as well, when Producer Don Young was at home in 2010 with a sick daughter, and had some time to research Jake's music online. He found that while there was a lot of press coverage, there was no thorough or complete representation of Jake's story. He got the go-ahead from E.D. Stephen Gong, contacted Jake's publicist, and flew out right away to Honolulu to meet with Jake to propose the collaboration. Tad Nakamura was the clear choice for director, with a trio of films about the Asian American and Japanese American experience under his belt (PILGRIMAGE, A SONG FOR OURSELVES and YELLOW BROTHERHOOD). But this was Tad's first feature-length documentary, and it sounds like it was a challenge to "present someone the way you see them. I got to know Jake over two years – how do you portray (in one hour) the person you got to know over two years?" While it was mentioned that Tad continues to tinker with the film – "until he's locked out of the editing room," as Jake said – it was clear by the audience's reaction that he and everyone who's worked on the film have powerfully succeeded in crafting an elegant and beautiful portrait of a young but already highly accomplished artist.

Jake was deeply moved by the film and evening as well – he spoke of being on the road for nine months of the year and hardly seeing his family. Being reunited with them in San Francisco and seeing the last two years of his life and his life story on the big screen brought him to tears, probably in part because the film reminded him (and us) of the journey and all the people who were involved in it. Jake took all that heart and poured it out for us on stage, beginning appropriately with "While my Guitar Gently Weeps," and moving to the classic "Akaka Falls," paying homage to Western and Pacific traditions. He followed with his own composition "Blue Roses Falling," before inviting Dominic "The Dominator" Pieranunzio (dominator.ukeland. com), a man who really knows his uke and the winner of the CAAM Ukelelestar contest, on stage for an amazing performance, which will hopefully join Jake's videos on YouTube soon.

Jake's younger brother Bruce ("my son," as Jake joked) then joined him for a "Wipeout" duet. Bruce is apparently the jokester in the family, saying that after the film, "I feel like I know Jake better than I ever did!" Later, the boys backed up their mother Carol, who sang a classic Hawai'ian melody. Bruce quipped, "Jake's been all over the world – but he always gives his family their three minutes of fame!" He also said, "huh, all this time, I thought this film was gonna be about me!" "Bohemian Rhapsody" closed out the performance. No, Jake – we will not let you go, no, no, no.

During the Q and A, Joel, a young musician whose interest in music was waning, asked Jake for advice. Jake got down on his knees to listen to the question, and ask Joel's name. He then spoke eloquently about music and life as emotional journeys. (I paraphrase.) "Music is called the universal language, but I think it's really the language of the universe. It's the purest and most honest form of communication. We have filters on speech, but music is pure emotion. Whether you are experiencing relationships with family, friends or the universe, we have the desire to express who we are. Tad hasn't slept in two weeks because he was trying to express something through film…The instrument is the illusion. Before you play a chord, it happens in here," Jake said, gesturing to his heart. "It's about stimulating emotion – the more you can feel, the more you can grasp – the more you can express. My advice is just to go out and experience life. Music is not about playing scales. It's about feeling. You have to feel life."

With that, Jake Shimabukuro, Doctor of Aloha, cured us all of post-Tiger Mom trauma.

We left and wandered the streets, satisfied, but hungry for more.

The last night of the San Francisco run of the festival, I was en-thralled by the mixture of a live musical and film in *Prison Dancer*, a web series and soon-to-be theater production. I spent the evening riding a high, talking to wonderful people like Mina Son, director of a film about Deaf Koreans, and wishing the week would never end.

Memoirs of a Superfan, Volume 7.7: Nothing Short
March 16, 2012

I sing America, from pro-life to grow lights.
I sing America.

Joseph Cao sings America – former Republican Congressman from Louisiana, who strived for a time to bridge the gap between our polarities, before being reined back in. S. Leo Chiang's portrait of Cao (MR. CAO GOES TO WASHINGTON, playing again this weekend in San Jose with Cao and family in atten-dance) speaks to this wound – of an Asian American immigrant, child of war and unspoken loss, struggling to be whole again in this new country, struggling to make wholeness through politics. One of my good friends, a passionate activist, recently told me she was an activist because "politics is about healing." My jaw dropped as I disagreed. "Are you kidding me? Seems more like a meat grinder." Maybe even the disease, rather than the cure. I'm glad there are some politicians who seem to be interested in the medicinal quality of their work, but that doesn't seem to be the norm. Or perhaps many enter for that reason, and then find themselves mired in the disease, the game, the muck.

Art is often about healing. You don't become an artist without having some kind of wound – "without the wound, there's no reason for the journey," as I've written elsewhere. Art is transformative. I would paraphrase Eli Kimaro's father, Sadikiel Kimaro, as he pondered the discussions raised by her film and journey (which just won the 2012 Jury Award for Best Documentary at SFIAAFF). Art is nothing short of liberating.

I sing America, from lion dancers to line dancers.
From pole dancers to prison dancers,
I sing America.

Inspired by the famous Prison Dancers of Cebu, Director Romeo Candido, Writer Carmen de Jesus, Producer Ana Serrano and their incredible cast brought a once-in-a-lifetime, simply phenomenal evening to New People Thursday night. I was particularly struck by 15-year old Lia Yoo of Ohio, founder of a Gay Straight Alliance Club, who raised over $10,000 to help fund PRISON DANCERS. She was one of the most eloquent 15-year olds I've ever heard, and I just know we'll be hearing more from her in the future. Hey Lia, just tell us when we can vote for you or buy your books! If you're a politician, then politics just might be about healing.

PRISON DANCERS is releasing webisodes (www.youtube. com/prisondancer and www.facebook.com/prisondancer). How bizarre and strangely liberating it was to see the original Prison Dancers. And now, to see art transformed into rehabilitation (if that's what it was) in prison, and then re-interpreted as art once more – this is nothing short of liberation as well. I'm probably known in these Memoirs for hyperbole and sermonizing – Stephen Gong called me "The Reverend" last night – but I don't think it's much of a stretch to acknowledge that we all face our prisons. In some sense, we've all been prisoners, and we are all still prisoners, in this world of suffering. The freest ones are the ones who know this, the ones who dance, anyway.

I can hear Stephen saying, "that's just too much, Ravi, that's too much."

I sing America, from Prop. 8 to anti-hate,
I sing America.

There is the tender heart, the warrior heart born in response to suffering and intolerance. How do we reconcile prejudice with love? Perhaps with a father saying, "I love you no matter what," to his daughter, coming out to him for the first time after college (NO LOOK PASS). There was a good amount of "Daddy love" in this festival, including Eli Kimaro's A LOT LIKE YOU to Patrick Wang's IN THE FAMILY (Winner of both the Narrative Jury Award as well as the Emerging Filmmaker Award), but also harsh reminders of brutal masculinity and aggression, from Mye Hoang's unforgettable VIETTE to Rithy Panh's THE CATCH, and Jang Hoon's THE FRONTLINE. Life and film raise questions about how to be a good man, and what to avoid, to actively fight against. These questions are nothing short of liberating.

I sing America, from umami to Obama.
I sing America.
I sing America, Ph.D. sons of janitor fathers,
refugees from Vietnam,
I sing America.

Eli Kimaro spoke last night of how words from a village on the slopes of Mt. Kilimanjaro in Tanzania resonate across Asian America, and indeed around the world. I told her the other day that her film should be viewed by the U.N. General Assembly. Her aunts should be heard by the U.N. General Assembly. We have a Universal Declaration of Human Rights, but we're still far from the actuality of their universal acceptance, and we keep creating situations that put us farther from their realization.

But there's hope. We are holding something dear, each one of us. The power of expression, of agency, of the mind/heart. The words for mind and heart are the same in many Asian languages. Holding them together, as one – is nothing short of liberating. I saw the promise of liberation in a young person's experience with being deaf, in Mina Son's MAKING NOISE IN SILENCE, winner of the Loni Ding Award in Social Issues Documentary.

Thank you to all the volunteers, staff, members and fans of CAAM. We're 30 years into a journey, one that is really bringing us all together, hearts and minds, mind/hearts.

I sing America, the secret America,
As yet unborn.
I sing America, the America of our global hearts,
I sing America.

It was a seven-game, or seven-blog-entry, winning streak that took me to the heights of communal feeling and aspiration. I was immersed in experience, fully in the moment, documenting an incredible week that inspired, transformed and lifted me. And through the internet – through Facebook, even – my writing found an audience. The social network had a role to play, in spreading good ideas. If we tuned into the right voices, perhaps we could resonate our way to a more enlightened future. But paradoxically, we needed to be enlightened to begin with, to know how to use this strange new medium that, like the ocean and Mu, could divide as soon as join our continents together. It was a matter of perspective, surely, but also a question of how we constructed our shores, and what we allowed to sail between us.

But I channeled, as best I could, the life of the festival through the filter of my Buddhist, unifying-at-best consciousness, and this awakened something within me. Something that had been half-dormant for so many years.

I wished my life could be like this most every week.

I wanted to touch people, to communicate something true.

I wanted to explore, express and relate – voyage through human experience, and bring back a bit of wisdom and love.

To create. To heal. To come to. To wake up.

To write – a word that began to sound more like "rhythm," a musical production of the heart.

An Elegy for Doctorbot;
Or the Big Short Circuit

Sometimes social networking can make real life relationships worse. For example, your boss could defriend you.

Awkward.

I knew something was up when I got a chilly reception at the company picnic. My CEO, K, simply waved me off without a word. The Assistant CEO was similarly cold. I stayed for a while, making small talk with co-workers, but the vibe sent chills through me. When I got home, I checked: yup, K's Facebook profile now sported the "Add friend" box. We were friends no longer, after over six years of working together. K had been a supportive clinic administrator. He was enthusiastic about my creative endeavors, and also my medical work, promoting me to the position of Medical Director in 2008. For my part I had consistently voiced my enthusiasm for the clinic and its mission of treating the underserved, even as I grew concerned about our staffing problems. We were contracted with the city to provide mental health care, and yet had the highest number of patients per medical staffer compared to any other city clinic, potentially leading to deficiencies of care. I advocated for my medical staff, and more importantly, our patients, regularly – but this led nowhere. We were still underfunded. And now, I was defriended.

In disbelief and anger, I went to the clinic's Facebook page, and unliked it. "So there."

A short while later, marshaling my maturity, I sent an email to other members of the leadership, trying to heal the rift.

Subject: I hope we don't let our disagreement turn into hostility

It appears that our difference over policy has spilled over into personal animosity. I apologize for any part I have played in this; I have been upset over the last two weeks, but this is purely because I feel my advocacy for patients is not being heard or even acknowledged, and this has been extraordinarily frustrating.

However, I didn't expect to be met with hostility and dismissiveness at the clinic picnic by members of the leadership team, and I was surprised to learn when I came home that I had been de-friended on Facebook by two of you.

Please know that I have respect, appreciation and gratitude for our relationships over the last six-plus years. You have all been tremendously supportive in important ways during this time, and my feelings towards you have been positive and sincere. Whatever becomes of our relationships after this disagreement, we will always have that time – which I think points to the sincerity of our shared purpose and values. I hope we'll have opportunity to renew those shared principles in the future.

All the best,
Ravi

I cc'd HR, and waited for a reply. I returned to the clinic's Facebook page, and re-liked it. I tried to locate that feeling inside myself, too.

The conflict had brewed for months. It started with a documentation issue that for me had implications for the doctor-patient relationship and good clinical care. I should start by saying it was either all my fault, or it was the perfect mistake to highlight the Kafka-esque absurdity of the system to which I'd pledged my allegiance. It was just the right crack in the pavement to get me looking for a new sidewalk.

Jaron Lanier points out in *You Are Not a Gadget*, his cautionary manifesto about the perils of the software age, "there's a danger that you will become entrapped in someone else's recent careless thoughts. Struggle against that!" I was entrapped by the careless, unconscious thoughts of others, from computer code to interpersonal codes to the very code of the health care system. Careless thoughts came from careless hearts, heedless of the love that must bind us. In the end, the way we'll screw up health care is to come between doctors and patients, to minimize the importance of their relationship and by devaluing personalized clinical judgment and attention in favor of cookie-cutter mandates.

Once I saw this, I had to struggle.

Careless Thought #1: Surveillance only enhances care

There has always been surveillance in health care – by other clinicians, supervisors, and auditors. However, the medical equivalent of the social network, the electronic health record, is an innovation that promises great good, but in fact can become a Trojan horse for controlling the doctor-patient relationship and limiting physician autonomy. The more a doctor has to conform to codes that have little to do with patient care, the more that they have to worry about an auditor denying funding for trivial reasons, and the more they have to change their clinical practice for non-clinical reasons – the more danger to health care. This is a substantial issue as we move towards truly universal health care coverage, and my problems with the clinic provide a good example of what is happening on the front lines of care. The electronic health record is not ultimately about good clinical care. It's about coding, documentation and billing.

Careless Thought #2: Software designers built systems for themselves, not the real relationships of doctors and patients.

San Francisco's mental health programs had switched to a new electronic health record, Avatar, a couple of years before. There were numerous problems with the system, most prominently that it turned trained clinicians into data entry technicians, clicking their way through screens and causing certain evaluations to take two or three times longer than the old paper and pen methods. I took to calling it Aggravatar. The other problem was that we were now being scrutinized by a central office which took to issuing bizarre edicts that turned our work into Byzantine constructions of mandatory falsehood. For example, the standard visit time for a patient visit was 30 minutes, divided usually into 20 minutes of face-to-face time and 10 minutes of paperwork. Someone in the central office saw a string of 20-minute encounters come up on their computer screen and decided we must be lying. They sent down a decree to all clinics that instructed us to vary the visit time entered by a minute or two for each patient. Our actual practice of seeing patients didn't change, but now we actually were lying, putting in random numbers to satisfy a computer program. One clinician described her staff room: "Hey, Frankie, give me a number!" "22-18-21-hut-hut!" would come the reply. There was now an uncomfortable extra presence in my exam room, making me feel self-conscious and spied upon every time I entered a patient note.

Then came the crack in the pavement. When I became Medical Director, I inherited the previous director's Cambodian patients, all survivors of the Pol Pot genocide. I was immediately struck by the profound depth and extent of their suffering. They had experienced more trauma and suffered more anxiety and depression than any other patients I'd ever seen. Overwhelmed, I felt I needed to provide them more support and care. I decided to start a monthly group, focused on Cambodian culture, mindfulness and lovingkindness. Soon, my patients said the group was helping them to feel better; they opened up to each other and to me, and said they were less anxious, that they weren't "thinking too much." The group became deeply meaningful to me as well, as my relationship to my patients and their community deepened. I would attend Cambodian New Year at their temple; we would celebrate Valentine's Day together with chocolates and laughter. We were connected; we were an IRL social network, attached to and benefited by each other's company. The group treatment was an innovation that didn't fit neatly into any one box: it was a large group, focused less on symptoms than on the creation of community. It required special attention and leeway. Careless thoughts expressed in code and bureaucracy, though, don't take well to innovation.

Near the end of 2010, one of my group patients died tragically in a highway accident. We talked about her life and suffering in depth in the group, and mourned her loss. Somehow, though, I neglected to delete her from Avatar's group listing. When I caught the error, after two groups, I notified our billing department, and they sent word to the central office to delete the notes and the billings for those two sessions. Problem solved – or so I thought.

This would have never been a problem had Avatar been designed with reality in mind. It was set up so that one would have to manually delete patients from a group when they weren't in attendance, instead of manually confirming their presence. This was very much more error-prone than the more commonly accepted (in mailing lists, etc.) "opt-in" method. I would have never submitted a paper bill for a deceased patient. Now, a bill was automatically generated by software if I didn't exert special attention. The careless thoughts of programmers were about to blow up into a full-fledged confrontation, with consequences for patient care.

Careless thought #3: The hierarchy is adversarial to doctors, and thus toxic to the doctor-patient relationship.

The billings were never deleted. A year later, another, higher office, the "Compliance Department" said that we had billed for a deceased client. We provided proof that we had requested the billings and notes be deleted, but they wouldn't hear us. They shot their big guns at our small ship, and decided to board. They would audit *all* the group notes. They were intent on finding fault and establishing "compliance." Moreover, there was the overarching threat that they would take money away from us. I was sure that at some level they were rewarded for taking back funding, even from an already underfunded clinic.

I had written all the notes in the way I had been trained in four years of my residency program: patients were identified by their initials, and comments were made in every group note about each patient's participation along with the overall themes of the group. This was the professional standard I held myself to, and it made sense. This was the information that I needed and that any clinician would need to make sense of what was happening in group.

However, Compliance disagreed.

Careless thought #4: No negotiating.
The hierarchy knows best, not the doctor.

Compliance instead wanted each note to justify the service to the individual patient. They wanted the group note to include details of the individual patient's affect and participation, but not include anything about other patients or the interaction between members. My notes were "not in compliance." For my part, I felt that they were asking for each group note to be an individual note, and one that would be of no use to a clinician trying to reconstruct the process and progress of the group sessions.

Even this idea that each note should "justify the service" was problematic. When I trained as a resident on the inpatient ward, we were given similar imprimaturs. As a result, our patients' progress notes read "suicidal...suicidal...suicidal" for a week, and then miraculously on day 8, "not suicidal. Ready for discharge." Progress notes could not document progress, because the system was not set up to understand the reality of patient care.

Similarly, Compliance was now threatening to defund the group, despite the fact that we were caring for 15-20 patients for very low cost and with significant benefits.

My clinic supervisors, for their part, did nothing to defend me or the group, or even empathize with my position. After rounds of mounting absurdities, I saw that my position as Medical Director was being disrespected and devalued. I was essentially upbraided for not simply accepting "blame." Frankly, I had better things to do with my time. My blogging experiences gave me the urgent feeling that I should spend more time writing, to possibly reach more people through my words than I could as a full-time clinician. I called for a meeting with K, the clinic's CEO.

**Careless thought #5: "My needs first.
Empathy and validation for you last, if at all."**

At this first lunch meeting, I revealed my wish to reduce my hours at the clinic and step down from my position as Medical Director, ostensibly to have more time to write. I didn't provoke them by listing my grievances with their handling of the note situation. My goal was to work two days a month (down from my 20 hours a week), enough time to continue my Cambodian group and also see these 20 or so patients in individual sessions as well, as before. The Cambodian community was a special case to me, one deserving of special attention and relationship.

It became quickly clear, though, that K did not see any value in what I proposed. He suggested that having such few hours at the clinic would mean that I wouldn't really be "engaged" in the clinic's life – despite the fact that others similarly carried limited hours at the clinic, and were valued colleagues. He also suggested that financially it would not be feasible, even though the monetary commitment would be negligible, given that the person likely to take my hours would be a Nurse Practitioner, paid considerably less than me. I became alarmed at the lack of concern for my patients, and the lack of insight into the value of this particular group and the special nature of my Cambodian patients' experience. And to top it off, he seemed to be absolutely inconsiderate of my special, unique contributions to the group and to the clinic. I could feel in his mind a sense that I was just a generic employee making a request. It's possible that he had devalued me when I didn't simply accept blame and roll over when Compliance reared its ugly head. I was a doctorbot. A malfunctioning doctorbot at that, not a person worthy of respect and consideration.

I was further alarmed when he sent me an email the week after which did not address my points at all, and once again showed no empathy or acknowledgment of the special character of the group.

I then wrote emails to my supervisor, and also to the Assistant CEO, emphasizing what I called the "moral and spiritual nature" of the work, hoping that someone would influence K.

Instead of being the squeaky wheel that gets a little grease, I became the nail that had to be hammered down, or pulled out of the ship entirely. I was defriended.

Careless thought #6: Truth? We don't need no stinking truth!

I wrote my conciliatory email after I found out I had been defriended. However, I had been asked by my supervisor to addend all my group notes to "be in compliance." I told her it was impossible to remember individual patient's affects from up to six or more months previous. She said I had to do it anyway. Though she didn't say it, it was clear that I was supposed to make things up – to lie – to look good for the Compliance Department. At this point, I was not keeping a medical record for the benefit of clinicians and patients, I was fabricating a *billing record* for auditors.

I stayed late, and spent hours adding addenda to all the group notes. With minor variations for each service date, I wrote something like this, over 200 notes in total:

Themes: As above (in previously written group note for a Christmastime group the year before)
Number of patients present: 15
Facilitators: Dr. Ravi Chandra and Sothiya (name changed for purposes of anonymity, my co-facilitator and Cambodian-speaking interpreter)

Patient Observations: Pt. participated and was attentive. Moderate dysphoria noted, with some range. Pt was appreciative of gift giving and receiving.

Intervention: Facilitators provided empathic listening and interaction, and Sothiya provided language and cultural linkage as well.

Response: Pt. was engaged and appreciative of this session. Pt. has personally reported that group intervention has improved depressive and anxious symptoms over time.

Plan: Patient plans to attend group, and will continue to discuss symptoms with Doctor and Sothiya in individual sessions.

This therapy group is justifiable to the patient on the grounds that they have been through a soul-shattering loss of family, country and culture in the Pol Pot genocide and subsequent severe problems while a refugee and immigrant, and ongoing problems with adjustment to culture, and family and health issues. By providing facilitated group interaction and support for patient's culture, language and mental health, Dr. Chandra and Sothiya hope to continue building a foundation of trust in the world, self-respect, ability to assert oneself and interact with others meaningfully; all of these were demonstrably damaged during patient's experience.

This appended note is being added under the duress of the Compliance department, should anyone question why this was deemed necessary. It is not actually medically necessary, but is required for continued funding to treat severely disadvantaged patients, one of the main reasons that this doctor went into medicine.

I knew I was asking for trouble – but the fact that I was being invalidated forced me to make my point. In my heart, I felt I was facing down – and in fact educating – bureaucrats who did not understand what I was doing, or the importance of my work. Still, I knew I was asking for trouble.

Trouble came first in an email from the supervisor who had asked for the notes, a woman who had previously praised my work, professionalism, and communication skills.

> I just reviewed your addendum notes for 2 clients. All of the notes are gravely not acceptable. You wrote exactly same sentences for all the sections (Observations, Intervention, Response, and Plan) for all group meetings for each client – this is "cloning" that we talked about. You also wrote personal statements that do not belong to patients' clinical documentations such as "It (writing this addendum note) is not actually medically necessary but is required."
>
> I need to ask you to re-do the addendum notes – as you already wrote them on AVATAR, we cannot undo them. Please submit the new ones to me first before you write them on AVATAR.

I wrote back:

> I am afraid I am not creative enough to make up (read «lie about») 15 notes for each group meeting, and individualize them all (as I had told her before). The notes as a whole do pertain to the patients in question, and do speak to treatment issues. What I write in the note as far as personal observations are meant for any health professional who reads the note and wonders why there is an addendum, so I think it is necessary. Certainly, I would need to know why this addendum is there.
>
> That's the best I can do, I›m afraid. Moreover, I have no time available to do anything more.
>
> I hope you can understand.
>
> Best,
> Ravi

From the get-go of this small-scale, but illustrative, fiasco, I had taken umbrage at non-clinicians telling me, as a doctor and as the Medical Director of the clinic, how I should write my notes, and thus how I should conduct my medical care. At best, the note should be a way to emphasize what we want to have happen in a clinical encounter. It should convey the most important details of the session to any future health care provider. It seemed clear to me that the auditor's vision for group notes did not support what I would want to have happen in my group sessions: an interactive group encounter, with all patients participating in some way, and supporting their communal endeavor. The auditors wanted me to document primarily an individual treatment. The problem is, if you separate it this way, you easily lose the flavor of what actually happened, the importance of the interaction as a whole.

It was worth putting my foot down about this issue. I didn't want my relationship with my patients to be distorted by bureaucrats, much less their ill-conceived (and impossible to execute) ideas about what to put into an electronic health record. I didn't want my autonomy as a physician to be constrained. I didn't want to be controlled, because I felt I knew what was best for my clinical practice.

The other thing I was sure of: I was asking for trouble.

Careless thought #7: It's CYA, not CFP (Care For Patients).

What I didn't realize is that my immediate supervisors would go to any lengths to avoid trouble. They decided to back out the billings for all the group meetings, thus giving back the money we had legitimately earned in caring for disadvantaged patients, in order to avoid confrontation with auditors.

It was a cowardly capitulation from my perspective, but perhaps a way to avoid further sanctions. Agencies live in dread of audits, which could be designed to encourage better care, but instead seem to be about punishment, assigning blame, and taking back funding. The auditor is a fault-finder. They perceive themselves as holding the "good," and perceive deviating agencies or practitioners as "bad." This adversarial stance perpetuates toxicity. Despite all the accolades I received during my years at the clinic, the management team now viewed me as a troublemaker and "bad." I was scapegoated. Instead of engaging with me, instead of commiserating with me about the problem and seeing it in the way I did – as a bit of bureaucratic nonsense – I was told "I cannot defend your notes." If I had been in their shoes, I would have said, "this sucks; they do not know your patients or your patient care, and they have set up some requirements. How can we work to meet their requirements without losing our medical bearings?" No, instead, I was the bad doctor with bad notes. If I stayed in my position, I would inevitably be transmitting the system's toxicity to my patients. This was incompatible with my healing mission. Empathic failure was at the root of most problems that came to me as a psychiatrist. I couldn't stay in a system that failed me empathically.

Careless thought #8: Power over Love, Hierarchy over Intimacy.

Ai Wei Wei is dealing courageously with authorities and entities that are usually more concerned with protecting themselves than in seeing him as a human being, or responding to his concerns. There are many Ai Wei Wei's in the world. People of conscience who see a problem and keep striving to draw attention to it, to be understood and taken seriously. In this little battle, I saw how even in a small organization, the archetype of the dictator can possess the person in charge, despite all the other positive qualities he had. Once some leaders take on the mantle of decision-makers, they put blinders on and tune into their own perspective. They unconsciously become divorced from the human element, and lose the capacity for empathy for those with differing positions.* In health care, this means that bureaucrats fail to understand the importance of the doctor-patient relationship, and in

---

* Renowned U.C. Berkeley Social Psychologist Dacher Keltner wrote about this in his 2016 book *The Power Paradox*, which I read long after writing these words. Keltner writes that people are granted power because of their empathy, but once in power, they lose empathy. Power corrupts.

fact, do their best to micromanage it and put it into some kind of binary box of computer code and power relationships.

Perhaps at some level, these leaders fear that empathizing with others "weakens" their position. How can your boss say "no" to you if they are empathic? The whole point, though, is that the request for empathy is a request that the boss take in a different perspective, and validate the requestor's experience. That potentially could be a transformative event – perhaps threatening, perhaps reinvigorating. And empathy needs to be part of the framework of Emotionally Intelligent Decision-Making. Expediency and efficiency are speed demons, helpful in their right place, twin guardians of Structure, that behemoth that imposes itself helpfully and not, in our lives. But empathy brings us back to the pace that life is truly lived, felt and experienced. It's a slow walk, not a speed race. It's a deep breath, not a flurry of decisions. It's a practice of holding the space for what's sensitive and vulnerable, something that flees in the face of cold-blooded pronouncements. Empathy brings us back to depth. The needs and virtues of the human heart cannot be plotted by bureaucratic calculations, or accommodate themselves to a dictator's demands.

The patient is vulnerable. Doctors and other clinicians help them with careful attention to the relationship. The clinician is the closest eye on the relationship. If the system loses sight of the clinician's instincts and insights, the patient will be lost.

Careless thought #9: Dissent? Defriend.

Inability to tolerate dissent, and inability to connect empathically with the dissenter, are not particularly noble traits, and it would seem disastrous in any organization – or even in a marriage or family. The discourse of differing opinions bears strong witness to the strength of an organization. In the end, it is not our ability to fall in line and salute that marks our solidarity, but our ability to understand and co-exist with diversity of thought. Hierarchies have their place, but it should be a limited one. Even Confucianism, which emphasizes order and rank

– with allegiance and respect accruing upwards – also recognizes that this order is based on reciprocal relationships from the older and more senior to the junior – relationships that are supposed to be founded on good will and benevolence.

Every contact with another human being is a crucible for our heart, mind and soul. Facebook is such a crucible, a visible medium of the in-between, the space between us. Relationships transmute themselves into a digital domain at some peril; the greater peril is that the digital supplants the real, presses the real into conformity with digital code, and causes the real some kind of harm. The same is true when we press the doctor-patient relationship into an online progress note. My share of the conflict was in expressing dissent in the first place. But this was purely out of concern that the relationship that I was protecting was being ignored or devalued. This was a threat that I took personally, and was personally shocked by what amounted to a lack of empathy on the other side. But if we can't make peace over such issues, what hope is there for the bigger obstacles in our path?

When empathy and compassion are not in the room, it compels our inner Ai Wei Wei to rise in protest.

And as Ai Wei Wei has learned, as every person who has had to stand up for the rights of others and demand their own human dignity has learned, the protestor, the healer, is rarely blessed on first sight. The blessing would be to recognize that dissent is a valuable perspective from a valuable other. Dissent makes clear a point of disconnection. Our greatest duty, then, is to connect.

K missed that point – and Facebook was the means for him to make his preferred relationship posture clear, the final careless thought. "Ravi disagreed with me, therefore he can no longer be my friend." He preferred to disconnect, because that, in his eyes, kept him safe and secure, independent and in control. It was a short-sighted, mindless view that was a step towards power, not peace.

Careless thought #10: My feelings – and my position – are more important than yours. In other words, I outrank you. Shut up.

My boss opened the meeting, our first since the defriend, by saying he was "very offended, and this would take a long time to get over." I said nothing, but thought this was a rather defensive way to begin. Were his feelings more important than the issue we were facing, or more important than my own feelings? Some would argue that the boss's feelings are always more important; that's just not the way I operated, though, not with my boss or with the people I supervised. He continued, outlining the proposals that had gone back and forth, observing that none of the other's proposals had been acceptable to the other party. He had basically proposed that at most, I take a month off (to travel to India as I had planned) and then return to my half-time position, a non-starter because I had already indicated I was placing my chips on my writing. He also suggested that if I *volunteered* my two days a month, that could be acceptable. I kept silent. I hope I'm a fairly generous and good-willed person, but to volunteer to do what the clinic was getting reimbursed to do by the county was more than I could take. Taking advantage of my good nature made me feel uncomfortable, to say the least. It was a manifestation of toxicity, and implicitly abusive.

He acknowledged my service to the clinic, and then, finally, said the magic words I'd been waiting to hear for the last two weeks, the words that I had practically coached everyone in the management team to say: "the Cambodian group is important, and has been a very successful treatment program." He affirmed that these patients were in fact particularly in need of special services, given their history. However, his solution was simply that someone else would carry on the group. This despite the fact that there was no one who could match my role – as someone knowledgeable about Buddhism, mindfulness and lovingkindness, able to discuss medication issues, and already with an established history with them. There was no sense that this represented a loss to the clinic, as well as to these patients.

Instead, he suggested that group leaders change all the time, and we shouldn't make a big deal out of it.

On the face of it, this was true. None of us should think we're irreplaceable. However, what I proposed had the merit of being the least harmful plan. We had a good thing going – why not continue?

He asked me, as if it were up to me, "how long of a transition would you need, working 2 days a month? Two months, six months, eight months?"

"Three," I replied. Three months after I returned from a month-long trip to India would mean that my participation in the group would end in February, with our annual Valentine's Day group meeting. It seemed fitting to end on a note of love and connection, even as we parted.

"So you agree to a three-month transition."

"I agree that this is what the clinic is prepared to offer."

I thanked them all for their support over the years, and left, as stoic as I was when I entered. But when empathy takes a backseat to expediency, one can't help but feel dissatisfied.

Later, the clinic's supervisor asked Sothiya, my Cambodian co-facilitator for the group, "why is Ravi so interested in the Cambodian patients?"

I told her she should have responded, "why aren't you?"

Careless Thought #11: The Hierarchy devalues the Mind and Heart

The hierarchy can place rules, order, rigidity and subservience over the values of the heart, individuality, innovation and flexibility. My mentor, Dr. Francis Lu, award-winning "father" of cross-cultural psychiatry, told me, "institutions are generally irrational unless proven otherwise." The narrative of the institution, or the leader of the institution, can wipe out all other narratives, to the detriment of all.

The story that I lived every day was the doctor-patient relationship. Founded on compassion, humility, knowledge and skill, it was at the heart of my work. Moreover, this relationship required appropriate respect and deference from all other parties on whom the relationship depended. I was deeply saddened to discover that my clinic did not live up to the values they espoused in idealized mission statements and marketing to their audiences, the city's mental health system and patients of San Francisco. And beyond the clinic, others in the city's mental health system also focused on their own needs more than the needs of patients.

One high level administrator responded to my concern about increasing numbers of patients for our limited staff with a decree that I transition stable patients to primary care doctors – never mind that they couldn't possibly receive the same level of attention from harried generalists. "Those patients *could* leave your clinic," she said. "They're just *attached*." She used "attached" in a pejorative way – but I saw attachment as the very basis of healing, as it was the foundation of psychological health. But hers was the attitude of most administrators. Patients were essentially objects to them, numbers on a page that could be moved from one column to the next. As we scale up health care through the Affordable Care Act, we must ensure that we don't shove the doctor-patient relationship, with its attachment, compassion, knowledge, wisdom and skill – its *love* – out of the clinic door. Without love, we are lost. We must ensure that the social network isn't about the network, but rather about the people, about how we love and care for each other. Otherwise, the whole thing will go down in a big short-circuit that promises efficiency, but is a quick path to dysfunction.

Perhaps all breakups are messy. Some of the greatest rock bands have split over artistic and personal differences. At least we'd made some good music. Now I was off to make a solo album.

Like Jeremy Lin, I have been traded away. Like Jeremy Lin, my contribution and estimated future contributions have been devalued. Unlike Jeremy Lin, I am not going to a team offering me millions of dollars. I am going to a very cluttered writing nook, and a precipitous drop in salary. He went to the Houston Rockets; I received the ire of my boss on the day the Rocket-man, Neil Armstrong, dies.

I am on a launching pad, destination uncertain.

Sidd Is on Facebook. Would You Like To Be Friends?

It all started 2500 years ago, in Kapilavastu, which later became part of Kosala, which is now part of Northern India. King Suddhodhana was frantically pacing, waiting for a message to come in on his iPhone. His wife, Maya, was traveling back to her hometown to give birth to their first child. It was a tradition, but a tradition that made him anxious. "Always a rule! Always a tradition! I'm all for mothers being comfortable with their relatives at such an important time, but how's that supposed to make ME feel! And it's not safe for her, either!" he exclaimed to no one in particular.

Finally, his phone purred. It was a text. "She's in labor – we're not even there!"

Suddhodhana typed furiously. "Where are you? Is she okay?"

"We're in Lumbini, King. Wait, she says she's gonna do it, RIGHT NOW!" Eyes bugged out emoji.

The King thought about calling, but thought that would interrupt the attendants, who were busy tending to Queen Maya. A few minutes later, he got a series of pictures.

The first, of Queen Mahamaya clutching the branch of an Ashoka tree.

The next, of a baby boy – a boy! – a few steps away from his mother. Was he standing? Or was that the attendant placing him on the ground? Later, rumors would fly, but no one would talk.

In the next picture, the boy looked like he was pointing upwards with his index finger, and smiling.

"Look at my little #1! He's a real master of all worlds, isn't he!" texted Queen Maya.

"Mothers," thought Suddhodhana. But then he looked at the picture, and a tear rolled down his cheek. "My son. My son. I want to make him a great man, a great leader of our people."

"I love you Maya. You both look beautiful," texted the King, careful to spell out the word "love" instead of their heart emoji. The moment seemed to call for whole words, even though they were going out of fashion.

"Hugs," she texted back. The King sighed. "I hope you didn't suffer much, Maya."

"Hon, us girls know what suffering is all about."

"Come home safe, dear. We're all waiting for you. I'm going to make life easy for you and our son. Did you decide on a name?"

"Siddhartha," she typed. "Siddhartha Gautama."

"Sidd for short. I like it." He posted the photos to Facebook, with the caption, "Siddhartha Gautama, newborn prince of the Shakya Clan, with his mother, Maya and attendants. Look out world! He's a conqueror for sure!" Next, he emailed the wise man, Asita, and asked him to pay the royal family a visit. "Your sage prognostications would be most valued, great sir. Please honor with your presence." He included the photos, with the birth time and location.

A vibrating phone woke the king in the middle of the night. "She's sick. She lost a lot of blood. We're on our way home." *Dear God. What next?* Many women died in childbirth in those days. Even the wealthiest households were not immune. Suddhodhana arranged for doctors and healers, and made sure that all the proper offerings were made to the Gods. Maya came home, holding Sidd, and placed him in his father's arms. "I'm not long for this world, love. Take care of him. My sister, Pajapati, will help you."

A few days later, she was gone. All Kapilavastu mourned; Maya was admired and loved for her generosity and kindness. "She was full of love," Suddhodhana tweeted, "and even her last act brought love into the world." Pajapati read the tweet, and cried. *Whatever I do in my life, I will honor you, dear sister. And this boy, this boy – he will grow up knowing that his birth caused his mother's death.* Pajapati gathered her thoughts. "@Suddhodhana – Love comes at great cost, my King. But love marches on," she replied. Suddhodhana put his phone down, and raced to Pajapati's side. They held each other, and wept. The court photographer caught the moment, and after running it by the council, posted it to the Kingdom's Facebook fanpage. There, it garnered almost as many likes as the pictures of the newborn Siddhartha with Maya. "Siddhartha is lucky to have a family that will nurture and protect him," wrote one citizen. He thought better of typing the thought, *Who protects us? Death and sickness overtake us all. We'll be lucky if the King can protect us from invasions and bandits.* For those were the worries of the day.

A few weeks later, Asita arrived, his loincloth and walking staff testament to his simplicity. He took one look at Sidd, and began to weep.

"Is something wrong, Sage Asita," asked Pajapati. "Do you see something horrible in Siddhartha's future?"

Asita wiped his eyes. "No, dear Queen. Quite the opposite. He will be a great teacher, a man who will lead the myriads from suffering to salvation. I weep because I will not live to hear him preach."

King Suddhodhana hid his displeasure. "Thank you, Sage. That is a very noble future, indeed. Please allow my attendants to make you comfortable. Whatever you wish for, I will make yours."

"Thank you, King. I only wish for your happiness, and for the happiness of all beings."

"Duty is the way to happiness. The prince will learn his duties. Discharging them will make him happy, and blessed in the eyes of the Gods."

Asita thought carefully. "Quite right, King. But be careful you don't confuse your duty with his destiny."

The hell if my son is going to go about dressed in a loincloth preaching love like you, old man, thought the King. *He's going to be a warrior.* "Destinies are complex, Great Sage. Leading souls to salvation is a difficult task. I will make sure he is up to it – by training him as only a

Prince can be trained. Then he can choose his own destiny. As the next King he can unite all the kingdoms, and set a shining example for the ages!"

Just then, the sun poked through the clouds and a beam of light fell on baby Siddhartha's face. Everyone was silent. A celestial iPhone snapped a photo, and the photo quickly went viral on the HWW, the Heaven Wide Web, also known as the Indranet. "#Cute! Looks like a keeper. I'm in!" commented Indra, King of the Gods. Mara the Tempter, commented simply, "We'll see. He has to get past me." Yama, God of Death, agreed. "He's going to have some issues with me. I already carried his mother away. I'm open, though, I'm open." "Yama, your big fat MOUTH is ALWAYS open, LOL," replied Mara. Yama chuckled. He liked gallows humor.

Asita smiled and withdrew. *This child's heart is stronger than his father's will.* Later, he tweeted Karuna, a fellow sage. "You'll never believe this. Everything is about to change! I just saw this amazing baby!" Karuna messaged back: "@Asita: Compassion's gate opens every time a child is born! All things are possible with the heart and mind. #Love". "@Karuna: Word. But you ain't seen nothin' yet! This is big, man, big!"

But change, Asita knew, wasn't just about one person's gifts. Change came about through the interplay of worlds, individuals, and time.

Sidd grew up sheltered, as a royal prince. King Suddhodhana, remembering Asita's prophecy, did his best to keep Siddhartha away from anything that might make him curious about the deeper mysteries of life. This boy was going to be a King, not a Saint, and Suddhodhana made sure his court knew it. He was only allowed to venture out of the royal compound with attendants, who made sure there were no scenes of suffering in his path. He was only allowed 30 minutes of screen time a day, and Suddhodhana set up a special royal intra-net that only linked to happy news. His Facebook newsfeed was carefully managed: cute cat videos and stories about the unicorns of the Indus Valley predominated.

But parental controls can't completely block reality.

One day, the Prince was playing with his cousin, Devadatta. Devadatta had a new bow and arrow, and promptly shot a goose. Sidd, in shock, pulled the arrow out, picked up the goose, and ran with it into the Court. Devadatta demanded the goose back. "Dude, I was going to play Angry Birds with that!"

Sidd scowled. "The goose is mine, now. I saved its life."

The King couldn't disagree. He couldn't break his son's heart. "Sidd, you're right. Saving a life is more powerful than taking it."

Sidd started posting pictures of the recovering goose on his Facebook wall.

Chicks loved it, to say the least.

Devadatta defriended him.

Another time, Sidd was hanging out at the Spring Plowing Festival. He was sitting under a rose-apple tree watching the plow stirring up earthworms, and birds coming to pluck the worms from the ground. He was struck by the cycle of life and death, and totally zoned out, entering a trance for hours.

"That boy sure can think!" Pajapati texted to the King.

"It's a little much, P. Get him out of the sun."

"That's just it - the tree's shadow didn't leave him all that time!"

"..."

The King worried.

Suddodhana decided he had to take more active steps to make sure his boy became a great conqueror. He had him sit in on the defense council deliberations, and other cabinet meetings. "Sidd, a smart guy like you can do a lot of good when you're King," he said.

"OMG, what a bunch of hypocrites and egotistical #$#@! They talk big - and for what? Politics and squabbling doesn't end death and despair for anyone!" texted Sidd to another cousin, Ananda.

Suddodhana saw Sidd's lack of interest, and became concerned. "It's time for you to get married, son."

Within months, Sidd was married to a woman he speed-dated at a MaharajaMatch.com meetup. Yasodhara was beautiful, intelligent, generous and kind: everything Sidd could want in a partner. She took up her royal duties with great fervor, especially the charitable work that Queen Mahamaya had started years before. Sidd joined in. They posted pics of their Grass Huts for Humanity building projects, their Meals on Chariotwheels events and their Date-a-Sadhu Fundraising auctions.

They did not post pictures of kids – because they kept putting baby-making off. Sidd remembered what had happened to his own mother, and just wasn't willing to risk it. Moreover, Sidd had a restless spirit. He knew he had to find out what life and death were really about, before he could think of bringing a child in the world.

"Unscrew the inscrutable? In the Palace? You're joking." Yasodhara kept sending him pictures of suffering: sickness, old age, and death. "Unscrew that."

"That's pretty depressing, Yasodhara."

"You of all people know life isn't all LOLs, Sidd."

They contemplated escaping their confines and going on a pilgrimage together. Yasodhara thought that would be unfair to their families and the people. "Listen, Sidd: you go. Let's have a baby, and then you can go on the quest that you've been thinking about your whole life. I'll raise the child, and you can come back and give the little one the low-down on suffering." Yasodhara knew that her husband would never be happy living the life of a prince. Maybe he just needed to get this out of his system. And if anyone could figure out the meaning of life, it would be Sidd.

"Thanks for understanding, Yasodhara. I'll do it."

Nine months later, their son was born. They named him Rahula, meaning "fetter" - to remind them all of their connection, their bond, to each other. Even though Sidd didn't need a reminder, this would be a good one. A reminder to come back.

Sidd left the palace the next day, in the dark of night, alone. He deactivated his Facebook account, sent one last tweet ("Sorry, folks. I have to leave for a while. I love you all, but life's too short to not follow your #dream. #Peaceout. #Endsuffering."), and suspended his iPhone plan.

Where he was going, there was no coverage.

Being off the grid was no picnic. It took a while for the reflex to check for notifications to fade, and Sidd kept responding to phantom vibrations from a non-existent cell phone. But these habits subsided, and Sidd started noticing his inner life. He lived an extremely ascetic existence, and studied with meditation masters who taught him techniques that took him to the deepest depths of awareness of his mind, body and feelings. Still, he knew that he hadn't mastered suffering.

He spent years in the wilderness. He starved himself, eating one grain of rice a day. He later grossed out followers by saying he had even eaten his own poo. "Good thing you didn't food blog THAT!" joked his cousin Ananda. Ananda had a perfect, photographic memory, which would be an advantage for remembering Sidd's later sermons, but thankfully he was spared from seeing Instagrams of Sidd's worst days.

Sidd became rail-thin, and was able to touch his spine by pressing his belly. His hair fell out, and his skin blackened from malnutrition. He was at the point of death when he collapsed under a tree next to the riverbank in Gaya. A village girl, Sujata, saw him, and took pity. She fed him sweet rice-porridge, and nursed him back to health.

Sidd decided then and there that he couldn't starve suffering out of his system. Suffering was more part of life than even food. When he regained his strength, he saw he could once again concentrate and think clearly. He could once again use the anvil of his mind to forge a way out of suffering. He sat under a peepal tree, and vowed not to move until he'd found the answer.

Meanwhile, his ascetic companions felt he had betrayed them. They left for Varanasi, disgusted with Sidd and his three meals a day.

As Sidd sat under the tree, well-nourished, his mind cleared. He saw all his past lives, arrayed in a succession of altruistic acts. Here he was, giving his life to save others, time and again. Here he was, giving away all his possessions. Here he was, giving offerings to the sages of ages past. A common thread, a life force, moved through all time. In altruism, he paradoxically found refuge from suffering. By easing the strife of others, he felt more connected to them, realizing they were all part of a whole.

He saw what caused suffering: the clinging of the self to notions of "I, me or mine." This craving, this emptiness, caused dissatisfaction. The "I" always wanted what it couldn't have, and felt stuck with what it didn't want. Contentment was a virtue, but it didn't erase the craving. Could you erase the craving at all?

Then suddenly, he broke free of all the shackles of space and time. His mind was filled with boundless peace, without craving or disturbing emotion. He saw all beings in various forms of suffering, living but never escaping the jaws of death. He saw the path out. He saw how all beings could be saved, but also how necessary life was to amplify the power of good.

Mara, true to his word, sent his daughters to tempt him, and armies to frighten him, but Sidd was unmoved. He simply touched the ground, and said, "As the Earth is my witness, I am awake, and beyond all suffering."

The ground shook in all directions, and Mara bowed.

He texted Yama. "Yup, he's the real deal."

Sidd was in a state of bliss for weeks, and wondered how he could teach this ineffable insight. "Who would understand?" Indra, King of the Gods, beseeched him to try, "because there are some with only a little dust in their eyes."

He compressed his insights into the most powerful bullet-point list that was ever made: the Four Noble Truths and the Eightfold Path. He memorized and rehearsed his message, and set out to find his former companions. They would be the first to know.

He found them near Varanasi, in Sarnath, a few days walk from Gaya. They saw him approaching, and grunted in disgust. "Here comes the slacker," said one of the five. "That full-bellied softie." But when he got closer, they could tell something had changed. They stood up and bowed, knowing that he was worthy of their respect, without knowing why.

When he opened his mouth, their minds immediately blossomed. Kondanna's eyes lit up and he smiled. "Kondanna knows, Kondanna knows!" said Sidd.

They got him a laptop, and he reactivated his Facebook account. His first status update was simple.

"I'm back, after six long years of arduous practice offline. I have found the way out of suffering. Here it is, yo!

Four Noble Truths:
1. Life entails suffering (Dukkha, or dissatisfaction)
2. Suffering has a cause (Craving, or delusional attachment to the inherent existence of a separate self)
3. There is a goal - the cessation of suffering
4. There is a path - the Eightfold Noble Path.

And what is that, you may ask?
1. Right Understanding
2. Right Thought or Intention
3. Right Speech
4. Right Action
5. Right Livelihood
6. Right Effort
7. Right Mindfulness
8. Right Concentration

I know that's a lot to take in. I think it's better if we get together and I explain in detail. And more important than these words is the actual practice I will teach. I won't be posting much here, because, well, face-to-face beats Facebook. Looking forward to seeing you all – family, friends, and seekers."

Life is about direct experience and companionship; Facebook isn't that. And the mind/heart deserves better treatment than the newsfeed. He didn't post these private thoughts. *No need to inflame the technorati with my first sermon.*

Facebook was tempting, though. He broke all records for shares and likes with that first status update. #Enlightenment was a trending topic for weeks. Maybe this would be a good way to get the good news out, after all. He was a little ambivalent. Facebivalent. Being off the web was essential for his awakening. But without the web these days, his message couldn't travel as quickly. And it would be hard to stay in touch with his friends. Wisdom told him to steer clear; compassion told him to stay engaged. He'd have to strike a balance.

A Middle Path.

He'd have to put the "e-" in Enlightenment. Or, better than that, Enlightenment in the "e-".

And Sidd wasn't just Sidd anymore. He was Buddha – Awake. And for the sake of sentient beings, he would #StayWoke.

Buddhism in a Nutshell

The Buddha's last instructions were his most important, delivered after 45 years of teaching and building his spiritual community. Indeed, I think they're the only requirements in Buddhism, or perhaps in life. "Be a lamp unto yourselves; strive on diligently," he said before he passed away. Keep going. Awaken, only awaken. Only you can fully know the world you experience. The Buddha's teachings give us tools to help us understand ourselves and go beyond suffering, but only we can apply them and see how they might fit our unique circumstances. The world has changed dramatically from his time – and changes every day – but the human mind is the same, vulnerable to the same problems, and capable of the same luminescence, if we learn how to tend it.

But Buddha, though extraordinarily wise and knowledgeable, never proclaimed that we should accept his teachings on faith. Rather, he said we should examine his words, and see if they ring true to our experience. More recently, the Dalai Lama has similarly said if science debunks any Buddhist teaching, the teaching should be discarded. But with each step, I feel more sure of the path he laid out, more certain of the principles he discovered. I test his teachings every day, and find them a thorough balm and boon, empowering and insightful, compassionate and skillful. In short, they help – and more and more are finding this out for themselves.

Many people, particularly in the West, come to Buddhism because they are suffering and wounded. Their hearts hurt, and they want peace. They see the welcoming smile of the Buddha, seated in meditation, and feel at ease. The stillness he offers is a relief from the turbulence they've experienced in the world and in their minds. And there is so much turbulence – the inescapable vicissitudes of old age, sickness and death; all the problems the mind encounters along the way. Failures of empathy; trauma and abuse, from family, religion and culture. Racism, sexism, homophobia and other forms of discrimination and bias. Fear, sadness, loss; the ten thousand joys and sorrows; the changes of an ever-changing world; the attachments we form and the ache they create; our longings and desires; uncertainty and insecurity; and the turbulences of greed, jealousy, hatred, and ignorance, acting on us as individuals and as a society. Buddhism offers a way to cope with these, and a means to lift ourselves out.

First, sit comfortably. If you can manage a cross-legged position on the floor or a cushion, great. If not, a chair will do. Sit as erect as possible, without too much strain. You should feel upright, but relaxed, with your belly soft. Bend your head slightly, keeping your chin tucked. You can keep your eyes open or closed, as you wish. If they're open, fix your eyes on a point just a few feet in front of you. Feel your shoulders relax. You can cup one hand into the other in your lap, or place your hands on your thighs, whatever feels natural for you. Next, turn your attention to your breath. Notice it as it flows into your mouth or nose, fills your chest, and pushes your abdomen outwards. Then watch your breath as you exhale. If your mind wanders, as is its nature, gently bring your attention back to your breath. When your mind wanders again, notice and label what your mind is doing – "worrying," "planning," or simply "thinking" – and bring your attention back to your breath. You can count your inhalations – up to ten, and back down to one again – if this helps you stay focused.

You can also picture yourself placing each wandering thought on a leaf, and watching as it floats away downstream. Or see your thoughts and emotions as passing clouds, with the clear blue sky your true nature. In this way, you can loosen your identification with these "secretions" of your mind, and strengthen the calm, still observer within.

Watch your breath like this for as long as you can. It's normal to get distracted from time to time. The goal is not to be free of thoughts, but to become more aware of what your mind does, and deepen your ability to concentrate. Training the mind like this is like training a puppy. The puppy may pee, may play, may wander away, but you treat it with love and kindness, and gently bring it back to your lap. In the same way, you can bring your attention back to your breath.

A typical meditation session lasts about 45 minutes, but it can be as short as a few breaths to a few minutes, or days on end spent in silent retreat. As your concentration increases, you can turn your attention to your bodily sensations, your thoughts and emotions, and ultimately to the nature of self itself.

The mind is a thinking machine, it produces thoughts. But remember, it doesn't create truth. We have to observe the mind, be mindful of it, become familiar with it. The Tibetan word for meditation, *gom*, means "familiarization." In meditation, you're "getting to know you, getting to know all about you." The Pali word for meditation is *bhavana*, meaning "cultivation": you are not only familiarizing yourself with your mind, but also cultivating wholesome, fruitful states. Your brain will change with your practice, as you cultivate wisdom, compassion and peace.

This is the essence of the practice called "mindfulness."

Mindfulness is "awareness of present experience with acceptance and compassion," and is turning up in many settings, from sports to education to health care to the prisons. Myriad benefits of mindfulness have been described and are being discovered: to reduce stress and chronic pain, treat heart disease, lower blood pressure, improve sleep, relieve anxiety and depression, break free of addictions, improve productivity, improve relationships, decrease stress and increase resilience and self-awareness for police officers and others, and on and on. Even without all the philosophical underpinnings of Buddhism, the basic practice of mindfulness meditation has much to offer. Many people feel some relief immediately, and the practical benefits increase over time, as the brain learns a new way of being, and helpful neural networks are cultivated. (Mindfulness meditation, like anything, is not for everyone. If you have any mental health issues, you should consult an experienced meditation instructor or your health care provider before attempting these techniques on your own.)

Certainly, we can see that mindfulness is better than its opposite, mindlessness – being distracted, being overwhelmed by emotions and experiences, and being ruled by habits and patterns which we repeat uncontrollably. Mindfulness or awareness is a translation of the original Pali word *sati*, which also can be translated as "recollection" or "remembering." As we grow in mindfulness, we are recollecting a deeper sense of ourselves.

We are actually composed of many selves, each of them playing a role. Mother, father, child, brother, sister, spouse, friend, enemy, critic, advocate, doctor, lawyer, teacher, patient – each of them with a story, a narrative. The collective narrative we spin is our "narrative self." But alongside this self, and actually residing in a different part of the brain, is the "experiential self": the self that is composed of awareness of present experience and bodily sensations. Mindfulness can help deepen and expand the experiential self, bringing us to greater happiness and acceptance of the present moment. The experiential self can give us room to have a dialogue with the narrative self, allowing us to see situations from multiple perspectives and not be tied to our usual story. As we grow in mindfulness, we become less identified with our thoughts and emotions, less attached to them. We stop reacting in our habitual ways, and can generate a sense of calm. Depression and anxiety lose their footing, and happiness grows with our ability to stay grounded in the present moment. Awareness and acceptance of our present moment is always precursor to changing our narrative, setting the sights for our story on the highest goal we can aim for: freedom from suffering.

But isn't suffering an unavoidable part of life? Isn't suffering the price we need to pay for grace? There's a saying in Buddhist circles: "Pain is inevitable; suffering is optional." And maybe part of grace is learning how best to bear our pain. Certainly, we need a lot of awareness even to perceive the scope of our difficulty. The suffering that Buddhism speaks of is dissatisfaction, discontent, and being ill at ease. We want what we don't have, and have what we don't want. Suffering (*dukkha*) arises, as the Second Noble Truth declares, from craving or desire: we desire to have the pleasant and to be rid of the undesirable; we crave for "becoming," uniting with the pleasant, and "non-becoming," or disuniting with the unpleasant. Another way of looking at it is an attachment to a view of the self as independently existing, and thus living and craving in ways one thinks are necessary to maintain and supply the supposedly independent self. We perceive ourselves as isolated; fearing this state, we attach to the pleasurable and avoid the unpleasant, in subtle and gross ways. This approach and avoidance are termed "greed" and "hatred," springing from the third poison, ignorance of interdependent existence.

Interdependence (or interbeing, as Thich Nhat Hanh calls it), is an awareness of reality that goes beyond surface appearances. Superficially, things look discrete. The chair you're sitting on, the food you're eating, the book in your hands, the lamp above your head. But if you look more closely, you see everything is composed of parts, and is co-created by many hands. Many people worked to harvest the tree, turn it into paper, make the paper into a book, create the roads and transportation to bring it to you, and so forth. And how did the tree grow? Interdependent on everything that exists. As Thich Nhat Hanh says, "There is a cloud floating in this sheet of paper." Also the sunshine, rain, tree, and earth. Distant stars created the atoms in the tree. Even physicists haven't found an end to the parts from which reality is constructed. Even we are constructed of many parts and influences, physically, psychologically, and culturally. A table is constructed of legs, a tabletop, and so forth. The individual parts don't have "table-ness." Only when they're combined do you have a table. The same is true of the self. You can break down everything this way. It all comes together to become the things we see and experience.

Beyond the purely practical benefits of mindfulness noted above, it also sets the stage for seeing the Second Noble Truth in action, and acts as support for freeing oneself from suffering. We see our minds in three states: being attracted to, repelled by, or neutral towards the object in question. We are spellbound by sensory experience and our craving to have or avoid it, all because of our delusion of independent existence. Because of our delusion, we suffer.

The idea is that we shouldn't be passive about this automatic mental activity. That would be like seeing a sinkhole in front of us but not stepping on the brakes. Instead, "practice as if your hair were on fire!" Your happiness, and indeed your life, depends on your awareness.

Any activity can be undertaken with mindfulness. It is possible to bring mindfulness to your time online. What happens when you watch your mind on Facebook? What is pleasant, unpleasant and neutral to you? What pattern are you engaging in online, and why? Is it helpful or harmful? What is happening to your self? Growing in awareness, what choices do you want to make? What's your story? How would you like it to unfold?

Even the samurai warrior trained in mindfulness and detachment, allowing him to concentrate on both the way of tea and the "art" of killing. You could be a "Mindful CEO," mindfully paying attention to your profit and generating inner calm while detaching from the health and well-being of your employees and sustainability of the environment. But this kind of mindfulness is not the whole of Buddhist teaching. Mindfulness in its best and deepest form brings compassion, wisdom and ethics to all of life's choices, and compels a new way of being: an awakened life.

Right Mindfulness is only one-eighth of the Eightfold Path. Two other factors are closely related to it, and with these form the aspects of **mental discipline** vital to an awakened life. Right Effort asks us to diligently cultivate the wholesome or skillful qualities of our Buddha nature (compassion, lovingkindness, generosity, and wisdom, for example), and extinguish the unwholesome or unskillful (greed, hatred, jealousy, selfish desire, and so forth). Right Concentration brings us to deeper states of meditative absorption and attention.

Right Speech, Right Action and Right Livelihood comprise the **moral discipline** aspects of the Eightfold Path. The unifying theme here is *ahimsa*, or "non-harm." As mindfulness grows, one becomes more aware of the effects one has on oneself and the world. There should arise a sense of conscience about one's actions, and a desire to do the good and avoid the harmful. Buddhists are asked to adhere to the "Five Precepts": not killing, stealing, lying, engaging in sexual misconduct, or indulging in intoxicants (which cloud the mind and could lead to breaking the other precepts). But according to some Buddhist teachings, even these are not absolute – sometimes it might be necessary to break a precept in order to prevent a bigger harm. So I stand by my statement that the only requirement in Buddhism is, as the Buddha said, to "be a lamp unto yourself." (Breaking a precept for a bigger purpose is understandably controversial; it seems best to not harm in the first place. But we're all only human. Acceptance of our imperfect nature, even as we try to improve ourselves, seems essential.)

To properly decide on Right Speech, Action and Livelihood, one needs to cultivate the **wisdom discipline** of the Eightfold Path: Right Understanding (or View) and Right Intention (or Thought). Right Understanding refers especially to understanding that the self doesn't exist independently, but rather interdependently. Right Intention refers to carrying positive, beneficial, benevolent intentions for one's practice and actions, including the practice of renouncing harmful desires.

Together, the Wisdom, Ethical, and Mental disciplines are eight spokes of a wheel that carries the practitioner towards enlightenment and freedom from suffering. The wheel rides on our first and most continuous action, our breath, which is always with us and always available as an object of awareness. It deepens inwards, into our mental actions and skills, our knowledge and understandings of ourselves and the world, and then outwards, into all aspects of our activity in the world. From our breath to our living; from our living to all of life; and from all of life back to our breath, a continuous circle of interdependence. Seen in this way, the Buddhist path is the path of learning how to survive and thrive fully, how to become ourselves fully, and how to make best use of what the Dalai Lama calls "this precious human birth."

My friend posts a cute picture of a squirrel staring up into the face of a small Buddha statue, its front legs splayed out on either side, as if prostrating or awaiting the answer to an important question. I write a caption: "Could you put it in a nutshell for me?"

Buddhism, especially as introduced in the West, can seem highly erudite and intellectual. That was likely part of its appeal to early adopters. There is an endless stream of books written by an ever-increasing and more prolific number of authors and teachers, myself included. Some teachings seem incredibly complicated, abstract and inaccessible. But there are also branches of Buddhism that are very straightforward, actually relying on faith in the Buddha rather than meditation practice. The Buddha himself supposedly adjusted his teachings to suit the mentality of each listener. Therefore, "be a lamp unto yourself" – but also, "have faith." Some of us need saviors and miracles, while others want to rely solely on their own senses. There's a Buddhism for all of these inclinations. But they all ultimately rely on the Four Noble Truths and the Eightfold Path. They all depend on the Three Jewels: the Buddha (the teacher), the Dharma (the teachings), and the Sangha (the community of practitioners).

Buddhism in the West largely depends on spiritual teachers and the teachings. In my experience, the third jewel, the Sangha or community, is relatively loose, free-form and eclectic compared to

Buddhism in the East. I think that's largely because many Westerners attracted to Buddhism have had difficulties in relationships (but who hasn't?), and so get more caught up in following teachers or learning the dharma. Sangha is critical, though. Thich Nhat Hanh has said "the next Buddha will be a Sangha." I imagine this to be very similar to Martin Luther King's "beloved community." But as my friend Betty told me, referring to Tibetan Buddhism, "there are three levels of Buddhist practice. Dzogchen (placing her hand low), Mahamudra (raising her hand slightly), and — Relationships (raising her hand to the sky)!" Relationships are the highest form of spiritual practice. Relationships and belonging are extremely difficult, but ultimately provide transformation and insight. Perhaps "Keep Calm and Relate On" would be another nutshell for Sangha practice.

The Buddha's own "nutshell" for his teachings was this: "Cling to nothing as I, me, or mine." It is an instruction that goes "against the stream" of our casual and usual way of attaching to ourselves and our experience, of identifying with our emotions and thoughts and even our projections. When we get into our cars, if we're not careful, we *become* our cars, acting as if we were a two-ton machine capable of great speed and power – instead of the soft, slow, vulnerable human beings that we are. Our egos are primed for inflation and deflation: this is clinging to self. We think we are our jobs, possessions, money, notoriety or fame. We think we are what we post. We think we are our virtual selves. Buddhism helps us see this habit, and break it. Don't cling to anything as I, me or mine. Always ask yourself who you really are.

Indeed, breaking our self-centered habits and developing better ones is another definition of Buddhism. I heard one Buddhist teacher say, ominously, "this practice is meant to break you." My experience is that meditation builds you, even as it allows the difficult parts of you to "break through." When our minds become still, deeper, hidden sources of suffering rise to the surface. What our conscious mind had swept under the rug in order to adapt and survive is released. Our vulnerability and weakness, all our broken places, become undeniable and present. Our self-centeredness becomes visible. Our only choice is to hold ourselves gently, as if we were holding a baby, and help this mindstream in the ocean of our psyche come into coherence with our whole. A more resilient you emerges, more free of greed, hatred and the delusion of independent existence, the seeds of suffering. The brain is "plastic" – it learns from experience and can be trained and retrained. Meditators build areas of their brain associated with attention, positive mood and compassion. When these depths are strengthened, we find ourselves moving towards greater stability and understanding, but we almost always have to advance through troubling terrain. We are broken of our delusions, but cultivate freedom from delusions.

As we practice, we notice the sources of our suffering and discomfort. We lose our taste for habits that are superficially pleasant, but ultimately dissatisfying. We develop a wish to use our time well. This is what sits with me most as I observe myself on Facebook. I weigh the benefits and potentials – staying connected with a dispersed group, raising awareness for political causes, helping raise funds for worthy goals, being informed by a circle of online friends – in short, all the active ways I use the site – against the perils – a loss of privacy, what it does to my mind and heart, what it does to my sense of relatedness with the world, the way I become a passive spectator to what passes for relatedness. I come to conclusions for myself, but at the same time, realize what's good for me may not be good for others, and what's good at this moment might not be in the future. This is the dialogue I have between my experiential self, aware of present experience, and my narrative self, which sees many possible stories in this world of great needs. The only task is to hold the possibilities fully and with equanimity.

The choices ahead for all our endeavors, technological or otherwise, should be guided by wisdom and compassion, and not by ego and habit, which can only lead to suffering.

As I meditate, seven words emerge from the depths. *Be kind. The only instruction is kindness.*

This is the most resonant nutshell of them all: be kind. Learning to be kind, practicing kindness – to ourselves, each other, and the Earth which we share – this is the task of our time, the ongoing mission of our humanity.

Whether Facebook helps us to do this or not is an open question.

Origins, Migrations and Pilgrimages

This is about everything
that won't fit in a status update,
everything
that won't be liked with a click,
everything
that can't be shared
except when I look into your eyes
and hold your hand.
This is my heart, beating.

Why had the Mother waited seventeen long years to again visit the land of her birth? There were, of course, other things to attend to, all this time. Every few years, she thought about it, but eventually there appeared some reason, some excuse, to prevent the trip. The Son had been busy with school and career, and Son would be required. She'd left India with him, and she was not prepared to return without him. As independent as she was, she leaned on him in the way you'd expect an aging single mother of an only child to lean. It wasn't dependency – no, no, not at all. But as far as traveling to India was concerned, it might as well have been. He was, at the least, the contingency that allowed her to keep postponing. For his part, he had never encouraged her to travel alone, and wouldn't have supported it, even if she'd ever floated the idea. He had an image of her being beset by unnamed difficulties there, and that wouldn't do. India was anxiety-provoking, the Unknowns and Knowns of travel there much more intimidating than either Mother or

Son had ever verbalized. India was time and stress. At least a month was required to see – and reckon with – family, and to see the sights that might connect them to the greatness of the land they'd left. Not to say that family itself wouldn't or couldn't do that – but family was much more complicated than sights, and responsible for most of the stress. Both family and sights were bound to leave deep impressions, inter-mingling in what one hoped would eventually be alchemy. Alchemy seemed to require pressure, drama and even trauma, though, in at least its preface. And perhaps this is why the Mother had waited this long. In a word: Resistance. To visit again would be to revisit what had been left behind, to come into contact with a story that had gone twisting on without her, like a top that had been set in motion and now was spinning even more furiously on its own. To touch it again would be to risk spinning oneself, caught up in its unnerving gambol. This wasn't a risk, actually: it was inevitable. Mother and Son had spun out of Mother India, but Mother India's string still had pull. Indeed, she had not just a string, but a gravity. Maximum charm and maximum need, massed together in a way that compelled fascination and despair. Resistance allowed a safe, distant orbit. But the Origin was important. She beck-oned, across continents and seas. A return was required.

The Son had been to India five years before, spending five weeks there at the start of a five-month pilgrimage through Asia, probably the most difficult five weeks of his entire journey. India was Inferno at times, alongside Paradiso in people, spirit, and seeds of transcendence. It was a hard passage, with difficult family situations, visions of suffer-ing all around, and a turmoil of consciousness that only underscored the need for peace, his reason for pilgrimage in the first place. But peace required contact with the difficult, just as preparing a feast required fire. What he'd gained on this trip was invaluable; India had deepened, changed, and inspired him. He wanted to share this with his mother. So in addition to seeing family, he would take her to the sites of the Buddha's life he'd visited on that earlier trip. They would also visit the village of her birth and childhood. She hadn't been there in fifty years; he'd never been there at all.

He had no wish to see his own birthplace. His mother was his birthplace, his point of origin, and she was portable. She had transported him across countries, across worlds, as she had transported herself. The story of her origin and migration, from a small village in South India to the richest country in the world, made his story possible.

And now, he'd left his job. She had no more excuses. India called, or pulled. The stars had aligned for them to complete the circle, return to origins, and start a new story.

She was born in the 1930s, when the British still ruled India. Her parents saw her beautiful face, and named her "Amrutha," meaning "nectar of the gods," after the ambrosia conferring immortality, because she was the first live birth after her mother's three miscarriages. She immediately became the apple of her father's eye, the favorite of his eight children. Her siblings often garnered his ire – he had a sometimes angry disposition and strict temperament – but never she. The others sometimes got beatings; she got praise and loving attention. She was a good girl, though, always eager to do her homework and please her teachers. She had a certain light, I imagine, knowing her now, the same light that endears her to me and everyone she meets – a friendly energy that greets the world with a smile and strength. That strength, that spark, ignited one day in her small village, the village of Koppa.

She became fascinated with the town doctor. She went to him, day after day, pretending to be ill. "Amrutha," said the perplexed doctor, "you're not sick. Why are you coming to see me?" She confessed. She was enchanted by his work. The stethoscope, divining the body's secret messages. The pen, writing spells on a prescription pad whose paper brought magic in the form of pills and potions. The white coat, elevating the doctor beyond priests and teachers. The doctor was a healer, born of knowledge and science but godlike in his powers, holy in his ability to help his fellow man. She had been through a terrible illness herself, malaria that had wracked her body and swollen her spleen. She had nearly died; she told me later that her father even put a mattress on top of her in an attempt to control her rigors. But she recovered, and now was taken with the possibility of being a doctor who shepherded the sick to life. She was further motivated by a scene that etched itself into her mind: a gaunt, poor man pulling crumpled rupees out of his pocket to pay the doctor. She felt saddened by his need, and vowed to serve people like him. The local newspaper reported that their district Minister, representative to Parliament, had promised a scholarship to anyone from the area who wanted to be a doctor. She wrote to him, secretly.

Her father was not so taken with the idea. He was a man of tradition. Even though his daughter was an excellent student – a woman should hope for nothing more than to be a wife. "No daughter of mine is going to the big city to mix with boys and become a doctor!" He was angry that she had written to the Minister – the Minister! – without his knowledge. What would the other villagers say about a man who couldn't control his daughter? His friend warned him, "don't send her to medical school! Do you know, the boys and girls there wash their hands together in the same bowl!" When the letter came from the Minister's office communicating his support, her father angrily announced his disapproval.

Amrutha was unbroken. She no doubt inherited her father's fury as stubbornness. She locked herself in a room, and refused to come out until he relented. A few years after Gandhi's fasts to quell violence, Amrutha was fasting to compel support. It worked. He couldn't bear to see his favorite daughter suffer; his will couldn't match hers. He asked her to come out, agreeing to her plan. She, still wary, asked him to concede in black and white, and sign his surrender to her terms. Perhaps she could have been a lawyer. He slid the paper under the door. She read it, nodded, and unlatched the lock. She stepped out into her future. Recovery from malaria was like a second birth – and this was a third. Every step she would take in this life would break new ground and take her to new worlds. But there would be trouble on the path.

Have I mentioned her father was traditional? He did send her off to medical school – but he refused to even give her a pair of sandals. Shoes were fancy and uppity, he thought. "Just a fashion." Her bare feet would remind her of her family and station in life. Soon enough, though, she asked for some money from another relative, and bought her first pair of slippers. She wore the plainest sarees of all her class-mates, and when she could afford to eat out, she would split a dosa and a cup of coffee with another young woman – they called it ordering "one-by-two." This meal could be had for a few rupees, still a big sum at the time. But she sang, she acted in school dramas, and through a strange series of circumstances, she attracted the attention of my father. He was an engineering student; his roommate was interested in my mother's roommate, and asked him to write her and arrange a meeting. That didn't work out, but my father's correspondence with my mother did. They began meeting; he fell in love with her.

She graduated medical school, but soon, tragedy struck. Her father became ill. She was the one to diagnose him, from his X-rays, speckled with the white seeds of miliary tuberculosis. Amrutha admitted him to a sanatorium. She took his pulse, counting his heartbeats against the second hand of her first watch, his gift to her when she became a clinical student. He would only buy a watch for her "when she needed it," to measure the pulses of her patients. Now she used it to measure his. She injected him with antibiotics, and watched as they failed. She, the doctor, the first one in her family to go to college, was unable to heal her own father. She held his hand as he lay dying. He made her promise to take care of her mother and her siblings. She was the breadwinner now, the most educated, the head of the family. He passed away; one world ended as another began.

Perhaps feelings of loneliness and grief led my mother towards my father. I'm not sure. In any case, she agreed to marry him. But he was from a slightly different caste than her, and so their relationship would never be approved by either of their families. When they finally did marry, it was a secret wedding. If it was revealed that she'd married a man from a "lower" caste, it would make it impossible for her to find a husband for her younger sister. My father encountered significant opposition from his family as well. When they found out, they demanded that he get married right away to a woman of their choice, and to leave my mother. They wanted him to marry a woman from their caste, a woman from a wealthy family to boot. He broke, unable to stand up to their demands. My mother was distraught, but could do nothing. So he married again. And in time, he had two children by his second wife. But my parents sustained a relationship. Divorce was unheard of. My mother became pregnant with me. After she gave birth, there were times of abuse. Once, he slapped her, hard, on the face – and a shock went through her body, clearing her mind of any desire to be with him. She said later that in this moment, she had a vision of the Buddha. She "renounced," emulating Shakyamuni, the sage of the Shakya clan.

But now I was in the world; and there must have still been some longing for things to be "right." My father came to the United States for graduate school, with his second wife and family, and brought my mother and me as well. She wanted to start her training in medicine; he mocked her, saying she didn't have the brains to get a professional visa on her own. Infuriated, she went back to India so she could apply for a visa independent of him. To do so, she had to leave me with him. I was less than two years old.

I was never at home in his house. Naturally, his second wife didn't treat me well. Once, I played with her son, a baby who was younger than me. I tickled him and called him "funny face." She heard me, grabbed him out of my arms, and slapped me. "Stay away!" She must have viewed me as a threat. For my part, I tried to be a peacemaker. I complimented her cooking at the dinner table. "Mmm. Good *musruanna*." (A rice dish with yogurt.) My father chuckled at the scene; she said nothing. I guess it is something that she cooked for me, and probably cared for me in other ways in those two years – but she definitely didn't mother me. I didn't even know what the word "mother" meant; I can't recall ever hearing it, until my father took me to his office one day, and pulled out a picture from a drawer. "This is your mother. She is coming to visit you from India."

Mother. I turned the word over in my mind. What did it mean? It must have been my first koan. A word that should have meant the world to me, was instead a world I had to discover. An origin had been grafted onto me, and in those early years, it held precariously; but it took.

A few days after he showed me the picture, my father took me to the house of a friend. I sat on a sofa, my legs sticking straight out, as if I knew the ground would soon be taken from me. Then the woman in the picture appeared. She looked at me with absolute love, serenity and composure – the first time anyone had looked at me that way. She was tall to me at the time, beautiful and glowing, with fair skin and a bright, colorful sari. There was a new dimension in my world, surreally springing forth from a photograph into my consciousness. I smiled and said hello.

My calm soon dissolved. We all got in a car, and my father told me, "Now you are going to live with your mother." She was silent. He drove us to her apartment, and I started yelling and screaming in what I recall was the first outburst of anger and fear in my life. "NO! She is NOT MY MOTHER! Don't leave me here! She is NOT my mother!" I still didn't know what "mother" meant. I only knew that my father was trying to leave me behind.

They had to push me to get me through the door. My father put me into a bed, and left, after exchanging some words with the woman he called my mother. I fell asleep, numbed by the shock of my first conscious migration. When I awoke, I walked into the living room. My mother was sitting with a magazine. She looked at me, again with a serene composure and love which I'd never felt before, but which I must have remembered from my earliest days with her. I had a hole in my life that I didn't know existed, and she filled it. She held her arms wide, beckoning. I went to her, hugged her, and cried.

I was four.

My father soon left for India. The next time I would see him was almost three years later. "Are you coming to stay with us?" I asked, gaily skipping next to him. "Yes, I will be coming back soon." It was the beginning of a long decade of promises made and broken, a string of disappointments that taught me not to expect anything from him, from anyone, from life. My mother divorced him, but stayed connected, thinking I needed a father, a man in my life. I did; but he never delivered. The hole in my life grew bigger, massive and cavernous, capable of swallowing every hope that rose from my breast.

It was another demonstration of my disconnection from the world around me, one of the dark scars of which I was too ashamed to speak. There were others.

My mother continued doctoring, tending to the poor in the United States as opposed to India. There were times her patients in the rural South paid her in potatoes and onions; but she put a priority on my education, and I ended up benefitting from the finest academic institutions in the country. Her migration changed both of our worlds. But the world we entered wasn't always welcoming.

When I was in Kindergarten, a white boy said my skin was dirty, because it was brown. I went home, and scrubbed myself, head to toe, with Ajax. After all, it made the tub white. Wouldn't it do the same for me? My skin turned raw, but stayed brown. I asked my mother, "why am I still dirty?" She looked at me, a little surprised. "That will not go.

That is your skin." I went back, and told the white boy. "I'm not dirty." "Yes, you are," he said, and ran off.

My mom told me never to use Ajax on my skin again. She didn't tell me what racism was. She didn't know much about it herself, at that time. We were just a few years here, living in the deep South – Tuskegee, Alabama, where she was doing her medical training. There were public schools and Catholic schools, all mixed race, legacies of integration. In those years, school was an oasis. A large and welcoming extended family, where I sometimes called the teacher "Mom" by accident. (I held the word all too close now, all too ready. It was always on my reborn tongue, even as "Dad" receded into dark silence.) I was carried along by the friendship of classmates and warmth of teachers. At home, there was the confusing absence of my father, but in those early years, I felt wanted, and special. The pinnacle of inclusion was the 4th grade. We lived in Nashville, Tennessee, a mile from the Grand Ole Opry. I rode the bus to school, and was easy friends with blacks and whites alike. I was Cub Scout pack leader, 4-H Club president, and public speaking champion. But I knew something was wrong. There was a disconnect, and I was somewhere on the other side, able to pass at times, but inside, feeling apart, even as I couldn't make out why.

My teacher pulled a black boy angrily out of class when he smooched his lips next to a white girl. She took the paddle off the wall, and I jumped between them. "You cannot hurt my brother!" I shouted. Maybe I'd watched an after school special the day before; maybe it was in my blood, a bit of righteousness that had passed from my mother's father, to her, to me. The black boy said, "man, you ain't my brother. Let me get my whoopin'. And don't try to kiss no white girls." Now, it's probably hard to imagine that any 4th grade boy would be allowed to kiss a girl under his teacher's eyes, but when the color line was involved, reactions were more intense on all sides.

Christina, a smart, pretty white girl, had a crush on me. In all shyness, I didn't know what to do with the attention. We sat next to each other on the bus; I reassured her I still liked her after her new glasses made her feel self-conscious; she was a cheerleader for me in the class spelling bee, and I was in awe of her smarts, looks, and kindness. One day, her little sister declared she was going to marry me – probably a sentiment her big sis had inspired in her. Their mother was not pleased about her daughters' interest, and forbade them from seeing me after school. I didn't have words for it, then, but these incidents of difference-made-visible lingered. I presumed I was unacceptable because of my brown skin. There was a color line, and I started to struggle with it, internally and inchoately. Needless to say, I never tried to kiss Christina. "Don't try to kiss no white girls" became the enforced rule, rather than "stand up against racism." Racism itself was never acknowledged or discussed, much less the idea of standing up against it. My nascent bravery went unnoticed.

Some whites struggled in their own way against the color line too. The Den Mother of our multiracial Cub Scout pack was white. Whenever my own mother was on call in the hospital, I stayed with her and her family, and was treated as a son. But still, something was wrong. There was a refuge of acceptance, in the classrooms, playgrounds and homes of friends, a refuge that the adults must have known would be challenged or evaporate outright as we grew. Still, no one spoke to me of race; perhaps they were shielding me, or perhaps they were in denial. Perhaps they all had hope that our futures wouldn't be affected or defined by the color of our skins. But somewhere underneath my conscious awareness, I felt there was something wrong. There was an emptiness, a separation, larger than the still-growing disappointment with my father. I was 10 years old, being carried along by unseen forces, a vulnerable heir to histories and conditions of my adopted country, conditions that would become a disconsolate fit, a subtle shaper of consciousness-to-come. The migrations continued.

From the comfortable nucleus of Nashville, we moved to inner city St. Louis where my mother was continuing her training rotations at the Homer G. Phillips City Hospital. Here, the color line was more palpable. The year after, we would move to the North. St. Louis was a fulcrum of our American voyage, in the middle of the country, and perched between tensions. Our journey paralleled the Great Migration of Blacks from South to North, yet another thumbprint of diaspora, disillusionment, and discovery. I felt at home and part of the group in an all-black elementary school in inner city St. Louis. The teacher, an African American woman, saw a spark in me, and tagged me to go to an integrated "gifted" program in the suburbs. My walk to school turned into a ride on a yellow school bus that took me from the gritty brick buildings of the inner city to the tree-lined suburbs surrounding the Kennedy Elementary School, from a class where everyone looked like me to a class where I was only one of two non-white students. Before, I played with all the kids at recess; afterwards, there were cliques, rivalries and aggressions I couldn't understand.

It was a lift academically, but a rift interpersonally. I lost a feeling of togetherness, and acquired a daily sense of migrating to another world, a world where I wasn't sure I belonged. The inner city had been left behind, devalued. My commonality with other dark-skinned children was rent; in its place, a confusion about how I was connected to them. I felt difference more than congruence with my classmates. The world had grown larger, and less understandable. My skin, my identity, my boundary of communication with the world, was in question. I was a fatherless child, and my mother's strengths didn't include a complete understanding of the world to which she had brought us.

My suburban teacher, another African American woman, tried her best to reach and engage me, involving me in the class play and trying to get me to take up a musical instrument. She also told us about how the "For Sale" signs went up all around her block when she and her husband moved into their house in a previously all-white neighborhood. "Why would they do something like that?" I asked her in all innocence. She burst into tears. I apologized, thinking I'd hurt her feelings. "No, it wasn't you," she said. But we never talked about what "that" was. Racism was still an unacknowledged force; even our teachers didn't feel free to discuss it. The force of division and trauma floated between us all, as yet unnamed in my life.

One day, near the end of the school year, I went back to the classroom of my inner city teacher, and thanked her. Despite the problems

I'd encountered, she'd created a miracle in my life. She hugged me, my head pressing against the bottom of her warm bosom. She was a mother, even at work, and she gave me another birth that year, another origin, but still one with an uncertain foundation.

I took my confused feelings of separateness north, to Flint, Michigan for the 6th grade. I remember amazing teachers who took my acquired distrust of school and homework and rekindled a love of knowledge. An African American man who took in my "why do I need to learn decimals when I already know fractions," and turned me into a kid who enjoyed math and computers. Another teacher, a white woman, who praised a short story I'd written, about Sherlock Holmes going to Hong Kong to solve werewolf mysteries. Teachers who inspired and pushed me to do a talk on meiosis, which I delivered in an amnestic, dissociated trance, waking up at the end in a sweat, looking into my teacher's approving gaze. It might have been my first meditative absorption. My racial identity was still unformed, but I was finding an identity as a budding scholar, an identity that could gain the praise and approval of teachers, black and white.

But I was also a geeky nerd kid who carried a briefcase, not a backpack, a kid who very often didn't have a clue. Race was an unspoken subtext to my striving. My mom and I socialized mostly with other Indian families, and occasionally visited a Hindu temple, but I didn't know what it meant to be Indian, much less Indian American. When we went on a summer field trip to the Koster archaeological dig in Illinois, one of the archaeologists proclaimed himself and other white people "*Homo sapiens sapiens*" – the "wisest of the wise men." Then he glanced at me and said, "I don't know what you are." My African American teacher and I traded looks, but we never talked about it. Neither of us could press him on his bias, we just assumed he knew what he was talking about. I assumed that I was different from him. (I learned much later that all humans are part of *Homo sapiens sapiens*, but not all of us are wise.)

We moved to the suburbs of Detroit next. In Junior High, I was one of two Asians in my class, and the one with the darkest skin. We were both bullied. I got called the "n-word" regularly, until I started hanging out with a tough white guy who became my bodyguard, when he wasn't bullying someone else. I watched *Roots*, along with the rest of the country, and the history of the world became clearer. But still, racism was something that black people experienced; I felt I had no cause to complain about "a few taunts." I must have been exposed to the Civil War, slavery, and the Civil Rights struggle, and I remember having strong feelings about race, but I couldn't express or work through these feelings. Where was Brown in a world of Black and White? I don't think I could even ask that question; I could only mentally check the "other" box, the "sometime-scholar" box, the "son of a single mother" box – all boxes that left me apart and adrift. Who was I? No one. Race, that most essential aspect of identity, remained subterranean.

My mother, voting against the cold and white snow, moved back to the South, and I stayed at a boarding school in the Detroit suburbs. There was academic rigor and inspiration, and also depression and isolation. I felt a vast distance between myself and my well-heeled classmates, most of whom were blessed with two involved parents. I felt disadvantaged and doomed, and fell into a forlorn depression. Our school counselor was more interested in making a computer lab than in helping us cope with identity formation, racism, sexism or homophobia, perhaps a premonitory note to the current battle between psyche and silicon. We were left to our own devices. I felt abandoned and alone, and told no one.

Instead, I read *Siddhartha*, and dreamt about transcendence. I read *The Autobiography of Malcolm X*, and took him to heart, deeply to heart, as I contemplated the evil of hatred and the importance of standing up for one's rights. My whole school went to see *Gandhi*, and I felt a new pride in being Indian, and hungered for the possibility of transformation, redemption and leadership. My ideals were awakened, but I had precious little confidence in my ability to put them into action. And race and racism were always at some historical remove; students had few conversations on how race affected us, our parents, our community. A white classmate said the only reason one of my black classmates did well was because "he had white blood in him." When I was accepted to Brown, another classmate said it was "because of affirmative action." He apologized, but it hurt. Our High School theater director had me pegged to play a role as the accented salesman in *Oklahoma*. I declined. He thought I fit the bill, but I didn't want to be seen in only that way. But I couldn't avoid being stereotyped. I was cast as Aslaksen by a Senior in his adaptation of Ibsen's *Enemy of the People*. Aslaksen was a sober man whose tagline was "moderation, moderation!" A classmate said, "that's perfect – that's just like you!" To him and others, I looked like a "moderate" Asian kid. Inside, I fumed with anger about everything from my father to racism. I identified more with the Doctor of Ibsen's play, a man who fought for truth against greed, a man who stood defiant, strong and angry. I identified with the hero, of course; even the tragic hero. But I wasn't asked to play that part. I wanted to make noise, but couldn't find my voice. That 4th grader who stood between a child and a teacher's paddle had gone silent. I stuffed the anger, turning it into depression. I became the stone boy, stoic and temperate, while underneath, emotions burned red hot and frictions gathered.

When Vincent Chin was murdered in Detroit during the summer after my Sophomore year, I was disturbed, alienated, frightened and angry. But there was no discussion in school the next year; only one of my Asian American friends voiced her upset. I stood up in small ways: I befriended an Asian American boy who was being bullied; denounced classmates who said cruel things about a teacher disabled by polio; disagreed vehemently with racist comments of other classmates. But I didn't step into "being" Asian American, because I didn't even know what that was. I had no role models, no language for what I was experiencing, only the sense that there was something deeply wrong and disconnected about my life. I assumed it was me, my fault, something I couldn't do anything about. I had to hold fast to my academics, hold fast to knowledge, in order to survive, make it to college, win. I submerged my discontents, but I was painfully aware and dissatisfied.

I became more aware when I visited my mom in the South, and a woman shouted at me while I crossed the street: "Move out the road, boy!" I became more aware when white teens, our neighbors in Alabama, joked about getting points for running over black people in their expensive car. I became more aware when even a female South Asian teenager called a boom box a "nigger box." I became more aware when I sat through a laser light show at Stone Mountain of Georgia in which Jefferson Davis was portrayed as a hero riding a horse, and President Kennedy and Martin Luther King, Jr. were portrayed only as initials on tombstones, while all around me, white people waved miniature Confederate flags.

By that time, I was aware enough to be angry, and aware enough to voice my anger.

By that time, I'd gone to college. Brown University, where I found community for the first time, an Asian American community, a community of young people of all races striving to make some difference in the world, a community of friends that through even the hard times, tried to be good to each other, to be related to each other. My racial identity found expression, on the path to its fullest, freeing, most possessive depth.

But sometimes, even now, living in San Francisco, a city resonating with diversity and liberal ideals, I still feel my identity is not fully worked out. I don't think I'm a finished product; I don't think I'm done. I don't always feel comfortably and continuously connected; but I know my feelings are not unique.

I don't think my skin is dirty. But it is injured. There's something wrong, where my skin meets the world, where the sensed world meets my heart, and disturbs it.

There is an emptiness, a longing, a search for healing, a need to be a part of healing the wounds I carry and witness. *Siddhartha* appealed to me in my youth because it told the tale of a journey to a place beyond suffering, a place I desperately wanted to go.

I'm still traveling, migrating, a pilgrim going from origins to places unknown.

❀

You haven't a father,
So I'll give you a brute;
A bruit for a heart
That beats wrong;
You aren't yet whole
So I'll make you a part
A part always searching for home.

The story's the thing. Events happen in real time around us, we wade in or watch; but our minds have to make sense of it all, chart a path through the mess. We make up a story. We have choices on how we tell the story, on how we view its angles, on how it can be viewed from different angles. We have choices, but then we must take a stand. Our internal stance, which informs our actions – makes us who we are, and shapes the moment we share. It proves us; it provides our proof. As the Buddha said, "with our thoughts, we make the world." With our story, we fashion the boat of our soul, to carry us across the sea of time. We set a course and sail; we check the stars, seas and charts, then keep taking aim until we reach our goal. This is our pilgrimage, the central journey to which all others are joined.

We must know where we're going; we must decide how our story bears us.

President Obama wrote a widely distributed note to author Yann Martel hailing his book, *Life of Pi*, as an "elegant proof of God." Martel wrote that this was an "insightful analysis" of the book. Now, I'm a huge fan and supporter of President Obama, but I find it quite strange to call a work of fiction a "proof" of anything other than the author's intentions and perceptions, much less God. Even the Bible itself (or any other Holy Book for that matter) can't "prove" God. God requires a leap of faith, or some kind of deep personal experience that is by its nature unverifiable. When an author writes a book, he is demonstrating his own creative capacity – manifesting his own God, if you will. What would God be, if not an extraordinary storyteller? Wouldn't he or she be a creative and sustaining force, much like an author to their characters and world?* So, reframed, I would say *Life of Pi* is an elegant proof of – Yann Martel. I am rather convinced of Yann Martel's existence, as I am of President Obama's, at least in this historical dimension. God is another matter, and ultimately beyond the scope of human fiction or philosophical speculation.

Yann Martel had a story to tell; his Pi had a story as well. There are stories underneath these stories, and not all of them are acknowledged or revealed by either Martel or Pi. It's possible that they found their way unconsciously into the tale, and these unintended meanings and contexts are ultimately born only in the reader's mind. The book is a positive print, with the reader carrying, in their mind, the original negative and a context that breathes its own life. Martel, of course, carries his own negative. One story, apparent in how the book was received, was that Martel used his agency to create something that many others valued. That's another desirable quality to which surely both Gods and men aspire. If there's anything that we're all dependent on, as much as air and water, it's the hope that others use their agency in ways that add value to our lives – and of course, that we will do the same. The more of us participating in this web of value-adding agency, the more likely that happy endings are possible. Martel set out to write a novel that was riveting, hopeful and flecked with spiritual significance to lift the reader into reverie, and to inspire meaning as the reader goes on to create their own story, just as Martel empowers Pi to use his own agency – to survive, and craft his own story of significance. To survive is to shape a story of life out of both the harrowing and happy strings of our existence, to make those threads a tapestry. Noah didn't build an ark; he made up a story, a narrative arc, and saved the world.

---

* Well, it is possible that God is more of an Actor than a Creator, so to speak, one Actor among many. But this is a topic to be taken up at another time.

Martel and Pi illustrate this weaving of threads, this building of ark and arc: the power of myth-making, and the power of a narrative to generate meaning. Martel constructs a world, and carries his characters through it, God-like. That his hero struggles, overcomes internal and external obstacles, and finally survives or even transcends suffering is a narrative arc designed to illuminate some precious pearl the author bears. The conceit of the novel, and the "surprise ending," so to speak (spoiler alert) is that there are two possible stories. One that is almost magical, involving the Indian boy Pi being stranded on a lifeboat with a 450-pound Bengal tiger that he must contend with and even conquer in order to survive. The alternative tale is told to appease some disbelieving investigators, and involves no tiger at all, but a series of ghastly incidents with other human castaways that demonstrates only the brutality and venality of human behavior in a world that is simply a battle for survival, bereft of compassion. Which is "the better story"? The investigators choose the one with the tiger. One presumes that, in parallel, we are to choose our own better story in life – and Martel has said, in essence, that story would be the one with God in our boat, much like the tiger with Pi. We need no "proof" of human brutality. Any casual glance at a newspaper will provide that. We need examples to the contrary, and here Martel provides a service, in the choices he makes, the tapestry of the tiger. We do have a choice in how we tell our tale. For me, it's not so much about God but in how we choose to make meaning, the meanings we choose. How we become authors of our own personal story. The spiritual meanings, the idea of God, can lift our human narrative into a domain of higher purpose. We may not be able to make happy endings – but we can set course and sail.

I never had time to read *Life of Pi* when it first came out, but got motivated by the impending release of the Ang Lee film adaptation and the fact that I was traveling to India myself. What better time and place to connect with a story of a shipwrecked Indian boy and the meaning of life, than on Buddhist pilgrimage in India? I read the book on and off while I traveled, even while I stayed in a lodge decorated with tiger heads in North India, and finally finished it when I returned to America. The minute I closed the book, my friend called me to tell me his wife was in labor, which gave real life continuity to the idea of people choosing stories and creating meaning; we do this everyday, and never more so than when we choose to become parents and care for another being. My job was to cover for my friend while he went on paternity leave, something which I reveled in doing, because it carried meaning in this interdependent, life-giving world, filled with both shipwreck and transcendence. The tendrils of affection around his baby-to-be extended through me; it was the wind in our sails. I was a small part of his lifeboat, the lifeboat of his family arc.

What is the tiger, if it isn't just a tiger? A tiger is ferocious and strong, the embodiment of power and threat. Amy Chua called herself a "tiger mother": a demanding mother who pushed her children to the limits in pursuit of her vision of excellence – and obedience. Some praised her for both her stern discipline and her stated desire to build strength; many others reviled her for advocating abusive parenting methods that had traumatized them and led to depression, anger and suicide rather than to excellence. Others said they knew their tiger mothers were flawed, even tragically flawed, but they loved them anyway. Certainly Chua's children attested to a great deal of love and support in their family, and even Chua said that her book was in part an attempt to show how she backed away from her most severe ways, and learned from her "cubs."[†]

But the tiger mother is one way that the tiger is in our boat. Chua's assumption is that tiger parenting – with high demands, high criticism, and supposedly high support – produces better outcomes. This flies in the face of much earlier research showing that the similar "authoritar-

---

† My response to Chua, available online, is titled "The Battle Hymn of the Teddy Bear Psychiatrist." This teddy bear has claws, too, I noted.

ian" style of parenting produces low-achieving, depressed, alienated children. And a more recent study showed that, among a large sample of Chinese Americans, supportive parenting (loving, affectionate, democratic) produces much better outcomes than tiger parenting. In fact, supportive parenting produces the best outcomes of all four possible combinations of critique and support (high criticism/low support = "harsh", high on both = "tiger", low on both = "easygoing", and low criticism/high support = "supportive"). Supportive parenting was also the most common style, deflating those who wanted to stereotype Asian parenting styles as existing predominantly in the tiger camp.[1]

The message is clear. The better story, the one we should choose – is the one with support. Compassion, kindness and empathy take us a long way to our best selves.

The Son had no recollection of choosing, but the Mother in his boat was supportive, indeed.

The tiger could represent our own violent and aggressive impulses. The investigators in *Life of Pi* perceive that "the stories match": the animals are a *roman a clef* for people surviving the shipwreck, and the tiger is actually Pi himself, pushed to the point of murder, an evil which he cannot psychologically tolerate and from which he must dissociate himself. The tiger represents his animal instinct, which keeps his senses sharp and his mind inventive. Bracing himself against an imagined tiger gives him a reason to live, and puts the worst of his own violence outside himself, just as overcoming and transforming our aggression puts us on a spiritual path. The best in us is revealed against this dramatic contrast.

The tiger represents the wildness of nature, everything that is out of our control and yet we must learn to contend with in order to survive. The tiger could even represent God, as others have suggested. Or perhaps Pi's relationship with the tiger is where we'll find God. God is, in part, the connections between us – the "holy spirit" – the collective force of our bonds, how we shape them and how they shape us. As Martel constructs it, there is fear, distrust and power here; but ultimately it is compassion, respect, and the knowledge that each party of the dyad is vital in some way. Indispensable, not to be destroyed or abandoned. Even loved.

It's the eye of the tiger, it's the thrill of the fight...just a man and his will to survive.

Survival on the open sea is the dramatic challenge of *Life of Pi*. What makes it possible? I would note that Pi is the beneficiary of much human care, hidden in a background of details: others have built his lifeboat and supplied it with a treasure-trove of food and materials vital for the journey. He is tossed onto it by sailors he doesn't know. He is never completely on his own. Beyond the boat, he is adrift on a sea that teems with life capable of supporting his. And beyond that, he bobs on an ocean that is ultimately connected to land, and people, his ultimate rescuers. He certainly masters his fate – he uses his agency to supreme advantage – but he lives only because of the context of life around him and invested in him. Compassion surrounds, envelops, and buoys him in all these ways. Perhaps one could read the interdependent, sustaining surroundings as one manifestation of the divine, just as his will to survive – his tiger – is another.

Survival requires an emotional rudder as well. The meerkat island is an oasis, and also a trap. Pi could have lived here forever, an island unto himself – but "no man is an island." He cannot exist in himself alone. And he cannot leave the tiger to die on the island either. Ultimately, his compassion for the tiger, though it puts him at risk, also rescues his humanity. If the tiger is his own excommunicated, dark shadow, he must bring it with him. Without it, he would not be whole. And at ultimate end, the tiger lopes into the jungle, without a look back at him, dissolving into the wildness where he belongs. Pi is with people, who compassionately tend to him. There is no need for his shadow to possess him.

Compassion frees us from the island of self, the death-trap of self-ishness, and pulls us into relatedness. Without compassion, there is no survival, no survival of anything recognizably human or remotely desirable. Compassion, and wisdom guided by compassion, are the contexts that makes life possible – for Pi, for Martel, for all of us.

In selflessness, our shadow dissolves.

I would say to Martel and President Obama that the cares and constructions of this novel are as much an illumination of Buddhism as any other religion – or at the very least humanism. Pi's existential survival is linked to his reconstruction and maintenance of a mind that is extremely mindful, compassionate, wise, and skillful, ultimately non-selfish and aware of interdependence. When we express these qualities, we are manifesting Buddha mind.

I once threw the I Ching, and came up with Hexagram #10. "Treading. Treading upon the tail of the tiger. It does not bite the man. Success." This came at the appropriate time, when keeping my head low and doing my duties was important to keep me safe from the retaliation of supervisors. I survived. Success.

There are tigers in our world. Within and without.

I dreamt of a giant tiger, stalking me through the halls of a building. It's sides scraped the walls as it advanced down the hallway towards me. I shut the doors tight, cowering from the threat. And then, in the dream, I thought, "Oh, I could have just offered myself to her."

In one of the Buddha's past lives, he says he came upon starving tiger cubs at the bottom of a cliff. He threw himself off the cliff so they'd have food to eat. It's hard to believe – but all these stories of the Buddha's previous births, the Jataka tales, emphasize extreme altruistic conduct. The monkey king who sacrifices himself for his clan. The rabbit who throws himself on a fire to feed a starving man. Altruism defies ordinary logic, but we have examples of it in all life. From the teacher who threw herself on her students at Newtown, saving them from the gunman, to soldiers who sacrifice themselves for their buddies, to the gorilla who tended to the baby who fell into her enclosure, to the dolphins who save humans from sharks.

The Buddha also once told his closest disciples, who were questioning him intensely, that in a past life they were all vampires, and that he cut his throat so they'd have blood to drink. Did the Buddha believe in vampires? I'm not sure, but I am pretty sure that at the very least he had a good sense of humor, teasing his overly eager, vampire-like inquisitors. It's certainly a story to rival the sacrifice of Christ: "This is my body…this is my blood…"

Altruism may be almost unimaginable, but it is possible. Some deep place in our hearts knows that self-sacrifice to save others is not only self-less, but also connects us to some immortal, undying place.

The Impossible, directed by Juan Antonio Bayona, shows us what is possible too. Based on the true story of a Spanish family caught by the 2004 Indian Ocean tsunami in Thailand, it is harrowing, and ultimately victorious despite terrible loss. The most important scene for me occurs when the severely injured mother and her son walk through tsunami debris. They hear a boy's cry from some distant pile of rubble. The mother starts to cry out, to try and locate the boy and help him. The son urges his mother to keep moving, to save them both. He is worried about her injury – the flesh on her leg is cut to the bone. "Look at you Mom! We need help!"

She looks at him and calmly says "Even if it's the last thing we do." Even if it's the last thing we do.

Lee Chang-Dong's *Secret Sunshine* is a poetic offering about grief, human will, and what connects us. A woman, Shin-Ae, suffers not only the death of her husband, but the tragic loss of her son. She finds solace in Christianity, for a time, is finally able to release her pent-up tears, and even moves to forgive her son's murderer. When she goes to see him, though, he is not a broken man, humbled by prison and aching for forgiveness. He smilingly says that he has already found God, and has been born again. God has forgiven him already; her gesture is unneeded. Has God worked a miracle, or has he robbed her of her triumph over her own hatred? Is the murderer such a sociopath that he bypasses remorse and guilt through "religion"? Shin-Ae's grief breaks free again, and becomes a maddened rage. She angrily leaves the Church, and shows the defiant force of her will. The minimalist ending – the camera pans the ground, showing sunshine mixed with shadows, a secret, secretive sunshine – gives us many meanings. A mother's love is as powerful as the sun; though shaded, it can lead, and it can blind others with its might. Perhaps – just perhaps – there is a distant, mysterious God whose movements are nonlinear and don't conform to human fantasy. There is sunshine in human grace that's not explicitly "God." A man who clumsily cares for Shin-Ae, even if it's mostly out of his own desire for her. The viewer's compassion for her, an implicit hope of redemption in our relatedness to her. Love, compassion, hope: the ties that bind us all. All of these are secret sunshine.

That the sun blazes, yet oft is hidden, gives it many secret ways to show its light.

The human heart is like this, too.

Our human sun blazes from the heart. Sometimes it shines secretly.

Traveling to India is being plunged into the holy and the vulgar, the inspiring and the excruciating, all at once. One could choose to focus on one pole or the other, but coming to terms with all of it is a real challenge, and practically the definition of enlightenment. I don't think you can fully awaken without being immersed in India. Or maybe being too immersed in India keeps you from full awakening. My experience of immersion and emergence is a pilgrimage tale in itself, a baptism and re-baptism in something I struggle with, love and hate all at once. Some Indian immigrants and children of immigrants refuse to go there, wanting to fully cast off her burdens and relate to what seems more relevant, less hurtful, to them. I don't seem to have that choice. Something in India calls to me; history, hope, beauty – even magic – and family ties. India seems to say "ignore me at your peril; this is what the world really is. Deal."

If you don't come to India, India will come to you.

After a day in the air, Mother and Son found ground in Bangalore, where they were met at midnight by Krishna, Mother's nephew, son of her older sister, dead for many years now, and his wife, Radha. They were a modern couple, in many ways – Radha wore a miniskirt to the airport, attracting stares from middle-aged Indian men who wore dress shirts and slacks even in the middle of a warm October Indian night. If she noticed, she clearly could care less what they thought. Mother had insisted on packing a flyswatter, and she playfully swatted Krishna on the tush, laughing. He was still a child to her. She had saved Krishna's life when he was a child, diagnosing his Rickets disease and prescribing a course of vitamin D, firming up his softened bones, allowing him to grow to his now near 6 foot height. He had never forgotten this act, one of the many ways Mother's choices had changed the course of her family's life. Now, more than fifty years later, Krishna felt he was still in her debt. "My mother has died; you are my mother," he would say. "You are my cousin brother," he said to Son, making their tie sound even closer than mere cousins. They were all family, but these bonds would become manifest and more tightly woven as Mother and Son spent two weeks in Krishna's home, two weeks that magnified years. To Son, an only child, "family" would acquire new meanings, as "mother" once did. It would not always be an easy engagement, but it would be enlarging. Family touched the heart in ways that friendship couldn't. Family, particularly Indian family, was ever present, never done with. Perhaps it could be put aside, perhaps even a barrier constructed. But the ties of blood and time meant that they all shared something. Their history was twined, and lengthy, even though they'd hardly seen each other over the decades. Whatever meanings would come of this trip, the meanings of family would reverberate, flow across and through all barriers. All the unsolved and perhaps unsolvable questions India posed would be refracted in many ways, but the prism of family would always have significance, telling proof of any answers offered. They had been and would remain continents and oceans apart, but they would soon carry a bit of earth from each other's lands, giving their hearts more ground on which to rest, and their minds more to ponder, as they would wonder about what had arisen, and what could arise, in the space between them.

Mother hadn't been to her birthplace, Koppa, in 50 years, a long half-century ago. The village of her childhood, her origin, called to her as she approached her 80th year. Krishna and Radha made all the arrangements, reserving a hotel in the nearby city of Shimoga for an overnight, as Koppa was over a full day's drive from Bangalore. As Krishna drove, the years peeled away imperceptibly; the travelers shimmered in anticipation of acquaintance and re-acquaintance with the humble face of their histories. *Sati*, remembering, embraced them. They arrived in Shimoga for the evening, and Son, expecting a powerful homecoming, tried to get Mother to describe her feelings about the next day's discovery. She was circumspect, casually downplaying the significance of the journey. "Oh, it's no big deal."

Early the next morning, they piled into Krishna's SUV, converted into a time machine, and drove the final three hours to Koppa. As they drove down a main road, Mother's eyes lit up. "There it is!" They parked, and she got out of the car quickly. Son had to scramble to keep up. She crossed the street without even checking for traffic, and exclaimed, "Those windows! Those windows!" She looked up at three windows on the second floor – spaced equally and each set under a triangle of A-framed roof – and broke into tears. "Those windows!" Son captured the moment on video, as he imagined her seeing this house and those windows every day as she returned from school those many years ago. The three "A's" of the roof could have stood for Mother's name, or marked the Alpha of her journey. Memories of her father, mother, and family were tumbling forth, as Mother wiped her tears. They knocked on the door of the house, and a mustachioed man appeared. As Krishna had told them, the new owners were longtime tenants of the house, and had bought it from Mother's youngest brother, Ajay, a few years ago. There had been some controversy in the family over the sale and its proceeds, since these involved only Ajay and none of the other siblings.

The mustachioed man led them all through the house, from the sitting room to the kitchen, from the downstairs bedroom to the upstairs bedrooms, to the courtyard, to the well, deep in a large backyard. Mother whispered to Son, after seeing the courtyard clutter, "my mother used to keep it much cleaner. It used to be so clean!" Son was not surprised; Mother had drilled him with "cleanliness is next to Godliness," leaving him to fill in the "and Mother is next to God" for himself. There was an origin for everything, after all, and Son realized that Mother came from somewhere – she came from here. Her habits had been forged by the cares of many generations before her, a fact that he could hardly hold in his mind; she seemed like the origin of everything about herself to him, but indeed she was not, completely. She was unique, surely, but also *a part of*; and he was *a part of* that too, though now far removed. His world got bigger in that moment. He had a village in his life as well, as it turned out, with a grandfather and grandmother who kept a clean house, a house with a roof pointing skywards with three A-shaped triangles, giving Mother habits, and foundation. Foundation that was his, too. Mother inquired gently about the purchase of the house, and assessed the current owners, favorably. The owner and his wife, for their part, offered their guests coffee in small stainless steel cups, as well as a plate of fruit and a piece of cloth, all Indian traditions of welcome. They smiled and bobbed their heads from side to side, in the Indian manner.

Mother wandered through the house again; Son took pictures of her inside the room where she'd staged her fast. She opened the doors as she had done on that day, six decades before. So many years had passed since that origin; she had created a world with her journey from this small village; a journey which began with her revolutionary step of going to college, and then to America; a journey for education and betterment that created Son's world, too. Nothing had been preordained here, there was no privilege that was simply played out. Quite the opposite. It was spontaneous generation from sheer will and effort, from mud roads to medicine. Here, at the navel of Mother's world, Son took in the enormity of it all. All the ways it might not have happened, all the ways it might have gone differently, leading to a very different life for them both, and possibly no life for him at all. His existence, his life, was utterly dependent on his mother's resolve, on her latching herself behind a door, and then emerging, days later, victorious.

The upstairs bedroom was filled wall-to-wall with clocks in various states of repair. Pendulum clocks; wall clocks; table clocks; cuckoo clocks. Some ticking, others still, all taking refuge in this room. This was part of the mustachioed man's business. It seemed fitting, to Son, this bottling of time in this house. Maybe this was where time began.

Mother looked around the sitting room and proclaimed, "I could come and sleep here, on this sofa!" The mustachioed man smiled and bobbed his head. Son's eyes widened.

As far as she had traveled, part of her still longed for home, to be under her father's roof, where time began.

They asked for directions to Mother's High School; a young man pointed the way, and then immediately asked them to stop to have coffee with him, a sweet gesture of warmth and hospitality, common currency in the village economy. Time didn't allow them to accept this tender but quaint invitation; the SUV moved onwards to their goal. Soon, they were being ushered into the office of the High School's Vice Principal.

Mother had a dream of giving scholarships to children from this village. About a dozen students achieved first rank on the government's standardized exams, the Vice Principal told her. Later, he would send Son their names, and she would write individualized checks, giving each of the rank students about $20, as a prize. It didn't sound like much, but $20 went a long way in these parts. She hoped to make this an annual scholarship, hoped that this would become an incentive for students to work harder, but much depended on communication with the school. Even in these days of email, this was not a guarantee. The village High School was still far off the beaten path in many ways, and probably not used to thinking of itself as having a connection to the world Mother and Son inhabited. It probably wasn't even sure that the connection mattered, a sad limitation of possibility.

"I want to come back here next year and give a speech to all the students, and give the scholarships to them directly," she told Son. She wished to inspire and give back to her roots, to complete the circle as fully as she could. Son could see that in that moment, she would be receiving so much as well. He wished it could happen, too.

If she could elevate this world, give it the possibility of her own voyage in life, she would, with her will. As far as she'd come, there was knowledge that she'd left a world behind as well. Though she had served the poor, she'd done so in the richest country in the world. The poor she'd originally hoped to serve were still in need. There was so much need, in this far-off world, but now it was just a little less distant from theirs, a thread of thought and love running between them. It was a stitch spun by the heart's loom.

Whether the stitch would take, here, was beyond the control of Mother or Son, but not beyond their hope.

Time would tell whether the beat of the village clocks would match the beat of their hearts.

They made their way to the village clinic. The young doctor was surprised by having visitors, as were the patients, who followed them down the halls and listened to their conversations. They looked at equipment – incubators, suction apparatuses, gurneys seemingly primed for deliveries – all of it ancient, like they'd stepped back into the 1960's. The doctor assured them that most of the clinic's needs were taken care of; this seemed hard to believe, though. Mother wandered through a room of "hospitalized" patients – the clinic doubled as a hospital – and she spoke at length with one elderly woman convalescing in a bed. Suddenly, as Son watched, Mother planted a kiss on the old woman's head. Dismayed, Son pulled Mother aside. "Be careful. You don't know what illness this person has, or if she's contagious!"

He worried about communicability. Mother was focused on its near cousins, communication and communion. Their trip had many moments of Mother making such impressions. Her long absence from this country seemed to require these gestures, part of her Grand Return. Joking conversation with a salesman that had him declare that she was "a grandmother" to him. She corrected him: "Don't make me old! Say I'm your auntie!" And then, at a bank, after a long, almost interminable conversation to set up a non-resident account, she considers giving the teller a key-fob as a parting gift. Son, reading the mild irritation in the teller's face, discourages it.

Mother was loved by many in the country where she'd resided for more than half her life, but the country of her birth had forgotten her, lumbering on like an oblivious giant towards its own weighty destiny, as if she hadn't mattered at all. These small notions – a kiss, a key fob, a display of personality – were ministrations and supplications of, and flirtations with the giant, the mother, Mother India, she'd left behind. Would she be able to put to rest the grain of guilt she carried over leaving a world behind? Would the Mother remember her? Would love win out over all the sorrows of the path she'd chosen, forty-five years ago? Who had abandoned whom? Her longing seemed the only indication of the rift.

Forget-me-nots bloomed as they traveled on, from origin to open road.

Mother, Son, Krishna and Radha had spent a long day in Koppa. Night overtook them, and day turned to dreams, as the SUV, once a time machine, now became a vehicle for a bardo. A critical mass of psyche gathered as they drove back to Shimoga, creating a confined, conjoined transition to a new relatedness: it was exposed, uncomfortable at times, but necessary and real even as it bordered the fantastic. Whatever misgivings would come of this, this ride had to be so.

Krishna was a successful advocate – the Indian term for "lawyer." He'd picked himself up by his bootstraps years ago, when he was still producing his older brother's films. They'd run into legal problems, and he found himself needing to learn the law to argue their cases. He decided to actually become an advocate, studying late into the night for years, and working hard as an intern. Radha was an extraordinarily supportive wife, steady through the strains that challenged their spirits. His generous spirit added further strains; he had taken his brother and sister-in-law, with all their issues, under his roof too. Krishna and Radha spoke to Son of all of these strains. Son was a psychiatrist, Krishna said – he should be able to help. Son resisted. Krishna was driving, and this was an awkward setting for a potentially dramatic therapy session; there were warnings of this in the air already. Moreover, Son was wary of the boundary, and didn't want to be pulled into advising his cousin. Krishna entreated Son, though; perhaps the long day of accompanying Mother into her past had created a need for resolving his own. With qualms, Son relented and listened as Krishna spilled forth about his life. Stresses of work, family and childhood all tumbled forth in a three-hour road trip that pulled them hazily out of time. The drive became intensive psychotherapy, a mourning of trauma and losses. Son offered insights; how childhood difficulties could be connected to current anxieties and tensions. He was thorough, direct and as kind as possible, but also felt like he was being used like a scalpel, all the other possibilities of his relationship with Krishna and Radha, his short time here in India, being subsumed into his utility and expertise for a mission he did not choose. He was asked for help; he offered it, but his words felt mean, sharp and cold, for the simple reason that they pressed his vacation into work. There was a resistance in him and a bite in his words, as if they knew they were dangerous to speak. Traumas had led to unmet needs that pushed Krishna into patterns of emotional anguish and pulling for more from others, including now, Son. This wasn't the ending Son had wished for the day, which had suddenly turned to revolve around Krishna, instead of Mother. But this was how family was. He was there for a limited time, and there were many needs that came to greet him, tug at his sleeve, and plead with him. Krishna's needs were only the first, an appeal for enlightenment and solace from a doctor and cousin, or cousin brother. Krishna and his family would be gracious hosts as well, but the trip to Koppa, the voyage back in time, was the beginning of discomfort for Son. He felt forced to wear an analytical hat, and a critical one at that, putting some part of him at odds with Krishna as a cousin, father and man. He liked him, but was now on his guard. Was Son now their doctor, or a family member? A younger cousin to be babied to his discomfort, or an equal? All the contradicting roles met at stalemate, and Son started to withdraw.

Son had played happily in the extraverted pleasures and chattiness of family reunion. He threw himself into taking pictures as Krishna's family celebrated the Dasara festival, blessing all their household technology, from automobiles to computers. When he bloodied his toe walking barefoot around the cars parked in the dirt outside their house, Krishna's daughters, Son's young girl cousins, turned into attentive urgent care physicians, washing and bandaging it, in a moment of tenderness that was touching to him. Sita, Krishna's sister-in-law and wife of his brother Ram, never let a moment go by without offering some food or coffee to Son and Mother. He was, in short, well cared for, enjoying the kindnesses and attentions of family – a rare experience for him, an only child raised in an often lonely land. He had nothing to complain about. But after the trip to Koppa, something turned inside him. He retreated into himself, and found solace mainly in the safe, comforting, familiar blue glow of Facebook, preferring communication with distant friends over now-difficult relatives.

An awkward therapy in the bardo of the traveling car turned into an awkward two weeks. There was a Buddhist pilgrimage on the other side, and it was looking more and more attractive, more necessary, by the moment.

For his part, two days later, Krishna said Son had "cured" him. If so, it was a cure by absorption, and likely temporary. The main lasting change was in their relationship, which was now drawn deeper and more complex. They were, indeed, family.

Son was on Krishna's turf, and respected that, though he soon began to bridle at tensions that were particularly poignant for him. Son was sensitive to anything that resembled masculine domination of the feminine. Krishna was father to two young daughters, whom he both loved and cared for enormously, and sometimes bullied and controlled, out of his exhaustive anxiety and drives. Son immediately sided with the two young ones. They came to him, in turns, and spoke until tears flowed. On one level, it was another version of the complaint of children all over the world: "my parents just don't understand!" On another level, they were newfound family, caught in difficulty; he felt pulled to help them, somehow, but there was little he could do. But what he could do, he did; he said words that, as Radha said, "went straight to Krishna's brain," since he was family, too. But this didn't decrease Son's tension. He walked on eggshells; they cracked and cut at him.

The daughters were so weary of their world that they had taken to Japanese anime and manga; the idealized world and relationships portrayed there comforted and inspired them. Krishna, of course, could not understand their fascination. They craved Western food at the mall; he couldn't bring himself to stomach even a sandwich, much less a slice of pizza. The older one wished she could spend time with her friends; her father refused her, fearing not only loss of reputation, but also rape at the hands of men whose type he knew all too well as a father and advocate. "I trust the woman," said Krishna, "but not the age." But the feminine was under siege in India; inside the house by a perhaps overly protective father; outside the house, by a vicious and degraded masculinity and stifling misogyny cloaked as tradition. Son related to the daughters' feelings of not being understood, their need for ideals and escape. He felt the cloister within the house and the dangers without; he could feel the need for escape and freedom himself. He escaped into poetry; what he wrote, he offered to the daughters. It was as tangible an expression of his heart that he could give; he hoped his sentiment would stay with them, though he might not see them again for years.

Manga-Bangalore
Nov 2nd, 2012

The world beats in Bangalore;
My young girl cousins love Subway and Anime,

And spout Japanese phrases,
Cowboy Bebop their lingua manga.
Like children everywhere,
they complain their parents don't understand them.
Like children everywhere,
they are inventing their own language
and creating identities that don't hew
to the shape of an ancient, but timeworn, culture.
The call of India seems in part a din,
Something to wrestle with as much as love.

Growing up is always a struggle;
escape, always on the mind.
So *Naruto, One Piece, Fairy Tail* and *K-On*
give them homes when Bharat's four walls
can't hold their spacious souls –
Homes for the heroines they yearn to be –
the heroines they are.
They carry their own compasses,
unknown to parents, class, or clan.
They want to go to peace,
but they travel through war,
I have hope their journey
won't suffocate.
Their hearts beat universal time,
and they need to breathe.

The weather was cool and comfortable, typical for this season in India, but family could create their own weather conditions; the rareness of meeting them all could bring heat to the surface, as love and concern mixed with sweltering frustrations. Son had a lot of fondness for Uncle Vishnu, Mother's oldest brother. He'd spent a lot of time with him on his previous trip, gaining appreciation for his humor and adventurousness. Uncle Vishnu, now in his early 80s, had lived a long stretch in England, working as a photographer and printer. He'd then retired to Bangalore; now he volunteered his time in "Gandhian social work" as he put it, including animal welfare organizations. He might not have been as good at his own welfare, though.

Mother had heard concerns that Vishnu was being taken advantage of by his tenant-caretakers or even by her youngest brother Ajay, and she wanted to see him, check up on him, and most of all, to deliver a message. Krishna arranged a driver, and Son and Mother set out for Vishnu's house, in a corner of Bangalore that wasn't far as the crow flies. But the crow didn't have to deal with potholes, mud gullies or open pits. Getting to Vishnu's house was the most difficult passage of their entire trip, but Son was determined that they get there; twice, as a matter of fact. The first time, they met Vishnu and took shrewd measure of his surroundings, having tea and a long conversation with his tenant-caretakers. Mother did most of the talking, while Vishnu and Son played with Son's camera. Son snapped pictures of his beloved Uncle, and was enchanted by old pictures on a shelf. He'd only seen a few pictures of Mother in her youth. On a college trip to India, he'd seen a photo of his Grandfather, and some of his other Uncle, Mother's younger brother, Ajay. Here were the first he'd seen of Vishnu; they were rare and welcome reminders of family history, and his Uncle's exploits abroad. Here he was, lifting weights, bare-chested and strong. Here he was, in his 20s, looking as handsome as a movie star. There was a small mirror on the shelf, next to the pictures, and a round wall clock, ticking away as if measuring the distance from the past. It was no longer strong enough to hold fast to the wall, so it came resting on the ledge. How much longer before it sank to the ground and stopped entirely? Son took a photo of the still life scene, with his Uncle framed in the mirror, next to his photo in youth, and the clock; a demonstration of time's arrow and cycle. Time began and time ended, but within a greater cycle of many beginnings and endings.

They brought Vishnu back to Krishna's house for dinner and a small reunion. Sita served Vishnu tenderly, taking pleasure in watching him eat his meal slowly. She looked at him with love, and affectionately brushed his shoulder when she got up to get more food for him. "How are you, Vishnu mama?" she asked. He had no teeth, but he was never without a story, and laughter came easily in his presence. Son remembered his animated, theatrical descriptions of his time in Great Britain and elsewhere, and his dramatic renderings of difficulties in India. This time, he was replete with photography advice for Son, some of it helpful, and the rest tolerated as well intentioned, as most advice from the older generations is tolerated. Son believed in context, the relationship of setting and subject, and the importance of the background. He might make the subject a tiny dot in the corner of his canvas. Uncle Vishnu would tell him to crop the "unnecessary" background, and bring his subject to full center. Son would listen, quietly, but heed the image he saw in his own mind.

The next time they made the trek to Vishnu's house, Mother's concern and frustrations came to the surface. It had been seventeen years since she'd seen her brother; this might be the last. What might have been sadness turned into a harangue. She ranted at Vishnu, telling him to be sure his will was done properly, so no one would take advantage of him. She couldn't protect him from death, though that's what she might have wished most; so instead, she was determined to protect him from lawyers and miscreants. Vishnu stood impassively, expressionlessly, watching Mother, as she repeated herself on and on. Make a will. Make a will. Make a will. Finally, Son interrupted.

"I think he heard you."

These words went straight to her brain, too; and she stopped.

Son marveled that he seemed to have certain powers in India that didn't seem to manifest as readily in the States.

Mother's words were appropriate, but it was clear to Son that Vishnu had already taken whatever action he deemed appropriate. As far as he was concerned, there was no danger. But perhaps he missed Mother so much that it felt alright to hear her go on and on about anything. Perhaps that was the photograph that fit this parting frame best, the picture of Mother he wanted to retain. She was his baby sister, still, and he allowed her to be front and center in the closing shot. Son, though, tried to take it all in.

Later, Mother said, simply, "he's grown so old." If she had felt her own age a bit more as she looked at him, she said nothing of it. They were mirrors to each other, drops of water separated by miles and years, but still reflecting their common source. Stubborn will had carried them both abroad; they had both gone far from their roots. They might deny their similarities, they had ample differences, but their bond remained, unspoken but observable to the interested eye.

They said their long, but still too short, goodbyes; a promise was made to keep in touch, and visit again, soon. Son knew this might not be possible. He rolled down his window and patted Vishnu on the arm, held his hand and memorized his face, trying to hold it against the passage of time and death. He felt emotion welling, as he looked Vishnu in the eyes. The caretaker's wife, looking on, wiped away a tear. Later, as Son looked at the photograph he'd taken earlier, he wrote.

> My uncle, 82, bald and wrinkled,
> stands next to me,
> reflected in a small mirror
> which stands next to photos of him in youth;
> here, in striped Speedo, lifting weights easily
> with his chest puffed out;
> here, handsome, with a friend, posing.
> The clock behind these mementos on his shelf
> is a reminder of ever-present motion.
> Photos and faces, eyes and time,
> circle and pull each other,
> the past and present commingling,
> perhaps they plead with each other,
> or have reached a happy or forlorn acceptance.
> I carry a trace of him forward,
> in my own circle of memories.

Ajay, Mother's younger brother, was no doubt upset. He had eagerly written of possibilities for Mother and Son's time in India, offering his home and time for the duration – but plans changed. Conflicts arose, personal and impersonal. The days slated for Ajay were given to Krishna and his family. And now, the visit with Ajay, his wife and stepdaughter were tacked on to the end of a long day of travel – first to Mother's high school teacher, now retired and living in Mysore (he pulled out decades old letters from Mother, and they reminisced about their long connection, a vintage and practically unheard of scene of relatedness through the years, in Son's eyes) – and then to Mother's youngest sister's house in Hunsur, a short drive from Mysore. Aunt Lakshmi had gathered her children and grandchildren for a feast and reunion; she had been widowed a few years prior. Son had pleasant memories of her husband, whom he'd seen alive on his previous trip, and her – she had strived to maintain a face of high-minded family accord in front of Son, despite acrimonious disagreements with Ajay that had kept them apart. "You should not hear of such things," she said to him then, sparing him from what was no doubt the ongoing bicker of judgments and grievances. This day of reunion, there were hints of underlying unhappiness between family members – a grudge here, mistrust there – but Lakshmi tried, with abundant food and pleasantries, to maintain her maternal realm. Mother sensed the tensions, and valiantly gathered the tribe in a circle, had them hold hands, and even tried, without success, to have them hug one another. It was her attempt to be a peacemaker; perhaps it could have been her role had she stayed in India, or perhaps it was only a necessary gesture because she'd left. In any case, their brief time with family demanded some attempt at harmony.

After lunch, Son spent time with Aunt Lakshmi's 11-year-old granddaughter, who was fascinated with him, the tall foreign stranger who was also a cousin; she gave her attention fully and unreservedly as only a child could. Son was charmed by her innocence, purity and curiosity. *This is what it's like to have a child look up to you*, he thought to himself. It was a feeling that made him want to be a better person, a feeling that most fathers could confirm.

She said she liked to read and write; Son challenged her to write a poem along with him. They both wrote of love.

She wrote, reflecting her ideals:

Love is a community
Which makes everyone happy.
Love brings people together
And makes hatred gone.
Love is like a sweet apple or a chocolate
We eat with joy;
And we should all love each other
and be in community.

He wrote, reflecting the shared meal:

Love is edible;
the stainless steel plates
of my Aunt Lakshmi's house
are a mirror for her boundless heart.
Rice, sambar, rasam, papad, and so much more
come from bottomless serving bowls.
Plates are endlessly refreshed,
reflecting a love that never stops.

I met her twenty-seven years ago, my mother's sister.
She speaks only a few English words,
but we both speak the heart's subtle, quiet language,
and my tongue savors her food –
What more need have we for a common tongue?

Love is edible,
and we are all fat.

Laughter rippled around the room at the last line, rippling across
bellies that had indeed seen Aunt Lakshmi's culinary attentions over the
years. Whatever their disagreements, there was no arguing over food.

She took Mother and Son to visit her best friends, the town doctor and his wife, who welcomed them with coffee and conversation, in
their house above the clinic where a long line of patients waited for the
doctor's cares. As they left, the wife took a large sandalwood carving of
the goddess Saraswati down from their mantle, and handed it to Son.
It was an extremely generous gift, perhaps overly so, and made Son
wonder at the synchronicity. Saraswati was the goddess of literature
and music, and was known as a patron to Buddhist practitioners. The
poetic *mise en scène* earlier in the afternoon had caused some other
ripple, perhaps, in a realm above. Love was edible and it also traveled;
here, in this distant, wayward home, travelers received far more than
they could give.

To prove this point, Aunt Lakshmi took Son aside and pressed some
large bills into his hand. As much as he wanted to, he couldn't refuse.
Refusing a gift would be refusing love.

The brothers Krishna and Ram, with their wives Radha and Sita, all
piled back into the SUV with Mother and Son. By the time they reached
Uncle Ajay's house, it was dark. Because of their past disagreements
with Ajay, the four stayed in the car, and only Mother and Son went
in, for a living room summit. Ajay expressed his disappointment at
the short stay; Son and Mother offered their apologies. Mother had
brought some small gifts for him and his family, and of course, Ajay had
his own gifts for Mother and Son.

He was Mother's cherished younger brother, practically a son to her. Back in the States, she would often call Son "Ajay"; they occupied adjacent neuronal loci of affection, the same place in the heart. Mother had recounted time and again how her father's death had especially affected Ajay, who had to break his father's skull to complete the cremation ritual. This memory sometimes brought tears to Mother's eyes. But their closeness meant that his actions could hurt Mother like no other's as well. He'd been divorced and remarried; Mother was understandably saddened that she hadn't even gotten an invitation to, or notice of, his second marriage.

But Ajay pressed small gifts upon them, offerings intended to appease his older sister and to connect them once again. For her part, Mother was quick to underscore her love for her brother, even as she emphasized her position as elder sister. "You're very intelligent, very smart and philosophical. You're just like Ravi for me. But I'm smarter than you." Ajay was silent. As Mother and Son finally got up to leave, Son reminded her of the one possession she had mentioned wanting to retrieve: an eight-inch tall, white porcelain sitting Buddha that she'd purchased – for three rupees – in her first year of Medical School. The statue had passed into Ajay's hands when she left India over 40 years before, but had stayed in her memory. The Buddha's calm, smiling countenance had sustained her through difficult times, though she didn't even know anything about Buddha or Buddhism then, beyond his embodiment of peace. Ajay looked a bit surprised, but then looked to a glass cabinet in the living room. The Buddha sat on the middle row, there in the very center, on the middle shelf, the heart-space. He had attained a place, and significance, here, too. Ajay pushed hard at the glass door, moving it aside, and reached inside to retrieve the figure. He wrapped it carefully in newspaper, and found a box that was just the right size. Son wasn't sure if he was sad to part with it, or simply sad to say goodbye to his sister. When Ajay handed the box to him, and said goodbye, his voice seemed to catch, slightly, before recovering into a smile.

In the SUV, Mother shed tears, and remarked, sadly, on how thin and frail Ajay appeared, how old he had grown.

Krishna jumped in to reassure her. "Don't worry, everyone is happy, he is well."

Son understood. "It's not about his happiness; she sees he's aging, he's not the young brother she remembered and cared for so long ago. Mother is sad that this may be the last time they see each other."

The car was quiet. Mother reached across the aisle and patted Son on his arm. Nothing more was said; but the heavens must have seen all. The skies broke open in fat raindrops that drenched the roads all the way back to Bangalore, a fit of grief over the years, gone their separate ways, and soon to end.

> Words, gone straight to space;
> Rain, teary monsoon, replies.
> Emptiness embraced.

If you tell your relatives in India that you like pomegranates, expect them to find a funnel and force-feed you till you burst. Son discovered this. Every day after he casually mentioned that he'd loved the curds rice with pomegranate seeds he had on his last trip, he'd found a fresh pomegranate on the dining table in front of him.

The morning after they returned from the trip to visit Mother's sister and brother, the morning after the sad, silent drive back from Mysore in the rain, Son was sitting quietly on the living room couch. Ram, Krishna's older brother, unceremoniously and wordlessly plunked a stainless steel cup full of harvested pomegranate seeds on the table in front of him, then turned and left the room. It was a quietly dramatic moment, like the tipping of a chess piece in some long running game, and a gesture of quiet respect and affection as well. Ram had been almost unheard and unseen during Son's time here, a ghost of himself, withholding and perhaps observing, from the shadows; but now he seemed to be offering his subtle approval, appreciation of what he'd seen in Son the previous day. Son wasn't some spoiled transplanted scion of the West; he had a relatable, feeling heart. The pomegranate seeds, hand-plucked by a cousin twenty years his senior, were a bow, a quiet welcome to a deeper level of home.

Ram did have many critiques of the West, and perhaps reason to be wary of Son. Five years ago, during Son's previous trip, he had bemoaned the rise of the fast food "pizza culture" – the culinary invasion that stood for everything wrong about globalization and the loss of Indian ways. Now he targeted consumerism and technology, decrying the incessant "buttoning" of the young into smartphones and computers, separating them from the world of life and liveliness Ram understood, and tethering them to things that seemed alive but were actually dead. The young were staring into the death of everything that made the world real for Ram, and turning away from each other.

He was an artist, a director of past renown; his life revolved around stories and people. Indeed, a week before Son left, Ram called him into his room; he'd had a drink or two. "Let me ask you a question. Has your mother come back to India to find a place to leave her body when she dies?" Son laughed at the creative and poetic thought. "No, I don't think so," Son replied. Ram continued. "Okay, so perhaps I am wrong about that. But I have fixed your marriage. I have found a girl in Shimoga and if your mother agrees, you will be married on the 5th of November."

Once a director, always a director. Even now, Ram was arcing for narratives to connect the dots; he sought his bullseye, his big reveal, looking at all the camera angles. Happy endings, of sorts, for Mother and Son alike. "I'll keep it in mind," Son said, glad he'd be leaving on the 5th. He would never find out how far Ram had spun this last story, a perennial demand of the whole family. "You must get married! You must have the FULL enjoyment of life," said Radha, neglecting Mother's full enjoyment of life despite being a single mother, and the fact that Mother was standing right next to her when she made this declaration. They supplied him with pomegranates; they no doubt would have supplied him with a "girl" had he asked. He reminded them that even

Ganesha, the elephant-headed god, was a bachelor. "No," said Krishna, offended. "His wife is Siddhi, awakening." *A good cover story for pushy relatives*, thought Son. But his relatives weren't the only ones fixated on "the marriage solution." A lawyer friend of Krishna's had pressed Son on his tour of the Bangalore courts: "has marriage not *occurred* to you?" "The thought has occurred," he replied; "but the event has not." At least this produced a laugh.

Everyone was working on some story, some fashioning of the world, mostly to suit themselves.

A recurrent theme in Buddhist and some New Age circles is shedding "the story." I once heard a renowned Buddhist teacher demand this: "that's just a story your mind made up! Drop it!" This has never sat well with me. I fully realize that many of the stories we tell do perpetuate our own suffering, and keep us in the dark about our truest nature. We should loosen the grip these stories have on us. We should learn to view our stories from the many vantages that a meditative mind gives us. Many of our stories do melt away under the light of observation, or at least become more fully visible. But one story must propel us, a story that involves us most thoroughly. It is the story of survival, the story of presence. The story of life, compassion and wisdom. These are all the same story – the story of a mind coming to critical mass, rearranging its atoms to create light, magnifying its molecules to manifest the transcendent.

We cannot be story-less; at best, we can choose our story.

Ram: "When I am on the journey, my body moves forward, but my mind goes back. When the body goes forward and the mind goes back, there is a tussle between them, a magnetic breaking which makes me feel a lot. In that feeling comes a revelation about the story. Even when

I am alone, in my room, I am always on a journey. The mind and body have different attitudes, different magnitudes. The mind wants to leave the Earth, the body wants to return to it. Imagination lifts me beyond. There is a tension between flying and falling, between the power of my mind and the gravity of the Earth, and I become light, like a bee, touching flowers and taking their essence. Then I become a fish in the ocean, wondering how the fish likes the taste of salt water, but the man doesn't. I lose my soul and get into the souls of others, the feelings of others. Like that, I will have a hundred feelings and a hundred imaginations, and I bring these back into my body. Then, in my body, I imagine it all in a different color, and write.

"I went to a hypnotist, and he helped me see my story. Throughout five lifetimes, only one attitude has carried me – that of an artist. Between flying and falling, I have soared through these lives. And now I am here, talking to you, and you are also flying. Maybe we have flown together before. We must have – we have – flown together before. Life is like that. The universe is like that. We are always carrying a story, creating a story. We are always flying. Somehow, we are together."

We unfold in stories, stories composed of everything the past has delivered, and germinating everything the future will bring. This moment is all we have, a seed that never gives out. When we recite a poem from memory, the most tangible line is the one on our lips, on this moment – but it's all there, the whole poem, the story we know and the stories we don't, all in our collective story, our collective psyche. We are psychonauts, flying through psyche and stories in intangible space, and making our own story, all at once. The mind goes backwards, readily; we become pastronauts. We wander into and engineer imaginations of the future; we are future-trippers. But in this moment, we must be still, like the seed, seeing.

Ram: "When you go back to the past, you can imagine the future. Like the cricket player, you have to step back a few yards before you bowl. The batter has to pull back before he hits the ball forward. That gives the acceleration. The more we can go back, the more we gather ourselves, the more momentum we gain, the more acceleration you can have. The farther forward we aim, the farther we must go back. We must go back not only into the past, but into ourselves.

"A nuclear bomb has to reach critical mass. Every mind is like a nuclear bomb. It must gather mass, construct itself, before it can explode. It's not a bomb to destroy. It's a bomb to enlighten. But the bomb you are preparing must have friction. Without friction, you cannot create the bomb. That's the thing. This is true of all writers. The more friction, the more enlightenment they can bring to society. This is the bomb I am preparing in myself.

"The writer, the director notices. I keep notes in my mind. The way everything changed when you moved to the back of the car and started speaking with me. The director has to notice all of this. The way you are holding your camera. The way the woman next to me is sleeping. Where we are going and where we have all come from. All of this is part of the story. But none of this is the story. The story carries all of this along."

At the Bangalore airport, Son discovers that not only had their flight to Mumbai been canceled – the whole airline has been canceled. Only in India. Kingfisher Airlines is no more, and they are stranded, a last minute surprise stranding that leaves him desperately scrambling for a way out, any way out. Kingfisher representatives direct him to Jet. He is grateful for the plastic ease of it all, his credit card keying the door open to his escape. Escape comes at high cost, but at this point, he would pay nearly any price to leave Bangalore, and family, behind. The next step would have been to call the American Embassy and report he was being held hostage. He'd helped Krishna's youngest daughter with her essay on *As You Like It*; now he knew the full meaning of its most famous line – "too much of a good thing." He'd had too much of family. He'd gotten a prodigal son's attention, for which he was grateful, but along with this gift came a big dose of outsize personalities and demands, cares and suffering. And despite his generosity, Krishna was probably glad to see Son leave as well. Son hugged Radha and Krishna goodbye, surprising them with physical affection. It was a genuine burst, but given the extra vigor of his relief in departure. Before he could approach Krishna's older daughter, though, Krishna threw an arm around each of them and curtly walked Son to the airport doors, pointedly preventing an embrace that might have invoked Krishna's displacement and probably, the taboo of male-female contact already breached when Son had hugged his wife. Son was welcomed, loved and wanted; but he had also gotten too close. There had been joy, warmth and love in each of their four meetings spread over 30 years. There had been an instant closeness and fondness from the beginning. But now, there was reason for tension as well, tension which came with the substance of a real relationship. And relationships in India were brawny compared to their anemic American counterparts. Relationships on Facebook were downright cachectic. Real world – whether Old, New, Third or Whole-world – relationships were difficult, but necessary. The difficulty itself was necessary. Deepening. Fertile, even.

"You cannot know sweet without bitter," Sita had said, between her servings of coffee, outsized affection in thimble-sized cups. Few would choose bitter; few would, at first glance, choose dislikes over easy pleasantries. But reality had bitter notes; it was like coffee itself, bitter and sweet, the full-bodied flavor and drama of being human in a difficult, divided, wanting world. Reality was a story of awakening. Shakespeare had it right; the Greeks knew the territory. Their stories would continue, even though this chapter was drawing to a close. The narrative arc hung incomplete, in midair, like a bridge still being built. Their meanings to each other would have to rise and be reflected over time and distance, as the arc rose over still waters. Son would send them books, a parting gesture: career guidance books for the young women, and a copy of the *Dhammapada* for all. Krishna would write back, gratefully, saying he was reading the latter every night, before dinner. Buddha's words comforted him. This was now part of the meaning between them, part of the bridge. Only with reality could Buddha's words have meaning. Only in reality, in the needs of reality, could a Buddha rise, between them. Their stories, being as they were – bitter and sweet, difficult and joined – required a Buddha between them. Required a bridge. You would not need a bridge without the waters to span.

Son remembered Persephone, beholden to the underworld because of the pomegranate seeds she'd eaten.

He, like her, would return. Compassion and conscience required it; these included the ties of family.

We grow, not only by looking at each other, but also by looking in the same direction. When they looked out from their hearts, Son knew they saw the same goal, the same destination. Peace.

And when they looked towards each other, they saw a bridge: hazy and dreamlike in fog, but somehow able to bear weight.

As their flight landed in Mumbai, Phil Collins was on the overhead: *So take a look at me now – well there's just an empty space...* Son wondered if this was an ironic comment on his current lack of regret in leaving Bangalore, or an early notice that he would in fact find reason to be nostalgic in the future. After all, the "me" is "empty space," according to Buddhism, empty of inherent existent and thus only existing interdependently; not just subtly confluent with the world, but composed of it. His self had changed already; he was more aware of contingencies of family and culture. India was a powerful and personal experience, the Earth Goddess twisting her hair and releasing a flood that washed away the usual way of seeing; she leveled the self. "Start again, here," she said.

The self is a mirage. You can fool yourself at home, seeming to be self-satisfied and self-sufficient, master of your domain. You can fool yourself at home, but not on the road. The road reveals an ungainly travel companion: the ego, in all roughness, isolation and defense. The ego that is empty.

So take a look at me now...

If you have less than a day in Mumbai, don't busy yourself with travels, wasting your time in cars and on sights seen by many, soon to fade in memory and importance. Spend it with fourteen relatives, most of whom you've never seen before, in a cramped room at the airport hotel. Order room service, and chat. Let the years flow and coalesce around the moment, distilling time and reinvigorating transcontinental alliances with the correspondence of eyes. Take in everything; let yourself be reflected and refracted through the pupils of all, and reflect and refract them in turn. Be a pupil. Let hearts beat in proximity and lungs breathe the same air, from one chest into another, a communion of soul, airy spirit that you'll carry with you into all future breaths though they may be taken thousands of miles away, mixing in with the salty air of oceans and the loamy respirations of soil. This is, indeed, what it means to breathe. Breathe; Be Earth; Be Heart. Anagrams so unavoidable and clear that they encapsulated the truth of being human, itself derived from humus, the word for earth. With our breath, we contact all breath, all earth, all heart. Son felt that, in the crowded hotel room, and would carry it a world away.

Mother and Son had last seen Deepa, Mother's last surviving older sister, some twenty-seven years prior. They had contacted her daughter in New York, who had contacted her sisters in Mumbai, who contacted their mother now living in a nursing home, and soon, a hotel room was arranged. Son's aunt and cousins, spouses, and their children, three generations of family – became familiar. Frustrations with situations and with each other were naturally trotted out; Deepa's grandson tried to silence the turmoil emerging from his mother and grandmother, but Son encouraged him to let it flow. No solution was expected, but some things just needed to be said, in this rare moment of expansive relief.

Even this small part of the evening would be cherished in some way, aches made communion and common woe. Son folded paper cranes with the children, and joked about Facebook with the adults. His cousin's husband, Jagannath, described his days, far-flung across the city from his wife, children and friends. "One window on my computer is always open to Facebook!" he proclaimed. In one of the most crowded cities on the planet, there was an urgent need to not be separated from people you actually did care about.

"Oh, Wastebook…this is much better," said Son, gesturing to the small village gathered round.

"Well, yes – but it took hours for each of us to get here," Jagannath replied.

Son considered it. It was true – but *this* was truer, he felt, than any online alternative. This – would last. Instagram impressions couldn't match real world imprints.

Even the parting had staying built into it. *Hugs*, Son thought, *never ended, worldwide.*

The next day, Mother and Son flew from Mumbai sunshine to Delhi smog, a plastic smog so opaque and thick it could have been used to drive a 3D printer, a printer hard at work extruding billionaires and beggars in bottom heavy, world-weary proportions. They found a taxi stand, and asserted themselves to women who tried to cut in front of them; soon, they were in a taxi, but driven by a man who didn't know where he was going. After stopping for directions, twice, three times, they found themselves in front of a grand hotel that seemed to be spewing the smog that blanketed the whole city. Clouds billowed forth from the entrance, making it seem like a portal to some supernatural realm. Finding out it was actually mosquito repellent grounded them finally in the reality of New Delhi, where money could build high walls to keep out human-sized pests, and chemical weapons to deter even the smallest intruders. This could have been the palace of the Buddha's father, designed to shield its inhabitants from suffering.

But even in paradise, there are snakes. Son gets into the elevator the next morning. A tall, lanky, middle-aged white man is already inside. Then a female hotel attendant boards, dressed smartly in uniform. The white man looks her up and down, like she was a dessert menu, before he tries to punch in his floor number. The button doesn't light. When the hotel attendant tries her hand on the other panel, it works. "You have the magic touch," the man says in a sultry, come-hither voice. The woman doesn't acknowledge him. She turns to Son, smiling, and asks, "what brings you to Delhi, sir?"

"I'm here to start a Buddhist pilgrimage," Son said, conscious of how far his aims were from the white man, who was still eyeing the rear end of the hotel attendant. *And I've just met Mara in the elevator.*

The pilgrims gathered in the hotel cafe after brunch. There were five of them, three women, including Mother, and two men, including Son. Shantum Seth, their guide, introduced himself and his team, and invited them all to say a few words about themselves. Irene, from Australia, said she came from the Tibetan tradition. Barbara, from England, practiced Zen. Patrick declared himself a spiritualist, interested in "altered states." Son mentioned his Buddhist practice, as well as how mindfulness and lovingkindness had influenced his work as a psychiatrist. Mother glossed her introduction, and spoke from the heart, perhaps too closely for a first meeting. She spoke of life, her suffering, and how Buddha had brought her peace; she wept. Son felt awkward. He was unprepared for the sudden overshare, the deluge of words and tears. But Shantum simply took Mother's hand, and held it for a moment, breaking the tension. He rang a bell, and they all sat in silence, before adjourning to gather belongings and prepare for their first day together.

They learned from television screens that President Barack Obama had just won his second term. Son was exultant. His country had chosen inclusion and commonality, sangha, over the party that seemed to emphasize division and moneyed interests most prominently. It was an auspicious day to meet pilgrims, and to form a sangha with them. But sangha, like family, was composed of individuals. And one of these individuals seemed ready to pick a fight.

Patrick's words broke the group's buoyant mood. "Obama's just another politician. They're all the same. It didn't matter who won the election." Son looked at him, weighing the days ahead. *Oh, this trip is going to be interesting.*

There was a stunned silence in Shantum's living room, the living room of his joint-family compound, where over a dozen people were gathered – the sangha of pilgrims, plus Shantum's brother, author Vikram Seth, their parents, and a Buddhist teacher and his daughter, visiting from America. All were jubilant about the news of Obama's victory, with renewed hope for the future. Shantum's mother, a former Supreme Court justice, had just praised the merits of the re-elected American President. The Buddhist teacher's daughter, a recent college grad, angrily sprang to Obama's defense after hearing Patrick's words. "I disagree. Elections do matter. And Romney would have led the country in a very different direction."

Son listened to the repartee. He didn't fully disagree with Patrick, but noted his timing was awful. He not only seemed to lack tact, but seemed to pride himself on his pugnaciousness. Picking fights wasn't a good way to make friends – but Patrick didn't seem interested in making friends, or even making nice. He described himself as Irish, but he'd grown up in America, and had no trace of an Irish accent, having moved to Ireland as an adult. There was something out-of-place about him, a mid-50's-going-on-12 alpha-dog ego on Buddhist pilgrimage, who held his fight even in how he described his citizenship. It turned out that he'd added the tour on a whim, after finding he had just enough time for it before his around-the-world ticket expired. He was the accidental tourist written in by a cosmic trickster. Son was relieved when he found out that he would be leaving after the first half of the pilgrimage. Perhaps, Son decided, Patrick was part of the difficult-personality-taper that he'd been on since Bangalore. It could only get better, right?

Ironically, Son had just published a series of online essays about dealing with difficult people. "It takes two to tango," "put on a gameface" and "use every opportunity for practice" were three bits of wisdom that came to mind right away. Easier said than done.

Shantum spoke after leading them through Birla House, the last residence of Mahatma Gandhi.

"Pilgrimage is my practice." He'd organized Thich Nhat Hanh's first pilgrimage to the sites of the Buddha's life in the 1980's, and the venerable monk had encouraged him to devote his life to pilgrimage. He'd led tours since then, and even became an ordained teacher in Thich Nhat Hanh's Order of Interbeing. "India hasn't changed in 2500 years. We can see what it was like then." Shantum had majored in Gandhian economics, and was still very devoted to the Gandhian village ideal of relationships, harmony and coexistence. "Gandhi reminds me of Buddha, at least in our contemporary life. And India will be your teacher, as it taught both of them. Don't try to work it all out here. The real journey begins at home."

Joseph Campbell famously said "you don't need to travel to the holy land. The holy land is within you." But it takes travel to really awaken what we hold inside. There are places, and there are *places*, made special by the history they've witnessed, thus becoming a portal to both history and transcendence. Visiting the Buddha's birthplace in Lumbini, his place of Enlightenment in Bodhgaya, the site of his first sermon in Sarnath, and the site of his passing in Kushinagar, along with such incredible locations as Nalanda, the phenomenal Buddhist university that flourished 1500 years ago, and several famous monasteries, one of which included the stone dwelling-place of the Buddha himself, now adorned with coatings of gold leaf from countless pilgrims, this was all like the ringing of a time-stilling meditation bell, resonating with breath and heart. And having Shantum for teacher and guide enriched the experience powerfully. He gave daily Buddhist teachings and led the group in meditation at each of the sites; he passionately educated them on the versatility of the cow patty as green fuel and building material, and sold them on his idea of a "bullshit conference;" and he gathered them, at the close of each day, to share their thoughts, "aha moments," and difficulties.

The pilgrimage, with Shantum's care, joined them all as sangha, but it also joined them to all others who had passed this way, over the course of 2,500 years, and of course connected them to the man whom they were all inspired by, the Buddha himself. In some way, the Buddha was still present, walking with them, helping them awaken.

And when the holy land within was awakening, it was possible to see the depths of the world without.

They flew first from Delhi to Patna, and got in the van that would carry them across the Buddhist path. Driving through the city, they saw myriads, a whirlpool of humanity, living on the street, in tent cities where bare-bottomed waifs sat on the bare earth. The roads were coagulated with life, strapped but scrappy. Mother, looking out of the window, touched Son. "Ravi, see. See."

If this was the India that hadn't changed in 2,500 years, one could see the reason for Siddhartha's burning need to understand the world, replete with suffering. That first van ride was like the fabled chariot rides of Buddhist legend: the old, the sick, the dying, piles of rubbish and the poor, most of all the poor, filled the eyes no matter which way one turned. It was life at its most elemental: basic, subsisting, making the best of what was. Mother, looking at the children: "I wish I could take one home with me." Mother and Son's hearts were opened by and connected to this land; they could not turn their backs.

That evening, Shantum asked them all to share their "aha moments." Patrick responded zestily. "Everybody looked so happy! It's like they were at the mall! I saw boys with their arms thrown around each other, and children playing games. Some people from the West just feel guilt when they come to India. But I don't think these people need our help."

How convenient for you, thought Son. He decided to counter, mindful of the tiger in the boat. "Looks can be deceiving. I had a friend who went to Burma a year after the protests that triggered brutal government repression. She also said 'people were smiling, they looked happy, it wasn't so bad over there.' I mean, what did she expect, that all the people would be groaning and moaning with the weight of injustice? The fact that many people in Burma and India are happy is a testament to their spiritual and community strengths, and the resilience of the human spirit. It doesn't take away the facts of disease, malnutrition, violence against women and children, political problems and so forth." *You see what you want to see*, he thought but didn't say. It was true for him, too, but at least he hoped he was aware of it.

Later, Patrick told Irene and Barbara that he thought Son was being defensive.

There's no better place for a pissing contest than a Buddhist pilgrimage in India, apparently.

Nothing annoyed a know-it-all more than someone who knew more, or who just knew *different*. Nothing annoyed someone who saw compassion as "guilt" more than someone who took compassion and connection seriously. Nothing annoyed the apathetic more than someone who would never give up. If compassionate masculinity enraged Patrick, and made him want to fight, Son decided he wouldn't be his fight-buddy, but would carry on being himself.

Still, there was something about Patrick. In moments, he looked like a churlish little boy who had just never gotten his share of hugs, and who was now simply looking for a way out of whatever limits and stresses were in his world. Thus, his fascination with "altered states," and his rejection of intimacy with people who might actually need his help, and thus, increase his stress. Thus, his fight with anyone who seemed to argue for such intimacy. He needed this boundary to keep him "safe," but it was precisely what caused him to lose the affection and kindness which he undoubtedly craved, somewhere deep inside.

If you saw love as too painful, weak, or misplaced, then power was your only move.

In Bodhgaya, after a long day of meditation and touring at the Mahabodhi temple, site of the Buddha's enlightenment, Shantum led them to a nearby village, once home to Sujata, the young woman who fed Siddhartha sweet porridge after his long fast, saving his life. It was a story of connection, intimacy and care. She didn't care for the ascetic Gautama because she knew he would be great. She cared for him because he was in danger.

Led by the flashlights of two children, the pilgrims followed Shantum into a humble house, and then to its top floor, an open-air rooftop. The inhabitants of this house were part of a vulnerable middle-class, not far removed from poverty. Patrick, as soon as he reached the rooftop, exclaimed, in character, "they're livin' in the lap of luxury! A rooftop under the stars! What a rich family!"

The children brought them tea and cookies, and Shantum introduced them to the owner of the house, Hari, and his family. He had first met Hari on that first pilgrimage with Thich Nhat Hanh. The monk had asked to meet a boy from the village who was the same age as the boy who brought Siddhartha fresh kusha grass to sit on before his enlightenment. He and his Order, and Shantum's pilgrims, saw Hari grow through the years, and even helped him with his needs; they were now helping with his children's education. Their help and care continued the human connection that existed between Sujata and Siddhartha two-and-a-half millennia before.

As they spoke, Son noticed Hari's young daughter flitting by the candles, her skirt dancing dangerously close to the open flames. He gently cautioned her. "Be careful."

Patrick sneered abrasively, "I think she knows!" There was a moment of stunned silence (something which seemed to follow Patrick's declarations) on the rooftop at the unexpected confrontation. Barbara, the Zen pilgrim from England, later called it "crushing." Son wasn't crushed, though; he would have been incredulous had the moment not confirmed what he'd already seen in Patrick.

The daughter pulled in her skirt and gave Son a grateful look. Son eyed the edge of the rooftop, and noted that Patrick was standing close to it. *It would only take a quick push...* The thought made him smirk darkly. *But he might pull me over, too. And "Murder on Buddhist Pilgrimage" wouldn't exactly be the best headline.* They would both be victims of outright aggression, even as they were both victims of Patrick's verbal push. The "Irishman" had mistaken Son's kindness and concern for patronizing, just as he'd mistaken compassion for guilt after their first day in Patna. It wasn't a big jump to see that Patrick most likely devalued kindness and compassion within himself as well. His mind didn't sound like a pleasant place to be, and surely led to his need for psychedelic "escapes."

Son chose to ignore him, and returned to the conversation with Hari, Shantum and the other pilgrims. But the next day, he abstained from taking dharma vows with Patrick and Barbara. It wasn't auspicious to walk through that special gate with such a difficult person. They would remain linked though, as all people are linked. And ultimately, Son's sentiments bent in the caring direction; he no more wanted Patrick to continue in his internal inferno than he wanted the girl's skirt to catch fire. There was no way to warn Patrick of his danger, nor would he take him seriously. Instead, Son simply applied water. He stretched himself to be kind to his fellow traveler, who wasn't, after all, all-bad. Son smiled and waved goodbye to him as he boarded the van taking him to his flight from Bodhgaya home. Patrick, looking a bit confused and wary, waved back. Son wasn't his fight buddy. So maybe Patrick was unsure, in that moment, who *he* was. That would be a good first step towards enlightenment, Son thought, for both of them.

Each path has a destination. When we journey, we keep the end in mind. There is only one glaring exception to this rule: death. We live on, heedless of our final stopping point. We remain oblivious to mortality, asleep to the final sleep, and numb to all the small choices that allow it to creep closer, infusing our lives with darkness. Yet compassion, and the whole of the spiritual life, is born from bringing death fully into awareness. Siddhartha Gautama was aware of death from his earliest years, and was touched by it in his first meditation as a boy, under the rose-apple tree, watching the birds pluck worms from the plowed earth. His first sermon was at Sarnath, near the holy city of Varanasi, where people came to die and be cremated on the banks of the Ganges, seeking release from rebirth, as the god Shiva had promised. Buddha taught a different way, not dependent on location, but on intention, effort and mindfulness.

Shantum led the pilgrims to the cremation ghats of Varanasi, city of the god of destruction, and they watched the bodies burn. No cameras were allowed, of course, but the somber scene blazed itself into their minds. The fires burned fiercely in the dark Varanasi night, the door to the next world crackling open in light and heat. The pyres were tended by rag-clad youth whose bright eyes darted between the foreign onlookers and the fires; they added wood to keep the flames high, death and life ushering and embracing each other, intimately, in the night. Son's eyes fell on a human arm sticking up from its inferno, hand clenched in some charnel mudra. It was little more than a piece of wood itself, fleshy fuel soon to be dust and ash. The flame itself lived, flashing red and yellow clamor, dependent on the morbid heap; when that was gone, the flame would be extinguished too. All life comes to an end. Birth comes inextricably paired with death, a code whose binary duality supposedly could be broken with the Buddha way.

The door to the underworld was open, and thoughts of death settled on them all. Not surprisingly, Irene became sick with gastro-intestinal illness a short while later, after visiting the village where the Buddha was struck with his own fatal dysentery. And that night, a dark shade settled on Son as he lay in bed. It was a ghost, he was sure, a cloak of death, which descended and covered him like a blanket. It was not a cause for struggle or even fear, but of watchful awareness. He allowed it to draw over him, lying still. He nestled with mortality; fears crackled forth from him like the cremation fires in Varanasi. Accidents, abandonments, failures, losses of love and life… This dark wraith was precisely what needed to be transformed, and there were so many smaller deaths possible in it. Losing heart, losing compassion, losing connection – these were all early signs of demise. The wraith could only be a messenger of these black possibilities, these terminations, congruent with the callousness of his clinic administrators and the aggressions he'd met in life and on the road. These deaths could not be denied or minimized. They were the signal fires, the escape fires, the heavenly messengers that had to be known, for survival's sake. He did not fight the darkness, but allowed it to merge with him, the shroud of winter that had to be borne. Though it was death, it was fuel for his flame.

Mother was dubbed "Ambassador Amy," which she added to the title Son had given her years before, "The Dalai Mama." From start to finish, she befriended air hosts and hotel attendants, street children and waiters, with her infectious sparkle. "I wouldn't get lost in the forest – I would talk to the birds!" she said, and Son didn't doubt it. Her energy would flag, walking from site to site, but rebounded as soon as a new chatting partner appeared. Within moments, she'd gathered their dossier, from marital status to birthplace to occupation, and given them her own capsule biography; for added measure, she dosed the young with advice and encouragement. "Guess my age!" she would command, all but demanding a flattering reply. The other pilgrims had to wait patiently as she worked the crowd like a veteran diplomat, which she was. Son played sidekick and straight man, handler and lookout, checking the rope line and mostly staying out of the way, Boswell to her Samuel Johnson.

The pilgrims go for a morning walk near Rajgir, on the same land that the Buddha walked. "Implant the earth with your love and peace," instructs Shantum. A gaggle of children surrounds Mother, tagging along and begging for chocolates and money. Mother takes one by the hands, and says "come, walk with me;" then she makes her move, trying to hug a boy who laughs and runs away. The other pilgrims are far ahead of her, and Son motions, urging her to drop her entourage, as Shantum's helper, a little annoyed, shoos them away. They turn their attention to "implanting the earth," but leave the children behind. Shantum extends his hand to help Amy across a small creek. Son knows better. She refuses. "I am independent!"

The scenes are repeated time and again. The pilgrimage was *places* to most of them; to her, it was that, but *people*, too. While the others did their best to implant the earth, she was quite effectively implanting the people with her own robust affection.

Ambassador Amy becomes Unstoppable Amy on Vulture Peak, site of many of the Buddha's most famous sermons. She initially sits down on a bench after walking a short way up the long slope, tired after a long day of walks in Nalanda and Rajgir; soon, though, an image forms of the Buddha preaching just a short, walkable distance away, and she marshals her strength, gets up, and strides slowly but surely towards the top. Thai pilgrims stop on their way down to talk to her; they ask her age, then smile widely and approvingly give her the thumbs up. Encouraged and vitalized, she summits her Everest, arriving at the Peak just as the sun begins to set. Various pilgrims – Burmese, Thai, Japanese – have left their offerings on the altar. Shantum, knowledge-able of Peak protocol, pays a small sum to the unofficial keeper of the space, and takes a candle imprinted with the Buddha's image. He hands it to Mother, and gives her a hug. She has earned it; she has won the mountain, as if it were a hopeful but skeptical teacher watching her progress.

On the road between Varanasi and Kushinagar, cities associated with the ending of life and victory over death, their van is caught in a traffic jam caused by a festival procession. They get out on foot, to get a better view. A swarm of men is dancing to loud music blaring from the back of a truck. Mother starts waving her hands and legs, metronomically, in time to the beat in her version of Dancing Matt, and one of the men, either ecstatic, inebriated or both, urges her forward. She steps out and dances, smiling, while a man with a stick pushes back the raucous throng. Mother is happy, excited, and alive. The scene, which might have verged on danger, was instead triumphant. Son replayed the video again and again, later. A record number of friends "liked" the image he posted to Facebook. Mother was a global celebrity for a moment, her spirit amplified and seen by all through a technological megaphone. It was as close to transcendent as Facebook could get, giving friends a dramatic glimpse of joy and goodness under the Indian sun: the Mother Goddess, dancing.

In Bodhgaya, Son had a dream. Mother, sleeping in the bed next to his, suddenly became the Great Stupa of Boudhanath, lying on its side, its unblinking, omniscient eye gazing at him, perennially.

Perhaps all my life is a circumambulation, he thought, as he drifted between dream worlds. Circling Mother was a pilgrimage in love, and he would always be walking, feeling her eyes on him, her presence guiding his steps.

The great monastery at Sravasti was their last pilgrimage stop. The Buddha spent twenty-five rainy season retreats here; this was his home more than anyplace else during his years of itinerant teaching, so it was natural that many pilgrims felt and honored his presence at this location. They noted the "kutis" of prominent disciples, including one traditionally thought to be Angulimala's dwelling place. Son had a special fondness for Angulimala, whom the Buddha converted to a life of nonviolence from one bent on accumulating spiritual power through murder. Angulimala means thousand-finger necklace. Angulimala had been told that killing a thousand people would make him powerful beyond measure. Buddha was to be Angulimala's thousandth victim, but Angulimala was instead himself struck, by Buddha's words and soul-force, and renounced violence on the spot. Buddha renamed him Ahimsaka, "non-violent one," and ordained him as a monk. Ahimsaka endured the abuse of the people whom he'd wronged, whose loved ones he murdered, without complaint. The Buddha told him this was his karma, coming home to roost. He eventually became a birthing assistant, whose very presence was said to ensure a healthy delivery. So did the world change through the Buddha's love and presence, through individuals moved by his example in word and deed.

Son was uneasy. His mind had grown deeply aware of numerous micro- and macro-aggressions, coming to a climax, somehow, on this very peace pilgrimage. There were the aggressions of father through abandonment, and society through racism, and sexism transmitted through the experience of Mother; more recently, there were the aggressions of clinic supervisors, the observed aggression of masculine against feminine principles in India, and tangles with Patrick. All of them *form fruste* of death, carrying death in their hostile intent. These sparked in him compensatory bursts of anger, his survival instinct and penchant for social justice pushing him to take some hot action. But these were in turn almost entirely subdued by his meditative practice and better judgment. Still, the conflict between his inner warrior/ troublemaker and his inner peacemaker somehow bloomed into an overarching sense of guilt, of having somehow wronged the world and thus deserving its aggression and disapprobation. Perhaps his karma was coming home to roost; perhaps the only way out was through, to accept the world's angers without struggle. Perhaps the contact with the transcendent union that the journey had aroused was coupled with knowledge of the existing gulf between us all, with guilt and heightened self-consciousness the only remedy for concatenated empathic failures,

failures in love, the cause of all woundedness and separation. Union vied with ruin, and his own natural aggressions seemed to boomerang into remorse at his own failure to successfully achieve the former, and self-blame for having anger at some parts of the world in the first place. As the group meditated in Buddha's dwelling place, bedecked with gold leaf from many years of pilgrims, Son thought of Angulimala, Ahimsaka, and sin, the "missing of the mark" of interdependence. Shantum asked them each to say something on this occasion of the last day of their tour. Son spoke to the group, but also to all the monks, nuns and laypeople, all the sangha who had ever gathered here, and all the people he'd ever known, everyone to whom he was deeply connected, in ways that could not be known.

If I have harmed beings through ignorance, aversion or greed,
If I have let myself down through selfishness of body, mind or speech,
I humbly apologize and vow to correct myself.
May all beings be free from suffering and the causes of suffering,
and may I assist in the great awakening.

Son had carefully plotted their voyage to the subcontinent and back: from certain engulfment with family troubles in South India, to a hopefully more liberating experience on Buddhist pilgrimage, and finally, over the moon with four luxurious days in Hong Kong. It was a journey from distress to comfort, Inferno to Paradiso, recapitulating his five-month odyssey five years before. Hong Kong was, of course, an ultra-modern city with ultra-modern hotels, including comfortable beds, air-conditioning that worked, and service personnel who were actually accustomed to taking care of travelers. It was a touch of heaven after a month of hardships made bearable and even enjoyable only by the spirit of the people they'd met and the glorious history they touched. India induced Paradiso in its own subtle way, but Hong Kong gave birth to it immaculately.

The desk attendant at the Harbour Grand Kowloon took an immediate liking to Mother, and sent a complimentary tray of exotic fruit to their room. Mother thrilled at the Great Buddha of Lantau Island, enthusiastically striding up the long staircase just as she'd climbed Vulture Peak. They met three of Son's lovely friends now living in Hong Kong, each from three stages of his life to this point: college, medical school and the clinic he'd just left. Reunions such as these boded well for the union he aimed for: conversations, shared enthusiasms, and sincerely caring relationships, all without a blue wall between them.

Their final night, after a long trek from the Great Buddha to G.O.D. (which could only be Goods Of Desire in this distinctly materialistic Paradiso) – where they paid exactly $108 in Hong Kong dollars for a shared meal, mirroring the 108 beads on a Buddhist mala, or the 108 desires that must be transcended before reaching nirvana – they lay on their beds, exhausted but happy, talking of their grand adventure. Mother decided it was a good time to confess.

"Before the trip, I thought I would just collapse and die in Bodhgaya, in the Buddha's arms," she said.

Son considered the revelation. Perhaps his cousin Ram wasn't wrong after all, when he posited that Mother was looking for a place to leave her body. Out of the silence, he spoke. "Were you disappointed?"

Mother laughed. "Yes. I was disappointed."

"We can go back if you like."

She laughed again, her body quaking in her adjacent bed, till she was almost breathless, but in a good way. When she could be serious again, she said, "Well, I was worried. What would you do with my body."

They each had their own journeys, but for this long stretch, they would travel together, each with the other in mind.

❀

Three weeks after they landed in America, a young woman, later given the defiant *nom de guerre* "Nirbhaya," meaning "fearless," was savagely raped by a gang of men in New Delhi. They beat her and a companion, and penetrated her with a steel pipe, puncturing her viscera and causing massive internal bleeding. She underwent five surgeries. Nearly all of her intestines were removed, being hopelessly damaged. She was septic, her intestinal wounds leading to systemic bacterial infection. She was flown to Singapore for further treatment, at the point of death, and finally succumbed on December 29th. Cousin Krishna's fears, leading to what seemed like excesses of caution and control of his daughters, were rendered understandable. The danger he saw became real; India was closer to *Clockwork Orange* than the orange, and peace, of the robes of a Buddhist monk.

A world away, Mother and Son felt like their own guts had been wrenched open. They were in tears or at the point of tears for weeks, traumatized by an inconceivable, hideous reality that amplified their sadness, anger and resentment at the land they'd just left. The fact that tens of thousands took to the streets in protest heartened them somewhat; the thirst for justice and reform made visible and vivid gave them a tincture of hope. Perhaps if they were there, arms joined with the protestors, they would feel the trauma transformed into determination. Instead, it just sat with them, darkness in the dead of December, reminder that ruin was much closer than union; sorrow a more certain companion than joy or triumph.

In the midst of this grief, Son returned to his Cambodian group. He revealed the clinic's decision, that he would only have three months left with them, and then someone else would have to take over. Several women started sobbing immediately, and Son and his co-facilitator sat struggling to hold their own composure. As he looked at their faces, some of them so sad and distraught they could not even meet his eyes, something inside him changed. He could not go through with this plan. He could not leave them like this. "I haven't discussed this with the clinic administrators before, but I could continue to lead the group as a volunteer. It wouldn't be the same – I wouldn't be seeing you all in individual sessions anymore. But at least we could continue seeing each other." They immediately protested: they wouldn't want to take advantage of him. He insisted that it would be his pleasure. He wanted to do his best to assure that these people, profoundly affected by adversity, people he had grown very fond of, would not suffer a loss of relationship and community that he could prevent.

He asked his supervisors about his plan to volunteer that very day, but wouldn't get an answer for weeks. K called a major meeting of administrators to discuss the request, and even then, took another week to approve it. Son couldn't help but feel that the reaction of animus to his initial call of alarm, expressed through defriending and verbal aggressions, still hung in the air. The question was not whether his service was helpful, but whether he as a person could be tolerated anymore. The answer seemed like "yes, barely" – but this was good enough. His supervisors who had ended up on the opposite side of battle lines they had drawn – they were not "all-bad," after all. They did, however, seem removed from his concerns at the front line of care. If they were ever to be truly allied again, they would have to find new purpose arrayed around the importance of relationship, the bond between caregiver and patient. There could be no healing without it.

We are all birth companions, separated by accident and chance, by our own limited vision, amnestic of our common origin. We travel in obscure fugue, struggling to be ourselves in our selfish, self-conscious way, but the self that arises from union eludes us. When we awaken to our relatedness, we awaken to life. When we plot our voyages with compassion, our journey can only lead us home. This is the story we must write, the odyssey we must live.

Son wrote, and wished his words could travel themselves, easily, to willing ears, and make the road ahead easier.

The Buddha sits in you,
heart-watcher.
Water the Bodhi tree
and awaken.

But it was winter. Dark, with only a promise of light.

Crow

A crow calls to me on a dark January morning. It is a dream crow, waking me, or a spirit crow, telling me to bear witness and pay heed. The dark messenger has been on my mind lately. I've been sitting with crows, spying them on the wires, watching them watch the Earth, counting them as they count the minutes and keep the time. I have been thinking about my depressed patients, suffering through the dark winter days, and contemplating the nature of crows, matching my soul against theirs and feeling a wordless, black, primal conduit open between us. The winter blues are black as crows. A pitch-black survivor of scorn and disappointment, the crow practically becomes me. The crows have taken notice of me. They stare at me with eyes as black as the night between stars. And out of this blackness, the spirit crow says, "it's time."

A Nature documentary calls the crow "a schemer, a scavenger, a dreaded omen of death." They are smart, precocious birds that can recognize faces; they teach their young to identify dangerous intruders. They mob predators, and can throw a hawk off its game. They talk to each other, having a language of over 250 distinct calls. They have social brains, and live up to five years with their parents, observing and learning. They are "wise guys and tricksters," who can make tools and use them in complex ways – the documentary shows a crow pulling a string, to get a stick, to get another stick, to get a piece of meat, and even shaping a stick with their beak so it could be a proper pick. A crow could pick locks, enter any dark place, and roost. Or just wait there, in the dark, unafraid. The crow's nest looks out over the ocean, sighting for land, skeptical of every mirage.

The crow's brain-to-body-size ratio rivals many primates; John Marzluff, a scientist who studies crows, calls them "feathered apes." This fatherless man sometimes feels like a featherless crow, a giant crow with black skin, black blood and most of all, a black heart, like the crow that Ted Hughes wrote about in his collection called *Crow*. His poems are nervy and unnerving. Crow is the tragic hero – death, life and struggle in a universe of strife. He is triumphant, and then fallen, all-powerful then vanquished. The darkness of defeat by adversity and opposition becomes redemption and rebirth, or at the very least, muse. Crow-black is the night before dawn, the void before creation. "When God crushed Crow/He made alcohol…When God said 'You win, Crow'/ He made the redeemer." Hughes' poems ring me like a bell, and then leave me cold with their audacious artistic pretense. Sometimes my own darkness wants to just sit, gather and grow, and not be collected into an *m.o.* But my darkness has character, reasoning, and a way of being, just like Crow. The crow in me is flattered, moved and bored by *Crow*. You reach for me in words, and you'll likely fail, says Crow. The crow has to be felt, experienced, lived. Still, I'm a writer, and I search for Crow in black words on a white page. I offer Crow the pen, and do my best to keep out of the way. Hughes did this much better and more completely than I; but when the crow wants to speak to you, through you, you listen.

Do you remember drawing crows as a child? A sun, clouds – and curved black lines that punctuated the sky, elevating the mind from the ground, flying into the unknown. They were beautiful and mysterious, the first creatures I could draw with any semblance of reality. Vincent Van Gogh's *Wheatfield with Crows* is an extrapolation and expansion of those childhood drawings; the crows connect a fertile, bright gold and green earth with dark heavens, sending us a brooding message that lifts from the canvas into our souls. The crows fly from a vivid, gleaming ground into blue-black mysteries above. These crows are like us; they are just like us.

A crow won't fit into a status update. A crow scorns the Facebook wasteland as a thin-screen happy place without depth or dialogue. Caws and cackles, even when tweeted, lose their environmental, sensory significance and portent. There's no there there, on Facebook. You might know a bird by its transcribed song, but that won't help you see its nest. You won't see it wing through the air, you won't see its soul.

There's something magical about birds; they are, in fact, symbols of the soul. They do something that we humans can't – fly. Only our thoughts can rise above our circumstances. In our imaginations, we fly. So birds are like our thoughts and feelings, soaring beyond our bodies. Sparrows, swallows, hummingbirds – we think of them as uplifting and delightful. Doves are the buoyant hope of peace. Vultures and buzzards are dirty morticians, feasting on death, reminders of the end of life, and also its renewal. They are life feeding on life, as we all must. Crows and ravens, with their dark color and dark manner, give flight and substance to our own dark imaginings and beings. They are common birds in my city, crossing my path frequently. The weather changes in San Francisco like the mind – clouds and wind to sun, sun to fog, and back again. The crows are always here, roosting on the roof, waiting on the wire, arcing across the sky. Here, foraging a scrap. There, watching. Head bent down, shaking and chuckling at the confirmation of some perceived folly. Always formal in dress black, they are a constant tribe of elders. The natives who've seen us come and go, who will outlast us and crow about it, if we don't kill the planet first. Judges in their dark robes, they always seem to be measuring the world. As I do, this January morning.

I've heard of crow funerals. They gather, sometimes by the hundreds, to look at and process past a fallen fellow crow. A bird that mourns and witnesses is a companion to us, a fellow traveler. We can wonder if it isn't all a crow funeral, when a crow is near. Some say they are not animals at all, but spirit beings. Traveling with them enlarges my spirit. They are a fulcrum between separation and communion, a gateway to a deeper reality and an invitation to perceive the world through their eyes. Through the crow's eyes; as the crow flies. They are survivors. We could do well to learn from crows.

The film *Tokyo Waka*, by John Haptas and Kristine Samuelson, tells of Tokyo crows, in poetic image, and exploration in weaving interviews that illuminate the sensibilities of the city, its people, and Buddhist and Shinto philosophies. A waka is a kind of poem with internal repeats, not unlike the way crows have been spaced through this season, for me. Crows are seen building nests from hangars and plucking at garbage bags; humans engage in countermeasures against the crows. Tokyo has a city department devoted to crow control and capture, and they have reduced the crow population by half. But a man says "it is quite telling we are unable to completely control crows." Nature always has the last word. Crows have an ungovernable, unstoppable persistence. You can't just show the crow the door and be done with him. He wants to teach you something, so he'll stay. As he chooses.

A Buddhist monk speaks philosophically of how crows and people send us messages about the nature of life: evanescent, driven by desire, with a sense of ultimate tragedy or futility. That last sense seems characteristic of Japanese culture. The saying "shi ka ta ga nai," or "it can't be helped," is common wisdom. Perseverance, despite difficult odds and disaster (the documentary lists the Great Kanto Earthquake of 1923 and the Tokyo fire bombings of World War II – both reduced the city to rubble and ashes), is a national trait. The city rebuilds, slowly, after each apocalypse. Another man in the documentary says "the Japanese will always remain serious and deep inside." Serious and deep is the essence of crow to me, so un-Facebook as to warrant the crow's consideration as the symbol of resistance to Facebook and the superficiality of the Silicon age. Indeed, the emblem of the Japanese National Soccer team is the Yatagarasu, a three-legged crow and messenger of the god Kumano. Harbinger of divine intervention, symbol of the sun and the dawn of renaissance, Yatagarasu is the first to clean up after a battle. His legs stand for Heaven, Earth, and Man. Crow stands on all three: dark, preternatural conduit, Hermes in black.

A Shinto priest describes the profound humility and respect felt by humans when facing nature: the awesomeness of a tree, the magnificence of a boulder, the might of the ocean. "This is where Shinto came from," he says. When I look out from the eyes of Crow, I am with the trees, boulder and ocean looking out over a misguided mankind that has neglected natural law, has forgotten the tribe of elders. An unnested Crow, I taste bitterness, certain of the wrongheadedness of the ways of men. I sit on the wire, and cackle as they pass.

A Cambodian legend tells the story of Owl and Crow. They were both first all-white, then Owl asked Crow to paint her. Crow was careful and artistic, flecking Owl's chest with spots and lining her wings with gold, brown and black. Around Owl's face, Crow painted a great heart. Then it was Owl's turn. Owl was jealous and wanted only to be the prettiest bird. She took her large brush, and with broad strokes painted Crow black. When Crow saw himself in the mirror, he was angry. "Because you did this, I won't let you see the light of day." That is why Owl only comes out at night. Crow flies whenever he chooses, and lands wherever he wants. He has grown to love black, he's made his color his style; but the taste of dissatisfaction has never left him, a reminder of disloyalty, devaluing and disregard. Paint Crow black, and you make him the scapegoat who sees through the illusion your mind has created.

Masahisa Fukase took to taking pictures of crows after his wife Yoko divorced him. His photographs are described as "reflecting the inner landscape of his heart; about the pain inside." The mortal world is shot through with vulnerability. Bruises are a given in life; trauma a vast narrative. Crows fly into this dark wounded space, and know it. But they do not, I think, in the end symbolize futility. They are, after all, birds, capable of heavenly flight, perhaps closer to God than we are. In Native American myth, Crow frees the Sun and brings light into the world.

In Tokyo, as the workday closes, the bells ring out a song. Misako Ichimura, interviewed in *Tokyo Waka*, is a homeless woman living in a park; she says she is "home-full", there among the trees and birds. She sings the words:

It is getting dark
The bell from the temple on the mountain echoes.
Let's hold hands and go home together.
Let's go home with the crows.

A bird that symbolized the heart after divorce – can also symbolize coming home, together. There is disappointment in Crow, and also
hope. If Crow is painted as black as unforgivable stain, he also has a key
in his dark breast-pocket.

Love.

Love

Love never goes sour
It just ferments, sealed in a cask,
Waiting for new drunkards.
Come, let's break open the tap.
– 7 likes, Sunday, April 20, 2013

But love does go sour. Love can go cold, hostile, and resentful. Love can go bad. Most of my anger, sadness and harsh judgments have come from disappointment in love, when others don't meet my needs for love and compassion in their actions towards me and the world, and when I don't meet my own high standards. A friend demonstrates through word and deed that she doesn't really know me, after years of friendship. A girlfriend judges me unwarrantedly and says cruel things. Far more disturbingly, a woman is raped in India. A young girl is shot by fundamentalists. A child is killed by a drone. And my own compassion can be hard to find when I'm pressed by a difficult moment. These failures of love, the personal and the global, the overriding of love by other demands – selfishness, defensiveness, anger, hatred, greed, power – each one mars me and sets me back. The only recuperation I have is to rebuild. Rebuild my love for my friends, rekindle my love for humanity, and find hope. I have to forgive, let go, and accept, because otherwise love goes sour. Forgiveness is part of the fermentation process for love. "The light enters you at the bandaged place," wrote Rumi, and so does love. Some days, it feels we're bandaged head to toe from the trauma we've been given. Forgiveness is not a trivial or idle thing, but rather an opening where wound meets air, where air meets lung, and lung lets heart beat and blood flow. Love and forgiveness are as vital to us as marrow and oxygen. Love knows sorrow, denies it, and then makes love from sorrow. This is why flowers grow; this is how the lotus blooms.

I think this is the only way that love knows, that we know love. Pain and loss are the surest forges for the deeper force of love. Some Christians are fond of saying "God doesn't give you any more than you can handle." And yet we're given pain that spills over our vessels, pours out over us and beyond our capacity. And in this dark moment, we have to love, anyway, or become bitter prisoners of dejection. Love can turn to vinegar, can dry to salt, from tears. Knowing this salt was once love is the only way to reclaim it. We season our sorrow with the salt of broken love, and find that salt, too, is necessary.

I realize my love is imperfect too. Sometimes so naive and open, vulnerable and apt to turn to hurt and fear; sometimes wise, wonderful and strong, flowing forth through my heart to everyone I meet, earth below and sky above. In moments seemingly absent altogether, turned to Crow. To this day, love is not constant, but I aim to make it more sure and certain, more aware of the obstacles before it. I've been a fool for love, tripping unexpectedly into passions of union, then falling back into the mundane separateness of self. Still, the experience of togetherness guides me, surely, towards interdependence, awareness of difference, and communication across boundaries. Once awakened to the heart, we become followers all.

> The experts feigning wisdom devalue compassion,
> thus displaying their foolishness.
> The powerful dismiss love,
> but love shows them their powerlessness.
> The mind forgets the heart
> But the heart keeps beating,
> believing and knowing
> the eternal law:
> Hate is never conquered by hate –
> By love alone is hate conquered.

The "eternal law" was reiterated and advanced by the Buddha. All of us can discover its truth in our own lives. What the Buddha said of love sounds like an early version of a sexy Motown song. "It is in this way we must train ourselves by liberation of the self through love. We will develop love, we will practice it, we will make it both a way and a basis, take our stand upon it, store it up, and thoroughly set it going." You go, Buddha! Let's set it going. Let's get it on.

Love seems non-controversial. It is recognized as essential motivation, a cohesive and expansive force that requires active participation and yields incalculable reward. Dante wrote that money shared is halved, yet love shared is multiplied, implying one economy that isn't subject to quantity limitations. Jesus instructed his followers to "love your enemies and pray for those who persecute you," and Martin Luther King, Jr. and Mahatma Gandhi heralded the transformative powers of love and non-violence, changing the world in their wake. Love is an ideal, subject of countless songs, and experienced by nearly everyone on Earth for some moments at least, although it's possible that not all are capable of feeling its sway. To write of it risks platitude and a surfeit of shallow, fleeting limns that hint at but don't fully capture or deepen our connection to the eternal law.

To advocate replacing hate with love is sublime. To actually do so is heroic. I don't know if it's possible that all aversion can be overcome, for everyone in every situation, but I do know that it's possible for nearly all of us to become more loving, to free ourselves more from the slavery of hatred and dislike, and further the bond of love.

But first – why do we hate? The answers are individual and varied, but they can be distilled to disapproval of others because we perceive they embody some trait or behavior that we take to be a threat to us, our loved ones, or some principle we defend. The *other* is not part of our tribe and is unacceptable in some way. In this way, we divide the world into "us" and "them," and quite frequently, the other side reciprocates. The third path, the middle path, of seeing commonality, is at once exalted in rhetoric and then abandoned in deed. Declared the most powerful truth, and then derided as weak. It is a muscle that needs to be strengthened and flexed before it can lift, yet it is the only muscle that can lift the Earth as one. Strengthening the capacity to love and find commonality is surely one of our prime tasks.

The Buddha was approached by Brahmins who asked him how they should practice, if they wanted to maintain their religion and worship of God, and yet improve their mental states. He taught them the *Brahma Viharas*, or Abodes of God. The Divine Abodes amount to four instructions in love, each working at the feeling of separateness and division that underlies our usual ways of perceiving ourselves and others. Cultivating them helps to bring us to experiences of oneness that can transform our subtle and gross tendencies to divide, and moreover, undercut the very sources of suffering. Metta, Karuna, Mudita, and Upekkha make the eternal law – internal.

Metta

Metta means "lovingkindness", or even more simply, "friendliness," "goodwill" or simply "love." I believe, intuitively and by experience, that metta is the foundation of good mental health, as well as the foundation of a good society. Jack Kornfield, Sharon Salzberg, and Sylvia Boorstein among American teachers have all written extensively about this healing emotion, and I have benefited immensely from their guidance in print and in person. I first began practicing lovingkindness during my residency training in Psychiatry. Every day for 45 minutes, I silently repeated the following phrases, suggested by Kornfield in his book *A Path With Heart*:

May I be filled with lovingkindness,
May I be well.
May I be peaceful and at ease,
May I be happy.

My mind kicked up immediate and persistent resistance, calling me selfish for wanting this for myself, and berating me for my obvious deficiency in embodying it. Kornfield warned of this common experience in his book. Yet I kept up the practice, generating metta for myself, trying to connect my mind and heart. Many have noted that Westerners, in particular, are inherently self-critical and even self-hating. This develops from experiences in childhood (of not being loved appropriately), a critical, competitive society and schooling experiences (which lead us to believe, falsely, that we should be valued only for our productive capacity or other attributes, rather than who we are as complete human beings), and more broadly, a culture which creates hierarchies and emphasizes individuality and status at the expense of community.

It took three months of extensive daily practice and a weeklong metta retreat for my brain to get the message. I still frequently have to dip back into self-metta to nurture myself in difficult moments, when feeling in conflict with others, or disappointed in them or myself. I find that it has gotten easier with time, and that usually, metta is available as a "ground-state" that guides my experience and actions in the world. If it's difficult to say these phrases for oneself, one can imagine some beloved person or even religious figure saying them to you.

After grounding in self-metta, one can change the "I" in the phrases to "you," and direct metta to others. First, pick a benevolent loved one, a benefactor in your life, and direct the phrases to them. You can think of metta spreading directly from you to them, almost like a light from your heart or mind shining on them. Next, direct the metta towards friends and other loved ones. It's natural to imagine them with smiles on their faces, sharing metta with you.

Usually, the practice then shifts to people we feel neutral towards, neither liking nor disliking. They might be hard to identify, because we naturally form subtle likes and dislikes to nearly everyone we encounter. You can try practicing this in the local cafe, supermarket, or on public transportation. Direct your attention to a stranger you feel neutral towards. Say the phrases, and genuinely wish their lives to be filled with lovingkindness, safety, ease, health and happiness. You may find that you may feel closer to even the neutral people around you.

Many people report that this practice actually makes them feel happy: our brains have built-in positive rewards for kindness and love.

After you have had much experience at generating metta, you can direct it towards the difficult people in your life. These are sometimes thought of as "the enemies," but there are many gradations of difficult people. Some of them are not outright enemies, and yet they can try one's patience and sanity all the same. And even our enemies deserve our love for several reasons. First, as Sylvia Boorstein once told me, "if the difficult people had love and happiness in their lives, they would be less difficult!" Second – because they are human beings too. (Of course that doesn't mean we don't need boundaries with difficult people.)

Also, we must be aware that we have more control over our agency in the difficult-person-tango than we have over our partner's. Adjusting our stance towards them can change the interaction in important ways. This doesn't mean tolerating abuse – metta directs us to care for ourselves, too. If we don't care for ourselves, we will be unavailable for others. Changing the space that the difficult person occupies in our own minds can take time, but is well worth it.

Finally, generate metta for the whole world and all beings in it. From the Metta Sutra:

> So with a boundless mind should one cherish all living things,
> Suffusing love over the entire world, above, below and all around, without limit.
> So let one cultivate an infinite good will towards the whole world.

For bonus credit (and I highly recommend this) commit the entire Metta Sutra to memory, and repeat it as part of your daily meditation practice. These days, we devalue memorization, but I believe that wisdom such as this can work in subtle ways, reorganizing our neural networks and becoming seeds of new perception. I find these words return to me at various times during the day, and that each day as I repeat them, I notice my mind weighing, holding and cherishing the phrases in subtly different ways that feel like a ripening, deepening, and flourishing.

The Metta (Lovingkindness) Sutra

This is what should be accomplished by the one who is wise,
Who seeks the good, and has obtained peace.

Let one be strenuous, upright, and sincere,
Without pride, easily contented, and joyous.
Let one not be submerged by the things of the world.
Let one not take upon oneself the burden of riches.
Let one's senses be controlled.
Let one be wise but not puffed up and
Let one not desire great possessions even for one's family.
Let one do nothing that is mean or that the wise would reprove.

May all beings be happy.
May they be joyous and live in safety,
All living beings, whether weak or strong,
In high or middle or low realms of existence.
Small or great, visible or invisible,
Near or far, born or to be born,
May all beings be happy.
Let no one deceive another nor despise any being in any state.
Let none by anger or hatred wish harm to another.

Even as a mother at the risk of her life
Watches over and protects her only child,
So with a boundless mind should one cherish all living things.
Suffusing love over the entire world,
Above, below, and all around, without limit,
So let one cultivate an infinite good will toward the whole world.

Standing or walking, sitting or lying down,
During all one's waking hours,
Let one practice the way with gratitude.
Not holding to fixed views,
Endowed with insight,
Freed from sense appetites,
One who achieves the way
Will be freed from the duality of birth and death.

Freud considered dreams the "royal road to the unconscious." I consider Metta the royal road to our highest dreams of what Martin Luther King, Jr. called the "beloved community," an inclusive society that amplifies affection and mutual support, even as it recognizes difference and individuality. Metta is the first and usually most powerful foundation for oneness, and a primary antidote for selfishness, hate, disaffection, and disconnection.

Mudita

Do you feel irritated at the achievements of others? Do you get annoyed when someone you don't like – or even do like – gets attention? Do you experience *schadenfreude*, or happiness when misfortune strikes someone else? Most of us experience these emotions fleetingly, particularly when we're feeling insecure about ourselves. Our minds are naturally built to compare ourselves to others. This may have served some evolutionary purpose in forcing us to adopt competitive stances towards our "rivals," but it mostly gets in the way of our happiness now, and moreover, is destructive to good relationships.

Mudita is "sympathetic joy," or joy in the happiness of others. Mudita can naturally arise, but it can also be cultivated, much like Metta. The most natural incidence of this occurs between parent and child, and there is even a word in Hebrew describing joy in one's children - *nachas*. You can imagine one's Mudita going out to others, and their happiness coming back to you, and thus making you happier. This is a virtuous cycle that can keep feeding itself.

Being aware of Mudita vs. schadenfreude is an important indicator of one's personal mental state. Schadenfreude might indicate a tendency towards selfishness, which is a fundamental cause of suffering, or it may indicate that a particular need is not being met. Identifying that need – for status, possessions, friendship, etc. – helps us interrogate it and bring it into relationship with our larger self.

Jealousy and greed are "long emotions" similar to love in the way that they can become driving forces for a lifetime of action. As mature adults, we can ask ourselves how we've been co-opted by these emotions, and what we'd like to do about them. How do they fit with our spiritual aims, or even our personal? Mudita is an antidote and countermeasure for our tendency to be small and self-centered, envious and competitive.

Practice being happy when your friends are happy. Practice being happy when even your difficult people are happy. Mentally exchange places with them, and experience what their happiness is like to them.

One situation in which I find it difficult to extend Mudita is when other people do harmful things that bring them joy. What to do in this case? When our deepest wish is for the other person's complete happiness and overcoming their bonds of suffering, we can work with Karuna, or Compassion.

Karuna

Compassion, or Karuna, is a deep and powerful emotion and motivating force. The bird of enlightenment is said to have two wings – compassion and wisdom – making compassion an essential part of a perfected mind. Like wisdom, it must be cultivated. It is the ingredient that most surely refines the mind and heart. Metta and Mudita both help us break down the walls between ourselves and others. Compassion compels us to take action across that breached boundary. We see the suffering of the other person, and feel it within us, as well. We literally "feel their pain" – compassion means "to feel with" another. Through modern neural science, we now know that this is actually true – our brains have "mirror neurons." We replicate what we imagine are the sensations of the other person within our own minds.

When we see suffering, there are possibilities beyond indifference and *schadenfreude*, and these can be thought to exist along a spectrum. Pity views the sufferer as separate and below the observer, and might even be expressed as scorn. Sympathy is more supportive, but there is still a gulf between the two, and no obligation to help. With empathy, the observer is making deeper emotional and personal contact, and tries to understand the perspective of another. Compassion is the crown jewel. Not only do we notice, see and feel suffering in another, and understand their perspective, but we also feel moved to do something to relieve their distress. Distress comes in myriad forms, from financial and physical, to spiritual and psychological. Compassion can work on any and all of these forms of suffering.

The most common statements of purpose I hear from my patients are that they want to love and help other people. Sometimes, the only happiness that a depressed patient feels is in helping a sheltered animal, for example. So compassion provides gifts to both the giver and the recipient. We feel each other's pain, and we can feel that pain being relieved as well. This doesn't mean that there's any form of selfishness involved in compassion – it's just proof that we are built for it.

I know that compassion is widespread, and yet it can always go further. We can notice our innate wishes to help others, and meditate on them, bringing them into fullness. The internet age connects us and brings us news from afar; it also creates a dilemma for us as we see others suffering. How do we help? How do we remain resourceful enough to help, and not get burnt out? And ultimately, what are the most meaningful ways to help others?

The internet can also be a barrier to compassion. Others complain about their suffering, and we can become defensive or derisive about those complaints. Our mirror neurons might not engage without a true relationship between ourselves and the sufferer. We can become inured, overwhelmed or apathetic to suffering as it appears on a screen. But when we harden our hearts, and stoke aversion, we move farther from transcendence and enlightenment, farther from our best selves. This is something to guard against as we spend more time with technology instead of people. I think we need to unplug as much as possible to generate deep compassion and connection. But the online world deserves our compassion as well, so this is necessarily an ever evolving dynamic.

Psychologist Dacher Keltner at the University of California, Berkeley, says we have a "compassionate instinct." Evolution is as much about survival of the kindest and most compassionate as it is about survival of the fittest. Compassion arguably enhances our evolutionary "fitness." We are drawn to compassionate people, and inspired to be like them. We are more likely to safeguard compassionate people and "the arc of history" bends towards creating more compassionate communities, which clearly aids our mutual survival. Enhancing our own compassion brings us more into alignment with broad, transpersonal, archetypal, or some would say, divine forces. Perhaps union with these forces is the "freedom from the duality of birth and death" that the Metta Sutra speaks of. The ultimate compassion of the Buddha is to break us free of the suffering of this earthly realm, and the birth and death it entails.

Compassion and kindness have been shown to speed recovery from illness and improve mental and physical health. They may even be correlated with increased lifespan. Compassion counteracts social isolation, which is a risk factor for heart disease and other illnesses, and is enjoyable, activating the pleasure and reward centers of our brains. Engaging in compassionate behavior encourages others to follow your lead, creating a chain reaction of good deeds.[2] Surely this is the basis for any working civilization. We are wired and primed to respond in just this way. Perhaps a social network could light a fuse of compassion that ignites us all – this certainly happens with donations to charities after disaster, for example. But the danger is that such click-and-move-on forms of compassion might not be deep enough for true transformation or all the benefits of compassion. I tend to think that these require actual relatedness and engagement between individuals in the real world. Ultimately, compassion is not simply an ideal to be held in one's mind. I believe it must be tested and honed in reality to fully ripen into an enlightening mind and take us towards transcendence. And relationship is the surest, and perhaps the only, spark for true compassion.

There is no single, simple, one-size-fits-all way to generate compassion in a technological age – this requires constant calibration, reflection and effort. But we have to keep Metta, Karuna and Mudita flowing if we are to reach our fullest mutual potential. Upekkha helps us do this, and helps us create the stability of mind to face all the questions and difficulties that the other Brahma Viharas can raise.

Upekkha

Upekkha is commonly translated as "equanimity" or even-mindedness. Whereas each of the other Brahma Viharas impels us to some kind of union with others, Upekkha asks us to stay still and retain a stance of observation. Equanimity is called a 'protector' of the other three Brahma Viharas. We can imagine becoming depleted if we are always impelled to action with compassion. Equanimity helps us gather our reserves, and plan for the best way to interact. We might also be repelled by the actions of others. Equanimity helps us maintain our composure, while we work to increase our Metta and Karuna for the other. Upekkha is also called "acceptance," and this is often easier to understand than "equanimity." Sometimes the situations we encounter are not amenable to immediate change, or may be completely intractable. Here, we have to cultivate acceptance, just as in the serenity prayer popularized by Reinhold Niebuhr:

God, grant me the serenity to accept the things I cannot change,
The courage to change the things I can,
And wisdom to know the difference.

Upekkha, as equanimity or acceptance – is also a form of love, an unattached, spacious love that can hold the whole Earth in mind, with its good, bad and indifferent aspects. The Earth itself is said to have extraordinary equanimity: it accepts the weight of all, and the spit, blood, and pus that are thrown upon it, without protest. We have seen how a mother's love exemplifies Metta; a mother also must have a great deal of Upekkha as well, as she may watch her child do things unskillfully but not intervene immediately.

As a doctor, the first three Brahma Viharas have become my strongest "muscles," and most natural expression of my caring for my patients. You become what you do the most, and being a doctor requires lovingkindness, joy for your patients, and compassion. Upekkha helps me stay grounded, patient, and forbearing for their long-term benefit. It grows out of the mindfulness and non-judgmental awareness that I try to cultivate as I listen to my patient's story. As they sense my acceptance and caring, they usually feel more relaxed, and willing to share the more difficult material of their personal suffering.

All of the Brahma Viharas guide not only one's own mental state, but also the relational space between us. They create a safe, supportive environment that is as free of harmful aggression as possible, a space replete with fruitful connection. Facebook is a potentially connecting space as well, and we could find ways to practice all of the Brahma Viharas, and even mindfulness, while we're logged in, becoming more pro-social in the process. Noticing our friend's status, we could conjure joy for them in their happiness. We could send them lovingkindness. We can comment in a way that extends compassion. We could try to generate even-mindedness and equanimity as we scroll through the newsfeed, striving to maintain a kind of detachment and calm that is a Buddhist ideal. If I were designing a Buddhist version of Facebook, I would replace the "like" button, with all its implications of status and favoritism, with four buttons labeled Metta, Mudita, Karuna and Upekkha.

Still, I think I find it much more fruitful to actually generate these mind states when I'm offline, and not being inundated with varying signals and random material. The Divine Abodes require mindful attention to fully blossom, something which is hard to come by online. Moreover, when these mind states are generated with real human contact in real time, they become much more powerful and meaningful, gaining a context that brings us to our best selves, our most related selves. In the real world, we have the emotional space to recollect ourselves, and form a loving connection. And ultimately, the Brahma Viharas are about real people in the real world, not their output on a screen.

When you see your friend again, in the one true world, offer a smile, let your heart open, and anticipate meeting their happiness with yours. Then you'll both share a divine abode, indeed.

Burning and Burnishing in the Facebook Flame

There are few, if any, of us that haven't been afflicted with a quorum of the seven deadly sins, if not all of them, at one point or another in our quotidian (or with them, perhaps Shakespearean) lives. There are some that even go for twofers, taking Pride in their Anger, Lust, Greed, Gluttony or even Sloth. I doubt anyone takes Pride in Envy, which might qualify it as the most deadly of the sins, having little to recommend it, except for the fact of its prominent, pre-empting placement on the ego's pain channel. Envy is not in the least pleasurable, unlike the other usual deadly suspects. Envy is where we most notice how small our bandwidth really is. If it has anything to say for itself, it is that it puts an arrow in the bullseye of our little-s self. Ah. This is where I live. So this is what it is.

What is it?

Like all emotions and behaviors, a case can be made for the evolutionary or adaptive origins of envy. It arises in the comparing mind. We evaluate others, assess ourselves, and decide "He has something that I want! She has something that I aspire to, that I should have, that is rightly mine!" As social animals, we have an instinct to strive for status and all its trappings. The individual with the highest rank presumably got the most mating opportunities, back on the savannas of our origin, or whenever status became more important, perhaps during the agricultural era. We certainly perceive the person with "more" of something as better off, safer and more secure, compared to our measly, insecure, wretched selves. Envy is insecurity turned hostile. And as Teddy Roosevelt said, "comparison is the thief of joy."

Envy arises as burning emotions and strident thoughts of grievance and grudge, coupled with aggressive intent to advance over the envied other, to knock them off their pedestal, and have what's duly ours. Envy is a split between us and them, a complementary duality of separation between us and our envied twin. They have it all, dammit. We are lacking. We feel, on our side, deficient – dejected, devalued and even humiliated by the other's perceived attainment. Our twin is ideal and perfect, and we are flawed, defective and broken. The flip side of envy is shame, often buried deep within us. If we didn't have shame, we wouldn't feel envy.

Envy is, no doubt, stoked by an underlying experiences of emptiness and deprivation, and a sense of unjust valuation by the world. It is perhaps an unavoidable by-product of our intense wish to be "somebody," be important, be loved, be secure and safe from the harm we perceive awaits us if we do not "become." Envy intensely etches our feeling of not belonging, as we substitute the goal of "winning," being admired and having possessions, for belonging, being loved and loving. Social media's gold standard of belonging is popularity. Lacking gold, we feel excluded and diminished, we feel shame at our inferior mettle, we envy those anointed by the precious aura of social media acclaim.

"It is impossible to be ambitious without envy," wrote Joseph Stein in his monograph on the topic. A case can be made for the inevitability of envy, in passing or as dark and persistent motivator. One can even argue that the game we're playing here on Earth could be advertised as "Jealousy: How Far Would You Go To Have No Other Gods Before You?" There's nothing wrong with ambition – but what should we be ambitious for? At what cost? What tempers ambition? Does the narrow pursuit of an ambition distort us? The fire of envy does more to burn than burnish us. In envy, we see our ambition, but also our disaffection. Our dissatisfaction. Our *dukkha*. Envy is quintessential *dukkha*. We have what we don't want and don't have what we want, a perpetual longing and misery.

Envy hardens our suffering, our separateness, our shame, our long-ing for perfection, our longing for more, our self-centeredness, into a bitter battle, staked against another. This is what it is. With envy, we gird ourselves against their "threat." Our envy deprives them of our affection, and we think this makes us strong. Envy is suffering, it is uncomfortable, but sometimes it can be perversely, if perniciously and temporarily, delicious in its aggression. Envy is suffering, but it rawly defines an existential truth. We are alone in our skins. How do we deal with this? How do we deal with others? Too often, we reflexively put up our dukes against who we imagine outshines us. But even as we burn, we dim our own light. Envy is corrosive to human relationship, and corrosive to our hearts.

Envy arises in the self and the self-in-relation-to-others, and both seem irreversibly amped up in the era of social networks. Facebook fans the flames for our comparing minds. The medium itself is made for shallow and frequent comparison, while real life gives comparison space to come to rest, to let go, or to relate more broadly. Envy is an ob-session, and Facebook makes obsessing all the easier. We find reasons to envy and obsess over people and qualities which normally would not bother us, simply because we are in contact. We could defriend or "hide," but we don't. There's something *desirable* about the madden-ing blaze of envy. We don't necessarily dislike the person, after all. We envy them, and need to stay in their orbit, if only as a lesser moon, or competing, lesser sun. This forces the issues of relatedness upon us.

We amplify and broadcast representations of ourselves, and receive the broadcasts of others. These are in turn fodder for entertainment, enlightenment, commiseration or private misery – sometimes all of the above in one pensive scroll of the newsfeed. "Of course I'm not so shallow as to be annoyed that my photo or status update isn't liked!" claimed one young woman – but she noticed. She's *not* shallow, in total, but most of us have our shallows, the sandbars where our boats come aground. It seems – and is – such a trivial pursuit, this tallying of likes. But then your friend's seemingly greater accumulation of social capital becomes an aggravating eyesore. Why, she has more likes! He has more friends! He is *doing something*, having fun, advancing the common good, being unique and creative – while I am just stuck here in my pajamas, staring at a computer screen. In this juxtaposition, we always lose. We are treated to or force fed "success theater" in our newsfeed, and find our own plotline wanting. Our mundane lives, where we all trudge through the never-ending school of OHS – Ordinary Human "Stuff" – seems torture in comparison to the highlight reel of our Facebook friends. All of these are subplots of the messengers from the pit that is bottomless and shallow at the same time: *no one loves me! I am not good enough!* I suck. Always have and always will.

You may realize that this perception is often a distortion on both ends. The other person is not as fully happy, perfect, brilliant and well-endowed as their Wall would have it. And it's quite likely that you are not as deficient as you think you are, in that moment. But *still. They have more likes. They have more wit. They have more, it seems, of everything that you wish you had.* To undo the distortion by saying that the grapes are sour, is, well, sour grapes. Let's face it squarely: you admire something in the other person. You admire that they are admired. But admiring, in this intimate moment between the newsfeed and you, seems to be showing up as hatred mixed with regrets, misgivings and shame about yourself. The spoonful of sugary admiration is dissolved in a quart of sour milk: it is grudging. You click "like" on their status update, and even add a cheerful, scratch-their-back comment. You groom them a little, as any lower-ranking chimpanzee would their superior. But inside, the sour milk festers. Wait a minute, you say to yourself. This isn't me. I am not this sniveling, resentful toad, lost in perpetual deficit. You check the mirror. *Or am I?* Even worse than being a toad is being a worthless toad. You keep checking the mirror, and keep posting, checking back frequently for the life-giving infusion of likes, that circular red flare on the world icon that means all the world: *notifications.* It seems like big numbers would be gratifying; when you get them, you might gratefully scan the list of "likers." But it seems to register only lightly. Soon, you're at it again. There's always that friend who has ten times the number of friends, who regularly racks up 3-digit likes, is always on point, and is funny, smart and even heroic. *What about me, me, mememe?!*

You find solace in the fact that occasionally, a special "someone" finally "liked" one of your photos. It becomes the closest thing to a digital hug. "Do you remember when we first liked?" No, she probably doesn't. But you do.

Slowly, you realize that you're not only wasting time, but also forming a habit, an addiction, to a slot machine that has been rigged for low, infrequent payouts for most gamblers. Just enough to keep them pulling the lever of the blue-walled bandit. Worse than that, you're creating a self, an insecure Facebook self, that invades your consciousness with its incessant demands for stimulation, distraction, validation and even conquest. Is this what I am? Is this all I'm made for? You log out of Facebook, renew yourself for a time in the real world...but something pulls you back. *Some* of this was fun, after all. And what are those friends up to? You have FOMO, fear of missing out...but even this is a brand of envy.

Pay close attention. This is the showdown at the Ego Corral. This could be the moment to mentally make your envied enemies list in your War Room of Personal Vendetta. Or you can sulk in your own private Cyberia, desultorily scanning the blue horizon for affection, attention and praise, narcissistic supply from the world outside. More maturely, it could be the time to recognize limitations – of yourself, of the medium. It could be a time to resign from this game, cash in your chips and move on, feeling like a loser, or a winner who saw through the Facebook scam, or both. Or you could tilt your Stetson and load your gun: only one self will survive, small-s or Big-S.

Or maybe it's not a showdown. Maybe it's an opportunity. Maybe you've just found the seed – the seed of your Buddha nature – planted deep in your wound. Time to fill your Stetson with water, and tip it to the ground.

The Tibetan verses on training the mind include the key instruction: "Drive all blames into one" – the ego. From this self-identification, the self-creating and selfish ego, springs all suffering. The ego can mistakenly think of itself as independently existing and separate. This ignorance of interdependence causes suffering to self and other, through greed (to preserve the selfish ego), and hatred (to defend itself against others). Of course, the ego exists for a useful purpose – it is our best attempt to cope with the predicament we perceive as our reality. We need an ego to cross the street, to avoid the harmful and chart a course for what we want. But the ego can become mired in self-centeredness, giving rise to the sting and stain of envy. And it is best to see envy as a stain, as something to be undercut and mastered; we do not exist pleasantly while in its torturing grasp. Envy is inherently antagonistic, a form of hatred. The mind has a tendency to obsess over things; envy is an unpleasant, lose-lose, antagonistic obsession. Like most obsessions, it can pass as the mind finds new amusements and ways to console itself, but it is important to keep the tendency for envy in mind, because it is an important signal of our suffering. If left unchecked, envy threatens to bring Iago out of our ego. But keeping our eye on envy might help us transcend suffering itself.

The first step, of course, is mindfulness of envy, to watch the mechanics of the mind. This is to develop an observer awareness of your thoughts and emotions, through meditation. We see thoughts and emotions clearly without overly identifying with them. Instead of *being* our emotion, we can *be with* our emotion. There usually arises a distaste for this state of mind and way of perceiving your situation: envy is distressing and unhelpful. Next comes cultivation of countermeasures. This is not just about dropping envy, but exploring, illuminating, and transforming it.

> *Where is this feeling of unease coming from? Why am I dissatisfied? What do I feel is lacking in me? Why do I feel that my friend has it "better," somehow? What do they have that I want for myself?*

We rubberneck our relationships, especially the difficult ones. When you envy someone, you make them a particular kind of difficult relationship, and you make yourself their counterpart – the resentful competitor. (I am all too aware that my name bears the same initials as the preceding two words.) Their existence and doings become a cause for your unhappiness and misery – which in turn harm only you, and not them – but could turn into actions that harm you both. The Wall can become a wall – between you and them, separating you, and thus a point of isolation, not exactly the ideal outcome of the so-called "social network." In fact, this construct – the Facebook Wall/newsfeed, is a marker of the boundary between connected others. Imagine a vast network of connected squares. Inside our cubicles, we put up information on the semi-transparent walls that surround us. This information garners attention, and makes us feel less alone. But somewhere over yonder, you see the walls of X's cubicle practically lit up with attagirl appreciation, while yours remains only occasionally lit. What do you do with yourself, in your cubicle, in your mind? What do you do with the real-world walls between you and others? These are the best questions to ask, the fruitful questions, the questions of the wisdom-seeker.

One possible way out is to channel your envy. After identifying what you're envious of (number of friends/admirers, a ridiculously joyous family or personal life, fame, attainments, talent, possessions, intolerable displays of happiness, great food pictures, an unending stream of awesomeness in activities displayed with absolute disregard for your secret wish to be included in any of them, documentation of a clearly superior life, etc., but I digress), you can set out to cultivate those things. Envy can become sincere admiration and awareness of the qualities of your friend that you admire, and inspiration for you to acquire or polish those very qualities. It can become sincere admiration and respect for your friend himself, as a unique human being, which seems a worthy and truly pro-social mission. At the very least, you can admire the way he Facebooks like a Boss. But it is important to realize that, of course, you can't be them. You can only become yourself. "Be yourself," said Oscar Wilde. "Everyone else is already taken."

This realization should empower you to find your agency – how should you use your power and resources to create yourself? What kind of self should you create? I think that's not so much about possessions, status or even achievements, but who you are underneath all that. The channeling of envy is a honing of desire – what do you want for yourself? What is your deepest intention for yourself? Who do you want to be? The imperative of our times is, I think, the cultivation of the self as a loving being. We can't get there without kindness. Envy, a form of hostility, is a major obstacle, the unkindest cut of all.

"What? Be kind? Be loving? I know that!" you say. "That's simple! That's obvious!" Well, it is and it's not. What seems like such a no-brainer becomes more of a task and even an unreachable ideal in our competitive, ego-driven society. After all, most people are kind *enough*, and that keeps society functioning as well as it does. But if we avoid furthering love, we can blow off our greatest opportunity to build ourselves and society. Each of us individually has tendencies to kindness and malice, and collectively, much potential in either direction as well. Every stone we add to the love and malice pots can bring us closer to wellness or warped-ness. It is our choice.

But isn't it true, as the song goes, that "you gotta be cruel to be kind?" Aren't there limits to being kind? If you devote yourself to kindness and love, won't you lose some "edge" that keeps you attuned to wrong in the world, and sufficiently reactive and proactive? Don't you need to be unkind when the situation "calls" for it? Don't you need envy and some level of cruelty to be "successful" in the world? Several patients and friends have voiced this fear – that cultivating mindfulness and love would "dull" them in some way, or turn them into blissed-out Stepford wives. But love doesn't mean passivity, or being inured to injury. Gandhi and King proved the transformative power of love; we can prove it every day. As the Buddha said:

Hate never ceases by hate.
By love alone does hatred cease.
That is the eternal law.

Envy is a curious mix of admiration, longing and hatred. When we hate, we become enemies of our own love. We travel the path of suffering. If we can dissolve envy in love, kindness, appreciation, acceptance and respect, we can find our common humanity and take down the walls between us. When we turn our kindness and love inwards, we can hold, nourish, and heal those wounded places within us that give rise to envy and hostility. Envy is shame turned outwards. Shame, like envy, arises in comparison; comparison to others, and comparison to some idealized self. We judge ourselves for every perceived "flaw." We are hostile to our very nature as imperfect, flawed human beings. We hate ourselves for being human, for being works-in-progress. We pretend we are perfect, online. We can't accept our imperfection, because we think no one else can. And indeed, sometimes we have been judged for who we are. All wounds are empathic failures. But the empathic failure, the failure of love, has to stop somewhere. We can cultivate benevolent, accepting, understanding attitudes towards ourselves and others. That doesn't mean dropping our standards. It doesn't mean not striving for improvement. It means being gentle with ourselves. It means being tender.

We can cultivate love.

We can cultivate kindness and compassion towards the ways we suffer, including envy and shame. We can be mindful observers of our emotions and stories, and not their victims. We can experience interdependence through loving relationship, and dissolve the small s-self, lifting us out of the quicksand of the self-centered ego.

Leaving behind envy, we journey towards connection. Healing shame, we become whole. Shedding the illusion of separate, small-s self, we glimpse the transcendent. Our subterranean, submarine emotions are resolved in a feeling of society.

And who do I become after that? Respectful companion. Resourceful comrade. Rooted in compassion. Romantic, colorful, rib-tickling creative. I like those RCs better than the resentful competitor, dripping with the poison of envy, feeling forever separate and alone.

Your Face Before Your Grandparents Were Born

Even when I'm on Facebook, I'm not on Facebook. I do not always know this, but I'm trying to recall. I type some words, share a picture or an article, and view and "like" the dispatches, declarations and witticisms of friends, made near for an instant. There are pleasures here, to be sure. Facebook is a comfortable, copious and captivating nest, with seemingly endless attractions for our social brains, always in search of stimulation, always reaching for connection and meaning. We are social creatures – language, tool-use, and socialization are three hallmarks of being human, and all three are – at least arguably – present in Facebook. These three are certainly not exclusive to human beings, but the capacity or desire to use Facebook is, at least so far. *Homo sapiens facebookus* rises. But the self that is on Facebook is not the true self. It is a slice, a snapshot, a careening rim-shot, a bubble from the depths, empty.

Even when I'm on Facebook, I'm not on Facebook.

The part of myself that seeks satisfaction from Facebook or other networked inspiration – is not my only self, nor is it the most true self. I disavow it, and seek to be myself elsewhere. Or rather, I marvel at the Facebook self as it occurs, the Facebook *daemon* or *machina*, and gain perspective by distancing myself from it, not as a retreat, but an advance into another self, a more spacious self, of ample rest and quiet curiosities. From here, I can see that other Facebook self: when activated, it's happily frolicking, interacting and playful. It is never awkward, and practically giddy with the thrills of cybervolley, an automated, asynchronous call and response with the object of its attention. But it is prone to moods: when passively consuming, it can turn curmudgeonly, dissatisfied, and unhappy. Something is on or something is off, in binary "1" or "0." Even analog can't contain the itinerant, wandering, universal self; how can this binary thirst? Thirst on, thirst off; satisfied or dissatisfied; the self judged satisfactory or not. I wish to delete the "like" button and get on with my life, stop considering the newsfeed and wake up to the real news, around me. Perhaps part of the trouble is in the "liking" itself – a play for my emotions and attention from a cold, metallic place pretending to be human. Google+'s "+1" is subversive this way, giving us a bit of distance and equanimity instead of emotion. Still, we are prone to count and compare. It all leads us in the same direction, the place where the Face, the *machina*, thrives.

I heard a man say he'd like to create a technology based on the attachment between mother and child. "What a boob," I think to myself. "What does he want, a double-D that plugs into USB?" Robo-mommy is not the way to go. Why would we encourage attachment to devices that don't live, devices that are extracted from and ultimately destroy what we should be most attached to? Mother. Mother Earth. Each other. Yet that's what's happening. It seems vital and necessary to limit this kind of attachment, not increase it. If we love our devices too much, we will lose everything. First ourselves, by distance and delusion; then the world, by poisoning the space that holds and feeds us, using it as a resource and stripping it of its sustaining power. It is not a trivial matter to create a digital self, to fool yourself into thinking you are "on" Facebook, that Facebook contains an early version of you as spiritual machine. Facebook is, ultimately, a fascination with what we presume to be the self, and a decay of what really matters, in form and substance, from the personal to the environmental. Your *machina* has a carbon, and a psychological, footprint.

But it is enticing, and it can function practically at some moments. We make it work, as well as it can. Our sociability and need for connection finds a way to use these intermediaries, these Faces and facile obsessions. Supposedly, about a third of singles use at least one of the many and proliferating dating apps and websites.[3] Anecdotally, it's probably much higher than that in San Francisco and other urban areas. All of us probably know someone who's met their partner through one of these, and swears by it. But that leaves two-thirds of singles who pass. It's not clear how many of these are the "permanently unemployed," so to speak, and how many are simply satisfied to meet people and date the old-fashioned way. I used the sites extensively many years ago, but stopped because of frustration: for some reason, I wasn't getting much in the way of attention or replies. The most popular flavors at the time were people who loved hiking and the Dave Matthews Band, not psychiatrists who loved thoughtful movies and slam poetry – and who looked like me. Go figure. Out of curiosity, I tried it again in the year of Facebuddha. Immediately, I noticed the *machina* at work. I clicked through picture after picture, occasionally stopping to read a few profile lines. I got an email asking me to upload a photo and profile of my own, so my *machina* could be subjected to the same superficial attention it was giving to others. I wasn't myself online; and how could anyone see the real me this way? How could I possibly see another person? It was an enticement to be unreal as a gateway to reality – a hope likely to be deflated, as it was before. I logged out, and unsubscribed from the site's email list.

If we're ruling each other out for superficial reasons, are we not becoming more superficial? When I am online, I am by definition more superficial.

Even when I'm online, I am not online.

It verges on modern platitude to say there's a good bit of being human, a large part of being oneself, that's just not part of the social network experience. Facebook may ultimately be viewed as 'training wheels' for socializing, or perhaps a useful safety net for those in danger of isolation. Similarly, online dating can provide dating experience. But neither is quite the real thing; they are simulacra and displacements. When we choose to pick people through an app, we may be avoiding the possibility of rejection, the necessity of courage and spontaneity, the beauty of falling in love with the unknown, the potential of discovering and creating the new. What gets left out of the online social experience may in fact be the most important part of being you. Facebook can take time away from engagement with our deeper selves, which requires contemplation, real relationship, and space. We must know the self, the real self behind all facades, beyond all *machina*.

Zen Master Dogen said, "To study the Way is to study the Self. To study the Self is to forget the self. To forget the self is to be enlightened by all things of the universe. To be enlightened by all things of the universe is to cast off the body and mind of the self as well as those of others. Even the traces of enlightenment are wiped out, and life with traceless enlightenment goes on forever and ever."

I doubt we can study the Self when we're mired, exhaustingly, in the Facebook performance, once a celebration, now a contrivance. If Facebook is a "thing of the universe" and cause for enlightenment, it is only by knowledge of what it is doing to us, knowledge of what it is.

The Facebook Bardo

A bardo is an "in-between," transitional state. According to Tibetan Buddhism, after death we enter a bardo, a transitional state before our next birth. Life itself is said to be a bardo, an existence between existences, an evanescent dream bubbling up in expression from some deeper stream of consciousness. There are bardos within the life bardo, when our usual ways of perceiving and interacting are suspended, and something different emerges. During our sleep, our dream is a bardo, a kind of consciousness between periods of wake. We row our boats, gently down the stream – and life is but a dream. Dreams within dreams within dreams – we wander like this, in a trance, inattentive, rarely conscious of the whole, rarely if ever focused on meaning, purpose, and the deepest intentions of the spiritual life. Buddhist teacher Jack Kornfield has said we "sleepwalk" through our existences, tuned into some private movie in our mind, not awake to the nature of our suffering: our delusions, obsessions, and unconscious behaviors that keep us from our highest, most transcendent possibilities. Meditation, by contrast, is a bardo that can awaken.

But we invent new ways to sleepwalk. We have invented the Facebook bardo – a dream-like state of consciousness where we lose inhibitions, become obsessed and addicted, are exposed to experiences that range from amusing to engaging to hostile to bizarre, and we are activated in novel ways that have the potential to be illuminating or destructive. Like the dream bardo or the bardo of death, we experience altered states. Our egos joust with information, emotions, and surreal experiences – we practically hallucinate. Just as in those other bardos, we face provocative images that are meant to stimulate. The Tibetan instructions for dying are to carry on and not get distracted or submerged by traps, and to in fact look past those traps to free ourselves from ego and delusion themselves. The bardo contains the possibility for enlightenment, but also the snares that will determine the state of one's consciousness after the bardo: one's rebirth into the next world. The Facebook bardo lies in sync with this – however, in Facebook's case, it is seems impossible to free oneself from ego traps entirely without exiting the medium completely. The same ego concerns and traps tend to keep getting reactivated through the interface itself. We remain unavoidably prone to comparisons with others. Envy, jealousy, greed, anger and desire can come even more quickly than in real life, and are unmitigated by the presence of others and the positive emotions of relatedness.

Facebook seems to have a direct line to our reactive, threat-conscious reptilian brains: why else would it have the potential to inflame us so much more than our friends themselves, should we happen to meet? Facebook inherently and unavoidably fuels self-centered thinking. Despite all our online interactions with others, and the ways we can promote community and commonality through the site, we remain sensitive to how we're perceived, "liked" and shared, disliked and distanced, as conveyed in digital signals and the red flare of the world icon. We are always alone with our screen, which has become our primary source of attention, which we want to be love. We want it to be the Facebreast. But it is all too often more of a wall, at best a mirror for our need than a door to its satisfaction. The Facebreast is empty. We can find love and connection in the real world in an all-encompassing way; this bardo has a flat, unendingly dissatisfying LCD limit. A friend can hug you; this screen won't, ever.

And this is the ultimate danger of the Facebook bardo: we don't meet our friends in the same way anymore, literally or metaphorically. Our very presence in the bardo, and our behavior on it, involves a distancing from and aversion to real world interactions. Facebook promotes satisfaction with online relationship, and dissatisfaction with real world relationships.[4] While it is arguably a great boon to friends and family separated by distance, or people who share mutual interest and identity who cannot be physically present with each other, the Facebook bardo becomes a way of isolating us from the community that exists near us, and perhaps prevents us from creating that community itself – by taking our time and presence from the real world, and also by activating parts of ourselves that are actually detrimental to community. We all are prone to antagonisms. These antagonisms, from trolling to snark to flame wars, are more likely to happen online, when we are not soothed and nurtured by physical presence and all its cues.

Technology can dominate our time and attention. Therefore, we must exert particular mindfulness in our interactions with devices and screens. We must be particularly mindful of this bardo. We are, most of us, on a slippery slope to frittering away our valuable time, and with it, our valuable mind, on distractions that dissatisfy and ultimately don't lead us towards transcendence or even happiness. We need all the help we can get – information, knowledge, skill, wisdom, compassion for ourselves and others – to marshal our defenses and make our stand for our own best inner light and hope. As the Buddha said, we must "be lamps unto ourselves." We need to light a torch to see the dangers and attractions of the Facebook bardo, certainly, but also must be aware that this techno-bardo keeps us from a full experience of our life bardo. That in itself should give us pause.

There are other techno-bardos, of course: the bardos of gaming, YouTube videos, and virtual reality, not to mention the less-enveloping techno-bardos of television and the cinema. Care is required in constructing these bardos so they are of benefit to us, because they do in fact influence the ways we think, act and perceive. The Facebook bardo challenges us to monitor ourselves – and for this reason can be helpful, as it can highlight and expose facets of personality and consciousness that we can then work on with intention. The danger is getting trapped in the medium itself, having our relational energies confined to its limited channels, and feeding the reptile within. But perhaps we need to know this dragon before we can tame it.

Logging in,
We log out of reality.
and enter a virtual world,
thinking it expands –
But we're narrowed instead.
We can only post and like;
lurk and write.
Every scroll is a drag,
a game that puts us in a trance.
Emotions and thoughts
float in some separate space;
We're no longer embodied, no longer embraced.
We mistake this delusion for some kind of fun –
The dim blue light
Distracts us from the sun.

You create an account, a profile, a virtual identity. Some say this is an opportunity to imaginatively try out personalities and styles, a form of art. Indeed, insecure adolescents[5] and adults,[6] who have a less stable sense of self, experiment with identity and idealize themselves online. But identity creation online can be an exercise in stepping away from ourselves, towards vanity, disinhibition or a false persona. A false self can be the gateway to significant pathology. Is our social media projection coherent with our real world self? Do we need to be someone else online, to feel freer, to attain popularity, to work at some part of ourself? Is our act here a swagger of brash identity and unabashed opinion, not true to our larger self or greatest possibility? Does our social media path lead us towards understanding, love and inclusion, or towards distraction, hostility, separation and aggression? What do we experience, in the bardo? Do our actual lives leech their reality, their substance, in favor of the insubstantial cloud?

My fear is that we fall into a trance and follow the online norms. We stop asking these vital questions. We become ungrounded, distracted from the ground of our deepest intentions. We become frustrated, dissatisfied, and ambivalent, and don't know why.

Distractions and frustrations of the heart

Of all the "hallucinations" that can occur in intimate relationships, jealousy is perhaps the most destructive. Psychologists have reported that jealousy is correlated with relationship dissatisfaction, and intuitively, we know this to be true. Relationships are made of trust; suspecting your partner of emotional or sexual infidelity erodes trust substantially for men and women alike. When we're jealous, most people (and women more than men, apparently) seek information about the supposed transgression. Facebook makes this effort dangerously a breeze.

Even before Edward Snowden laid bare the U.S. government's massive internet surveillance program, we had invented words for the new or enhanced personal surveillance capabilities that Facebook offered: *Facestalking* and *creeping* were part of our RSA (Relationship Security Agency) mandate. Amy Muise and her colleagues have done extensive research on the phenomenon, and reported about it in papers with provocative titles such as "More Information than You Ever Wanted: Does Facebook Bring Out the Green-Eyed Monster of Jealousy?" The answer is, very likely, yes. While their original paper demonstrated that trait jealousy (or innate tendencies to jealousy) was the most powerful predictor of "Facebook jealousy" (on a scale created to assess the experience of jealousy in the Facebook context), a significant portion of Facebook jealousy was positively correlated with time spent on Facebook. Muise speculated that this could work in two ways – people who had more trait jealousy likely spend more time on Facebook to check up on their romantic partners, and that spending more time on Facebook could in fact inflame jealousy, by exposing people to their partner's suspicion-inducing activities and relationships. The anecdotal accounts of the study participants were telling. "(Facebook) definitely invokes a false sense of jealousy." "I was already a bit jealous and insecure, but I think that Facebook has definitely made me much much worse."[7]

Facebook certainly doesn't seem to help those afflicted with jealousy, and it may actually bring out latent jealousy in those not normally susceptible. A later study by the same authors, showed that undergraduate women who reported jealousy in their relationships were more prone to creeping.[8] They spent more time on Facebook monitoring their partners on days that they felt more jealous. (The same was not true for men. This is thought to be because while men experience jealousy just as much as women, they tend to cope by avoiding triggers and suppressing emotion – a scenario which has been noted by others to potentially account for their more violent retaliatory responses to jealousy.) This would seem to predispose jealous people to a vicious cycle: jealousy leads to monitoring leads to discovery of more triggers which leads to more jealousy…and on and on, until the relationship self-destructs, one imagines. Facebook creeping has been described as addictive. We just *have* to know the truth – does he love us or does he not? Any trace of anxious or insecure attachment is amplified by the medium. The social network can paradoxically drive a wedge between us and our intimate partners. Relationship intimacy was also negatively correlated with perceptions of one's partner's use of Facebook.[9] In essence, we may feel that our partners are 'cheating' on us with the site itself! That hour a day you're spending on Facebook – is time away from your relationship. Your partner notices.

Romantic relationships are, by definition, committed and exclusive. They are also notoriously unstable at the outset, with trust ideally growing with time and mutuality. Information posted online can particularly trigger negative emotions (jealousy, anger, disgust and hurt), especially among women.[10] Those early in relationship (less than 3 years) were prone to having Facebook-related conflicts and even breakups.[11] Perhaps, as relationships age and mature, Facebook-style social network monitoring could enhance trust or at least not detract from it – but young people on the site now have to contend with the fact that their partners will see and potentially suspect everything that they post, or even that their friends' post involving them. 67% of one sample even monitored *ex*-partners using the site![12] Not surprising, but telling of our human disposition. Significantly, ex-partner monitoring is associated with more distress, longing, and lower personal growth.[13] Defriending, or staying off the site completely, aids in the healing process. Being trapped in this bardo allows obsession and longing to fester.

But there is a noted sea change of accepted possibilities in young adult relationships in the 21st Century – including the so-called "hookup culture," the death of courtship, delayed marriages, and open relationships. In sum, these represent a vast social experiment whose driving principles are that people should be always sexually open, socially open online as well, and never jealous. I may be wrong, but I believe that very few can contort themselves into all three of these boxes at once. It may be a desirable ideal to never be jealous – but one study reported that 75% of respondents actually tried to make their partner jealous at one time or another![14] One could hypothesize that evoking jealousy invites reassurance and assertion of relationship, and may be a natural part of courtship behavior. However, the social network is a totally new environment for our age-old emotions. While it may have been playful and alluring to casually flirt with a stranger while your partner watched, or tell him or her about some other person's interest, this would seem much more provocative when concretized and textualized in the Facebook environment, because the relationship boundary cannot be immediately and comfortably restored. Jealousy becomes disembodied online, taking on a life of its own. I doubt that many would consent willingly to having themselves pried and scrutinized continuously by their green-eyed partner; or that we would find our relationships more desirable as we become green-eyed at blue screen indiscretions. Indeed, Facebook "intrusion" is correlated with relationship dissatisfaction, mediated by jealousy and surveillance.[15] Creeping suspicions and insecurities cause us to creep, and we surely lose our peace of mind.

Jealousy, I think, not only extends to one's romantic interests, but also to our Facebook friends more generally. We might think that we're becoming part of some in-group when we join the platform – and indeed, we do develop a bit of familiarity with the people who remain active on the site. But it's just as true that we notice as the people we think are our friends display and even praise their *other* friendships prodigiously. It's hard to take our eyes off the fact that people who profess to like you – like other people more! We are on the outside, looking in, jealously and dejectedly. It feels at best like a "soft defriend", or at least an "underfriend." We are dumped back into the emotional wilds of High School again. We often take their exclusion of us as an implied or outright aversion to us. Click to display cliques. Unlike. Certainly, maturity instructs us to let go of this jealousy and hurt, and find other ways to restore our relatedness – but as the social network reminds us of our frustrated relationship desires, it disappoints.

Beyond the jealousy we feel towards the perceived closeness of others, social media offers new ways to be actively cut out. When we're dropped from the group text or email thread or even publicly shamed and ostracized, we feel a new and intense form of isolation. A message unreturned, a status or comment unliked – these are also forms of isolation. Even our own "normal" behavior on the site – we read many more posts than we acknowledge by clicking "like" – is an expression of aversion and a way we (unconsciously and inadvertently, usually) isolate each other. It's akin to turning your back on someone at a party. There's no way around this, of course, but the uneven apportioning of attention on the site wears on us, and is inimical to closeness. Every time you scroll past your friend's post without interacting – you are, in effect, shunning them, shrugging them off. Perhaps there's some meta-, digital form of relating that is being shaped by new media, one that we have to simply accept. I can't bring myself to like it, though, no pun intended. There's the mirage and promise of relationship, and the reality of the frayed fabric of community, with abundant gaps where our relational desires go unfulfilled. I can't feel good about scrolling past you without interacting; but I must. The cost of a "like" is tens or hundreds of virtual "shrugs," for most of our likes are outweighed by indifference, an indifference which we consciously or unconsciously register, and which chips away at our sensitivity, creating a far different climate in the Facebook bardo than real world interactions. There's a toll on our conscience and goodwill, and a subtle hardening of the heart that works against the softness and openness we perhaps thought we'd enjoy by joining the site in the first place. One man tried to solve this dilemma by creating a bot that would automatically "like" all his friends' posts. Facebook caught on, and banned it. Only "authentic" likes allowed, only authentic disinterest propagated by every scroll. Every scroll past is a scroll-by shooting, a subtle murder of relationship.

All our activity on Facebook amounts to creeping, in one form or another. We eye our friends and lovers, take account of them, their interests and activities. We shun them, passively and actively, and are shunned in turn, but are often embraced just enough, intrigued just enough, to keep us returning to the bardo. The only way to free ourselves from the sticky ointment of the Facebook fly-trap may be to avoid it entirely. As with any bardo, awareness is our main ally in our quest for enlightenment.

How ironic that jealousy and exclusion, the emotions of isolation and loneliness, are amplified in the network that is supposed to bring us together. The so-called social network can remind us of all the ways we're not included, not socially favored or engaged, not friended in the most important ways. Is this love? Is this where we want to be?

Beyond the silent scroll-by shrug, beyond jealousy and exclusion, social media can become a venue for outright anti-social acts and hostility. 6.6-17%[16] of adolescents reportedly experience cyberbullying, with perpetrators, victims and victim-perpetrators typically reporting significantly higher use of social media. Nancy Jo Sales (*American Girls: Social Media and the Secret Lives of Teenagers*) and Peggy Orenstein (*Girls and Sex: Navigating the Complex New Landscape*) detail how social media and internet pornography impact vulnerable girls seeking popularity through sexting and bardos such as Snapchat, which can become prime mechanisms of shaming and ostracism. Girls pressured into sexting suffer more anxiety, depression and trauma than girls pressured into actual sex, writes Orenstein. Our online interactions are often disinhibited and aggressive, allowing power, trolling and bullying to advance over love, compassion and kindness. Without the cues of physical presence, antisocial behavior is unmasked and amplified. Researchers found[17] that internet trolls exhibit the "dark tetrad" of human behavior: sadism (taking pleasure in others' suffering), psychopathy (lack of remorse and empathy), narcissism (egotism and self-obsession), and Machiavellianism (willingness to manipulate and deceive others).[18] Trolls only represented 5.6% of the sample but they can do a lot of damage, particularly to the vulnerable, children included. "Do not feed the trolls," but the trolls still bite. In the social network, we are exposed to the worst possibilities of dysfunctional interaction. This bardo can hurt.

Disinhibition can hurt perpetrators too. Harvard University revealed in June 2017 that it had "rescinded admission offers to at least 10 students who shared offensive images within what they thought was a private Facebook group chat. The students posted memes and images that mocked minority groups, child abuse, sexual assault and the Holocaust, among other things."[19] The cerebral cortex is still developing in teenagers, so there's less check on impulsive behavior, mostly generated by the amygdala and limbic system. Teens are more swayed by peer pressures and the wish to be popular. They are exploring identity, and being offensive or crude to appear tough, mean or "humorous" can be more appealing. This can translate into a gross lack of empathy for the targets of their behavior. The internet doesn't currently provide much of a check on impulsivity or trolling. That can only come through relationships grounded in the real world. In this case, that would mean adult and peer supervision. Adult supervision through parental controls and monitoring. Peer supervision through norm and boundary setting. It's all an added level of intensity surrounding childhood and youth. In the bardo, though, finally, all bets are off. There are countless ways for teens to hide their social media world from prying, caring and responsible eyes, to forget that they can cause harm to others with their own carefree, sometimes careless, thoughts.

Distractions and frustrations of the mind

It's hard to shake the Facebook bardo. Posts can linger in the mind, even more so than human faces or sentences from books.[20] Mickes and colleagues convincingly argue that updates are memorable because they are gossipy, pithy, complete, and spontaneous emanations of the mind that our social antennae are geared to tune into. They are coming from a "friend," and by the very fact that someone has posted them, they usually have some emotional charge. This emotional charge is likely responsible for their stickiness as well. They are often entertaining or annoying, a TMZ of TMI. The Buddha taught that the mind experiences sensations and perceptions as pleasant, unpleasant or neutral. Stickiness itself may become an unpleasant sensation over time. Why are we pestering ourselves with these neural stick-it notes? What is their cumulative effect? Why, when I think a thought, should I have a notion to post it? We're probably hard-wired to value the production and consumption of wit – but really, must we sink to this? When I bring mindfulness to bear, I find both production and consumption in this realm to be obsessions that aim at maintaining social relatedness, and even ourselves, in some digitally expansive, but ultimately superficial, form. Lingering only on what is superficially attractive to us by definition imperils our depths. The hallucination has dangers. We become what we do. We may have a natural affinity for personalized stick-it notes, but they can't be sustaining, any more than remembering the words "War and Peace" is more profound than reading War and Peace.

The garden of pleasures, the new "happiest place on Earth," is not always pleasant. 85% of one sample of undergraduates reported some level of Facebook-induced stress.[21] No doubt, there is the possibility of social engagement and support for one's difficulties online.[22] But some significant research indicates that those who are distressed tend to be dissatisfied with the responses they receive on Facebook.[23] Those with low self-esteem seek reassurance online, but often end up feeling that they don't belong and are a burden.[24]

Each individual has to come to their own reckoning of their personal cost/benefit ratio of being on the site, and use it to guide their interaction with the techno-bardo. For this, we have to be aware of dangers. The online world can be a safe refuge from the real, an easy way to check out and check in. But just as the challenge of the real requires more of us, it can offer much more as well. As a psychiatrist, I know that face-to-face supports, while sometimes difficult to initiate and maintain, provide an incredibly powerful positive influence. They are how we have formed attachments throughout our evolutionary history. When we try to change the ways we connect, we are in danger of losing real connection. When distressed, the right person, rather than the right post, is the best remedy.

Stress is a challenge to well-being. A study by Kross and colleagues showed quite definitively that the more time young adults spent on Facebook, the worse off they felt.[25] Subjects were texted five times daily for two weeks to answer questions about well-being, direct social contact and Facebook use. The people who spent more time on Facebook felt significantly worse later on, supporting a causal connection. The effect was small but significant, even after controlling for factors such as depression and loneliness. Interestingly, those spending significant time on Facebook and also reporting moderate or high levels of direct social contact also reported worsening well-being. The authors hypothesize that comparisons and emotions triggered by Facebook were carried into real-world contacts, degrading them. This despite other data showing that direct social contact improves subjective well-being. The Facebook bardo worsens our feelings about ourselves, and might damage the healing power of real-world relationships.

A frequent stress of the online world is information overload. Not to mention that a lot of the information we take in is the intellectual equivalent of junk food, coming at us in high quantity and low quality. No doubt, the mind needs both stimulation and rest, and the right kind of each. But we're addicted to stimulation, and we're clearly in a world where distraction and overload are all too available. We must take active measures to find rest. Nicholas Carr, in his book *The Shallows: What The Internet is Doing To Our Brains*, makes a clear case that being online erodes our ability to pay attention and develop our depths. The "literary mind," produced by engrossment with books, for example, is deposed by the scanning, clicking-and-jumping internet mind. As attention wanes, mindfulness and happiness suffer. We cannot be "aware of present experience with acceptance and compassion" (the definition of mindfulness) when we flit by a series of status updates like the following:

31 dead and 200 injured in Baghdad
Homemade popcorn with butter and garlic powder
Giants pitcher farts on the mound
A shooting at MIT
Bwahahaha
We got posted on YouTube

I collected this sequence as a found poem, "Facebook Newsfeed" – but it illustrates the scattershot nature of information we're fed, incoherent and practically psychotic in sum. A typical day's hallucination on the site. (Twitter seems even worse in this regard.) We're roadkill on the infobahn, unless we find the exit ramp. The info-glut rut runs counter to the deepening of our neural grooves. The longer we stay on, the more our brains are brined. Mindful attention here tells us that the newsfeed is an often slop-filled trough. Communication and information overload is thought to mediate the loss of self-esteem associated with more time spent on Facebook.[26]

It's not all bad...is it?

I dwell on Facebook as a trap; yet I must acknowledge the allure and benefit in some situations. Active interaction is correlated with feelings of social closeness.[27] (Passive consumption of Facebook, though, leads to dissatisfaction, mostly mediated by increasing envy.[28] Since all use is a mix of active and passive interaction, it's easy to see how Facebook use can negatively impact feelings of well-being in the long run.) It is an easy source of information about the world and what one's friends are thinking about and dealing with. It can be a reasonable way to get support. Individuals who are isolated or have a need to connect with an online community, due to illness, for example, find benefit and solace here. Social media can "serve as a spring board" for the "more reclusive...into greater social integration."[29] Facebook communities can help break down the stigma and negative stereotypes of illness.[30] (But alarmingly, it could also remove the stigma from negative behaviors, such as alcohol and substance abuse, and make them more acceptable, especially to minors.[31] One study found that "portraying oneself as a drinker is considered by many young people to be a socially desirable component of identity" on Facebook, thus helping to encourage alcohol abuse.)[32]

Facebook updates might help us identify those in our community who are depressed[33] or stressed,[34] and encourage us to help them in some way or enable health care providers to identify them. In a geographically mobile world, it can be a way of maintaining some form of contact, dissatisfying though it might ultimately be. Older adults may get cognitive benefits from interacting online.[35] Shy people tend to like the site and spend more time on it, one study claimed.[36] Perhaps the site encourages the shy and socially anxious to communicate, and provides some relief – but still, one wonders if this comfortable, stay-at-home solution is the best remedy for these conditions, which ultimately require some level of discomfort to truly catalyze change. Online interactions can be managed and are relatively risk-free. However, socially anxious people are not only attracted to Facebook, their need for social assurance is more likely to make their Facebook use become intensive and problematic, interfering with school and social activities.[37]

The rich get richer on Facebook. Those who have secure attachment styles tend to get more social bonding and social capital online. The avoidantly attached do not benefit – the poor get poorer. Some poor do benefit – those who are anxiously or ambivalently attached do get some benefit from spending time online, though as mentioned, this time seems to come at a cost[38] in school and social activities.

Some researchers are more sanguine than suspect, and clearly, my concerns are "against the stream" of the billion-and-counting daily users and high profitability of the site. Emotional disclosure, even through a digital medium, might provide some novel form of intimacy, although one could argue that it more likely serves the function of easing internal anxiety than truly creating a bond. Psychologist Adriana Manago found that larger Facebook audiences predicted higher life satisfaction and perceived social support,[39] although one wonders how this weighs against other research showing that more narcissistic individuals are more satisfied with their activity on the site. More narcissistic individuals tend to have larger audiences and could therefore perceive themselves as having greater social support. The less self-involved could understandably have smaller audiences and become more dissatisfied as they use the site. And how positive is it, after all, to think of one's online community of "friends" – as an "audience"?

And I would argue this audience and its effects on us are largely a mirage, a hallucination and ego-inflation with questionable authenticity. Facebook offers tantalizing contact with many others, but it places us on shaky ground. Studies show that between 40-75% of us would accept a friend request from someone we don't know.[40] Another study showed we are more likely to friend people we don't know if their photograph or name are appealing.[41] While most seem to use the site to bolster their real world relationships, it quickly becomes true that we have little real contact with the vast number of people we interact with online. When our friends comment on their friends' statuses, this may show up in our feed. Our boundaries are being lowered, imperceptibly, and this can't be without consequence. The main dangers are being oblivious to how we are being spread and viewed, and the growing insubstantiality of our connections. The larger our audience, the larger our reach, and the larger the feedback to our egos. Hence the inflation, and hence the addiction. When we're bitten in this world, we're more likely to want to stay in it, like hungry vampires seeking the blood of an adoring public.

A passage through the underworld

We can see ourselves, trapped on Facebook, as attention-vampires and werewolves for news, gossip and stimulation, zoned-out zombies in a newsfeed trance. Our passage through the Facespace can then be seen as a kind of underworld pilgrimage, lost in the self. The after-death bardo-underworld's traps and challenges supposedly determine the nature of one's rebirth. The Facebook bardo plants the seeds of the equivalent: our need and wish to be born into another Facebook experience. Whatever is pleasurable to us, what we feel we can't do without – pulls us back in, as surely as our desires, angers, delusions and perhaps more noble concerns supposedly pull us into our future lives. Facebook – Facecrack – is addictive. The Buddha said, "the mind, in contact with pleasant experiences, develops desire." We begin to crave the stimulation and simulation of contact that Facebook offers, and become addicted. Kittinger and colleagues say that "the use of Facebook may contribute to the severity of symptoms associated with internet addiction."[42] Indeed, Facebook addiction looks similar to substance abuse and gambling addictions on MRI scan.[43] Moreover, Facebook, Twitter and other social networks incentivize and reward posting updates. Instead of cultivating inner balance and peace of mind, we're cultivating impulsive tweeting and sharing, the snarkier and more inflammatory the better.

But even as it reels us back in, it frustrates us: the more one uses Facebook, the more dissatisfied one might be with one's friends![44] A study by Rouis found that those who spent more time on the site were least satisfied with their friends. It is unclear whether this is causative or correlative with underlying dissatisfaction – perhaps those dissatisfied with their friends are driven to spend more time on the site, looking for a fix. We've seen how Facebook use lowers subjective sense of well-being, and increases dissatisfaction with the self. Another study, by

Sheldon and colleagues, showed that feeling disconnected from one's social group did motivate increased Facebook use – and this led to some amount of quick relief and feelings of connection.[45] It is unclear how long these feelings last, though.

Dissatisfaction does fuel just this kind of addictive relief, as anyone who has struggled with any form of addiction knows. There's usually an initial rush that soothes the dissatisfaction, enough to keep us coming back. Then we find that the addictive activity doesn't meet our underlying need, and in fact makes us feel worse afterwards. When we feel worse, we're driven to repeat the cycle, seeking to repeat our high. This is the common cycle of addiction. Practically by definition, Facebook "rebirth" is driven by the dissatisfactions of loneliness, emptiness, envy and boredom, all part of our human condition. We have a wish to connect, but choose this beguilingly easy route. We could choose to explore our dissatisfactions and needs, and come to terms with them – but more often we keep trying to chase them away. They fuel addictive behavior. We are always hungry for something more, and find it difficult to come to rest. Sadness and depression are correlated with spending more time on Facebook.[46] It's not clear if either leads to the other, but other studies show that Facebook can make people feel worse about themselves in comparison to others. One could surmise that some people, once dejected from whatever cause, end up spending more time on the site, addicted, to chase their losses, and end up feeling worse.

The wounds of separation and abandonment underneath our dissatisfactions leave their calling card, propelling repetitive psychic activity, often without awareness. Waking up to the wound, the pattern, the addiction – causes a shift in how we relate to the world, including Facebook. Upon reflection, we find that Facebook is often a poor and lazy way to deal with our aches. Our humanity, and our healing, requires more of us.

❀

Young users may be more prone to the online obsessions and delu-sions of the Facebook bardo. Tiggeman and Slater in Australia found that the more time teen girls spent online and especially on Facebook, the more they internalized "the thin ideal, body surveillance, and the drive for thinness."[47] Certainly, one could speculate that, as with jeal-ousy, those with tendencies to evaluate themselves this way would be drawn to the site, but the causal link makes sense. Eating disorders have spread globally with the influence of media messages about thinness. Facebook potently spreads such media messages. The focus on self-presentation, self-portraiture and comparison can clearly be distress-ing provocations to the self-conscious, vulnerable and insecure. Other researchers conclude that maladaptive Facebook usage (defined as excessive social comparisons and seeking negative social evaluations) predicted increased bulimic symptoms and episodes of overeating.[48] It's not just that we get trapped into "rebirth" on Facebook – but it may exacerbate our distortions about ourselves. Already prone to compari-sons and negative self-evaluations, we find ourselves inundated with them by the newsfeed. We overstimulate our worst tendencies, and real world consequences result. Reality becomes unreal in this Faceprism. Facebook use, like substance abuse, can damage.

Another measure of the unreality of the Facespace is that we are far more likely to express positive emotions here, and present ourselves as being better off emotionally than may in fact be the case.[49] We hear many people talking these days about "authenticity," and yet we are committed to inauthenticity or only partial disclosure when we use the site. There's a reason we call it Fake-book. Most people screen out anything that might be unacceptable, preening for their public. The highlight reel of perfect lives and activities tends to make us feel ashamed of and dissatisfied with ourselves, and less likely to expose our vulnerability.

Those that do expose vulnerability tend to acquire an aura of their own: they wear their wounds like proud tattoos, and we oblige them as much as we can. But their disclosures often don't make us feel more comfortable to disclose. Nor, necessarily, should we. We cover our complaints with our sleeves, and show them to our own, private, real world doctors – who have more balm than a few online comments could provide. We project a separate, usually happier, more confident life on the site. The continuity we have in the real world, the communication between light and shadow, the way a real self is necessarily constructed as a whole – is not found in the virtual self we create.

Who are we, online? Who are we, together?

Social interaction on the site can lead to more expressions of acceptance and fewer of prejudice, some researchers say[50] – but it is unclear whether this is authentic change or simply another distortion and example of conforming to the smiley-face creed. I'd like to believe it's mostly genuine, giving us a glimmer of hope. Certainly the individuals who maintain contact tend to be positive and more accepting towards each other, but this may be a strictly intramural effect: reserved for those online in one's own group, or those whom our group promotes. Are we creating a bubble of perceived camaraderie that doesn't translate to reality? Or does the most popular camaraderie fall short of widening the reach of deep and true compassion?

There are George-Zimmerman-sympathizers and Justice-for-Trayvon-Martin-activists in real life and online. Facebook hardly became the forum for them to communicate or resolve their differences. There are plenty of examples of the opposite – where our differences become grounds for defriending. And if any of our differences are more accepted by our friend circle – we don't get the chance to experience that acceptance in living, breathing form. There will always linger some doubt about our acceptance, when we're reduced to digital interaction. Our acceptance here is a less-than-fully-authentic, perhaps no better than a shrug of "I'm okay, you're okay, I'll be on my way." We should aspire to more than that – if not with a greater number of people, than with a few, more deeply. That would be infinitely more real than the distorted dream of identity we're weaving online.

> A comment thread is not the tapestry I seek.
> Love's loom shuttles heart-to-heart;
> Looms larger than "likes."

Early in my psychiatry residency, I discovered that my patients could create feelings in me, beyond the appropriate caring reactions. Some patients, by the way they expounded on their accomplishments and knowledge would cause me to feel insecure. I described this to my mentor, and he immediately recognized it as a case of "projective identification." These patients were narcissists, with a tendency to overvalue themselves and devalue others – and I had a complementary "hook" in my psyche for feeling insecure around such people. As soon as I recognized what was happening, the sensation disappeared, and I could productively work with them.

What is Facebook but an incorrigible narcissist, always telling you how wonderful they are? And no wonder that many people become unhappy with Facebook: they are being "hooked" by a form of projective identification, from a collective source instead of any single person. A provocative study from Singapore highlights the very problem. Test subjects found to be low in narcissism actually perceived their friends' lives to be better than theirs, and subsequently rated their social well-being lower. More narcissistic people tended not to do this, presumably because they robustly overvalue themselves to begin with. Moreover, these narcissistic people tended to get a better view of themselves from others' perspectives, while just the opposite was true for the least narcissistic individuals.[51] Facebook seems to be better for self-centered people!

Of course, it may depend on what you view online. People who updated and viewed their own profiles during one experiment reported greater self-esteem.[52] We like to look at ourselves; seeing this evidence of our output is enlarging – or inflating – to our egos. We tend to collect and promote evidence that supports our significance, and withhold anything that contradicts our value. So naturally, looking at our profiles and updating our "selves" boosts us. But by definition, this is a self-involved activity, bordering on solipsism. Facebook encourages self-centeredness. And as soon as we compare ourselves to other people's grand projections, we are prone to feeling small, unworthy, resentful and envious, more symptoms of self-centeredness.

We entered the bardo for *more* connection, but our journey here leads to *less*. We may join our friends momentarily in their happy cyberspace, but we can't dwell with them there, together. There is an unbreakable wall, an absence of presence, that prevents full communion. We can – and must – hold each other in our minds, but this doesn't really happen in a newsfeed trance. It's only as we reflect on our friend connections offline, and as we renew them in reality, that we can elevate our thoughts consistently. If we stay locked in the Facecrypt, we may find that our good feelings for ourselves and others are endangered by the barrage of vectors of disconnection, which keep springing forth, unbidden. We cannot maintain ourselves for long in this airless, often vapid, space. Supporting this notion, another study looking at a longer period of social network activity found that increased Facebook time was correlated with lower self-esteem and worse adjustment to college.[53]

Extraversion – being primarily concerned with external considerations and outward activity – naturally corresponds with increased Facebook activity.[54] "Extraverts seek out virtual social engagement, which leaves behind a behavioral residue in the form of friends lists and picture postings," said Gosling and colleagues in a paper from the University of Texas. No doubt that extraversion is an often useful quality for individuals and for society; but having a space that is dominated by extraversion cannot be beneficial to all. Most of us have tendencies towards intro- and extraversion. Our introversion, our capacity to enjoy our inner life and be gratified by it without comment or connection from the outside world – is under extreme pressure by the Social

Network. This is a practically deforming possibility of Facebook, that we lose or devalue the inner life, the qualities of quietude and solitude that must be nurtured and encouraged to flower and give benefit to us and even the world around us.

A crucial component of inner life, sexuality, is a key case in point. A woman displaying sexual references on her profile may increase her male friends' sexual expectations, yet simultaneously decrease the likelihood that they'd want to date her.[55] Extraversion as expressed in sexual display is not correlated with desirability for longer-term relations, apparently. One's ability to maintain sexual exclusivity is presumably questionable if one makes online references to sexuality. Jealousy is presumably a potential here, as well as good judgment. One wonders what else is best kept private. What some consider reasonable fodder for the public eye may in fact make them less desirable even as a friend. The very fact that one is disclosing the inner may be cause for concern to some, even in this time of extreme externalization and amplification of the self. Disclosure is certainly part of intimacy; but how special of a friend would you be if you were as willing to disclose publicly as much as you share privately? How trustworthy is that? Now, certainly, very few people are this open – but this contrast between the power of intimacy and what happens when the private is diluted should make us reconsider the value and effect of most public sharing of the inner life, ranging from one's errant thoughts and observations to one's sexuality. Certainly, we can feel less alone when we share; stigma and shame recede under the open, accepting sun. But aren't our inner lives worthy of a conservation effort? Why share X,Y or Z at all? Why share on the internet? What kind of trip – what hallucination – beckons us here?

More powerfully, what could be exacerbated as we sojourn on the site? Both narcissism and low self-esteem are positively correlated with spending more time on Facebook.[56] The latter seems to be worsened with increasing time on the site. One could imagine that narcissism could similarly be amplified. Certainly, insecurity and need for popularity drive increased disclosure on the site – all of these often come along with narcissism as well. Self-involved people do indeed tend to be more active and have more self-promoting content, as you would expect.[57] Facebook is a dream come true for the self-involved. It is a dream about them, a bardo that allows them to indulge their habit of high self-regard – and that flies in the face of enlightenment, which requires compassion and care for others. No wonder that today's young adults have the lowest empathy scores compared with young adults over the last thirty years, with a corresponding increase in narcissism.[58] There are likely multiple causes, including declining civic participation, but certainly our online environments such as Facebook might actively be breeding against empathy and for narcissism. (See my later chapter "Narcissism: The Opposite of Belonging.")

But if our choices can make us worse – choosing differently can make us better.

The bardo of selfing

Of course, the major thrust of our voyage into a social network like Facebook is not just attempting to be social, but attempting to be *self*. By posting updates, photographs, links and memes – we are trying to create a self. We are "self-ing." As human beings, we tend to want to affirm ourselves and confirm our identities, and we do this by any means necessary, online and off. But online, this element of our nature is heightened to sometimes grandiose proportions. We want to prove ourselves, be seen in a certain way by others, or even more basically, reify and assert some part of ourselves. But transcendence requires us to overcome our self-centeredness, to let go of our selves, which goes very much against the bardo-stream of the newsfeed, whose overarching imperative is to self, and create a false self, at that.

The peace of mind required to let go of our selves is also imperiled by the Facebook bardo. Instead of promoting rest, contemplation and tranquility, we are compelled to post and look for validation. We are activated by the posts of others, which may or may not be conducive to the Brahma Viharas; more likely, they are distracting appeals for attention, keeping our minds busy but not truly soothed; reactive and not reposed. Instead of letting go of self, we create self. We grasp at all beacons of self, instead of recognizing them as sirens leading us farther from home. The self on Facebook is, all too often, not the self on the path to freedom from self. It is a self that wants to be solidified in silicon, made immortal and universal in the Cloud – ultimately an impossible task whose pursuit fuels the isolation and restlessness that led us to the bardo in the first place.

Frustrated desire

I once heard a Tibetan monk describe the final stages of the after-death bardo. A consciousness, floating free, sees a man and woman making love. The carnal attraction is too much to resist, and the consciousness is drawn in, taking birth as the product of lust. Our desire-filled choice pulls us into our rebirth.

Desire is, of course, an important expression of the human psyche, a motivational force and "glue" in relationship. Desire seeks to bring us into contact with the desired object or outcome, merge with it, even possess it. Traditionally, in Buddhist terms, the goal is to either eliminate desire or transform it into a more transcendent emotion, such as love, compassion or equanimity for these objects and objectives. Perhaps this transformation marks enlightenment itself.

The Dalai Lama writes of positive desires (those with social and spiritual benefit – for example, the desire to become enlightened),* and negative desires (purely selfish aims). Psychiatrist and noted Buddhist writer Mark Epstein explored the topic in his book *Open to Desire*, subtitled *Embracing a Lust for Life*, which pretty much says it all. He argues that the problem is not in desiring, but in clinging to our attachments, and expecting others to fulfill our desires.

Desire is a subtle, powerful and mysterious force, and our desire for relationship compels us into social networks. Our "lust for life" sets us happily liking, commenting, posting, and tagging our way into contact

---

* Buddhists seek to cultivate *bodhicitta*, or the desire to attain enlightenment for the benefit of all beings.

with social peers. And yet somehow it is a limiting limerence. We dance electronically, at a distance, and our deepest desire is almost sure to be foiled, for all the reasons set out above. Imagination, fantasy and yes, even mystery, are necessary for desire's full flower – yet on Facebook, we seem to know too, too much. The private nook that a potential lover occupies becomes narrower and narrower as they become more public and known. Celebrities evoke romantic desire in their pristine known-ness, and their elevation by the director's lens – but our Facebook friends have a tendency to become ordinary. Our friends have a special glow; they show us a different facet of their personality every time we see them. But they become flat and boring when they're always accessible. Our minds need space for enchantment to weave its spell, even the everyday enchantment of friendship.

Even celebrities can suffer from overexposure. Our friends may retain an interesting appeal – but compare this to the feeling you may get from a casual encounter with someone who evokes your desire, whom you are not connected with online, and whom you may never see again – as we may never see anyone again. This knowledge of the evanescent, the mortal, limns and expands our consciousness, if we choose to be aware of it. But there's hardly room for a *Before Sunrise* in the Facebook-tinged world – no surreal supra-bardo of heightened intensity that won't come crashing down as soon as you start to scan each other's walls. The Moon is stirring because it is a regular sight, yet distant, stoic, and evocative. Who pines away for their frequently posting Facebook friends? Their very availability makes them un-available to our lusts; even contemplating Facebook dating can seem almost incestuous. (I mean, would they post about it? Tag you in date-updates?) This, despite the fact that there are apps such as "Bang With Friends" that attempt to hook up friends who are mutually interested sex-partners-wanna-be. I generally feel so friendly and fond of my Facebook friends that I would be somewhat shocked if any of them harbored overt sexual wishes towards me, and were willing to telegraph that notion into a third-party app. Call me a romantic, but desire loses its magic and mystique when reduced to an app with a checkbox next to your name. It's like filling out a job application – "I will do all of the following."

That being said – that the Facebook Commons subverts erotic desire – it is true that complimentary, flirtatious and amusing direct mentions and interactions do keep a certain fondness in the air. So keep that coming, Kristina Wong.† It is the nature of the mind to be affected by the attentions of others, even when these attentions come through the Silicon Curtain. But this e-zest cannot compare to the subtle stirs of a real meeting, with all its ripples. The real meeting gives off the sparks and actual fire of desire, but also the full-bodied physicality, exclusivity of attention, and irreducible drama that must come from *presence*. Flirtation in the Matrix is a kind of tryst – a Matryst, if you will – but it is ultimately a hallucination. It is an indication of keeping the other in mind; there is a context and subtext of relatedness and affection (what the Greeks called *storge*). But it disappoints *eros* (their word for romantic love), certainly, and is such a limited form of *phileo* (friendship) that it may not even qualify for the term. Keeping up with one's Facebook friends may speak to a certain kind of desire, and it may feed our need to incarnate them in our minds, keeping us from what we fear would be our empty, lonely, boring lives. But it also keeps us away from that fertile expanse of quiet, calm and mindfulness from which deeper connection, even love, arises. And a LOL can't match the sight of a smile. Our heart-desires are stirred, for a time, but cannot be fulfilled.

Keeping up with the feed becomes some strange duty and distraction of modern life. Our desire for our friends' presence can wane, our obsession with ourselves rise. When we meet our mortal, special, desirable friends again, in the real-space of the real-world, it seems a brief stopping-point on the way to seeing them in their "true" virtual

---

† Kristina Wong, illustrious performance artist, has, I'll make it official, a very serious mock-crush on me. Or at the very least is capable of dramatic displays of affection that are highly endearing. I highly recommend her movie, *Wong Flew Over the Cuckoo's Nest*, about Asian American women, depression and suicide. www.KristinaWong.com.

existence, in the illusorily immortal newsfeed, where our interactions become but inputs to vampire-minds craving the blood of fresh stimulation and the means to feed our egos. We can remain stuck in an online trance, where we can always exert control over our relationships, which if experienced in their real form, would by their very nature, transform us. Indeed, they're the only thing that ever has. "See you on Facebook!" we say on parting, forgetting that on Facebook, we don't really exist.

It may sound strange for a Buddhist to yearn for a romance of the real, of anticipations, imaginations and silences; but this romance is far better than the romance- and art-lessness of Facebook. We need the spaciousness of reality, with its meaningful absences, vacancies and emptinesses to really have a chance at sensing the fullness that lies dormant within it, within us. Desire, romance – these are only vehicles that convey us to the space between us, where interdependence breathes freely. The experience of interdependence – of love, of compassion – needs degrees of freedom and space that evaporate as we persist in the logged-in, scrolling state. "Desire itself is movement, not in itself desirable," as T.S. Eliot wrote. But it is a close and necessary contrasting cousin and portal to love, which is "itself unmoving, only the cause and end of movement."

Perhaps, ultimately, the Facebook bardo will be seen as one of the tempting traps of the life-bardo, a hallucination that endangered the most precious possibilities of this human birth: to love each other fully; to relate to each other fully; to help, completely; and to transcend the ego's petty, ruthless charms. Instead of sangha, though, here we practice a form of abandonment of others, under the guise of affiliation; it is a hallucination of friendship not worth the crumbs of a madeleine. We practice attachment to self. In this bardo, our normal ways of relating, reacting and being present are suspended as we slip into the crack of Crevassebook. The only way to stop our slide are the ice picks of logout and deactivation.

The Facebog, the Facebother – is not our true home. And it can take us away from our best, enlightened, connected, interdependent selves.

Like Cronus devoured his children, Facebook devoured Instagram to prevent usurpation. But the swallowed child lives on, creating a photographic bardo that shares much with his Titan (perhaps Titanic) parent's dream realm.

We log on to connect and express ourselves, and along the way strive to manage the impression we make on others. We can create a false and idealized self, with all its consequences. We archive our lives and escape our reality. We become immersed in the sometimes glamorous lives of others.[59] Instagram and Snapchat can provoke envy and jealousy. (In fact, Snapchat elicits more romantic jealousy than Facebook; the emotion, at least, is no ghost.)[60] If our self-worth is contingent on approval from others, we may use Instagram intensively for validation and comparison, with usually problematic results, including low self-esteem[61] and loneliness.[62] Following strangers on Instagram is correlated with negative comparisons and depressive symptoms.[63] Exposure to "fitspiration" (or what some would call "fitshaming") images triggers negative mood, low self-esteem and body image dissatisfaction.[64] Similarly, viewing and worshipping celebrities online is highly correlated with negative mood and body dissatisfaction.[65] Instagram users, unlike users of other social media platforms, have a high prevalence of so-called "orthorexia," or narrow and obsessive dietary habits in pursuit of "health," reinforced by the Instagram food pic and celebrity culture.[66]

Posting, lurking, liking, comparing…Instagram impinges on our egos and time. The Instagram bardo, like Facebook, has the potential to distract, overwhelm and confuse our potential for transcendence.

Leaving the Facebook bardo can lift mood and perceptions of well-being. Researcher Morten Tromholt of Denmark found that after taking a one week break from Facebook, an experimental group had higher life satisfaction and positive emotions.[67] The effect was especially pronounced for "heavy Facebook users, passive Facebook users and users who tend to envy others on Facebook."

Staying in the bardo is bad for you. Holly Shakya and Nicholas Christakis looked at 5,208 adult Facebook users over two years, measuring life satisfaction and mental and physical health over time.[68] All measures were worse with Facebook use, suggesting a causal link. This link depended only on the quantity of Facebook use, not the quality of use (i.e. passive or active use, liking, clicking or posting). The researchers concluded "exposure to the carefully curated images from others' lives leads to negative self-comparison, and the sheer quantity of social media interaction may detract from more meaningful real-life experiences. What seems quite clear, however, is that online social interactions are no substitute for the real thing."

As clear as all this research seems to be, a whole generation is simultaneously being swallowed by the attractions of the social media bardo. This diversion from real life will leave lasting impacts on many, and indeed global society. We have invented something new, and a new way to suffer.

Sidd thought long and hard about Facebook. Wisdom had told him to stay away from this site and others. But he thought compassion was telling him to stay logged on – to spread his message and stay connected with community.

Now, he reconsidered.

Compassion, as surely as Wisdom, he realized, was telling him to get people free from the Facebook bardo. Facebook, in fact, was not just another bardo. It was an ego trap within the life bardo. Only in life was there a possibility of transcendence, an experience of interdependence through real world relationship. Transcendence through technology was only a mirage, a distraction, a snake-oil pitch that would keep us away from our spiritual quest, even as it offered a temporary balm.

Regarding the dream unreal,
I vow to let go –
Attaching only to
the boundless truths
of wisdom and love.

New Ways to Crave

"The disease is suffering. The world is medicine. So what is the self?" The Zen teacher looked around the room impishly, a slight smile tugging the corners of his mouth. Then suddenly and without warning, he *thwacked* his staff hard against the wooden platform on which he was seated, startling the gathered audience. He answered his question in a grim and gravelly growl: "Maybe that."

Like most Zen lessons, I had to sit with it to understand it better, the sound of the staff and the conviction of the teacher rumbling in my mind. Was the self something to be struck down, broken? If so, what remained? Or are we to struggle recurrently against the excesses of the self and ego? Or was this a dramatic but misguided instruction, overly relying on punitive discipline instead of love? I don't know that there's an absolute answer, but many relative ones, as we must all weigh the activities of our hearts and minds and come to our own reckoning of whether thwacking the undesirable or rather cultivating the desirable brings us to our best "selves."

Transcendence, enlightenment, selflessness: these are desirable. What holds us back is revealed in the first two Noble truths: suffering and the cause of suffering. Suffering is caused by the mistaken view that the self exists inherently and independently, a view stoked by all our self-centered ways and an ego that thinks first of itself. Thinking we exist independently and separately, we crave sustenance from the "outside" world, even as we defend ourselves from it. Out of this craving and its underlying insecurity comes greed (to enlarge and maximize ourselves), hatred (to diminish others), and jealousy and envy (both to compete with others). Anything that fosters an experience of separateness, isolation, and emptiness is fertile ground for the growth of self-centeredness with its insecurity, craving, and destructive emotions. The Dalai Lama says "if one wants to be happy, practice compassion. If one wants others to be happy, practice compassion." The converse is also true. If one wants to be unhappy, practice self-centeredness. If one wants others to be unhappy, practice self-centeredness.

When we are active on Facebook or even texting our friends, we do play at connection to others. Sometimes our sense of separation is briefly soothed. Engaging with our screens, we amuse or inform ourselves, and our mental and emotional activity temporarily relieves our feeling of disconnectedness from the world, or even our self-centeredness. But as our minds itch to check our phones, to check our notifications and messages, to see if our comments are liked; as we restlessly watch the hit counters on our YouTube videos, blog posts and Kickstarter campaigns; as we stare at a blank screen blankly, waiting for some signal that we are heard, that someone out there sees us – in that empty space of longing and exile, we experience the perilous void of our modern, cyber lives. We check Facebook in the middle of the night to find out if we are somebody. We have an irresistible desire to check notifications on everything from our dashboards to our underwear. We're even told to take our measure in bits and bytes, to value the "Quantified Self," what I would call a modern oxymoron. Can the self be found in a string of 0's and 1's? Can it be found in a hit counter or a number of likes? I hope we'd say no. Still, we keep looking, checking, counting, craving. Lacking.

We are distorted by the desire for validation in our digital dream. Our frail human frame has been lost against a vast technological canvas that alternates between inclusion and dismissal. It has promised to enlarge us, but in fact makes us feel small. Our inventions dwarf us, more than the skyscrapers we've built. This boundary between human and machine, this man-thing interface, is a territory prone to isolation and alienation, precisely because we are futilely trying to connect through this unpeopled abyss. We seek secure attachment through screens, but are left longing. We have invented a new way to crave, endlessly and insatiably. We have invented a new form of suffering. With this tantalizing possibility of connection, we feel more acutely the lack of it. As MIT media sociologist Sherry Turkle says, we are "alone together." And as we try to find confirmation of our be-ing online, we experience only emptiness.

But this emptiness must be seen as an unnatural variant and inflammation of the existential alone-ness that comes with being human. Perhaps here, with our screens, our separateness can be understood for what it is: the manufactured illusion of a self-centered psyche. But what a hard-core and recalcitrant illusion it is! Our happiness lies in seeing through it, in overcoming it to find a more solid ground. We can stay stuck in suffering, or we can strive for transcendence.

We can make a choice to *thwack* our craving, self-centered selves. We can seek to understand what it is we're looking for when we stare at the empty screen – and indeed, "who" is looking. We can try to understand what our selves become as they fetter themselves to an online world. Most importantly, we can cultivate an experience of interdependence and relationship with the real world, the only way out of our exile. We can give ourselves a reality check. We can open our hearts, and we can love.

The disease is suffering.
The world is medicine.
So what is the Self?
That which loves selflessly.

Boundaries of the Self

A boundary is a dividing line, a margin of contact, and a container. A personal boundary marks the point at which we are, in some understandable way, separate. Crossing the line can be a violation of privacy and integrity. But we also communicate across the boundary, making it not so much an unsurmountable wall, but more of a dynamic, fluid, transitional space, like a cell membrane that carries nutrients inwards, and does its best to keep toxins out, all the while marking some notion of cell/not-cell. Our own boundaries mark self/not-self. Our skin marks a boundary which is easily recognized as our most essential; and even this is a porous cover. When we're touched on this boundary, it can signal trust, comfort and love. Or danger. Beyond the limits of our physical geography, every culture gives individuals a certain amount of safe space. It's not polite to stand too close – this can be threatening to the other person's boundary and feelings of safety. Our senses mark another boundary: what we hear, see and feel touches the membrane of our broadest frontier, our ken. What we perceive with our minds is perhaps our most expansive limit. Our neural membranes receive all our senses, and the universe impinges on us at this inner line. Synapses ripple, our membranes pulse, and we touch the world with our mind. The furthest star of your imagination caresses your receptors as surely as the baby you hold dear. It's no surprise that there are more neural connections in your mind than there are stars in the universe. We hold a universe of possibilities within us. In this way, each of us is ultimately boundless, free, in communion with everything that exists. The molecules in every breath of air you breathe have been around the world, breathed in and out by countless other beings. And long, long before that, the atoms that formed these molecules were created in the heart of one of those distant stars, just like every part of this stardust-you. The story of any one of us would involve every other, mostly unknown and unacknowledged, gravities which bend light into our very eyes.

Still, we do find it uncomfortable when others are in our zones. Despite our ultimate continuity, we need to shield ourselves from each other, from unwanted and excessive turbulences and disturbances. Despite the possibilities for limitless sharing and openness in this internet age, we still feel a need for privacy, shelter, and space. It's been argued that privacy is necessary to have a self at all; without the boundary, there is no self. Without the partition of privacy, we would be always forced to squirm and conform in the inevitably controlling gaze of outsiders. Freedom to be ourselves requires privacy, and we cannot be free with others unless we have that internal freedom. Certainly, our communion is infinitely more intriguing when we're intimate with an interior, private life. It's not surprising that writers and intellectuals like Zadie Smith and Stephen Marche (each famously writing, in *The New Yorker* and *The Atlantic*, respectively, about their disenchantment) find Facebook to be distasteful. The life of the mind, a writer's sensibility – are necessarily introverted. The writer values the solitude from which depth emerges, and is usually thoughtful, and careful, about what the world sees of them. Not everyone is so introverted, and even writers have to cultivate this quasi-sage like state with its more regulated boundary between the observed world and the observations they make of it. A writer makes his or her narrow road to the interior, and returns with insight that's not possible under the lamp-glare of constant self-presentation and scrutiny. Even the performance artist who values public display requires some refuge from it.

All these notions of privacy are not so much about propriety, but about preservation of the self, which would seem to require active work these days. We may have to start a charity called The Self Conservancy to protect the endangered habitats of our mind; we may have to learn how to be a Humane Society to our own human nature. Our selves, our boundaries, are in danger of being flung apart into the cybersphere of sharing, with unrecognized losses, sold only as gain.

But it seems natural and desirable to share – we are social creatures, and "social media" thrives on our deep wishes to be seen by others and to see them in turn. But sharing inevitably raises questions about our boundaries and notions of propriety. Sharing, which used to denote dialogue between friends, now means staccato signals in text and photo. Sharing has lost the specificity of reception by a known other, and is now a broadcast to an audience. Telling everyone is telling no one. Since the self is interdependent, and how we share and how we are received impacts the self – it is clear that we are altering the very nature of the self by the way we choose to communicate, and what we choose to put out into the world. The medium is the message, and the medium may depose the self. This, alone, should give us pause as we venture into what is proclaimed to be an inevitable future of "social" sharing. I have to believe that our selves are generally resilient, and we will find our way in this vast experiment, but there are dangers here that require us to be wise. We are, after all, *Homo sapiens sapiens*, the "wise humans," our first self-selected screen name which hopefully won't turn out to be braggadocio. The online world will be a good test of us, but so far, we're all over the map, exploring every possible niche of behavior, Lewis and Clark of the uncharted cybergeography of self.

It's becoming more common for students to become Facebook friends of teachers and mentors. This is an obviously awkward potential intermingling of professional and personal display, and boundaries. Students' perceptions of their professors are, in fact, influenced by their professors' Facebook content. In one study, different kinds of professor profiles were created, and students were asked to evaluate them. Social professors were viewed as inappropriate and less skilled – but entertaining. Politically active profiles evoked strong and often negative reactions from students, even compared to religious, family, and professional-oriented profiles.[69] How does it alter, enlarge or diminish the teaching role to engage in Facebook contact with one's students?

Relationships change us – how is the teacher-student relationship changing? Is this a tolerable and useful boundary crossing, or a boundary violation? What of the student who later becomes a professor? What happens to their online trail of self? What will it mean to public eyes when they have a professional role, or when they are applying for a job? Our selves have been enlarged, and in a potentially harmful way, when we create a Facebook persona and go wide.

What is appropriate to share, publicly? What is our boundary, and what is appropriate to offer up to the boundaries of others? Medical professionals have traditionally given a lot of attention to this line of inquiry. The discipline of lengthy training, the oversight of licensing boards, and most of all, the importance of the professional's conduct in the care of their patient give these professions a healthy dose of caution. They are supposed to exert care in maintaining an appropriate regard and distance for the benefit of their most important audience: the people they treat. One can imagine the old-time, small town general practitioner being very zealous about his personal conduct. Everything he did could potentially affect his reputation and ultimately his ability to care for his patients. Now, Our Town is Our Facebook-and-Twitter-feed, not to mention emails and texts which could easily become public. As a person, I have posted political, poetic, and personal material. Later, I wondered how any of these might alter the views any person might have of me, as a psychiatrist or otherwise. Being a professional usually exerts a damping effect on behavior, at least in some contexts. Perhaps we can call it refining, at best. Self-consciousness approaches new levels when our actions approach immortality and potentially unlimited reach online. *Self* changes even as we turn this new form of self-exposure over in our minds.

Professional schools are concerned with the propriety of display – many have proposed guidelines about the use of social media and have admonished students for inappropriate posts – but students sometimes resent this feeling of being watched and controlled by the hierarchy. "When do I have to be professional, and when am I allowed to be an individual?" they ask. There is a yearning to be a Facebook Boss, a professional @lete on Twitter. This completely ignores the point that by displaying ourselves, we are changing our individuality itself, perhaps even losing a precious quality of individuality – the "in" in individuality, if you will. What we have is more of an "outdividuality": the inner and private have been devalued in favor of display. The professional may be the last holdout outpost and advocate for the bounded self. We may here see a useful model for conduct in the digital age.

But institutional guidelines can make students feel that their social lives are being hamstrung. Pharmacy,[70] veterinary and medical students have all been studied for their perceptions of being watched and monitored for online unprofessionalism. Professionals-in-training can feel resentment at being observed and being accountable to third parties, or even feeling "controlled" by their institution.[71] "Students perceived society to be struggling with the distinction between doctors as individuals and professionals," write Finn and colleagues. Students sometimes feel that being watched is a burden and sacrifice, and intrusive to boot.[72] But someone is always watching, especially online, a point that some choose to ignore. One quarter of young doctors in one survey made their Facebook profiles totally public. 37% of these revealed their sexual orientation, 16% revealed religious views, 43% indicated their relationship status, 46% showed themselves drinking alcohol, and 10% actually showed themselves intoxicated. Veterinary student disclosure of personal information was positively correlated with their need for popularity and negatively correlated with their awareness of consequences.[73] Another large sample of veterinary students showed that a third of them had "high exposure" of personal information, with significant disclosures of unprofessional content such as "substance use, obscene comments, and breaches of client confidentiality." The earlier the students were in their training, the more likely they were to have high exposure in their online profiles.[74] Vaguely knowing that some doctors drink to excess is one thing; knowing that yours did so last night is another. Perhaps the notion that every professional has a duty to the image of their chosen profession is quaint – but it is, in fact, true. Our collective trust in the healing professions is maintained out of continuing respect for the behavior of their members. The professions depend on substance, are built on real-world care, but are carried by image. Trainees may chafe at this kind of all-encompassing responsibility, but it is still a strong and necessary consideration.

80% or more of one sample of medical students and first-year physicians felt their colleagues displayed themselves unprofessionally on Facebook. Relatively few were aware of their institutions' guidelines about online behavior.[75] One medical school dean supposedly delivers a lecture during orientation week illustrated with publicly available – and unprofessional – photos and status updates from Facebook.[76] His message is to clean up, and quickly. The white coat extends to the blue screen, apparently. Is this a gain, or a loss? Does sharing any and all content deliver us to some better place, interpersonally and personally, and should we be wary of any infringement on this possibility? Does the doctor who shares their drunken photo or off-color comment feel more connected and thus more stable? Isn't having fun with one's online life a reasonable request in modern times? Or is it the reverse? When does social sharing become narcissistic, self-destructive – indeed, destructive of the very idea of self – and is any of it necessary? How a professional – how any of us – answers these questions changes our experience of self and boundary. A professional identity was once reserved primarily for work; Facebook creates an identity accessible by anyone around-the-clock, creating mini-identity crises and potential for embarrassment or even harm.

Our self is different from our image, but it is continuous with it. When the image becomes static and displaced from the self – it can threaten the viability of the self, or at least its professional incarnation. Our output becomes permanent, and rebounds to us, eventually. Sexual indiscretions might be damaging to a politician, but sexting might carry a higher valence. Anthony Wiener's behavior calls into question not only his fidelity and morality, but also his judgment, impulsivity, and ability to maintain his boundaries in a way that a string of affairs might not. There's something undeniably wrong with the self that's willing to share the private this way – but to an anthropologist from

Mars, wouldn't all sharing be a little suspect? What is that insistent share button in my mind all about? When did I acquire it, and when did it acquire a hold on me? It's like we've all taken some strange cyberdelic drug which has made us think that everything we do, see and think is worthy of public consumption, made us think that we must make everyone in our social world regularly aware of us in just the way we like. We're pushing up against each other's walls and creating a world where other people's boundaries matter less to us than our ability to penetrate them. Perhaps we grow tolerant and aware of difference; perhaps we gain something in knowledge of each other and the world; perhaps we grow in disaffection with the medium and each other; perhaps all of the above. In any case, our selves have changed, and what we are together, has changed. There is a dramatic difference between the self of deep relationships, and the scattershot self of postings and receptions of postings. If we aim at making ourselves "transparent," we will cease to exist as we are. We will be only what our profiles confirm us to be, and forever confused about our true nature.

And what does it mean to my boundaries and my self when my relationships, likes and activities are "monetized" into ads that follow me from screen to screen? In this way, the social network distorts the boundaries of the self through greed. Facebook is not a non-profit enterprise. It exists to maximize profits to shareholders. There's nothing inherently wrong with a profit motive – as a psychiatrist I make a profit by providing a hopefully valuable service. But I don't press my patients for stock tips; I don't offer them discounts if they wear brand-name logos. I don't get a kickback from the companies who manufacture the medicines they take. All these would be ways that I could "monetize" my interactions with my patients, and all of them are considered unethical and transgressive of the doctor-patient boundary. On the Social Network, though, we implicitly agree that we have no boundary, and that the Network can make money from our information using any possible means. Clearly, we are being exploited. Our selves and boundaries have become financial resources, losing their power to be sources of psychological health.

The boundary is the threshold between me and you, me and the world. For my threshold to remain open and pliable in a reasonable way, I must feel sure that what comes to my ken is not some form of assault.* My professionalism and my personhood instructs me not to assault others on their thresholds. Facebook, Twitter and their ilk afford the least assurance of my boundary of any communication platform we've created so far, both for my side of it and what I see of others. The self gets muddled as I scroll, and questionable and even invasive as I post. I define myself in some important way, yet I'm often stripped of the context of a real relationship, and thus am in danger of losing my self entirely. How often do we hear someone say "I wasn't myself today"? How are we ourselves at all anymore, posting, LOL-ing, and thinking about what we'll post and LOL about? Will we be ourselves, or will we become our displays? Are we already part-Borg in the way we have allowed the medium to define a new self-hood and new boundaries for us? If we begin to think that we are what we post, that we can truly know ourselves or others in this way, we begin to lose touch, literally and figuratively.

I can't believe the authentic self can thrive with such constant projecting. I can't believe that our friends can truly flourish in our minds without enough separation, enough of a boundary, to allow reflection and genuine fondness. If absence makes the heart grow fonder, what happens to the heart when we're always in thin-screen contact, close and yet disjointed in our relationships? What does it do to us when we substitute posting for meeting in more tangible, personal ways?

When we meet, a context arises, a depth of relatedness which includes social niceties and kindness, in themselves crucial components of the boundary membrane between us. Facebook strips away that

---

* These words were written before Facebook Live made it possible to broadcast literal assaults in real time. This exposes us to the violence that exists for some of the world's citizens, and opens the door for compassion. It also made it possible for some to seek attention through acts of violence and even suicide. Without an audience, I doubt these sadistic, exhibitionistic incidents would have occurred. Certainly, thousands wouldn't have been traumatized by them. Huston Smith's advice on psychedelics might well apply to the cyberdelic. "Once you get the message, hang up the phone."

context, and engages us, directly, word-and-image-to-eye, close but in a potentially harmful way. Without the other person in our sights, we become disinhibited. We say and do things online that we would never say or do in person, sometimes to sadistically harm our audience.

We are cheek-to-jowl passengers, lured to a train not of our choosing, going to some unclear destination. We invent a novel form of familiarity, which does not make us family, fellow travelers, or truly friends. Every moment on the train, we are potentially subject to offense and ephemera. We are subjects to whatever experiments the train's engineers decide to run on passengers. (Facebook regularly adjusts its newsfeed algorithm to make the site more alluring. In 2014, Facebook revealed that it had manipulated the ratio of positive and negative posts half a million users saw in order to test the effects on the users' emotions. *The New York Times* wrote "to Facebook, we are all lab rats."[77]) We are occasionally informed of some detail we think significant, but mostly are numbed by a flow of boundless self-projections.

Just as professionalism is called into question by careless posting, even our individuality and community is at stake in this new world. If I am to experience boundless union – it must be through love, it must be through meditation on the real, it must be through the enlightened bliss of real contact and generosity of spirit. It cannot come through the strange, self-altering realm of Facebook and social media, where the mind mingles with the tawdry, trivial and transformative, all at once, and to little end. How we treat each other, at the boundary, and how we construct our boundaries – defines us as social beings, and as a society.

Only our goodness must be unbounded. Facebook opens the door to the less-than-good, the less-than-related, in ourselves and others, and therefore, fails us.

Junk Food Snaps and Instaspam

If we have sight, we are looking all the time. Every moment of our waking lives, we observe the world around us. We orient ourselves, take stock, gather information, contemplate, and even rest in communion with our visual environs. When we take a photo (or make a photo, in Ansel Adams preferred, less aggressive, more creative, phrasing), we are memorializing a moment, immortalizing it, to reminisce, document, comment, share, or enlarge and strengthen our identities, including our technical, artistic, and (I would argue) spiritual capacities. I've rarely felt as alive and in the moment as when taking pictures on tour. Taking a photo helps me see, reminds me to look more carefully and skillfully, and appreciate the people and world around me. Like the Burmese daub golden thanaka bark paste on their faces as sunscreen and cosmetic, I feel that my photomaking presses a loving light of consciousness on my subjects, and brings them more deeply and surely into my mind, or perhaps through it, to the universal mind, or timeless universality. In photography, the photographer can disappear, becoming only a conduit for pure awareness. In photography as in Buddhism, my goal is a merger between self and subject, awe/enlightenment/transcendence through communion and union. When I look at my photos, days, months, or years later, the shutterbug moment of long ago can create a pleasing mix of appreciation, warm curiosity about my subject then and now, and meditation on life. I enjoy looking at others' photos as well. Such an eye for color, for light and shadow! Such a heart! Such bravery! Such humor! Such artistry! Such a moment, transmitted from eye to eye! I appreciate other people through the visions they share. We are not omniscient or all-seeing, but good photography does enlarge our vision, and through vision, our hearts and minds. The world as it is, or at least the world as I see it through my lens, is what must be accepted, reckoned with, loved. My photography has sometimes been a nuisance to my traveling companions, but I've always wished that everyone could enjoy their moments as much as I do when immersed in my film or digital romance of the camera. There's another RC I cherish.

There are some moments that I've regretted not capturing with my lens, but I find those instants emblazoned on memory, imbued with an almost spiritual significance. Perhaps it's "the one that got away" that I am determined to hold onto anyway, or perhaps it's the closest I can come to eidetic memory: occasional, but elevating. Perhaps it's a reminder that it's not the photo itself that's so important, but actually being fully present in the moment. Photography is thus only a portal to transcendence, not transcendence itself. But if we need a technological door to love and wisdom, awareness and sensual appreciation, I vote for the camera.

That being said, I find I don't need to share many images. I don't belong to Instagram or Snapchat. I have occasionally dumped images on Facebook, posted an occasional photo on Twitter, but more and more, I don't see the point. Curation of my photostream is just too much work, too much self-involvement. And while I appreciate the work of many photographers, I don't need to keep up with their latest work. As for the rest of you – I wish you well on your photographic odysseys, but I'm sorry, I have no need to watch your lives unfold, curated, snapshot after endless snapshot, selfie after selfie. I must observe my own life. Why observe yours? Let's be serious: I don't even have enough time to look at my own photos, much less yours. If I want to see incredible photos, I'll go to a gallery, or visit an artist's website. Why would I want to pester others with images from my life? Maybe someday I'll get around to sorting through all my travel photographs and compile a coffee table book. Until then, some of my friends and occasionally my patients might get a favorite image on a holiday card, a small present of my past, an inspiration for the New Year. The physical token, even if thrown away, seems more valuable than a digital downpour that washes away meaning in an ephemeral flood.

Who are all these folks making pictures for, anyway? Themselves? Friends? Family? Followers? I can make a case for the first three; the fourth seems inflated. But then again, why shouldn't my cherished image spark joy for some distant other? The problem comes when I hinge my joy on likes and shares, and feel crushed or overwhelmed by cruel, disinhibited comments, or not being noticed at all. This is a new way to crave, to compare, to envy, to feel dissatisfied. To suffer. Indeed, the reward centers of teenagers brains light up when viewing "liked" photos. Researchers noted "viewing photos with many (compared with few) likes was associated with greater activity in neural regions implicated in reward processing, social cognition, imitation, and attention."[78] "Risky" photos seemed to shut down the cognitive control areas, possibly because impulsivity overwhelms higher brain centers responsible for modulation of those impulses in young (and yes, older) people. Having our own photos liked feels good, and we can even feel drawn in by photos that have garnered likes from others. But this ego inflation and inflammation can just feed our comparing minds, taking us away from the more humble joys of simply taking a picture for ourselves or a few specific others.*

Still, I feel some joy when I see a child composing a photo with a smart phone, learning to see. But then, I heard a girl describe how to get followers on Instagram. "Well, first you have to take really good pictures!" It was cute, but also sad. She was already hooked on the idea of having an audience, being Instafamous. The picture was only important in the quest for popularity and prestige. The private goals and spiritual possibilities of photography easily get lost on this deforming mission. Underneath the girl's words, I could hear the fear of not being

---

* You can buy 100 likes on Instagram for a dollar from vending machines in Russia, and probably soon from a mall near you. Buyers beware, though. There are reports that hackers might be distributing code via Instagram comments. It's not just you and mom sending each other messages on Drake's Instagram feed.

popular, and I feared the crushing effects of the pressure to perform. "Take some pictures for your mom or dad, kid," I wanted to say. Show them to your friends. Someone who likes you for who you are, not what you do. But in some strange way, this child and many others are both being parented by the internet, and using it as a mirror. If it is a parent, it is not a benign one. If a mirror, then a funhouse mirror.

To say that not everyone subscribes to my idealized view of photography as art and spiritual undertaking is an understatement, to say the least. We need boundaries to avoid being besieged by images that don't exactly help on the Eightfold Path. Right Viewing could be a corollary to Right View. All this requires awareness and conscious choice. But all too often, we sleepwalk with our obsessions, addictions and neuroses, waking up only to find that we have lost time, and a bit of our minds, to junk food Snaps and Instaspam.

Sometimes we lose our mind to other's addictions, not our own. Others take and post our image – leaving us to contend with how we feel about our potentially unflattering faceprint on the web. What if so-and-so sees this? An employer? An ex? A lot of pressure can come with the click of a shutter, especially for a young or self-conscious mind. Sometimes we lose our minds quite publicly. Imagine a person with Bipolar Disorder, posting manically and nonsensically. Imagine their shame when they come down, and realize what they've done, what they now look like online. Will their friends accept them? Will they be kind and understanding? Or abandon them? Even if they are accepted, it can be hard to shake a digital shadow. The online world leaves us uncomfortably open to others' opinions and control.

Some choose to explore different identities with their Instagram accounts, keeping a "Rinsta" or real Instagram separate from a "Finsta" or friends-only/fake Instagram. The more public Rinsta broadcasts them as they wish to be seen at-large. The Finsta can express private or even unsavory thoughts to people who would understand. This gets complicated, as private isn't always private. Pictures can get stripped of context. Everything shared becomes fair game for one's later regret or abuse and judgment by others.

We fill our feeds with image gluts. Selfies seem like the high fruc-
tose corn syrup of our diet: they're everywhere, but they might not
be good for you. Group selfies are more favorable, each participant a
human shield for the others from accusations of narcissism. But how
much self-display is appropriate? How much emphasis should we put
on our looks? Rates of dental cosmetic surgery are on the rise, apparently because people want to look better in selfies. As a teenager, Danny
Bowman locked himself in his room and took over 200 selfies a day, in a
quest for the perfect image. He had been bullied online with comments
about his nose and skin. He later tried to commit suicide, and was diagnosed with Obsessive Compulsive Disorder and Body Dysmorphia,
or delusional distortions about his appearance.[79] (Bowman thankfully
did recover to become a mental health advocate for young people with
the U.K. Group Fixers.) Teenage angst about acceptance and looking
"right" can become terrifying insecurity, vanity, or both. But at the
other end of the spectrum is the artist Cindy Sherman, whose self
portraits courageously open a window to personality and the human
condition. Then there's Kim Kardashian West. She published a book
of selfies (*Selfish*, natch), because, why not? I'll leave it to her fans and
art critics to debate the significance of her work. Celebrities do have
to sell themselves. But what is it like to live in a world where so many
are trying to become Facebook Famous or Instaperfect, or feel famous
and perfect for a moment through the likes on their photo feeds? Some
even hire fake paparazzi and put themselves on the covers of their own
tabloid, to be "Celebrity for a Day."[80] Others share food pics they find on
the internet to show off meals they didn't have and avoid the shame of
sharing their actual, less brag-worthy meals. Is it validation, narcissism,
belonging, entertainment, art – or a new way to crave, and a distraction
from our true self? Reasons may vary. Some people now use any meeting as an excuse to pull out their phone and snap a quick proof. I like
to think that this comes out of an almost manically social, excitable,

fun-loving and lovable nature, always trying to make the most of the moment, albeit for display. But assertion in selfie pushes away other possibilities for the moment; I wonder if their underlying human insecurity, if not actual narcissism, is attempting to push away the thoughts of others and even their own unwelcome thoughts with an avalanche of upbeat images, enlarging them to VIP proportions. In any case, selfie taking remains so desirable it's spawned a cottage industry, from the selfie stick to smartphone cases with LED lighting and special grips, to Casio's *zipai shenqi*, or "magical weapon for taking ultimate selfies," the most popular selfie camera in China. At $1000, it promises to "make your face slimmer, skin whiter and eyes bigger" for that perfect "K-Pop star" or "anime" look. Apps such as Meitu and Facetune can prettify those on a more modest budget. (More on selfies in the chapter entitled "Narcissism: The Opposite of Belonging.")

The endless stream of self-images leaves us open to being dangerously fixated on our looks. The narrow and excessive focus on a certain kind of look ignores the reality that beauty standards are largely a cultural construct. We have choice. When we apply narrow standards, we ostracize many, and make ourselves miserable. We feel unacceptable, even to ourselves. Media images amplify the problem. On social media, when we view our physical appearance as the only way to get acceptance, attention, success and self-esteem, we are bound for failure and suffering. Looks may make a first impression, and unfortunately play a significant role in everything from hiring to dating to higher office, but character and personality are far more important for long term relational and personal success. And looks change, making them an extremely unreliable foundation for self-esteem. Over time, we all shop at Bag, Sag and Beyond. The selfie generation will be getting their monthly BSB 10% off mailers in about 20 years. Will they break through vanity (disrupt it) to greater acceptance of aging and varied appearance? Or will botox and cosmetic surgery rates skyrocket, as they have for the last decade?

As with all fixations, there are backlashes which may prove balancing in the long run. #Uglyselfies promotes acceptance of our bodily reality by showcasing the ways we're all imperfect. That love handle can get internet love with #uglyselfie. But if we're feeling unloved and insecure about our looks, is the internet really the antidote? Wouldn't a personal touch be better? The more we depend on devices, apps and distant others for validation, the more we will hurt. The picture we broadcast is a plea for attention, but we're often not paying attention to ourselves, the person holding the camera. If only we could be *wabi sabi* about our looks: love our ordinariness and imperfection, because we are all ordinary and imperfect. So is the whole world. The digital dharma of "perfect" machines and pristine code seems to promote perfectionism, though; we are bound to be affected by it when we migrate online.

Sometimes, a photostream helps to establish bona fides. Grindr, the gay male dating app, for example, allows you to add Facebook and Instagram links to your profile, to impress and reassure potential connections. In the same way, being "seen" online, having a web "presence," be it Instagram or a web page, feels essential and substantial these days, particularly for those trying to create a "personal brand" or launch a business venture. We amplify our image or bypass our insecurities with online certainty. But how is the new norm of image-making and web-presence-creation affecting us? Our time and attention has to be diverted from some other place – call it the interior, the inner life, the space where we can come to coherence of identity and purpose and cultivate peace and transcendence. The inner technology of the heart doesn't need an app. It just needs a chance.

But images might be a way of working with the interior, not just avoiding it. Photographer Minor White said photography ultimately depicts the "inner landscape."[81] The #Insideoutchallenge Instagram campaign seeks to make mental health issues visible by having sufferers paint themselves artistically with makeup that portrays their inner states, and caption their photos with descriptions of their anxiety, depression, bipolar disorder, etc. I believe that taking and viewing photos has the potential to hone and heal inner experience just as surely as writing, playing music or watching films. Photography, just as any art, has the potential to transmit empathy. But we can't be blind to what we're doing, so to speak. We have to be sensitive to how our activity changes us and moves us along in life.

Susan Sontag's surfeit of images has become a deluge. The firehose has become a tsunami. There is no refuge, unless we make it. In her classic volume, *On Photography*, she called for an ecology of images, of making them and taking them in. We must each arrive at our own sensory ecology, to conserve our minds. There is no end to images, but there are limits on our time, sensibilities and sensitivities. Anything can be photographed. One could conceivably make a case for every image as art, document, display or experiment. Photography can be spiritual. Deciding how and what you wish to share, view, and store in your image cloud, is now, more than ever, an essential task of human development, and ultimately a question of the spirit, as well. Why am I doing this? To what end?

The Social Network Is an IndigNation

Is anger the sandpaper
Smoothing rough wood?
Or rough wood
Waiting for polishing cloth?
Is anger
Answer or lie?
Defilement or truth?
If anger is a truth
It's only half-truth
Aching to be whole.
A hunger
Crying for bread.

Among active users of Weibo, the Chinese version of Twitter, anger is more viral than happiness, sadness or disgust.[82] Twitter itself is close cousin to Angry Birds; we launch angry tweets to topple our adversaries. Anger, researchers found, travels more quickly, broadly and definitively across the social network than the other wan-by-comparison emotions, tying users together in tighter bonds of hell-yeah-me-tooism and retweeted rage. The internet is the angernet, a handy transmitter to broadcast one's discontent and fury, and connect with discontented others in a rising chorus of ire-amplification. Complaints are contagious. Notes of protest propagate prolifically, passionately palliterative punctuation points of public pique, replicating clonally and sometimes pandemically, perhaps more polemic than poetic. Anger pops. What arises as a means to overcome one's own powerlessness, isolation and weakness, to rise up against a menace, a survival-brain boost of energy, is naturally strengthened when joined in tribal, primal scream. There is, always, strength in numbers. Oppositional Facebook rants and hashtagged Twittriol are as attractive as they are polarizing, drawing the like-minded into their magnetic "like" orbit. Anger is pure unbridled power, pushing an individual's synapses into full alert, and readying the body for a fight. We all are easily enticed and entrained to the flow of anger's yellow bile, which draws us to our most vigorous heights of surly strength and wished-for vanquishing of the triggering, and thus dangerous-in-our-minds, offender.

It is the most active, urgent and actionable of our emotions. When the conditions are right, or perfectly "wrong" and therefore unacceptable, they spark us to righteous rage, and a bonfire is sure to follow. When conflict catches us, we catch fire. Social discourse is most powerful and noticeable when people unite against a common threat. Social media has become a spontaneous, rapid response engine – an auxiliary amygdala – that can quickly take aim at issues and incidents that are felt viscerally by hundreds, thousands, or even millions. Clearly, the consequences for racist, sexist or homophobic comments and actions have changed dramatically in recent years. The anger of the masses – the conscience of the masses – holds leaders, businesses, and governments more accountable. All seemingly for the better. Online activists defend social media as if it were their mother – or messiah. They point to concrete examples where a chorus of tweets and posts cause real world change. L.A. Clippers owner Donald Sterling's withdrawal from the NBA after his racist comments drew widespread disapproval. The book deal of the Trayvon Martin juror that was cancelled after online protest, a notable Twitter-takedown. George Zimmerman, who shot Trayvon Martin, who was charged only after an online petition forced the issue. The outpouring of social media messages after the Mike Brown shooting in Ferguson, Missouri. Emerging protests the world over that are enhanced and organized with social media tools. All are examples of a population's anger crystallized and made crystal clear on liquid crystal displays.

The people can speak, and in numbers, be heard. Attention can be focused. Conversations started. Social media can turn heads, and if the expressions of anger are noted by a receptive party or government, they can catalyze change. In a democracy, the will of the people is a force to be reckoned with – and now, Facebook and Twitter can make that will known with immediacy. The nightly news spotlight is increasingly aimed by trending conversations on Twitter and Facebook. The complaints of the community can become nothing less than a call to conscience, and certain, palpable evidence of communal mood. Important issues of civil and human rights resonate around the world, share-by-share, tweet-by-tweet.

The power of righteous rage and indignation is undeniable. Is it not moving us closer to solving the problems of racism, sexism, homophobia, and other forms of discrimination, persecution and bondage? Isn't social media part of a sea change in the life and strivings of humanity, reinforcing and advancing our highest values? The land of social media is an IndigNation and InsubordiNation. Aren't these nations required, if we are to have a United Nations of Conscience?

Certainly. Dictators, oppressors and one-party states have reason to fear rapid communication and dissemination of ideas, and even more so, the easy spread of anger against them. Social media pushes creatively against control. Censors may impose some limits, but people find ways to skirt those prison bars. The network, the loosely organized or completely unorganized online "flash mob," is taking aim at hierarchical power structures across the globe. If people power is a forbidden fruit, then social media seems like a blossoming orchard of possibilities. It is a genie that can't be put back in the bottle, a necessary torch to combat the darkness of ignorance and tyranny. Perhaps, even, a spur to enlightenment, as our newfound connection can inspire us to rise above greed and hatred, and towards compassion and wisdom. Our collective compassion and wisdom certainly will determine our fate. Anger is part of our struggle to make sure that there is an end to all forms of the gulag. In case of emergency, break silence.

Anger is a vital component and provocateur of our egos – and must be heard, met and resolved in our advance towards a healthier, more inclusive society. Anger disrupts the status quo – and the modern mantra of technological change is "disruption." Anger spreading through social media may be the ultimate disruptive force in our global tweet-à-tweet. Facebook and Twitter are conveyance mechanisms for our angry prayers and insistent demands. We become the "hearer-of-all-cries," the bodhisattva responsive to the suffering of all, the bodhisattva who delays enlightenment to help others become free. When we feel and observe anger, we recognize suffering. We are reminded of the First Noble Truth – "Life entails suffering." Something deep within us is compelled. We become restless until we find the cure for what ails, the remedy for the wails and woes of a world in distress.

Anger comes to us readily on smartphone screens and social media apps, reminding us of the frustrations of our friends and the world we share. No princess can sleep happily with a troublesome Facebook post, an irksome tweet-pea, under her mattress. They are reminders of the journey, more immediate and personal than a newspaper, because they are being served up by someone you know. They can be a litmus test of our spirit and resolve. If enlightenment, or even community, is our goal, then we must learn to listen to the angers of others, and understand our own.

But as our eyes trip on peeve-after-peeve, we recognize that social media anger can be a burden. I can rhapsodize about anger in theory, appreciate it when used for causes I care about, value my right to use it as well – but in practice, viewing an anger-filled feed gets old quickly. Here's what we can step in when we log on: there's anger at spoiled, snooty 20-somethings ("spit in their drinks!"), government in general ("our government is bought by corporations"), Rand Paul ("why would we vote for a candidate who hates government?"), insurance companies ("spent 2 hours on the phone with Blue Shield"), Bill Maher ("Racist!"), rapists (video of alleged perpetrators being beaten by crowds in India), trolls ("Eff these racists who sent death threats to Asian American students"), bad airport food ("I hate this crappy airport burger!"), amenities ("worst WiFi experience ever!!! And the coffee sucks too!!!") and even angry rants about angry rants.

There is no firewall for the ire-wall.

We all get to our emotions honestly, and have every right to express them. But do we really need to permaculture our peevishness? All these issues need to be communicated, in principle – but when they come as a barrage, the medium becomes a source of dissatisfaction in itself. We discover we want peace, not peeves. To find it, we must return to the real world, relationship, and responsibility for one another, and leave this shallow texting engagement with little context. Our anger needs relationship. It requires empathic reception. Facebook and Twitter can't provide these fully. A 140 character rant or even a 500 word update can never give you the full 360. We can feel validated by likes and comments, vindicated by our ability to voice our annoyance, but these do not take us where we need to go.

We must touch the flame of anger, but then explore more deeply to understand the fuel of rage. There are no easy answers here. We may rather be right – and angry – than related, but related we must be. Through all our views and experiences of anger, we can create a mosaic to help guide our relationship to ourselves, the world, and each other. Where did this anger come from? Where did it lead? If I wasn't feeling anger, what would I be feeling? What is underneath my anger? How do I want to heal this suffering? Anger is not the answer; it is a question. "Who am I?" "Who would I like to be?" As telling as it is, anger is not our whole story; but on social media, it can seem like our only note. A shrill and possibly dangerous one, at that.

Anger can become hatred and then hostility, one of the three poisons that Buddhism warns against (the others being greed and ignorance of interdependence). The Stoic Seneca wrote 2000 years ago "a mind that becomes a slave to some passion must exist as though in a tyrant's realm," cautioning against anger's possessive and destructive potential.[83] A mind prone to anger, a mind that reignites its anger with swipes and taps of a screen, is not creating a path of peace, is not journeying towards enlightenment. Anger comes between us, dividing as often as it unites. It is a call to be heard that might make us deaf. Buddhist teacher Sogyal Rinpoche said, "Anger blinds us to 90% of reality." The 10% that we see may be the most important to us, but it is still only a sliver. We fiercely defend our beliefs, ideologies, convictions and oddly calcific idea of self. We become drunk with rage, and our newsfeed bartenders are always ready with another round.

As we become enraged, irritated, and annoyed, as we are distracted, entrained and entertained by anger – we create a habit energy that reduces our capacity for peace. "Habit energy" is also called "karma," the "throwing power" of our actions. Karma is the rut we make for ourselves, the mental groove we deepen. Where does the newsfeed rut lead us? As much as I like to keep my ear close to the ground of my friends' concerns, I find that hearing them in this way can take me farther from the ground of reality, relationship, and resolution. Absorbing their anger, I feel like their emotional waste basket. I don't want to be the angry bin. I want to help them, but can't across this screen.

Anger is the call of identity, of self-hood, which waits for the response of interdependence. Anger is a call to be seen and heard; it can be a call to be one. Anger may call for a just world, but anger, in itself, is not just. We cannot be just until we become love, until we cultivate love in all our actions, attitudes, relationships and institutions.

Love is the real social network, the foundation of society. The IndigNation is not a land I would choose to live in, but perhaps we can pass through this state, journey on, to a country of heart.

Vince Horn
@VincentHorn

Following

6:51 AM - 10 Jul 2017

7 Retweets **25** Likes

The Magic of Awkward

2013. It's a warm mid-September night in San Francisco, nearing dusk, the faint glow of the setting sun still lighting up the overcast sky, throwing a cool, appreciative light on the city below. It's the time of the Autumn Moon Festival. My friends have other plans, so I decide to moon gaze on my own. "Rice Paper Scissors," a Vietnamese American pop-up restaurant, has taken over the back patio of Virgil's, a nearby bar, and I'm eager to try the food. The communal nature of the patio is beckoning as well – an opportunity for conversation with someone new. I order my dishes – bún chả and pâté chaud, a Vietnamese noodle salad and pastry – and sit, eager for a recapitulation of a certain Hanoi rooftop, six summers ago. No one seems available for conversation, so I read liner notes from an Ozu film I'd just finished watching. Ozu's films are full of almost unspoken melancholy, the sweet, silent ache of children leaving home, and parents aging and dying. They are often about loneliness and loss, abandonment held in the frame of social graces and kindnesses which are so comforting and alluring to me, automatically inducing a sense of wistful longing and nostalgia, the fertile space where love can grow.

When I took my mother to Japan a few years ago, it seemed as if our whole trip was written and directed by Ozu: the quirks and mishaps of our adventure playing out against the backdrop of caring between us, within a society that was friendly, inviting and respectful to us both, a colorfully painted diorama for the foreigners in a foreign land. Here she was in a yukata, at Dogo Onsen in Matsuyama, uneasily preparing to take her first Japanese-style bath. She pouted to me out of her discomfort – "you always make me do these things!" She leaves, and I sit sipping tea, chuckling to myself with a shake of my head: she's my child for a moment, and I'm the one in charge, bossing her. She comes back from the baths even later than I, having finally enjoyed her time after being helped by another woman inside; I was left to worry about why she was so late, fearing an accident. I am the child again, worried about his aging mother.

Here I was, searching for an eyewear shop in the middle of the night because I'd stepped on her glass frames. She'd carelessly left them on the floor between our futons, and I'd carelessly stepped on them. The shops are all closed, so I buy scotch tape at a convenience store and mend the frames myself by lamplight, and cagily think of a plan to maneuver my mother into a repair shop for a more permanent fix; she is reluctant to spend money, especially at my behest. It must seem like her choice, if it is to work at all. "Let's walk this way. Oh, whaddaya know, here's a eyewear shop." The next day, I carry out my plan, and true to form, she refuses to opt for the more expensive fix. "Scotch tape is fine. It'll hold. I can get it fixed for free at home." So for the rest of our time in Japan, her frames are held together with tape I rewrap regularly, as if symbolizing not only the frugality I've known from her, but the way we've made do, bricolage, under less-than-ideal circumstances all along. It's a study in contrasts. We're at the pinnacle of comfort, a vacation in Japan, yet we have broken glasses and we're eating pasta and pizza because they're often the only vegetarian meals to be found. But – we eat, and are thankful. During one such meal, she dispenses advice to a college-age Japanese woman. "Stay in school and don't get pregnant," she says. The woman doesn't understand, and I restate my mother's words, barely able to suppress a giggle, imagining the bemusement of an American co-ed taking in such guidance. But to my surprise, the young woman does take it all in, and then bows her head to my mother. "Thank you. I respect you," she says, drawing out the word "respect" for added emphasis.

Finally, here we were, on our last day in Kyoto, and I tell her she can't keep insisting on carrying her own bags and being so independent. She's getting older; she has to let me care for her. She looks at me, amused. "Yes, I will," she says, in a sing-songy tone that says she won't. Worse – I get a stomach bug, and for a few days, she has to care for me.

Things happen, things change – but we remain, with the same feelings, subtly wishing for a world that's gone. The rug is slowly being pulled from under us; we might notice, but can do nothing. This is the feeling of an Ozu film, and the feeling of life when you care for others. Caring for others reminds us of falling short. We can deny the feeling, or we can try to stop ourselves from caring; but this too is a loss.

The bar's patio is spacious, but nearly full with diners. I am sitting on one of the few available chairs, next to two women who stare for almost 20 minutes at their smartphones, pecking at them ("buttoning") and occasionally showing each other their screens and commenting about this person or that. "Facecrack," one of them says. I'm a little annoyed, though I probably shouldn't be, that they are not paying me any attention. When one picks up a menu, I break in, trying to make conversation. "Have you had anything yet? I really liked my meal." The one with the menu doesn't even make eye contact. "Yes, we had the noodles." In a moment, they're back to their smartphones. I'm struck with a sudden fury, and decide to leave. I don't even say goodbye. Where did this anger come from? Driving home, I could have opened my window to shout, "I'm mad as hell and I'm not going to take it anymore!" *Network* has a lot in common with the Social Network.

There are whole books and volumes emanating from moments such as this. On one level, it's so easy to characterize. Either "they were lame" or "he was lame" or "they were iHoles" or "he was an a-hole" or "they were just hanging out together and didn't want to talk to anyone else" or "young women are always fearful, usually of the wrong things." On another level, more complicated: a congruence of social anxieties and immobilities, and my haunting, repetitive wish to be easy and familiar with everyone. A slight hunger for another's attention that might be characterized as needy, demanding, or simply too *expecting* of others. And of course, there are those smartphones in the gathering dark, shedding light that blinds the women to the real lives in front of them; their own lives. It's a *petit* trauma – a small, empty, everyday abandonment. Ozu would probably call it an example of decay, and he would be right.

But, as I've learned, expectations are only prelude to disappointment. We're left to balance the wisdom of acceptance of things as they are, of limitations; and also the call to compassionately challenge those limits.

Erin comes to my office, describing in full detail her pattern of deep closeness and intensity with friends, followed by distancing. They seem to ache for her even as they are exasperated by her withdrawals; she, in turns, feels guilty and unforgivable. The breakups are hard, makeups near impossible. Any step she might take back towards them would either require a full *mea culpa* and the indulgence of friends, or yield another distancing eventually. So she is caught, feeling doomed to live her life with aching loss and an overwhelming sense of having failed at what was most important. Her friends, dozens of them, send her birthday wishes; they sit, unanswered, in her inbox. A friend writes to say he's visiting from out of town; she doesn't reply. Her anxiety kept her isolated, filled with doubt and self-critique.

"Have you seen *Man on a Wire*, the film about tightrope walker Philippe Petit?" She hadn't. I described the film, about the man who spectacularly walked across the gap between the Twin Towers in 1974. "A relationship is a lot like a high-wire act. You're afraid of being on that wire, so you stay on your side where it's safe. But you always want to get to the other side, and you're miserable where you are."

She looked at me. "So I should just get on the wire?"

"I think the key is realizing it's not *you* on the wire. It's the relationship. And the relationship is kept on the wire by both you and your friends on the other side. You're here. You're safe. If they accept or reject your overtures, you will still be safe. The relationship may fall into the safety net – and there is a safety net. You can keep building the safety net with your compassion for yourself – being kind to yourself, remembering that relating is uncomfortable for everyone at some point, and caring for and soothing yourself emotionally. Every relationship needs our safety net of self-compassion. If the relationship falters, you each will be okay. Your feelings have been hurt, their feelings may have been hurt – but if you both work at it, you can help the relationship cross the gap. It's awkward, but it's workable."

"But if I'm awkward, if I'm not me, if I'm not *up* and comfortable and likable – it will be awful. I couldn't do that. It would be too disappointing."

"Awkward is a normal state. It's probably *the* normal state. When you know this, you can discover *the magic of awkward*."

The Buddha said there are three ways the mind could perceive an object or situation: it could be seen as pleasant, unpleasant or neutral. I could make a good case for a fourth perception on contact: awkward. Ambivalence, like and dislike, a feeling of being trapped – awkward is a variant of the unpleasant, but somehow more intimate. It also has more potential. Awkward gives us a way to work with the unpleasant, to give it a creative spin. We can become artists of the awkward, where we could at best only tolerate the unpleasant. When the unpleasant becomes simply awkward, suffering becomes a predicament instead of a sentence, and we might almost welcome it. As Buddhist teacher Joseph Goldstein famously says, "it's not *what* you are experiencing that's important. It's how you *relate* to it that matters."[84]

We are broken apart by awkward and its variants. Yet at the same time, we are all trapped in the same room together, observing each other *awkwardly* and trying, sometimes, to make *awkward* conversation. Our instinct is to head for the hills when the unpleasant shows up, or even take arms against it or even ourselves. Almost everyone, from teenagers to grown adults, fears the awkward, uncomfortable silence. We flee awkward into carefully composed, comfortable, asynchronous interactions in cyberspace, making reality even more awkward. But the best strategy, I think, is to stay *with* the awkward. International relations and most diplomacy, even when seeming to take the most certain footing through solemn declarations and strident, confident demands, is by definition awkward and delicate. There are opposing, antagonistic goals and strategies; there is history, fraught with misgivings and unforgivable failures of relationship, including outright hostility and aggression; there are needs, some of which can be spoken and others which remain unacknowledged and unexpressed. There is more in the moment of meeting than meets the eye. This moment is like a riverbank, swelling and nearing flood. It is a seed with a vast history and limitless potential, all awkwardly compressed and silently held by the assembled parties, unwilling, awkward, ensemble cast for the always-running movie of life, each frame shot by a camera with a slightly telephoto lens, making the space seem narrow and small. It would be cozy, if it wasn't too close for comfort. Each scene is a seed of the whole. Actors enter and exit left and right, into mysterious spaces onscreen and off, all of them filled with potential.

A rich man walks through a crowd of the poor. There is awkward disconnection, little diplomacy, but much room for thought. Another man has a trying time with family, but stays connected, in mind and heart. A woman is raped and murdered in India. There is a call for justice, but the legal system finds the situation awkward. Support is enlisted, yielding clarity, through complications that only steel the resolve of petitioners. Strangers sit next to each other at a bar patio, avoiding contact but still desiring it, sometimes reaching for it through a smartphone screen. The awkward must be recognized, accepted, and challenged, all at once. It is the divide between us all, the divide between us and a better world – but the divide also connects us. It could be the dead spot where nothing grows, where dangers exist; yet all land can be revived with our care. The awkward marks not only the expanse between us, but also the space within us that needs connection and belonging. The awkward is an opportunity to put down the baggage of our story, and create a new one, with the person before us. *Haven't we met, somewhere before? No? Yes? Well, I guess we're meeting now. How are you, in this moment?*

Each of us has the potential to change the awkward. We have the agency to create the scene we're in. We can discover the magic of awkward; even, sometimes, its small miracles.

There's a Hanoi rooftop in all of us. We need only climb the stairs.

Repairing Reality

Hey, there, Angel with your head in the Cloud –
Won't you take a good look, around you –
Look up from that phone, there's a blue sky above
The Earth all around –
No txt could be more profound.

had a bad feeling about Facebook for some time, but leaving it was an ambivalent, stuttering process that took almost a year and a half. The first stutter came on July 20th, 2013. I'd given a short talk at the Asian Art Museum just two days before on the psychology and poetry of collecting. Several friends came to see it, and several more people came up to me afterwards to ask questions and introduce themselves. A handful of strangers were even kind enough to buy my poetry book as well. I felt grateful for friends and institutions that supported my artistic work, and that I could in turn support with my efforts. It was a real world, connecting event. By contrast, two days later, I realized more fully that Facebook was a minimally supportive and connecting factor for me, yet I was supporting it with countless hours of my own time. There was an aura of contact with community, and occasions of positive, insightful interaction, but overall – this was a bust.

The inciting event was a post that struck me as offensive. It came the day after President Obama had delivered heartfelt remarks on the verdict in the George Zimmerman case, on what it felt like to be a black man in America. Trayvon Martin "could have been me, thirty five years ago," he said. Most people, myself included, took it as a moment of honesty and straight-talk from the Educator-in-Chief. One of my friends, though, took it as a moment to slam the President on drone policy.

> So I gather the guy who drone-bombs children made a powerful and moving speech on why it's bad to kill children, because it stops them growing up to be someone like him. Did I miss anything?

This garnered 52 likes, three shares, and 25 comments in short order. Most of the comments amplified my friend's opening salvo, and the few that took issue were dealt with in a wordy, caustic combination of dialogue and diatribe. Now, in principle, I fundamentally agreed with my friend. I had also raised my voice against drone policy and other forms of militarism. I had just read my poem that referenced the topic the previous week at a Buddhist open-mic in Oakland ("A Peace Prize winning President sends missiles and drones/potent proof of roses and thorns"). And I no doubt have posted edgy material on my own Facebook wall in the past. We could both likely vie to be authors of the *Zen and the Art of Arch Statements* monograph. But her words rubbed me the wrong way. The timing was off. Her statement and the comments of her supporters were far too one-sided and disconnected from the moment for my taste.

And moreover, my reservations about my friend's acerbic pugnaciousness had only been exacerbated by her past Facebook stridency. I'd labeled her the "link-wielder," after she attempted to rebut an article I'd posted against sexual trafficking with a number of links to blog posts and articles slamming *New York Times* columnist Nicholas Kristof, the author of the article. One of them was written by a highly respected and award-winning scholar, Gayatri Spivak, who suggested that sexual trafficking was simply another form of migration. "Then so was slavery!" I countered. This was not a dialogue. Where we might have had, in the past, a conversation about the subject, leading to mutual understanding, we were engaging in black-and-white, right-and-wrong polarities about subjects that were tinged with a substantial amount of gray. It was the radical left's equivalent to the right wing's "you're either with us, or with the terrorists!" Social media quickly turned into a polarized ideological purity test. She and some other friends could feel free to paint Obama as a "war criminal," as one put it. I didn't feel that added to any debate, which had to also include what the foes of the American state were doing to their own people in their march to bring down the U.S., create mistrust and fear in society, and advance their goals. Instead of conversation, we had confrontation.

Real life had brought similar instances, but Facebook confrontations were invariably worse. This same friend, the "link-wielder," had participated in a panel discussion about militarism a year or so after 9/11, in which another panelist declared, and my friend concurred, that she had celebrated while watching the Twin Towers come down on a television screen, because this represented to her a righteous blow against an American Empire which had caused global destruction. I understood that perspective, but I could not in any way rejoice in the killing of three thousand civilians. I had protested the retaliatory responses of the Bush administration in every way available to me at the time; I have always had an abiding and deep disgust for military solutions and other exercises of Empire; but this was too much. At the time, I just winced. One young man was so outraged by their statements that he shouted the speaker down. The speaker and my friend, in turn, argued back vociferously with the man, who was obviously further angered and distressed. He left the room, and I followed him, trying to connect with and soothe him. When I returned, I told my friend that her comments in reaction to the angered man were not exactly the pinnacle of non-violent communication, which she had on other occasions championed. She looked saddened by the unforeseen effect of her bravura performance, and nodded her head. But obviously, that moment hadn't changed anything.

It was more important to be "right" than related.

And that was the tagline of most Facebook postings. Opinion trumped discourse, a sure predictor of anti-social un-networking. Even

I didn't appreciate someone who had rudely disagreed on one of my Facebook posts. I politely asked him to stop, and then when he got angry, defriended him. I did tend to agree with the politics of most of my Facebook friends, and had often learned from them. But it was, ultimately, the most extreme echo chamber imaginable – and not a true discussion. The most frequent and popular political posters tended to be much younger than me, and in some kind of competition to be as radical as possible, to vent as acidly as possible. Granted, Facebook provided community and support for people who might have otherwise felt isolated in their beliefs and identities. But it also effectively isolated those of us who were, if not blandly moderate in our views, were at least more balanced in how we chose to offer them to the world. At least in person, as in the post 9/11 discussion described above, we could get a full sense of each other. Real life leveled us all – the space between us was continually created, and not "locked in" by texted proclamations. Our struggles and regrets over struggles were held somehow, and not dismissed and devalued, as they tended to be online. In-person conversations, even disagreements, could produce a basic sense of inclusion that the online back-and-forth couldn't.

My time was too valuable to waste on this level of interaction.

As much as I wanted to value connection with others, even and especially with those who prided themselves on their activism, I could no longer support the fundamental selling point of the medium – that my thoughts and interests needed to be shared and known by many others, and their thoughts and interests needed to be known by me. Frankly, I didn't much care that you thought Billy Joel's "Always A Woman" was sexist. I didn't absolutely need to see you angrily denounce the "enslavement of animals by pet owners." (I get that you were deeply concerned about the rights of vulnerable animals, but...we love our cats and dogs, and they love us. Sometimes that's the most love that any of us, pet or human, manage to find. We mammals are mostly built to love; but you can't hug out your differences on Facebook. Cats and dogs are just plain nicer, most of the time. It made me want to see more kitties in my newsfeed. But sadly, I guess I'll have to admit that I didn't absolutely have to see that twerking cat video. Twice.)

All these posts were from people I liked well enough, and who generally liked me. This kind of exchange, though, did not bring us closer. Exposure to a Facebook feed did not equal intimacy, although it could seem deceptively close. The communicative boundary became nonexistent, but the boundary is necessary for true connection and community. Facebook took me from bounded mindfulness to bombarded distraction, not the best state from which to develop compassion, wisdom or relatedness. Any of the bits of random information on the newsfeed might have some potential to help us become wise and close, but we can only travel that path in continuity, presence, intimacy and community, not part of the scattershot, fragmented and opinion- and display-intensive nature of relationships in the medium.

But intimacy and community are what I still longed for. They are present when I'm physically with someone else, when we're actively creating common ground, when we're united in common cause, when we string together a succession of moments and experiences into a continuous, free-flowing, substantial relationship. When I can feel somewhat more secure of our connection, reliability, and mutual interest. When others can feel more secure of me. That is what we long for – to really be known, held, valued, and considered. Each of us deserves that. And Facebook – well, Facebook fails us this way. I didn't want a datastream, especially of ephemera. I wanted people.

I'd had my middle-aged Facebook fling, experimented with the cyberdrug – and I'd had enough. I wanted to get clean again. I couldn't completely regret my indiscretions with the always too-loose wi-fi connection, but my marriage to reality couldn't brook any more digital dalliance. If there was to be social promiscuity, I wanted to make it more memorable and meaningful than the casual stroke of a never-coy newsfeed.

I typed "Out out damned Facebook!" in the status box, and logged out.

❀

Next came furtive email missing-you missives to a few friends, and within days, I had rounded up dates for the next few weeks. Dates, not updates, would be my new motto. I reflected on the fact that I had probably spent, at worst, about five hours a week on Facebook. I decided to at least match that in "social engagement" – meeting with friends, but also community service, lectures, discussions, classes and other activities that involved me directly with others, as individuals and groups. My sense was that this would provide a much more reasonable basis for personal satisfaction, and would do much more to add to my community.

I also received notices, like siren calls, about other social network sites, such as Path – which promised more private and personalized sharing than hanging out in the crowded downtown that is Facebook. Path limited a friend group to fifty, and an inner circle of only a handful of people. There will be no end to the permutations of the social network. Architizer, for architects. Doximity and Medscape, for doctors. Ravelry, for knitters. Buddhist Geeks, the online "sangha in the cloud," for Buddhists. Couple, for couples. Happier, for people who wish to share their "happy" moments, and be inspired by the happy moments of others. LinkedIn, for – well, whoever it was that used LinkedIn, and whatever they used it for. Blind, for those who want to anonymously compare net worths and compensation packages. Seriously. And even mini-groups subdividing Facebook itself. Secret groups, and topic- and goal-oriented groups all have their fans who claim these smaller arenas give them a level of intimacy that the newsfeed doesn't. Interest groups might serve a function – but in the end, they also narrow identity into a niche and can never allow us to feel fully accepted. In time, we might forget what full acceptance really means, as we're left only with a hazy longing for belonging, always out of reach.

All of these have the same theme: to turn our need for connection into a utility. And at worst, to amplify our need for "visibility" to grandiose, bordering on narcissistic, proportions. At least most of the professional and hobby sites seem to preserve a sense of boundaries, and are goal-oriented, more like the moderated bboards of the past.

(Ravelry is, in fact, moderated.) But trying to squeeze general related-ness into any online framework is inherently reductive and destructive, as my experience and research have clearly shown. Even the small, se-cret groups on Facebook can't match the connection and presence of a real world relationship, and might in fact promote a form of withdrawal from and aversion to real world relationships. Perhaps there will be a moment when we all say, collectively, "what the hell are we doing?" Or maybe each of us had to find our own personal limit. *I'm mad as hell and I'm not going to take it anymore.*

I had found my limit. And I was probably soured for good on all digitized social networking.

Facebook took my social media cherry. From now on I would be a digital monk.

There's no app for having lunch with a friend. This kind of shar-ing – is caring. Companioned meals might be a cure for many ills of the heart, certainly deserving of an NIH study grant. Even if we link up in GoogleSpace,* eyeing or i-ing our Glass avatars, it won't feel as special as time devoted to our friends in that age-old gesture of friend-ship: breaking bread together. Perhaps the popularity of Instagram and Facebook food pics says more about the wish to convene over even the sight of a meal than it does about the picture-taker's vanity. We send digital meals like the Chinese burn fake money for the dead. The money ensures that the proper heavenly officials can be bribed, and photoblogged meals bribe our friends to allow us into the pearly gates of their memory. Wafers of Instagram communion seem to be a major component of our most modern religion, Cyberism. It's perhaps the most nourishing possibility of the digital age, or at least one that takes aim at two almost universally held sources of emptiness: loneliness and

---

* Or now, in Facebook Spaces and Oculus Rift, where you can create your own avatar and interact with Facebook friends. So exciting. Oculus Rift is indeed a rift from reality.

hunger. But the digital can never be substantial fare in either case. We must share a table. We must lock eyes. We must smile and laugh, we must talk. Millennials dying fifty or more years from now won't wish they had sent more texts, or blogged more meals; they, like us, will wish they'd had more conversations, more – now this is really old school – more friendships. And what is a friendship if it isn't a conversation carried across a lifetime of shared meals? I wonder sometimes, in my corner of the Silicon Valley, whether this most basic of human activities will need rehabilitation workshops in the future, because our skills are being displaced by screens.

Our instinct to create that special love between friends, *phileo*, through conversation and presence is jeopardized by a utilitarian view of relationships. We think of people only as means to our own ends – specialists of one sort or another, or audience members – who are here to supply our egos. A New York Times article bemoaning the dearth of friends after 30 quoted one woman: "I take an extremely efficient approach and seek out like-minded folks to fill very specific needs."[85] She could be filling vacancies at a company rather than making friends, from the sounds of it. She explained, oh so charismatically, that she yearned to have enough friends to fill her party invitation list. Gee, where do I sign up?

She, like many of the over-30's described, were facing loneliness, the fundamental human problem. We all are alone in our skins, and must come to terms with that. We can't dispel this state by hanging out in crowds, online or in person. Seeking out friends to fill our needs is a little like trying to fix global warming by adjusting the thermostat downwards. It might make you feel more comfortable initially, but the problem goes deeper than that. We have to open our hearts, and start seeing people, fully. We have to see the source of our needs. We have to see their needs. As a bonus, we get to see and be ourselves more fully in the process.

A patient once said I was in the room to help him "process his thoughts." I had the immediate image of myself as some kind of kitchen appliance, a Thought Processor. Here I thought I was trying to relate to him as a whole person, and trying to be a whole person myself, and he thought I was a blender. He probably thought of himself as the complementary Thought Spewer. Objectification is nearly always unpleasant, and it often indicates an unhealthy way of viewing and interacting with oneself and the world. The more I'm seen as an individual, and not as an expensive utility, the better the patient's prognosis, and the more I can do for him. The person who objectifies and therefore devalues is on a sad, lonely, isolating path, one that can only be mended by love – but love often feels wrong to him, because he has devalued, and never loved, himself; he's never been loved for being himself, but rather for what he did. The idea that "I value you only because you do something for me" limits us and others. This is true in the therapeutic relationship, and it is true in friendship as well. When we value our "friends" merely as contacts, votes, donors, connections, fillers of party invitation lists, or in some way, our unpaid employees, we cease being related in all the deeper ways that make life meaningful.

A recent ad for esurance advocated "people when you want them, technology when you don't." Playful, perhaps, but achingly true to the narcissistic, utilitarian disposition. When you start thinking "What could Joe possibly say that you couldn't learn from a blog post," or "my Facebook feed tells me all I need to know about Joe," or "it's so annoying and inefficient to make time to see Joe" – you have devalued Joe and reduced your own possibilities in a way that you might not even perceive, an unwitting chit for internal climate change. The Sea of Love is in danger of being dried up by the fast and hot – but false – Sun of expediency. We think we're saving time by tending to our relationships digitally. We forget that when we make time for our loved ones – we actually make time. A meal with a friend expands time supernaturally. Our hippocampal neurons are hungry for moments we create with another; they swell with the solace only a friend can provide. Breaking bread banishes emptiness. Even a crumb from that table stirs the heart.

With a minimum of go-between screens between us, I manage to have lunches with four friends, a potluck with half a dozen others, two dinner and movie dates, and a retirement dinner for one of my beloved mentors – all in eight days. It's as if signing off Facebook has created a synchronistic ripple in space-time: the World Wide World was welcoming me back with open arms, and suddenly I have a full social calendar, without having to do too much to arrange it. My Bohemian writer/ philosopher self emerges, christened by rekindled friendships, and I take to languid meals and leisurely conversations like I'd been made for them, which I suspect I was.

Gina and I reconnected over seitan and grilled cheese sandwiches at the Dolores Park Cafe. We'd had a delicious two-hour conversation at the beginning of the year, but then she decided she needed to work for the next five months and wouldn't have time for me. Ahem. I was perplexed and disappointed, and thought I'd have to add her to my collection of koan-ships: the women who compelled me in some way, but who remained hesitant, distant and cool. "What is the sound of one person getting no response?" was the essence of the koan-ship. Naturally, Gina was a therapist, as most koan-ships seem to be. She was also interesting, intelligent and beautiful, as most koans are, implanting them in my mind, tinged with uncertainty and mystery, as they decide which way they'll turn. If my interest should stir, the koan transforms it to patience, reminding you of her independence, and the need to win her allegiance with yours. I've learned to appreciate a good koan, because the alternative is to be annoyed or give up entirely. It is a mild, everyday form of awkward, whose challenge I accept. I hoped satori would come after long silences, with seitan and grilled cheese, on a sunny day in San Francisco. The signs were encouraging, as we traded news of our lives. By the end of another long conversation, I had hopes for friendship again, and the sense that there was something valuable, here, between us, but its unfolding was still a mystery.

I hadn't seen Meg in a long time, either, but she was no koan. She was solidly placed in the camp of friends, enthusiastic in our interactions, even if they were spaced months apart. She made lunch for us both – quinoa and chicken, rustic carrots and yams – and colorful conversation that traipsed from Atul Gawande's latest in *The New Yorker* (she was a huge fan, as was I, hoping that his smart-Indian-guy-aura would rub off on me; remind me sometime to sing you my Atul Gawande song) to Sean Parker's Middle Earth themed wedding in Big Sur. I joked that she had caught me up on the newsfeed from which I'd logged out, but in a much more attractive way. Maybe this would be the best way to morph the feed, have it digested and read to you by your favorite anchor. We hugged goodbye, not knowing when we'd see each other again, but knowing that we valued each other, and this was not something that could easily be changed. Our friendship was secure, and would carry and hold over long silences and absences. And that feeling substantively filled those absences. "The heart grows fonder," as the saying goes; perhaps this is the only way it does, in presence and absence, pulled fonder, wider and more at ease, growing ever more mindful of the subtle sways of our interdependent world.

This was true in long conversations and meals with all the other friends in the homecoming-to-reality tour, as I called it. We laughed with each other, learned from and of each other, and took note of each other's lives. We give each other gifts of time and presence that couldn't possibly be matched by the sideshow being played online. Linda, pregnant with twins, is just as lovely as ever. Our years of friendship grow, stretching toward a lifetime. Kate, whom I befriended at the counter of a restaurant near my office over a year ago, regales me with stories of her life as a teacher and Cambodian American. Tony Nguyen, a friend who is producing and directing his second documentary film, fills me in on life and work and commiserates with me about the dissatisfactions of the online experience. I watch *Fruitvale Station* (about Oscar Grant, killed by a transit policeman) with two friends. We are all on the verge of tears and there are sobs all around us; it is a powerful shared experience, underscoring the importance of all shared experience in the real world, commensurate with the preciousness of life. A potluck filled with tales of friendship in the city, a retirement dinner replete with heartwarming stories about my mentor, all these times shared with friends and colleagues – these *are* life, not *about* life. Why would we ever think that a "convenient" online alternative would be more fulfilling, or even a helpful adjunct? We must watch our temptations closely, and guard what's most dear. Perhaps the Facebook fling will, in the end, highlight what's truly most important, and compel us to forge a truly, and not superficially, closer world. The newsfeed barely gives us shadows on the walls of the cave. We must go outside.

The night before the 50th anniversary commemoration of the March on Washington, I have a dream. I am circling the block trying to board a bus, but all the busses are full. I want to hear a speech, somewhere, where the busses would take me, but I don't know what the speech is about. I keep circling, and am lost in the crowd. I wake, and think to myself, that yes, we are all aching to hear some transcendent word, together. It must be in our genetic code to want to gather, and move, as one. As much as we mistrust each other, as much as we've disappointed and harmed each other, we have held each other more. If that isn't transcendence, I don't know what is.

The transcendent is not transmitted in words, but in the spirit between us. Not through our speech, our texts or tongues, but through us, all of us, our lives and loves and losses. It comes not out of us, but with us. Not above us, but between us. We dwell in transcendence, we exist as its catalysts and beneficiaries. The Divine Word comes in our names, our beings; we should not try to reduce it to a screen. Our friendships carry the potential for depth; when we reduce our interactions to anything less than full-bodied, full-sensory, full-feeling encounter, we endanger the space between us, the spirit between us, and our own possibility.

We are held by what is – not held back. The space between us needs our attention; cyberspace is no substitute.

We wish to be memorable; we spark at wisdom. We pride ourselves on pithy declarations and fortune cookie epigrams bursting out of our be-ing like magic, like a match struck in darkness. A thought catches fire, and bursts into a small sun, captivating us. We wish, we need, to raise up our radiant torch, our bright emissary to be admired by all. It is like a burning bush on a mountaintop, in that moment. So we touch our flame to the internet, and glow.

Wise and hip, cool and connected. Seen. This is what we want to be. The internet is amber – it is the ambernet – preserving us, creating us, giving us substance. We post, proving ourselves in some way. Our thoughts seem like manna to us. Why wouldn't we share?

"Food is good!" his mind proclaims, after a delicious meal. The thought comes with punctuation, clearing his mind and making him feel he should declare it to the world. It would be a perfect and popular update, he's sure. It was a universally held core insight, after all, that should be shared. Then: "Why?" The latter thought, he decides, was true wisdom.

We are on a learning-journey, moving towards wisdom and en-lightenment. Our "sparks" are only evidence of our need for the real flame, in real space and real time, between us.

Almost as soon as I mock the words of the advertisement that advocated "people when you want them, technology when you don't," my computer crashes. It's the most complete crash I've ever seen – the screen goes black, the power button does nothing, the 'sleep' light just winks on and off, and something inside the silver slab chirps, like a mouse squeaking one last protest before it's squashed. "Eep." It's an-other sign: people are essential, technology is a mirage. The universe is turning me again towards the real world, the dream of people, and away from the mirage of things. The great Zen Master in the sky has rapped me with his stick: "pay attention!"

One of the three marks of existence in Buddhism is impermanence. People, mountains, the universe as we know it – all will
pass. But technology seems particularly prone to give us reminders of
loss. Magnetic blips and silicon chips can spark and the arc of a narrative
evaporates, and not even to a Cloud. There is a queasy empty space in me
now, as if part of my self is gone. I've identified with the fruits of my labor, and with technology itself, subtly thinking that I was independently
existing and permanent in this state – I've "selfed" – but I've built a house
on shifting sands. Non-self, or interdependence, is the second mark of
existence. I've thought of it as reassuring, a reminder of connection, but
now I see it as a reminder that when we lean our selves too heavily on
any of our projections, we become more dependent than interdependent,
and we are more likely to suffer – and suffering is the third mark of existence. Buddhist teacher Wes "Scoop" Nisker puts the three marks this
way: "Life is hard. It all changes. Don't take it personally."

True, my suffering is limited. I have some assurance of recovery – I
think my hard drive hasn't failed, and I had recently backed up all my
data – but I know I will feel safer if and when my writing is published,
in the real world. Until then, I will make sure to add at least another
level or two of backups, and perhaps even print a copy of my drafts, not
leaning on any one leg again. But the red flag of impermanence, of insubstantiality of all technological projections of the self, and ultimately,
of all the ways we reify ourselves, is clear. I may feel safer when my
book is published, copies dispersed widely, but it would be a mistake to
identify even with this, to think I'm any "more" because of it.

Here is a lesson in not-clinging, non-attachment. My Schrodinger's
Cat of a computer will announce itself soon enough, and until then, I
dwell in uncertainty, the most constant force of them all, and rely on
the interdependencies of reality. I make an appointment at a nearby
Apple Store Genius Bar, with a person who is, in the end, more reliable,
capable and valuable than any device.

Technology is merely a tool for human creativity, a crystal-
lization of human capacity, and not worthy of worship in its own
right. Paradoxically, it's still a capacity I crave. I borrow a computer,

and continue to write, feeling soothed by the contact of my fingers with a keyboard. I remember the last line of Randall Jarrell's poem "The Death of the Ball Turret Gunner" ("When I died they washed me out of the turret with a hose"), and picture myself fused with my computer, spitting words like bullets from my turret gun. I defend myself, my world, with my words. And as surely, I create a new world with them, words flowing from my fingertips like lava from Mt. Kilauea, hissing land into a cold but welcoming sea.

When we see each other, when we connect, that new land becomes a bridge, something between us. Whenever we meet, we create new land. Facebook, ultimately, is a Facebridge. As unsatisfying, limiting, distorting and potentially harmful as Facebook is, we do need bridges. We can't help but share. This writing, this sharing, face-to-face, in the real world, is essential to me, even as I do my best to attach warmly, but not anxiously. We must relate; we must talk; we must meet.

I have no choice but to play out this share, with you, with the world, until there's nothing left, until I'm gone, gone, gone, gone across the great bridge of forever, gone beyond. I will use all tools at hand, but always stay focused on the goal.

Gate gate paragate parasamgate bodhi svaha!

Gone, gone, completely gone, totally awake, fulfilled!

Technology, at least, is replaceable, if not as completely reliable as it seems to promise. People are as reliable as they can be, but totally, heartbreakingly, irreplaceable. A beloved patient of mine dies suddenly from complications of a chronic illness. Another patient's grandfather dies. In Washington, D.C., twelve people are killed by a gunman, who then kills himself. Death is on my mind nearly every day. When I am with my patients, the old questions of my early days as a medical student rise again. How can I help this person live? How are they dying, now?

I saw the patient who died suddenly just two days before he passed. He came late to the session, and spoke almost exclusively about how the

TV show *The Sopranos* inspired him. The only thought in my mind as he spoke was the last scene of the last episode, the screen going black. We didn't have time to discuss that ending; and then he was gone, too. Was it a premonition? The question haunts me. But we all know that our screen will go black, someday, even if we have trouble facing this fact. When we do, we must resolve to use our time well.

My patient also spoke of love. He spoke of how important his friendships were to him, and how he once more longed for a girlfriend.

What better way to use our time than to move towards love? On this, we must stay intent.

Wherever my patient is now, I'm sure he's still moving in that direction, steadily.

The night after I get the news of my patient's death, I have another tiger dream. My recurrent dream, of a tiger taking over my office, has changed. This time, I return to my office, and the tiger has grown old, white-haired, and emaciated, as if saddened by my absence. She howls a cry of longing and relief as she sees me again, and greets me, placing her paws on my chest. I hug and pet her.

The harbinger of threat and death – has become a symbol of love. I've befriended the tiger in my boat.

Love lives on, surely.

Thuy was a smart, interesting woman I'd met at an arts event. We became Facebook friends, and I rarely saw her in the real world. When I did, I noted she was often more withdrawn in real life than her chatty, witty, provocative Facebook persona. I lamented our rare meetings. "But we see each other on Facebook," she replied. "Facebook is the glue."

If Facebook is the glue, I thought to myself, *I want the horse.*

The verdict is announced for the surviving four adult perpetrators of the Jyoti Singh/Nirbhaya rape and murder. Death by hanging. I am saddened to hear that the youngest man, just 20, wailed when he heard his fate. His cry echoed the screams of Jyoti Singh as the men tortured her. They heard her voice, but instead of compassion, they gave her brutal aggression and cruelty. Power and hatred ended life. If love is to live on, it must be active and powerful itself. But hanging won't prevent future rapes. Indeed, the day after the verdict is announced, I hear that a six-year-old girl has been gang raped by Indian teenagers. The same day, three Jammu and Kashmir police officers are accused of raping a minor, and a canteen owner is charged with kidnapping, raping and imprisoning a college student for twenty months. Rapes continue apace, one every twenty minutes or so in India. Grimly, the rape train is the only one running on time. The shock and outrage felt around the world in December, 2012 has not deterred a culture of rape, but it has focused a nation's attention. The death penalty has never deterred crime, but perhaps the men will be seen as casualties in the ongoing, undeniable civil war of gender that grips India. But winning the war, for the good of all genders – and not just courting public opinion or publicity – will require deep reforms across all sectors of government, law and society, ultimately establishing a new relationship between all peoples. The subjugation of women and girls that allows them to be seen as powerless others to be despised, used and oppressed – as objects to be utilized – is unconscionable and abhorrent, the very opposite of relatedness, the feminine principle that should live in us all, men and women alike. It must end. Only then can Nirbhaya, meaning Fearless, take her ultimate, most transcendent name: Ashoka. Without sorrow, without suffering. Without tears.

The world cries for our help. And hurts us. It is a wounded thing, wounding.

I remember my female cousins and relatives, all the women of India. I remember my mother, her journey and the obstacles she faced. We are all connected. My life depends on theirs, though we may be worlds apart. I cannot loose these bonds, nor do I want to. Somehow, they must be strengthened, and turned into a source of strength for us all. We are all pilgrims, migrants, transforming the land as we go, creating the space that holds us with our every movement, thought, and deed. Love and presence, companionship and compassion – these are the reeds that sustain us, the water that carries, the music that moves.

The Embodied Self, the Embodied We: The Network Called Society

For legal purposes, communication delivered in any form or medium is considered speech. But speech, in its most primal, essential, potent form, is the spoken word, delivered face-to-face, person to person. Right speech, part of the Eightfold Path, is not just non-harmful speech, but embodied speech, one could argue. Speech, bereft of context, physicality, and presence, enters an altered state. It becomes a kind of game input meant only to stimulate synapses, causing them to frolic, inflaming or informing them into some heightened state of arousal. But it has lost the depth of relatedness and sensation that being with another person naturally conjures. There is a romance of the real, a creative, evocative, desirable, vast possibility of perception, engagement and connection that is at a remove in the virtual world, which is itself rife with disconnection and disembodiment – a push away instead of a step toward, or with.

There are advantages to the disembodied or less-embodied propagation of information. No doubt, our social evolution has risen on printed word and ideas disseminated through technologies that collapse distance and time. We can't imagine a cohesive, coherent modern world without books, movies, radio, television, the internet, and smartphones and what they very often bring us. My words as an individual can be seen and heard by a potentially vast number of people with the press of a button. Scenes unfolding on a square in Cairo, a suburb of Damascus, or a street in Kenya can reach the entire world, demanding attention, response, and some form of relationship. This is a profound and powerful development in human history, and is to be lauded. Even so, there is the danger of overstimulation leading to apathy, the danger of short attention spans leading to a lack of focus, and the danger that the squeakiest or (in the internet's case) most visible wheels are not in fact the ones needing the most grease. All these dangers point to the limits of human capacity, or rather the persistent needs of being human which cannot be met by even the most powerful and transformative technology. We lose ourselves when the human scale, human needs and the human touch disappear against our vast and growing fascination with technology.

When we sit in front of a computer, or become engrossed with a screen, we are putting down our bodies in favor of a narrowly mental process. Our online activity may be intellectual, it may be emotional, it may be engaging, it may even seem vitally important and pressing in that moment – but it is disembodied. Our visual and mental field becomes limited to a small rectangle of light, and we lose contact with the world around us. (Sometimes to disastrous consequence. In September, 2013, a man murdered another man on a MUNI train in San Francisco. Detectives stated that he had pulled and aimed the gun repeatedly before he shot, but was totally unnoticed by other passengers, whose eyes were on their digital devices instead.[86]) This is an inherent devaluing of reality, and very often, a devaluing of the people we're with. I regularly see couples together at a meal, but instead of talking with one another, they each stare into their smartphones. Some fight this tendency with games. In "smartphone roulette," all members of a dining party stack their phones at the center of the table. The first one to succumb to the urge to check their messages or answer their phone picks up the tab. Here, we recognize that technology is a dangerous siren, and we invent means to resist it, but we've also given up: someone will in fact pick up their phone first, and then all the others will be off the hook, free to unhook from their surroundings and friends into a disembodied state. This scene of decayed modernity is ironic on many levels. The process of eating and sustaining the body is interrupted by a craving to feed the addicted mind. The very reason for coming together with and valuing friends, which might be dubbed soul-sustenance, has to now compete with devices that carry the implicit message that other people, elsewhere, and information, elsewhere, are more important than the physical presence of those gathered at the table. Surely, one of those people gathered is typing out a status update, tagging all the others at the table and proclaiming "having a great dinner with Nancy, Richard, Tom and David!" The diners are, *de facto*, neither "with" each other or really "having a great dinner," at least by my definition. The uploaded photographic evidence, of entrees and facial expressions, completes the disembodiment. As MIT media sociologist Sherry Turkle has said, "sharing is now being." I share therefore I am. Pics or it didn't happen. We deceive ourselves into thinking that nothing truly is, that we don't really exist in our own minds or the minds of others unless we impress ourselves and others with a virtual presence. We'd rather be virtual than here. A father pays more attention to the smartphone in his hand than to the son he is carrying. The son will know this, consciously or unconsciously; perhaps the disembodied parent is the new face of emotional abandonment. Relationship, and society, is built on the presence and attention we give each other; the attention we give to our screens and our virtual selves erodes our social bonds, and even our ability to create them. The frictionless embrace of technology lures us from the necessarily hard-won rewards of reality.

We most need embodied relationship and embodied community – sangha – for our most difficult conversations. And yet online interactions amplify the dismissive, disembodied and destructive. My most popular blog posts often deal with subtle racism and stereotyping. While they garner a great number of likes and shares in the social network, they also trigger a torrent of abusive comments, sometimes causing me to disable comments. Without real-time, physical interaction, with all the cues (facial expression, tone of voice, social milieu and so forth) that tend to soothe the emotional brain and connect rather than inflame – many people are likely to become disinhibited and "flame" the person who makes them uncomfortable. Psychologist and Emotional Intelligence guru Daniel Goleman coined the term *cyberdisinhibition* for this very effect. There is an implicit recognition of mutual vulnerability and a resonance of commonality and respect when we meet, face-to-face. Embodied real world presence tends to inhibit and refine our aggressive, base impulses; the social network and online interactions can loose the disinhibited, the dysregulated, and disembodied. Our culture is already rife with polarization. The social network can divide into opinion networks, each suburb vying only for power, volume and control, not accord with one another. We harden ourselves with intransigent, insensitive opinion, and make sangha that much harder to attain. We disembody our capacity for "we," and with it, an inclusive society. The disembodied "me" is amplified, with resultant narcissism and unhappiness.

If the "literary mind" of meditative, focused attention is imperiled by the online experience, as Nicholas Carr argues in *The Shallows: What the Internet is Doing to Our Brains*, what do social networks do to our social minds? I think true sociability, and society, require an "other-ing" mind, a "we-ing" that arises from embodied presence. Surely, we are reminded of others in our social networks, but at our screens, we are of course alone, focused on self and only a sliver of the other, through their textual avatars. This slice may be just enough to soothe, but it is not enough to free us from ourselves, and place us solidly within the community of belonging, the sangha. We fall short of the experience of interdependence, a prerequisite for enlightenment.

We embrace ourselves with selfies; our moment in the sun isn't complete without one. We "self," create a self, with our selfie. Each picture seems to solidify us, make us more real, more visible. It seems like harmless fun, and perhaps it is – but it is also an inflation of the self, grandiosely ballooning us into what we imagine is a more exalted state. When we find ourselves wanting to emblazon Facebook walls with a stream of our images, tattooing ourselves into cyberspace, we are distancing ourselves from the more modest and humdrum reality of life in an attempt to amp our stature, to ourselves and to others. The selfie is a presentation or display, a wooing of our inmost admirer. But this very amping up of ourselves is a distancing and displacement of the moment we inhabit, another form of disembodying. Narcissus stares into his image on a smartphone, Venus carries a new hi-tech mirror, and ancient wisdom about the perils of vanity seems cliché, passé, old school, and uncool. We have our pleasure, but this pleasure is decay. We fall in love with our presentations and pretensions, perform our personas, and stop really seeing, accepting and loving ourselves and one other as we are.

Even the undeniably cute stories we post about our toddlers, endearing as they may be (for a time), and however much they demonstrate our real bond, can wear out their welcome and should cause us to wonder whether we are "keeping it real" as we might claim. The broadcast of status updates may be a form of creative expression, and the toddler-tale touching in its particulars, but if we are too gladdened by likes and comments (and who wouldn't be?), we lose contact with the moment we're broadcasting. "My moment with my child" is different from "my moment with my child instantly shared with 5,000 people." The latter must necessarily be more about propping up, inflating, or soothing an insecure self. Insecurity is a natural and widespread state of being; the question is whether sharing and virtuality are appropriate remedies. Certainly, there's heart-warming tenderness here that seems to merit broadcast, and parents have spoken unstoppably about their children since speech was invented – but the medium seems to inherently push reality aside by its volume and reach. Some parents share stories of their children with their 5,000 friends before they've shared with their partners! Shares are understandably addictive for both sharers and recipients, and therein the danger, that the sharing, or even the willful manufacture of shareable items, displaces the real relationship they supposedly exalt, yet another example of the irony of the share. Parents fill blogs with captured images of sandwich bags they artistically decorate and give their children daily, unique bento box preparations, or tableaux of their sleeping infants in evocative dreamscapes – prompting some commenters to call them the greatest parents in the world, while others say they are the most self-involved. I'm all in favor of artistic creativity, but I personally draw a line at wishing others to dote on every detail of my instantly broadcasted life or relationships with others. There is not only a question of the boundaries of the children and other individuals being broadcast, but a "hey Ma, look at me" quality of grasping for attention that I can't believe is healthy for the broadcaster.

But then – why do we do it? Beyond seeking attention, beyond inflating ourselves, beyond vanity and narcissism, beyond trying to soothe our egos with a virtual, but disembodied, self?

Sharing is not only being, but a way of connecting, an attempt to create intimacy. These updates-in-the-box, tiny windows into our lives, can evoke sentiment, a welcome respite from our days of tense routines. They are breaks from absolute isolation, even as they give us solitude with a screen. A book is a massive "share" as well, an attempt to artfully transmit knowledge and experience, and represent the writer engagingly to readers; it is also an attempt to create familiarity and intimacy as well. And when we share on these scales, we want not just to go viral, but Ebola. The difference in mediums is important though. In the book, there is more of a boundary, more possibility for the reader to digest the material and form a context by themselves, to probe more deeply with a "literary mind" as Nicholas Carr put it in *The Shallows*. Indeed, the writer also benefits in all these ways as well. As a result, both reader and writer form a deep connection to the substance of the book; it can come close to embodied relationship, one mind keenly engaging with another. Reading a book delivers you to interiority, and when we meet in person, our interiorities can touch, the very definition of intimacy. See, how even those words can feel almost too close? Lo, the power of words.

There is an undeniable intimacy in the Facebook share as well. The parent-shares about their child work so well because we all have receptors for this most primal intimate relationship; they can become fodder for our consideration of our own relationships and lives, and not only a disembodying and displacement of the original relationship. But this requires active and conscious engagement with the people in our own lives. Every step in the virtual direction is just as likely to tug us away from engagement as it is to remind us of its importance. We can lose ourselves in our disembodied, displayed performance, instead of finding ourselves and each other in the embodied romance of the real. We are shelled by shares, which seem all too exterior, devaluing the intimacy of the interior. Louis CK tells a story about parents at a dance recital with iPads and iPhones in front of their faces, watching the screens instead of their children, preparing to send their children into cyberspace. "I'm not going to watch this. But here – you watch it!" Here, the parents have completely disappeared, existing only as broadcast antennae to children who exist only to garner them likes and views in the Social Network. The pride and intimacy of parenthood has decayed into this sad absurdity of disembodiment and lack of presence.

We share our happy or sad moments, but we are often out of tune with those who receive us. When we broadcast blithe joy to someone in pain, our communique is disembodied and self-centered. And someone is always in pain. Should they tell us of their distress, what text message could bridge our divide? Texted concern might help, for an instant, but falls far short of presence. It could be enough, to get us by, but as we settle for less, we might lose our stake on the real thing.

We reach for Facebook out of boredom, loneliness and the wish to be seen and connected. Yet engaging with Facebook leaves the deeper sources of our isolation and alienation unaddressed, and in fact, inflamed. Boredom and loneliness are states of void emptiness, forms of disembodiment and even abandonment by the moment and by others. In each is a requirement for love and presence that is not being met. How could a social network fully ease this form of suffering? It might soothe it for a time, or provide a bridge over it for those unable for physical reasons to have relationship, but it cannot completely connect us in the way the real world does.

The internet tugs at your sleeve. Your smartphone vibrates, a bright screen captivates, and you find yourself wandering on silicon streets. You feel a heady excitement, a tantalizing possibility of connection, of conversing with others, meeting them virtually, and most importantly, being seen and held in their minds. But as close as it brings us to what we desire most, the Social Network leaves us high and dry. There is always a gap of desertion, a space of failed presence. Emptiness, disembodiment, dissatisfaction, and suffering.

> I am "all over" the internet, but nowhere to be found.
> Cyberian exile is complete and profound.
> "Connected" to everyone, but alone at my screen
> I'm dissolving into a Silicon dream.

Thich Nhat Hanh says "technology helps us run away from ourselves. We don't have time for ourselves. We run away from our family. We run away from nature. We run away from Mother Earth. We try to forget ourselves by running away." He asks, "can we create a technology to remind us to come home?" In the last few years, we have mindlessly adopted the culture and credo of the Social Network. Or rather, that culture has flooded over us. It is our task to mindfully find a way to float our way over the deluge, to build our arks and regain the solid ground of the embodied, related self.

Pachinko parlors became popular in postwar Japan, a way of escaping the disconnected corporate grind into a kind of focused solitude, not unlike a video game or Facebook. In Ozu's film, *The Flavour of Green Tea Over Rice*, the pachinko parlor owner himself warns "pachinko shouldn't be regarded as fun. Otherwise the world wouldn't improve." We may need our fun and distractions, but technology is much more powerful and potentially warping than pachinko, part of the tsunami of isolation and disconnection that is modernity. Relationships are difficult, and not always fun, but they can bring us to ourselves most surely when we work to understand each other – from India to San Francisco, Bangalore to Bodhgaya, the doctor's office to the CEO's suite. And, as Venerable Master Hanh says, "understanding is love."

The goal of Buddhism is enlightenment, a shedding of self-centeredness. Meditation helps us cultivate wholesome, healing qualities of calmness and curiosity about our inner and outer circumstances. This is the technology that "reminds us to come home," and actually brings us there, step by peaceful step. And we most certainly shed our self-identification when we relate deeply to others, extending our hearts to them in compassion. Embodied relationship brings us to awareness of interdependence, awareness of interdependence will bring us to love, and love, surely, will bring us to enlightenment.

The Flavour of Green Tea Over Rice follows a couple through their quarrels and distancing from each other. Near the end of the movie, the husband is called away on a business trip to Uruguay, but the wife doesn't even see him off; she has left the home in anger. But the plane has engine trouble and he is forced to return, in the middle of the night. His wife greets him, now remorseful. They prepare a meal together, and make up over ochazuke, their comfort food. "A married couple should be like green tea over rice," the husband says. "Intimate, familiar, primitive and relaxed." The Social Network, I would argue, is ultimately none of these things.

Relationship is extraordinary and mundane at the same time, like green tea over rice. It is also notoriously fragile. As Issa wrote, "this dewdrop world is a dewdrop world, and yet..." It might be grandiose to see the world in a dewdrop, but to see the dew in the dewdrop is the beginning of wisdom.

When we see the space between us, and know it as fertile ground – when we don't run away from it to a disembodied state that alluringly seems more expedient, easy, amped up and glamorous – we come to know ourselves. We come home.

Smartphone Stepping Stones: But to What?

pictured myself growing old with my humble flip phone. I saw myself as the last man on Earth with one, an eccentric holdfast to the turn of the century, skeptic of the cybergospel and the paradigm of constant contact made possible by the smartphone that would, in my mind, make us dumb. I would be a Salingerian cyber-recluse, refusing to answer texts or scroll through emails as my date, seated in front of me, scrolled through hers. "Put that away," I'd demand of my distracted partner. No, I would be a living monument to the real world, a reminder that it was possible, desirable and even vital to maintain the space between us, a space that allowed deeper connection. I wouldn't succumb to the barrage of constant "communication" – I would be an ambassador of conversations, long walks, and dinners spent looking into my friends' bright faces instead of a bright screen. I would fight assimilation with all my might.

But all things change.

My Samsung flip phone came unhinged. Literally. One day it flipped, and then it flipped out, snapping practically in half at the seam to which I had grown attached. My attachments were coming apart at the seams.

I obsessed over the attachment. I drove to my carrier's store; they told me they were out of flip phones, but another store had them. I called that store, and they didn't. They searched all the stores in the Bay Area – and none of them had flip phones in stock. The current was against me. Still, I held fast, determined to stay in place even if it meant I would have to row hard upstream. I called customer service directly and ordered a replacement flip phone. I thought I would soon be confirmed in my eccentric, resistant-to-change ways. I had invested almost four hours in my attachment. While I should have been frustrated at the attachment itself, I was only frustrated at the time wasted at getting me my fix.

My cell phone was a running gag with patients and friends alike. One patient, a young man in his 20s, playfully mocked me, and regularly urged me to upgrade. He played Otto Gross to my meager Jung, but his Dionysian temptation was a smartphone, not sexuality. "I don't want to be that connected," I told him. Friends who texted me soon regretted it, as I made it clear I was *persona non texta*. "20 cents a text! You owe me!" I joked with them. "Why would I spend almost a thousand dollars a year to maintain something I didn't really want or need?" I would argue. "That's more than many people make in a year!" Some of my friends even came to admire my compact, sleek, functional phone, and in moments of clarity, complained about their own devices and dropped calls. "How inconvenient," in a world where we were led to believe everything should be friction-free, I'd say to myself. I thought I'd reached a stable plateau of standing still while the world moved on, and fell apart, around me, victim to false hopes and misleading marketing.

Then my "upgraded" flip phone arrived. It was 20% heavier and bulkier than my old phone, even thicker and heavier than a smartphone. It was ugly. And, of course, the universe being what it is, the new iPhone was introduced the next day. Superfast processor, fingerprint sensor – whatever. It didn't matter. It was time. No more whinging about my broken hinge; no more complaining about costly data plans; no more balking at change and modernity, like some techno-fundamentalist. I was being pushed, herded, shoved into the smartphone era by planned obsolescence. And soon enough, I was embracing and eagerly anticipating it, surfing the web for artsy custom cases before I could even order the phone itself. I was hooked, but hooked to a new thing and its tantalizing possibilities. Even so, one friend welcomed me to "the world of phones that are good for everything except being a phone." Even the converted become jaded. The earliest adopters acquired doubt. The latest ballyhooed smartphone advance is called "the flavor of the month," and we each find our comfortable, two-year contract plateau, which then annoys us with unfulfilled promise. We continue to restlessly crave.

Still, as Jaron Lanier writes in *Who Owns the Future?*, "the non-technical ideas of scientists (and regular Joe's like me, I'd say) influence general trends, but the ideas of technologists create facts on the ground."[87] A small number of visionary technologists, combined with the understandable, evolutionarily-pressured cravings of millions for easy communication and cool gadgets, has created an unavoidable stampede for smartphones and Social Networks. 2007, the year of my pilgrimage backwards in Buddhist time, was a turning point – the iPhone was introduced and Facebook became particularly prominent. Yet my own resistance and ambivalence to these creations is not a design flaw or a speed bump. What I feel is felt by many in their own way. The very push to be "connected" at all times and at any cost reflects how distant and alone we feel and are being made to feel by urbanization, mobility, increasing work hours, staggering economic inequality, emphasis on individuality and loss of community ties. We rush in for the quick fix to soothe our ache, then bemoan what we've lost, and perhaps never had. We are alienated precisely because we are sociable; it is our basic need for real world intimacy that is alienated. Online connections cannot repair this breach, though they can soothe it, feed it, for a time.

But we have choices. Perhaps our real world, living, social "technologies" – friendship, community, kindness, love – our inner technologies – can start to respond to those other pressures. Instead of simply creating an artificial space of superficial contact through gadgets and apps, reducing our "friends" to utilities, audiences, or appendages, perhaps we can create ways to see each other as whole, and really be with each other. We will have technology – but people, and the Earth itself, must remain at the center of our vision, for our minds and hearts to bloom to their fullest potential.

The new iPhone isn't available for order yet; and it will take weeks after that to be delivered. For perhaps a month or more, I will revert, atavistically, to landline and laptop, answering machine and voicemail. I take to singing Paul Simon and Ladysmith Black Mambazo's *Phoneless*, about the most tragic state known to 21st century man. But my pockets are delightfully empty, my mind spaciously free, unencumbered by techno-itches to check for messages and reassurances of connection. This is a welcome, restful home. We can, of course, live this way. When we do, we may find it preferable. But how would the young react, those who have known nothing but the smartphone, Facebook, Snapchat, Instagram, Twitter and their cousins? We are adaptable, but we don't always find different ways comfortable. Are we adjusting to a way of life that pulls away something vital from us? Are we frogs in a pot that is only slowly coming to a boil? I am a little hopeful when a friend tells me of her son, frustrated and breaking into tears as he tells her he feels he can't control his addiction to Facebook and his desire to stay in touch with friends online, and then relieved when she makes him deactivate his account. Perhaps the young are not so different from me, after all.

I remember another technological vision and myth that guided the late 20th Century. The Death Star was the pinnacle of military power for the Empire in George Lucas' "galaxy far, far away." But I believe that the real Death Star wouldn't fire a laser to destroy a world. It would shoot a ray of ignorance and delusion, spawning selfishness, hatred, greed, apathy and spite. And this is the danger of the technological age. That we learn our devices too well, and forget the art and beauty of being human; we forget how to nurture ourselves in solitude, that great partner to companionship and love, and lose ourselves in the cheap thrills of busymind and constant contact-without-contact. The danger is that we forget ourselves, and never see each other fully; that we grow apart and more averse to each other in full nuance, complexity and presence. The danger is that love will lessen; that way lies death, indeed. "People when you want them, technology when you don't." We must ask ourselves – where is the Death Star's beam in our lives?

A Tibetan monk said it best, in the short film *Shangri La* by Adam Smith. "My first day in America, when we arrived at the airport, we thought 'Wow. America.'" He continued, "we lived in a small village, we didn't have electricity, no proper water, no proper road, no transportation." Moving to America, "land of opportunity, freedom of speech, freedom of religion" turned his experience "totally upside down." But he laments his newfound lifestyle, wherein he had all manner of things, but didn't see his neighbors for months at a time. "In the Western world, you can have a very luxurious life. You have so many things, and then slowly you lose your mind."

This is precisely what's at stake – when we value "luxurious things" or a virtual medium more than reality – when they displace our reality – we are in danger of losing our minds, closing down our hearts, losing our synapses for deep relationship, openness and curiosity. Ambivalence and skepticism in the age of social networks are essential to transcendence: they are the signs of attachment not to a way of life that's "old and outdated" – but a sign of appropriate attachment to the only way of life we've ever known and for which we are adapted, a way of life which has been leading us towards peace and transcendence for as long as we've been human. Our relationships are our ground. The interior is our foundation. The real world, Mother Earth, is our home. Kindness is the only instruction. We must be sure they don't slip away.

We must build them, precious land in the sea of the unknown future, the future that awaits us on all sides of our loneliest moments, spent reaching for someone or something to dispel our discomfort and discontent, something to release us from suffering.

Zen Master Hakuin said, "It is like a man who is seeking fish. He must first of all look in the water. Fish are a product of the water, outside the water there are no fish. Just so, you who wish to seek Buddha must first of all look into your own mind. Buddha is a product of the mind. Outside the mind, there is no Buddha."

In our loneliest moment and our most connected one, just adjacent to it – is truth. In these moments, in your mind, your body, and in the space between us, is Buddha.

Seek.

Love.

The Internet? Neti, Neti

February 12, 2014. I type "1 Hacker Way" into my 2005 Prius's GPS. Nothing. Apple Maps on my months-old iPhone tries to send me to Menlo Park Street or Menlo Park Avenue in Tracy or Ventura, California. Nope. Google finally gets it right, placing a pin near the 101 in Menlo Park. I get in my car and drive, under my own power, listening to an actual CD bought at an actual live music concert in San Francisco, feeling a bit like an example of a "Triple Package" of quaint, on-the-way-out humanity, not yet outmoded by self-driving cars, digital downloads and virtual experiences. But it's humanity on a mission. I'm trying to find my way to the house that Mark Zuckerberg built, the Facebook headquarters, in the belly of the Silicon Valley whale. Cynthia Lin croons "I am in love," as I travel to the epicenter of "likes" for a mini-conference on "Wisdom, Science and Social Media: Bringing More Heart Into Communication," sponsored by Wisdom 2.0, Soren Gordhamer's group trying to bridge wisdom traditions and tech, and Facebook, which is ostensibly trying to be the bridge between us all.

Facebook wasn't even on the map just a few short years ago, literally and figuratively. My GPS hasn't caught up to the reality of its ascendance, and perhaps, neither have I. I drove by this spot when it was just an open space, on my way to the bridge across the bay. Now a giant sign gives me the "thumbs-up" welcome to a large, modern campus of two- and three-story-tall brick and stucco buildings, looking for all the world like a small community college, except this community keeps tabs on about a fifth of humanity. The transformation of this space was the prime physical manifestation of Facebook's mostly ethereal, cloud-based transformation of the world. For the skeptical, it is ground zero of the Zuckerborg invasion.

Where once there was essentially marshland, there is now a Tower of Social Babble. Facebook has built a new world online, and changed the real world as well. Just like someone visiting the developing world years apart, a traveler who'd left Earth in 2006 and returned in 2014 would say "everything has changed!" Technology has completely renovated our external, internal and relational environments. And we've been delivered something far more penetrating than new skyscrapers, malls or subways: we've received the implants of our smartphones and the incessant wish to post updates and check for notifications on Facebook, Twitter and the full spectrum of internet sirens. No one needs to call my smartphone anymore. My smartphone calls to me, asking me to check it, connect for a moment, and drown out the existential alone-ness of being human. The smartphone is a tool for disconnecting us from our humanness, as much as we use it to connect us to one another. We use the online world to escape our mundane existence to a disembodied, non-corporeal one – our technological form of spiritual transcendence. We use Facebook, Twitter and smartphones to distract us from our sadness, boredom and human reality, a reality where heretofore we have found timeless truths. But now, with modernity pressing on us, we find reality too uncomfortable to bear, so we are eager for ways to push it away. Others say that the tools of the wired world will bring us to those timeless truths more surely and rapidly, by reinforcing our ideals and giving us ways to act on them. They hypothesize that our presence online will allow us to engage with reality and the issues that concern us in far more depth and breadth than ever before possible in human history. With the introduction of the iPhone and the massive expansion of Facebook, 2007 marked the beginning of a high-tech earthquake that has undone our landscape. We are still reeling, in excitement, bewilderment, and in some cases, dread of all these alterations and upheavals. What do they mean to our selves and our society? This is a question vital to our survival and sanity, not to mention our actual spiritual transcendence.

I find my way to Building 15, where a succession of extremely cordial greeters meets me. One directs me to a row of iPads, and instructs me to find my name on a screen and register. As I click, swipe and slide, I'm presented with a thirteen-point nondisclosure agreement that only a lawyer could properly parse. I sign anyway. The greeter then points me to the concierge's desk on the other side of the room. A Black woman aptly named Moses hands me my lanyard and points me towards the Promised Land.

My group of a dozen or so early arrivals is ushered through the locked doors, and we find ourselves in a staging area between the various conference rooms. Against one wall, there is an array of drinks and snacks: twelve kinds of tea, four kinds of coffee, four glass-doored refrigerators filled with every non-alcoholic beverage imaginable, and shelves of sweet and savory snacks, from granola to Nutter Butter. The other wall is The Wall: a giant, touch-sensitive interactive screen showing a map of the world. This is like the War Room for the Facebook cause, or an imposing advertisement of its conquest: part cheery metric, part creepy awareness that all this data and more is readily available to the programming wizards (and presumably the NSA, should they want it), and part massive documentation of the ubiquity of the Facebook experience. The Wall tells me there are about 1.25 billion users of Facebook. Touch a country, and the Wall tells me how many computer and mobile users that country has. Touch another menu, and target-like circles appear, one circle for each user, pink for women and blue for males. ("How are transgendered people identified?" I wonder to myself.) Touch one of these targets and the Wall tells you how many friends the user has. The more friends, the bigger the circles around the target. Presumably, some other screen could draw lines between all users, making a map of social connectivity through the site, identify the most powerful influencers, the most isolated. As a psychiatrist, I wonder if someday I could touch a circle and get a mood or distress reading. Perhaps, instead of me, this information would be used by a pharmaceutical company to market medications (or vacations) to dispirited users. That presumes that people actually display their most significant misery on their Facebook walls. Even wanting to do that seems problematic to me, as a psychiatrist and believer in real world, embodied relationships that have the capacity for truly holding and soothing emotions. Squeezing yourself onto your Facebook profile is like squeezing an elephant into a thimble. It can't be done, and life is lost trying.*

The Wall is stunning, though. It's a phenomenal representation of the reach of this social network, but ultimately it's only a thin slice of the data that's actually collected by Facebook. The Wall is the Facelandia population graphically gathered for an abstract selfie. Many of my fellow conference attendees take pictures of it. I was told I shouldn't take pictures, so I don't. Instead, Donna, another conference attendee, instructs me on how to take a proper selfie in front of the fridges topped with Facebook logos: "hold the phone in your right hand! Stand here! Angle upwards! Now click!" I'm satisfied with everything but my face. No wonder I don't take selfies. With my shaved head, I look like a monk-cum-dentist wondering what he's doing at the candy store. Maybe to find out if this is what's causing all the cavities. Perhaps to offer fluoride, and hopefully not bromides. I look at the selfie again. Well…maybe I could pass for Mace Windu, about to take on Palpatine/Darth Zuckerberg. Yeah, that.

I am not an enemy of Mark Zuckerberg or his Facebook Empire, though. I appreciate what he and his team have done, and am in awe of the way that so many people are connecting online through his site, Twitter, Instagram, Snapchat and all the other social networking sites that have proliferated in the last few years. There's clearly a huge and almost insatiable craving to communicate and share in this new way.

---

* Algorithms could pick up on broadcast distress. But since the ultimate cause of distress is disconnection, what if the social network actually worsened the problem? Social media use could be a vicious circle, adding to the problem rather than solving it, leaving us sadder, madder and lonelier.

Facebook fills the isolating niche created by modernity itself, and has understandably become the dominant, elephant-in-the-room social network. We are a social species. Our biological and cultural evolution, and even our survival, has always depended on our ability to transmit information, knowledge and wisdom to one another, and along with this, our ability to love and care for one another and form cohesive communities. Of course, our survival also has depended on the ability to identify threats and respond to them appropriately. Facebook can be seen as just another manifestation of these evolutionary imperatives. I also see Mark Zuckerberg and his cohort as (profitable) prophets of online connection, the Chosen Ones who represent the collective American psyche's response to 9/11 and the ongoing challenges to our civic and communal life. In a world of newfound danger, the 9/11 generation found technological ways to establish contact, a sense of safety, trust, camaraderie and shared identity. That the NSA's mandate overlapped precariously with these ideals is another subject entirely, either unhappy synchronicity or subterranean, even subconscious, conspiracy based on fear instead of love. But both forces vie through technology, as they do throughout life. Post 9-11, we needed to amplify the messages of both solidarity as well as control in the face of destructive forces of division.

But it is complicated. Thich Nhat Hanh has said that "technology is neither good nor bad," implying how we use it makes the difference. I agree, but offer this counter-proposition: "technology is *both* good and bad." We have to be rigorous in our examination of all of the potentials in our very personal relationship with this fancy newcomer in our midst.

"Facebook, and social networking, are here to stay," people assert. There is an aura of inevitability, permanence, invincibility, overwhelming vastness and unlimited potential that technology has acquired, which generates camps of true believers, evangelists and acolytes, as well as apostates, agnostics and atheists. Technology has become a religion in its own right. Cyberism promises total transformation to its adherents. Through the uses of devices and apps we will make the world "perfect." The streets of the techno-future may not be paved with gold, but they will supposedly be steered by driverless cars – freeing us, presumably, to check Facebook more often (and theoretically making the streets safer by handing the wheel to a more reliable driver – it's a hint at how we are losing trust in each other, and finding machines a dependable alternative. One auto company spokesperson noted that people are "more interested in driving their smartphones than driving their cars."). Alexis Madrigal, technology editor of *The Atlantic* suggests we won't even need to drive our children to soccer practice anymore. We'll just let Google do it. Nannies mediate some parents' cares and time; why not technology? Why not, indeed. Relational "efficiency" through technology seems like an experiment in abandonment, to me. Some will be resilient, others less so. Only time will tell. "Who's mommy's best friend," asked one dad of his five year old daughter. Without skipping a beat, the girl replied "her cell phone!"†

Through Cyberism, we will also exalt the "quantified self" and monitor every aspect of our physical and mental being in order to delete what we don't like and magnify what we do, turning ourselves into programmable machines. We will live as "centaurs," integrated with and dependent on technology, as Clive Thompson puts it in *Smarter Than You Think*, his enthusiastic exaltation of the promises of the high-tech highlife that reads like a Song of Songs about the glorious relationship we will have to our devices and apps, and how they will be used to solve all our most vexing problems, from the oppression of dictatorships to understanding how proteins fold. And the New Testament of Cyberism will no doubt be headlined by Jesus Christ Superborg, the AI guaranteed to master or even redeem our human imperfections with flawless, silicon logic. Perhaps Google or IBM will figure out a way to make JCS a compassionate, as well as a powerful, thinker and actor. But if JCS is invulnerable, a perfect machine, it will never match the emotions, sensitivity and creativity that comes from our fragility. Without a body, how could it ever love? Without vulnerability, how would it

---

† Some might correctly note that we already have practically driverless cars. They're called "public transportation."

truly need and depend on others? How would it care for others, or even conceive of care? How could it ever be affected by another being in all the physical and emotional ways that make us who we are? Its logical "perfection" couldn't match these magnificent aspects of our already extraordinary human scale, a scale that some engineers feel they could and should exceed with a device. A perfect machine would still be a machine, in the end, but one with vast power. With great power comes the possibility of great, even cataclysmic error. Technology can, and will, be used to harm as well as help. JCS, or any AI, could easily be used as a mechanism of exclusion, exploitation, control and manipulation. And there are values inherent in technology that may amplify harm without our full awareness or consent, subtle assumptions that we buy into that end up eroding and devaluing the most precious qualities and possibilities of this human life, among these, empathy, compassion, and love.

Others posit seriously, and with no small amount of hubris, that we will upload our consciousnesses into the Cloud and live forever in a virtual reality. (Presumably, we would order babies through a drop-down menu.) But without bodies, could we really be us? What is consciousness, anyway? Mind is more than our neural circuits. There is no such thing as an individual. We are nothing less than all our relationships to each other, the earth, and the universe. We won't be uploading all of that anytime soon. We're barely living it.

Clive Thompson points to many advantages and uses of technology that he thinks should lift us into enthusiasm rather than apprehension. While he's right to point these out, there are significant holes in his argument, and in the whole framework of Cyberism, or the belief in transcendence through information technology, which can be summarized in five dualities. **Cyberism devalues emotion for cognition.** Thoughts are deemed more important than feelings. But meaning comes from both thoughts and feelings, and we must contend with and cultivate in both domains to be whole. **Cyberism devalues psyche for brain.** By assuming that we are composed of simply our biological neural networks, it denies the spiritual and relational components of consciousness. **Cyberism denies the physical body for digital presentation of self.** The body is at best an object in cyberism, not a central component of our identities. Our bodies become shadows of our online personas. **Cyberism devalues the lived community for disembodied pseudo-relationship.** We become more engaged with virtual companions than we are with the people who live in our neighborhoods and communities. Instead of building trust with people we share space with, our real-life companions, we build an evanescent "ambient awareness" (as Thompson puts it) of distant, virtual "friends." Our hours online come at a cost. Our neurons need neighbors and neighborhoods to flourish to their fullest potential. Our psyche needs a physical sense of citizenship and shared identity. **Finally, cyberism displaces the Earth and environment for an escape to a virtual world.** Our online gambit has a price. We ignore the carbon and human footprint of our technology and online interactions at our peril. As we value our shiny technological creations more, we must view the Earth increasingly as a resource rather than as our only home. Perhaps the problems facing us require technical assistance and advantage, but the solutions seem to lie predominantly in the former rather than the latter of these pairs, in the "matrix," if you will, of embodied, empathic relationships grounded in the real world.

If Clive Thompson's *Smarter Than You Think* is the Song of Songs of Cyberism, this book, *Facebuddha*, might be seen as a Book of Psalms in the Bible of Humanism, a song of praise to the power of love and presence, a personal lament at the difficulties of real world relationships, but also a song of thanks for their necessary and redeeming difficulty. *Facebuddha* also mourns for what seems to be slipping away as we lose sight of each other behind screens. It's ultimately a call to rise to our highest, transcendent potential, beyond our self-centered egos, and not lose our minds to apps and devices. This volume is a love poem to the space between us, a space we create by relating compassionately to one another in the real world, a space I feel is imperiled by the diversion of our *eros*, the feminine principle of relatedness, into the big blue Wall where we can never be fully related. We must be wary of how our affections are transmitted and mutated by this interloping mediator.

"Technology is a tool," people say. To which I reply, "so is a screwdriver, but you wouldn't use it to change a light bulb." This tool needs to be carefully held, understood, and even bounded. When it is not, it is a certain cause for suffering, personal and global, secular and spiritual. Almost everyone would agree that a technological intermediary is a poor substitute for love. Yet we are participating in the sharing of love and other emotions, information, declarations and declamations through staccato bursts of text and image, actively migrating our relational selves online. Yet we ourselves are not ultimately staccato. We may be somewhat stochastic, but most of us ultimately strive for continuity, coherence, wholeness and peace. In the Buddhist context, we strive for enlightenment, the fusion of compassion and wisdom to vanquish suffering and the causes of suffering, and to help others along that path as well. My explorations have taught me we cannot be whole online. Social media fragments us, pulls us into an ethereal dimension, a bardo, where all too often, our self-centeredness predominates. Jealousy, envy, and narcissism bubble. When we feel excluded from the attentions of others, we feel sadness, resentment and shame. Studies show that the more time we spend on Facebook, the more dissatisfied we are with our friends, and with ourselves. Facebook apparently causes, and does not simply correlate with, low self-esteem and depression. Facebook does, de facto, mark our petty egos, and at best, can make us aware of our broken places. At worst, it can create them. The blue wall cannot, however, mend our brokenness or fix our human problems. In the end, it is too shallow for long-term comfort, and a diversion from our greatest possibilities as social beings who require each other in ways incapable of expression on any small screen stage.

But social media is a tool. Staccato declarations of self and opinion can be useful. Activists use the internet to combat racism and sexism through hashtags and trending conversations on Twitter, for example. Those involved find it gratifying and powerful, even as it attracts trolls (read: cybersadists) who threaten and abuse them. But at the roots of sexism and racism are devaluation and isolation. All the "isms," all our wounds, come from some form of empathic failure: failures of love, understanding and empathy.

The internet seems inherently devaluing and isolating to me, ultimately arranged around the self separate from others. How can we heal our wounds and get to love and relationship with this limited tool? There is a reaching for confluence and interdependence with others through the activity of the mind (and sometimes heart) but it is ephemeral and devoid of physical presence and the comforts and reassurances of touch and sight. In the end, you are at your computer screen, alone. You might connect with others on your topic of choice, and this can be gratifying, but it can only contain what is transmittable online. Twitter and Facebook might then be seen as self-networks, more than social networks, because they are by nature self-centered. By amplifying the self, they support a disembodied selfhood arrayed around a bounded, screen-sized image of the world that takes the user away from full-fledged reality imbued with a sense of belonging and togetherness with others. A part of the self interacts with parts of others, in a way that can't quite get to full appreciation and acceptance of the parties involved, much less the others who choose not to be as vocal. We are still left, after the Twitter dialogues and hashtag activism, with a pressing need to find validation, inclusion and connection in the real world. The only balm for the injuries we have suffered at the hands of others, would be to transform their ignorance, malice and lack of compassion. That would mean overpowering their self-centeredness and our own, through relatedness and related communication. I don't think the dialogues on social networks can approach this level of engagement. It seems banal to say this, but perhaps it bears repeating in the age of social networks: we are more than our opinions. And sometimes our opinions get in the way of being human. We end up wanting to be right rather than related, a sure path away from happiness. Can the online dialogues change our relational environment, make racism, sexism, gay hatred and other forms of prejudice less acceptable? Perhaps. But the rubber meets the road in real-life, real-time relationship.

Excessive self-centeredness is recognized as a source of suffering in all wisdom traditions. I would argue that deep, embodied relatedness is vital to becoming human as well as transcending self-centeredness. We are more than just minds staring at a screen – we are physical beings as well. Companionship, the path away from devaluation, isolation, empathic failures, and their attendant suffering requires more than a mental abstraction. Our mind consciousness is deeply dependent on body consciousness. Both consciousnesses are at risk when we migrate our hardest, but potentially most rewarding conversations online.

Unlike a conversation in a physical space, there is more chance for exclusion and misunderstanding online. Twitter dialogues seem less grounded to me, and thus less capable of the deeper connection and transformation that comes with shared struggle and physical presence. Twitter is fast, though – and that is its attraction as well as Achilles' heel. And it elevates some voices that might not otherwise be heard. It brings attention to issues that might otherwise be overlooked. But it is both a help and a hindrance to the development of wise relating. How do stoicity, restraint and measured communication fare in this medium? As a psychiatrist, I worry that internet conversations – or inflammations – won't lead to real world trust, commitment, commonality and community. A gap develops between the online inflation of self and the real self, which must struggle to right itself through the imbalance. "It's like life through polaroids," wrote blogger Jenn Fang of Reappropriate.co in a personal communication. "Moments of emotion that are sequentially started and paused as you wait for the next Tweet or Facebook like." Resolution is nearly impossible, especially on controversial matters, either within the self or with distant others, because true, full empathic connection is out-of-reach. We can amplify aspects of our suffering with punctuated public declamations, but technology cannot elevate us to psychological or spiritual fullness. We need different tools for that.

The Cyberself, with its Cyber-love, Cyber-anger and other Cyber-emotions, might augment love, anger and emotion in the real world, but it can just as easily lead us away from their full development, resolution and reward. Love and anger require full reception and exchange for fruition, not available online. Self-driving cars, and self-involved Facebook and Twitter, may take us away from love, not towards it. Personally, I like the experience of driving. I resist being driven by an app whose GPS map is ambivalent, at best. I know the way to my heart. To reference *Star Wars* again, "I got a bad feeling about this..."

If we had to design a world from scratch, it would have to be one where we cared for others: our partners, our friends, our families, our children. Caring for another is the only way out of self-centeredness, which lies at the core of our unhappiness and most of the problems of the world we inhabit. Certainly, caring for others is not problem-free. But it is transformative. "Here comes everybody" (a la Clay Shirky, author of the book by that name) can never as powerful as "here comes somebody." But this is my view, this is my story, as someone who has loved others, and who has been in turn transformed by them. Just one person can practically rearrange your molecules, and by loving them, you can rearrange theirs.

At heart, Facebook makes "somebodies" into "everybodies" or even "nobodies." On Facebook, the somebody in us is unavoidably disappointed, separate and craving for contact.

A woman strikes a meditation bowl, and the ringing quiets the gathered crowd. We enter a large conference room peppered with motivational banners that read "Fortune Favors the Bold," "Focus," and "What Would You Do If You Weren't Afraid?" Arturo Bejar, Facebook's Director of Engineering, is the first speaker, and is as enthusiastic a representative of the Facebook way as anyone could be. He outlines his foray into "compassion research" in order to make Facebook a more hospitable place for relationship. Much of his work has been focused on how to help users communicate with each other in the classic awkward online situation. For example, your friend posts a photo that you find objectionable. The "Report This" tools that were in place were dissatisfying to users. Bejar and his colleagues realized that polite communication over such missteps was the route to maintaining civil connections. A set of stock report-back phrases were designed to help users bridge their gaps. "This photo is embarrassing to me," "this makes me sad," "I don't like this photo of me," and "this photo shouldn't be on Facebook" were tested and approved. The user on the other end would get a notice to "please take down this photo" along with a customizable and hopefully connecting message. Allowing emotion-rich messages tripled the number of people messaging about awkward situations. Bejar emphasizes that building empathy into communications, allowing users to see different perspectives, led to positive feelings for both parties. In another project, Facebook hired an animator to build cute new emoticon packs for its messaging app. This has led to a treasure trove of information about what emotions people in different countries communicate online. Interestingly, Americans score lower on love-emoticons and higher on anger than much of the rest of the world. I don't know what messaged love has to do with real love, but this bit of data did give me pause.

When Bejar speaks of his attempts to help users navigate offensive and bullying posts, I'm reminded of the boundary issues inherent in Facebook that have spoiled the experience for me in the past. We can't control what we're exposed to. Opinionated others find their way into our feed, and even a "friend" can annoy. But Bejar and his team are working on this issue. They want to make the "box" happier. But what if the box is the problem? The medium is the message, after all, and this medium is an unusually limited representation of relationship, self and other. Disagreements are part of all relationships, but on Facebook, they become divisive diatribes instead of dialogues. A generally conciliatory, diplomatic, perspective-taking viewpoint doesn't fare well amongst the colorfully provocative flamethrowers who see the world in black-and-white, certain terms. We can sometimes report or object to offensive posts, we can ignore them, we can "hide" offensive posters, we can defriend - but none of these bring us closer to the kind of relationship that can truly accept and hold our differences, or even, possibly, to transcend them.

But our last speaker, social psychologist Dacher Keltner, is enthusiastic about the potential of the online world to deliver us to positive emotions. He considers transcendent "awe" the pinnacle of positivity. He is working with Facebook on ways to mainline awe into our online experience. He tells us that awe is generated when one encounters something one's knowledge structure can't make sense of. We are overwhelmed by a sense of something larger than ourselves, and our sense of self is quieted as we merge with the grand. Over the millennia, spiritual awe has become secularized. Edmund Burke proposed in the 18th century that the sublime was to be found in every perceptual moment. 19th century philosophers rediscovered expansive emotion in nature. Muir, Thoreau, Emerson and others found spiritual heights in the woods, mountains, and shores of America. A sense of perceptual vastness is evoked when looking into the Grand Canyon or up at a giant sequoia. "Me small, world big," we register, and yet feel part of that bigness. Keltner posits that evolution gave us awe because it helps in building communities. We become better community members when we have felt awe. Our self-centeredness evaporates, and we-centeredness rises. We feel part of a bigger picture, and are drawn into a grander view of life. Awe makes us humble, more curious and intellectually open. He cites studies that suggest that eliciting awe can make us more generous and helpful.

And then he cites the Facebook "lookback" movie as an example of online awe. This application, launched at the ten-year anniversary of Facebook, stitched together a user's most popular photos and status updates of their time on Facebook into a 30-second movie, set to stirringly sentimental music. Some of my friends were touched by the memories. Others saw it as a bizarre marketing ploy built with the assumption that we didn't have lives before or outside of Facebook, designed to promote attachment to the site by appealing to our narcissism. Some were startled by photos of traumatic times that were "liked" and thus popular by algorithmic standards. At the very least, I found the movie a questionable example of awe. I ask Keltner how he dealt with the paradox that he was advocating awe mediated by a computer screen, while tracing awe to religious experience and encounters with the natural world. From Sequoias to screens seems rather anticlimactic, a prime example of the decay embodied by the Old Man of Crete in Dante's *Divine Comedy*, with his head of gold and iron feet.

"I agree and I disagree," he said. "Symbolic representations have always been part of mediating awe. Stories, pictures and paintings have always been used by humans." They have always been a part of "awe."

It was a good answer, in that the lookback movie did connect users tangentially to the bigger Facebook story. Still, I wondered, what exactly was that Facebook story? After all these years, I was still unsure about what Facebook was. Was it an incredible tool for connecting people, a value propagation device, an innocuous amplifier for "shits and giggles," a relentless timesuck, a political organizing mechanism, an annoying distraction from the real world, a spur and engine for narcissism, or an insidious mechanism of assigning social rank via the "like," "follow" and "add friend" buttons? Has it enhanced our relationships or has it harmfully invaded and displaced them? Keltner and Bejar highlighted the positive. Can we put up with the negative and embrace only the positive? I doubt it. If so, we would have to emphasize the broader dimensions of our lives and stories beyond the internet.

The human story, I think, is ultimately about relationship – and this is why I find Facebook so problematic. Transcending our self-centeredness begins with deepening our relationships with others, through compassion, love and spirit. We can't ignore the ways Facebook falls short of this story and our potential, and the ways we fall short when we get caught in its relentless ego-traps. Hindu sages negated ideological frameworks by reminding themselves that the transcendent was beyond conceptual rationalizations. "Neti, neti" – "not this, not that" – they would say, as they sought to negate worldly experience and cultivate nonconceptual awareness. Cyberism, and Facebook, are such concepts and frameworks of the worldly. Facebook awe seems far short of the realization of the sages, to put it mildly. Of course, the spiritual plane de-emphasizes all worldly things. Our modern danger is that the worldly, through technology, has become so inflated, intrusive and pervasive that it assumes a presumptuous pedestal. We are worshipping a false god, in other words.

The Buddha famously transmitted "Zen mind" to his disciple Māhākaśyapa wordlessly, with a smile and gesture, in spiritual communion. He plucked a flower, smiled and looked at Māhākaśyapa, who smiled in turn, uniting with him in peaceful bliss. If such transcendence is communicated with presence, how are we to regard our online engagement except as a diversion and devolution?

Bestselling Swedish philosopher and internet theorist Alexander Bard, author of *The Futurica Trilogy*, has said both that "we truly become human beings through the internet," and "the internet will change us completely even in the essence of what a human being is," as if we were not human before the internet. To him, "the internet is the Holy Spirit," and "the internet is God." By creating the internet, we are creating God.[88‡] Needless to say, Bard has not to my knowledge produced any credentials to speak on either the Holy Spirit or God. Considering

---

‡   More recently, Virginia Heffernan breathlessly wrote in 2016's *Magic and Loss: The Internet as Art* that the internet, "as an idea rivals monotheism," and that it is "an integral part of our humanity...the latest and most powerful extension and expression of the project of being human." Also: the "Internet (is) so abstract and powerful that we glimpse it...the way we see the face of God in the interstices and lacunae of the Torah." Talk about hyperbole and a half. But these ideas of technological transcendence have been percolating for some time. Heffernan quotes Marshall McLuhan: "Electric circuitry is Orientalizing the West. The contained, the distinct, the separate – our Western legacy – is being replaced by the flowing, the unified, the fused." Personally, I see more "magic," divinity, mystery and art in a single human being than all of the internet combined. All its servers, fibers and screens can't match the eyes that behold it or the minds that create it. And "the flowing, the unified, the fused" is accessible through the doors of our perception just as it is to those in the East. The concrete, literal West, though, seems to need a physical proxy for the transcendent. Years ago, an Indian sage said to Ram Dass of LSD, "you in the West are so materialistic; you needed God to come to you in the form of a pill." Now, the internet is our hallucinogen, taking us to an altered state which we mistake for true transcendence.

there's just as much evidence to call it the devil as God, and you see how absurd the proposition is. I think he confuses our technological foray with a spiritual one precisely because we are attempting to make a relational story online, and relationship is, ultimately, a spiritual quest. Also, he is clearly in awe of the internet and technology. Our relational pilgrimage, though, cannot be completed on internet confines. Our journey only includes technology because it is here with us, and thus requires us to be mindful and make choices. We must not be swept up blindly in its cause, or diverted by its spell.

Huston Smith writes in *The World's Religions*, "if you traverse the length and breadth of the universe saying of everything you can see and conceive, 'not this…not this,' what remains will be God." The internet? Neti, neti. The internet, and social networks, as informative, awe-inspiring and buoyant as they can be, cannot substitute for transcendence. Transcendence, like love, comes through deep experiences of interdependence and relationship, experiences we can only cultivate in the real world.

As we line up for lunch, a woman declares to me, "I heard your question! But we can't throw the baby out with the bathwater!" I smile and nod, but think to myself, "what's the baby and what's the bathwater?" As far as Facebook is concerned, I want to paraphrase Elaine from Seinfeld. *The Facebook dingo got my baby!*

On the evening of the same day as the Facebook conference, I attend a press screening for a film nominated for the 2013 Best Documentary Oscar. *The Square* followed Egyptians through the Arab spring and what has been characterized as "The Facebook Revolution." Their protests, centered on Tahrir Square, led to the overthrow of Hosni Mubarek, then the military government, and then Mohammed Morsi. It's an incredible, moving example of people coming together to change their lot. Their future is still unclear. One protestor acknowledges that it may take years or decades to reform the Egyptian government. But the seeds have been planted. The people are awake.

Facebook and Twitter helped sow the seeds of change. Images of police and Army brutality galvanized Egyptians and people around the world. Social media was used to organize relief efforts. People in squares throughout the world were inspired by the courage of the Egyptian people. But I was most moved by how Egyptian protestors related to each other through the struggle. They loved each other. They were kind to each other. They argued with each other, but they stayed connected despite disagreements, particularly in the early days of their revolution. There were touching moments of acceptance and change between Egyptians in different ideological camps.

The Egyptian revolution wasn't, ultimately, a story about Facebook or Twitter. It was a story of relationships between people, and a story of relationship to a space, Tahrir Square, where people could be with one another and find their common ground. Facebook and Twitter might have been accelerants, but they were neither the spark nor the fuel for the fire that lit up Egypt's streets. The sparks were in the compassion of the people's hearts, and their passion for justice. The fuel was their long-standing sense of connection with one another, their hard-won understanding that their situation required change, an understanding that was born out of relationship, conversation, conviction and shared sacrifice.

One can't help but think of the American context. How related are we, in America? How will we come together more fully to face our many challenges if we don't see each other, know each other, and share in each other's struggles? As a psychiatrist and humanist, I feel the online gambit is not enough. We need our Squares. We need better relationship. We need civil society and civic engagement. And it's not that we should strive for better relationships in order to have a revolution. The real revolution is relationship. The real revolution is love. This revolution must be lived, not texted, Tweeted, Facebooked or Snapped. Social networks might be part of the ladder, but the ladder must be kicked away.

It must be transcended.

Hanoi Now, Hanoi Again, Hanoi Forever

Hanoi. A hot summer night, May, 2015. I've come to Vietnam for the second time, this time with my friend, Tony Nguyen, to mark the 40th anniversary of the Fall of Saigon, and catch the spirit of a country united after long civil war on April 30, 1975. Tony's short documentary film about his mother and himself, their refugee story, and their sometimes difficult relationship, with silences and unanswered questions, has just won an award at CAAMFest, as the Asian American film festival in San Francisco is now called. One of the reasons he made his film (*Giap's Last Day at the Ironing Board Factory*) was to get closer to his own mother, Giap. He also describes the difficulties of growing up Asian American in Indiana. Tony's quest for identity, belonging and understanding runs deep in his soul, parallel to my own spirit. He is the kind of friend Henry Adams wrote about. "Friendship needs a certain parallelism of life, a community of thought, a rivalry of aim." We have the first two, hands down. Our "rivalry of aim" requires traveling and conversation to flesh out.

We eat crab bún riêu, a noodle soup, at the Old Quarter night market in Hanoi. After a young woman takes our order, a severe, cross-looking elderly woman delivers our bowls with an expression so sour it rivals the cut green limes on the plate between us. Tony and I start talking about smiles. You see, I'm all about the smile.

Apocalips

A smile returned is a tilt-a-whirl
Throwing me into a fit of ecstasy
Needed proof on a cold gray city day
Of inclusion in humanity.

We push each other away
To the partition of peripheral sight
Dread and indifference keep us safe
We create no-fly zones of subtle spite.

But how meaningful it is to breach that wall
To allow the other to matter!
We sometimes feel safer in solitude
But society is sacrificed on that lonely altar.

I smile to strangers, babies, cats and dogs;
It's my most aggressive flirt!
Only a war of upturned lips
Will apocalypse avert!

Tony's got a great smile, and he laughs at most of my jokes. He's a good guy. But he doesn't just give his grin up for anyone. He plays his heart close to the chest, whereas I tend to wear mine on my sleeve. I'm closer to the spirit of that Nat King Cole song, *Smile*.

Smile though your heart is aching
Smile when your heart is breaking...

He says that I just need to respect people as they are. I reply, of course, I respect their right to not smile. I'm a psychiatrist, I know people are not always in the smiling mood. The burdens of reality and history can weigh down the sunrise of the smile. I get that some women are rightly annoyed when they're told they should "just smile." I know that some culture's norms lean against "the American smile." There's a Russian proverb, "a smile without a reason is a sign of idiocy." But the smile also makes us happier, and spreads joy. "I just gotta be me, Tony, I just gotta be me." Tony brings up one of poet Bao Phi's characters from *Sông I Sing*.

Bác Trâm doesn't reply when you say cám o'n for the bowl of phở. It's just her in this place, from nine a.m. to midnight, so it's her right to take your money and give you your basil mint bean sprout lime platter and hate your guts from the safety of the kitchen. One night when she's bored she'll tell you she hasn't been back to Viet Nam since her husband died, she'll ask you if you have a job, she'll ask you if your girlfriend is white or Vietnamese as if those are the only two choices in the world.

I tell Tony that when I travel, I know I stick out like a sore thumb, with my brown skin, my Hawai'i beach hat, and my fanny pack. This may be the one time I see any of these folks, so I'm gonna smile. I am my mother's son. We're both quite fond of people. Sometimes, unfortunately so. Locals here see tourists night and day. Why not be an ambassador of good cheer? "If I was going to that restaurant Bao wrote about, I would smile every time, until 10 years later, that woman would smile at me. I'm in it for the long haul."

When we get up to leave, the old woman comes to clear our table. She looks at me. I smile at her. She pauses, and with what looks like extreme effort, she pulls the right corner of her lip sideways. I'm sure she doesn't understand a word of English, but it's as if she heard us hotly debate our *very* important issue, and rendered her judgment in grudging approval of my perspective.

I nudge Tony as we move away, touch my right index finger to my tongue, and make a mark in the air. "Score one for Ravi!"

He shrugs his shoulders, and soon, we're talking about something else.

But I hold onto that old woman's smile. Might be even better than the bún riêu. And it was really good bún riêu. Just don't tell her I said so.

My last night in Hanoi. Tony has already departed, headed to visit his relatives in Cam Ranh. I'll go to Cambodia in the morning. It's also 40 years after the fall of Phnom Penh, and the beginning of Pol Pot's genocide. I am going to Phnom Penh to pay my respects, and to bear witness in some small way to the healing and hurt that still linger there, rivals for the future of this tragic yet hopeful country, origin of my patients' long journey.

But tonight, I have a date with Yasue. We meet at a wine bar, at a table under the stars. Eight years before, on a Hanoi rooftop, Yasue introduced me to Facebook. Three months before this second meeting, I deactivated my Facebook account. This time around, she introduces me to the bigger social network.

Alcohol.

I haven't had a drink in over a decade. I was never a big drinker, but I stopped during my psychiatry residency because alcohol interfered with my sleep. But tonight, Yasue chooses a bottle of red, and I join her. "A jug of wine, a loaf of bread, and thou…" Perhaps I'll need to write *Faceboozer* next, but tonight, there's no writing to be done. Just the two of us, enjoying our second conversation in a decade, catching up and making time. We're making time for each other, and it seems we're actually making time itself. Two conversations spaced eight years apart are worth more than all the years of Facebook in between.

I deactivated Facebook after finally getting fed up with the political diatribes. After the *Charlie Hebdo* attacks in Paris on January 7th, 2015, many in my community didn't focus on the horror of the killings. Instead, they wrote screeds against *Charlie Hebdo*. While most of the world went #JeSuisCharlie ("I am Charlie"), these online activists ran their ball down the court with #JeNeSuisPasCharlie ("I am not Charlie"). Many distinguished literary figures and political activists carried that flag as well. They accused the cartoonists of *Charlie Hebdo* of being right-wing, anti-immigrant racists, insensitive to the plight of marginalized French Muslims. Some said the cartoons were an obscene insult to all Muslims. They felt that the West's vaunted freedom of speech was truly reserved only for the powerful – even as they used their freedom of speech in every venue to which I regularly paid attention. They misinterpreted cartoons, claimed all of France's whites were racist, and racked up the likes and shares like nothing I'd seen before. From what I'd read, *Charlie Hebdo* was actually a progressive – even Socialist-leaning – pro-immigrant magazine in a tradition of French satire that stuck its finger in the eye of any kind of orthodoxy. I could understand how some – or perhaps even most – Muslims were offended by *Charlie Hebdo*'s depictions of the Prophet Muhammad. I could understand how marginalized Muslim youth could be radicalized and motivated by *Hebdo*'s cartoons. But I didn't think the cartoons were motivated by racism, but rather were a withering critique of violence in the name of Islam. To the *Hebdo* cartoonists, I thought, violence itself was the desecration of Islam, a religion that heralded peace in its very welcome. As-salāmu 'alaykum. "Peace be upon you." Wa 'alaykumu as-salām. "And upon you, peace."

I didn't exactly disagree with my friends on the prevalence and importance of racism in the world. Self-centered power was the root of so many ills in the world, racism among them. But I thought they were just plain wrong about this incident. None of us could say we truly understood the French context of *Hebdo*, yet this didn't stop my online friends from charging into the fray. The unspoken false equivalence of *Hebdo*'s use of offensive free speech and the terrorists' murder spree was sickening to me. And I needed some time and space to mourn. Instead, I read comments like "Grieve the dozen people killed, but recognize they trolled with their work and trolled hard." Grieving was just a side note in their pre-written chorus about racism, preached to the choir. Racism is important for me as well, but I couldn't bring myself to write a one-size-fits-all narrative about the world. Okay, well maybe I could, about self-centeredness at the root of the world's problems. But then again, sometimes self-centeredness was a response to self-centeredness...so the narrative gets complicated. The other one-size-fits-all narrative I found useful was the unacceptability of violence. Any takers?

More importantly, I noticed how people on social media got attached to their opinions. Even reduced to their opinions. I was attached to my opinions too, and it wasn't good. The Buddha supposedly said "people with opinions just go around annoying each other."

I would rather Hanoi Yasue with my humor.

She was engaged to be married now, and about to move. We talked three hours nonstop, especially about family and the concept of "home." My friend Nguyen Qui Duc had told me he never felt quite at home. In America, he was a refugee. In Vietnam, he was a Việt kiều, or expat returnee. In either world, he felt out of place. I told Yasue that as an immigrant myself, I often felt less connection to place than to people. A place was just the stage for our meeting. We made home for each other in our hearts.

When the check comes, I pick up the tab. Yasue protests. "You're the guest! When you're in someone's home, you let them treat you!"

"Well, you're about to get married and move! It's only fair that I treat you!"

She acquiesces and takes a last sip of wine. She concludes our conversation.

"The world is my home."

Beat.

"You'll be picking up a lot of checks, then."

She throws her head back and laughs.

We rise to part ways. I don't know when I'll see her again. Maybe in five years, maybe in twenty. But it's enough, somehow, to share this moment. Time has stopped, there is no time, there is only now, stretching into forever.

We hug, and part as friends.

I want to press my heart, gentle against the heart of the world; and dance.

Narcissism: The Opposite of Belonging

What the world, needs now, is love, sweet love...
And why is that? If there's anything I know, as a psychiatrist practicing over a dozen years, and a human living almost 50, is that most of our human problems come down to empathic failures. In my life, in my patients' lives, in the lives of the world, significant others have fallen short of empathy and understanding at the most crucial times. I've fallen short of perfect empathy myself in many cases. But these empathic failures can come down hard on the vulnerable. From governments that don't care about the well-being of all their citizens, to institutions whose priorities don't include human relationships, to parents who fail to fully love their children, to brethren and sistren who fail in kindness and love, to our own minds, not loving and accepting ourselves as we are: it all causes damage. This is not saying we should simply blame those we think lack empathy for our cause or case. They are only human, after all, products of their own histories and facing their own challenges. Ultimately we must all take responsibility for our inner lives, hopefully with the help of loving others, including therapists, spiritual leaders, teachers and other professionals, family and friends. Sometimes we have to accept the world's limitations, and find happiness despite those limitations. But the buck stops here, in your own heart. We must strive to be the change we wish to see, as Gandhi said. Cultivating transcendence really comes down to cultivating your own intentions in life, based on your personal situation and who you need to be to face it.

Empathic failures are generally caused, in my book, to some form of self-centeredness. Self-centeredness, known in its extreme form as pathological narcissism, is a major cause of suffering in our world. If we were to state self-centeredness as a value, it would be "me first," or "my needs are more important than yours." Self-centeredness overvalues oneself, and automatically, consciously and subconsciously, devalues other people and groups. This overvaluing of self turns into racism, sexism, homophobia, and all the other forms of discrimination and violence, as well as the self-centeredness that imperils the planet and life as we know it. The isolated, self-centered ego is fearful of and hostile towards others. Compassion is the opposite of self-centeredness. As the Dalai Lama said, "if you want to be happy, practice compassion. If you want others to be happy, practice compassion." I would respectfully offer a corollary: "If you want to be unhappy, practice self-centeredness. If you want others to be unhappy, practice self-centeredness." Along with self-centeredness come envy, hatred and greed, which are not exactly the "eulogy virtues" *New York Times* columnist David Brooks writes about.

We start off self-centered because we have to be. In infancy we make loud demands for food and nurturance, and believe the whole world revolves around us and our needs.* Most of us grow out of our self-centeredness. Others get stuck there, by nature, nurture, wound, will or some combination. There is a healthy narcissism, of course, a healthy self-regard and self-love that allows us to maintain ourselves and our needs in balance with the needs of others.

All the world's major religions are guides to breaking through self-centeredness and pathological narcissism. The Ten Commandments could be read as prohibitions against valuing yourself more than others (along with directives to properly value God and your parents). Hence, don't kill, lie, steal, or commit adultery, all of which could be seen as self-centered acts harmful to others. Christ perfects egoless-

---

* Babies are typically also full of love, and are looking for love as well. Unfortunately, many of us lose our love. The erosion of our loving nature goes along with an amplification of self-centeredness.

ness, in advising us to be meek, turn the other cheek, judge not lest ye be judged, and love our neighbor as ourselves. The early Christian Gnostics taught that original sin was considering oneself separate from others – implying the truth of interdependence and the failings of the selfish ego. The Quran commands believers to "seek for mankind what you want for yourself," imploring the believer to expand his or her view. Hinduism holds the highest praise for those who return love for hatred, and teaches that those who regard "all creatures as one's own self" will succeed in attaining happiness. Rabbi Hillel said "what is hateful to you, do not do to your fellow man. That is the whole Torah. The rest is just commentary." Native American and other aboriginal religions have deep awareness of the interdependence of all living creatures, the earth, and the cosmos itself, calling on humans to live in harmony with nature. Tibetan Buddhism's mind-training exercises instruct us to "drive all blames into one" – the ego. All these philosophies teach us to keep the needs of others in mind.[89]

I suppose one could argue that these are all just ways that society tells us to stay in line and be sensible, good citizens. There's nothing wrong with being a sensible, good citizen. But these philosophies also call upon our better angels, and require us to press for society to be compassionate, just and merciful. Self-centeredness is harmful to society, but is also ultimately harmful to us as individuals as well. It creates conditions in the world which devalue compassion – and when compassion is devalued, individuals are devalued. Selfish acts also inevitably cause rebound actions which come back to haunt us.

But in a self-centered world, sometimes people feel they have to be self-centered, just to get their points across, just to maintain themselves and advance. Someday, I hope we'll all get to the point of mutual disarmament. We'll let down our selfish defenses, and open the doors to our hearts. I think it can happen, if we're not afraid of vulnerability and the possibility of shame, if "winning" an argument isn't our highest principle, if the material world is not the only ladder we're climbing, but rather the ladder of our hearts. I have hope, but I'm not so naive to think that everyone shares my values.

Social media, like our human mind, is "two spirited." (More on this in the next chapter and in Appendix 2.) One the one side, it is a bastion of grandiose self-centeredness. On the other, it is a beacon for compassion and generosity, taking us out of our own worlds to the bigger world we share. Which is it for you?

A year or so ago, one of my patients, a young woman in her mid-twenties working in a tech-related field, said to me "Snapchat is an empathy engine. I can see the world through the eyes of someone a world away!" She described news stories, or Snaps, from a young man in Africa. "Maybe she's right," I thought to myself. As we psychiatrists know well, caring begins when we really hear another person's story.

Social media, then, can be just another way to hear the voices of distant others, see their faces, and begin to care. Examples abound. The world was moved to see images of Aylan Kurdi, dead on a Turkish shore. Omran Daqneesh, the little boy in the ambulance, bloodied by a Russian air strike in Syria. The shooting of Philando Castile by a police officer, captured by his girlfriend and broadcast live on Facebook. "Humans of New York" posts images of New York residents (and now, residents of other cities) along with stories of their lives, and has over 18 million followers. In all these cases and many, many more, human suffering goes viral on social media platforms, triggering empathy, generosity, and action. Social media can start conversations that reverberate in relationships and on the nightly news. In the best case, these conversations lead to understanding and empathy.

At the same time, social media seems inherently narcissistic. Facebook is a form of display: self-presentation and self-curation. When we are in the Facebook matrix, we often end up caring most about how many likes we get on our latest status update or selfie. Many present a grandiose "highlight reel" of their lives. Facebook is what another young patient of mine called "success theater." "I've just been named to Forbes 40 under 40 list!" "Here I am on my fantastic vacation!" "Here I am at this incredible event!" "Here is another example of my amazing wit!" "Here is yet another picture of my adorable and perfect toddler – my perfect partner – my perfect life!"

I know, right away, the defenders of social media will object. Social media is only a tool, they'll say. It can be used for good or bad. For every example of self-centeredness, we can point to other examples of genuine sharing, caring and relationship. People do share vulnerability and distress online, and this brings connection. Sheryl Sandberg touched millions by writing about her grief after her husband Dave Goldberg's tragic death in an accident in 2015. We may first hear of a friend's illness on Facebook. We may find community and support for our identities online when it is lacking in our real world lives. At important times, I certainly found a supportive and vast Asian American community on Facebook.

Does social media inherently promote narcissism and other problems of the self? Or can we use it for good, to achieve the opposite of self-centeredness – concern for and understanding of others? If the medium is the message, what is the message of social media?

As I've discussed and demonstrated in this book, we use social media for several reasons. We are social animals. We have inherent needs for social contact, belonging and validation by others. Social media sites are popular precisely because they scratch this inescapable itch. Whether they can satisfy or even truly soothe our need to belong is another question. Narcissists have an inordinate need for fame, popularity, and admiration, beyond "mere" belonging. Social media provides a stage and an audience, tantalizing for the narcissist. Social media relationships can be numerous but shallow, a perfect combination for the attention-seeking narcissist. People also use social media out of curiosity and the desire to experiment, and a desire or almost lust to have connections, apart from mere belonging.

Reasons we use social media:
1. Belonging and a quest for secure attachment
2. Self presentation and a desire to be noticed
3. Curiosity and desire to experiment
4. Desire or lust for connections

When social media becomes narcissistic:
1. Belonging becomes fame/power/control
2. Self-presentation becomes solipsism, fascination with the self and excessive display
3. Curiosity becomes envy
4. Desire for connection becomes greed for followers

People also use social media for self-presentation, which can support either the need to belong, the race for popularity and admiration, or self-expression for its own sake. Yet self-expression almost always pulls for an audience reaction, and can hardly be divorced from the wish to be heard and popular. On social media, it is possible to be heard and popular for even superficial self-expressions.

When we amplify ourselves on social media, we invariably feel a craving for recognition. Surely, at least some of that craving could be termed narcissistic. Because online validation is usually intermittent, we are left with unsatisfied craving, and likely some amount of insecurity. Every time we post and interact, we fret about how we're received. How did I come across? Did I show too much pride? Did I make anyone angry? Did my humor make the other person uncomfortable? Was I right about what I wrote? What will they think or say about me? You can see I keep it pretty busy up here. But as psychologist Jean Twenge, co-author of *The Narcissism Epidemic* and author of *iGen: Why Today's Super-Connected Kids Are Growing Up Less Rebellious, More Tolerant, Less Happy–and Completely Unprepared for Adulthood – and What That Means for the Rest of Us*, told the audience at the 2017 Annual Meeting of the American Psychiatric Association, "if you worry about whether you're a narcissist, you're probably not one." She also said "only children are not more narcissistic than those who grew up with siblings." Phew.

Like gamblers in Vegas with a slot machine, we keep playing the blue-walled bandit in hopes of a payoff. So narcissism, characterized by excessive attention-seeking for the sake of supplying an insecure or grandiose self, seems part and parcel of the social media experience. Indeed, high levels of Facebook use are associated with higher levels of narcissism, extraversion, neuroticism, and low self-esteem and self-worth.[90] The more self-centered, insecure or disconnected you are, the more time you likely spend on Facebook, trying to get a fix. The distressed, though, tend to end up dissatisfied with their Facebook experience. But some studies also show a positive effect of time spent on Facebook, in enhanced self-esteem, emotional closeness and sense of belonging.[91] Las Vegas pays off just enough to keep us coming back. But just as in Vegas, you might be likely to lose over time.

Does Social Media attract narcissists, or is it making all of us more narcissistic? Are we the frogs in the social media pot, unwittingly being brought to a narcissistic boil?

A 2017 meta-analysis of 25,631 participants from 16 countries (half from the U.S.) showed a significant correlation between grandiose narcissism and the number of Facebook friends, intensity of Facebook usage, and uploading photos.[92] (Grandiose narcissists have a high opinion of themselves and believe others should admire them. This is in contrast to vulnerable narcissists, who while having a high opinion of themselves, are also insecure, defensive, resentful and likely to become aggressive when they feel shamed or insulted.) In countries with large "power-distances" (more hierarchical societies), which discouraged narcissistic display in public, social networking sites seemed to unmask narcissism. There, grandiose narcissists were more attracted to and active on social media. Social media is an irresistible magnet for the grandiose narcissist's exaggerated sense of self and need for admiration.

Other studies have shown that narcissism predicts increasing Facebook use over time (at least for men),[93] and that interacting with one's Facebook profile increases narcissistic scores in the short term at least.[94] Higher levels of narcissism also predicted more time spent on Facebook, as well as more self-promoting content.[95] Together,[96] these data suggest a reinforcing spiral of effects. Narcissists are attracted to social media, they are more active in specific ways, and their behaviors are often reinforced and validated by their online communities. Indeed, Facebook addiction has been correlated with narcissism.[97] Facebook users overall are more narcissistic, more extraverted, and have higher self-esteem than those who don't use Facebook.[98] (But more extensive Facebook use results in lower self-esteem.)

We are inordinately exposed to narcissists online, because narcissists have more friends. And as we've seen, they tend to post more as well. So while narcissistic traits or the full-blown disorder might be present in only a few percent of the population, we encounter many times that share in our news-, Twitter-, or Instagram-feeds. The online environment is skewed towards narcissism. Social media can thus be the narcissist's wheelhouse, and once we're in the wheelhouse, we may all be nudged towards narcissism and self-promotion, nudged towards the *wild wheeeeee!* of me.

Alternatively, non-narcissistically inclined individuals might find themselves dissatisfied in the narcissist's garden. There is some evidence that this is the case. The more time we spend on Facebook, the more dissatisfied we are with our friends,[99] and the more depressive symptoms[100] we have. People who use Facebook passively (and thus less like a narcissist) tend to become dissatisfied. If you feel ambivalent or negative about Facebook and other social media, you're probably not a grandiose narcissist. Not to say, of course, that if you're satisfied with your social media experience, you are narcissistic. You may have just found a sweet spot that I never found.

There are two specific and very popular ways to use social media that I think highlight narcissism: the selfie and the "angry."

The Oxford Dictionary's Word of the Year for 2013 was – "selfie." Smartphones are basically cameras with an occasional calling function. The average millennial will take around 26,000 selfies during their lifetime – more than one a day, probably many more during their prime selfie years.[101] (But hey, old folks like me get into it occasionally too!) It's estimated in 2016 we collectively took over 93 million selfies a day – and that's on Android alone![102] Selfies can be fun, they can document a moment or a meeting, they can be humorous or ironic – but doesn't holding up a phone and looking at our own image seem a lot like Narcissus at the pond, just before he fell in? Apps such as Facetune and Meitu help "make your ugliest selfies look beautiful." As mentioned in an earlier chapter, "Casio sells a special 'prettifying' phone in China. It is flying off the shelves at $1000 a pop due to high demand. The phone is nicknamed *zipai shenqi*, or 'the magical weapon for ultimate selfies,' and it 'makes your face slimmer, skin whiter and eyes bigger' for that perfect 'K-Pop star' or 'anime' look."

But recent research[103] demonstrated that people in selfies are perceived (at least by people who don't know them) to be more narcissistic, more extroverted, less open, less socially attractive, and less trustworthy compared to photos taken by another person. Caveat Selfie Taker, indeed. But if we tend to rate selfie-takers – at least those we don't know – as more narcissistic, less trustworthy, and less socially attractive – why are we taking so many selfies ourselves?

This goes back to our question: is social media making us more narcissistic?

It does seem that norms are shifting. Selfie taking is in vogue on social media. Everyone's doing it – so why not? We are "liking" selfies of people we know and don't know, to cement our social bond with them, to scratch their backs. That inevitably leads to more selfies. Research also shows that we are more likely to befriend people online if their profile pictures are attractive, even if we don't know the person in real life![104] Narcissists tend to use profile pictures that are deemed more attractive and showcase more personality[105] – and thus we're more likely to befriend them. Given the halo effect of attractiveness, or how we are subconsciously biased to think attractive individuals are more intelligent, kind and trustworthy, and given how important visual attractiveness is in making a positive first impression, is it any wonder that we have become selfie-obsessed in a society where images – and image – have become ubiquitous? Even if selfies are at least somewhat self-defeating, we still pull the slot-machine arm in an attempt to feel good about ourselves and make others like us.

But as we normalize and promote a behavior that most of us objectively consider narcissistic, are we not becoming more narcissistic ourselves? And simultaneously making ourselves and others feel insecure?

Selfies are popular online, and the angries are even more popular. As I have written about in a preceding chapter, anger is the most viral emotion in social media. Among active users of Weibo, the Chinese version of Twitter, anger is more viral than happiness, sadness or disgust.[106] I've called Twitter our auxiliary amygdala, fast-reacting defender against perceived threats and insults. We check Twitter and Facebook to find out what the internet is angry about today. Online opinions are often skewed, because they are personal and because the medium involves cyberdisinhibition, or disinhibition due to the lack of physical presence and cues such as facial expression, body language and tone of voice. We say online what we would never say face-to-face. Facts are faulty, reasoning is biased, and emotions are strong.

Anger is part of the fight-or-flight defense mechanism, triggered when the limbic system senses one's survival is at stake: one's life, mind, identity, loved ones or principles. With social media, we become part cyborg: the auxiliary amygdala is attached directly to our own. Many a person goes to bed angry, arguing with an article or post they just read online.

Anger is always justified to the person who is angry. Anger is perhaps necessary, and in any case, practically unavoidable in the course of human relationship. But anger, and particularly hostility, has downsides. Sogyal Rinpoche, Buddhist teacher, says that "anger obscures 90% of reality." Perhaps it focuses on the 10% of reality that is distressingly important – but our emotional agendas can hijack all other considerations. And of course anger is an attempt to be heard and seen. But anger is only resolved with understanding and empathy, which are hard to provide online.

I deactivated my Facebook account because I realized that online, people tend to get attached to their opinions and their anger, manifestations of self-centeredness. Indeed, I was getting too attached to my own opinions as well. The online environment is perfectly suited to expressing one's opinion – this is an aspect of self-presentation – but it is not well suited to listening, especially to opinions that are unpopular. Popular and angry messages are heard and validated in the heat of the moment. Messages that bridge divides or offer alternative views are dismissed. There's a saying in Buddhist circles: "the world is divided into those who are right." You can be right or related, right or happy. On social media, we often choose to be "right." Relatedness and happiness are shown the door.

Social media is often called a toxic echo-chamber. Our country has become increasingly polarized. Social media seems only to have made a bad situation worse. If I can only be happy when I either "win" an argument or when everyone agrees with me, I'm making what psychiatrist F.B. Steele calls a "bad bargain with the universe," one that guarantees unhappiness and also elevates my needs over all others. This mob mentality might be called herd narcissism. Not all anger is narcissistic, of course, but an environment where anger is valued and rewarded certainly promotes self-centeredness over empathy and compassion.

An internet cartoon[107] portrays someone calling their partner to bed. "I can't, this is important!"

"What?"

"Someone is wrong on the internet!"

So often we get caught up in righting the "wrongs" of the world with our opinion. But angry opinion is perhaps the most narrow and narcissistic form of our identity. We are more than our opinions, but not usually so on social media. Needing to be right is the self-centered opposite of being related.

Jung wrote "Were it not for the leaping and twinkling of the soul, man would rot away in his greatest passion, idleness." I have a great fondness for idleness, being given to meditation, leisurely conversations and long, slow films. It's an exquisite, fertile rot. Is it idleness to think the world must revolve around you and your smartphone? Perhaps. Or perhaps it feels empowering to those stuck in their cubicles or living rooms, to press the walls of their womb and have the world delivered to them for a fee. But to me it seems a self-centered rot, helpful for some, but like Ozu's pachinko parlors, a cause for sadness, not exultation. A sign of decay, not advancement.

The woman who cuts my hair regaled me with stories of millennials approaching her with ideas for scheduling apps. Some already schedule via Facebook Messenger. "They don't want to pick up the phone and call!" One even wanted to put her in an on-call truck to bring her services directly to those in need, all with the touch of a smartphone app. "It's the way of the future!" he said.

"Yeah, maybe you could cut his virtual avatar's hair while you're at it."

Others told her that in the future, hair styling would be done by robots. "How's that supposed to make me feel? And how are you going to get a robot to be as detailed and careful as me?" she asked. *How are you going to get a robot to have a conversation and relationship like the one I'm having right now*, I wondered to myself. *I mean, that's what keeps me coming back, to be honest.*

The urge to make the world more "convenient" for the self is a move towards self-centeredness, and away from interdependence with other living beings. Perhaps we love our apps and will love our robotic creations – but could they ever love us back? The less we find love in the world, the less loving we will be; the more self-centered; the more dissatisfied and lost.

I don't think these young people are trying to be self-centered or de-emphasize people, *per se*. They're just trying to hustle. But the drive to hustle sometimes out-hustles our better angels. We forget that the "leaping and twinkling" of our souls is sparked by other souls, in inspiration, companionship, and warmth.

Social media is not just a medium. It is a new religion. The Tweet is our Call to Prayers. We thumb our Phones like Rosaries. Food Porn is our Communion and our Offering to the Cloud. The Status Update is our Sermon on the Mount. The Selfie our personal Anointment and Beatification. Facebook Messenger is our Messiah. The Apple Store is our modern Cathedral, our Silicon Sanctuary. New Emoji are released to the fanfare of a new Pope. But is social media the temple of the self, the shrine of personality, or is it what its supporters say it is: the best chance for humanity to come together, the best possibility for us to transcend self-centeredness?

A year after she told me Snapchat is an empathy engine, my patient had a relationship crisis. She felt awful that she hadn't truly understood her boyfriend. I looked at her and nodded sympathetically, harking back to her earlier words. "Relationships are the real empathy engine."

Evidence suggests that social media, on the other hand, is largely an engine for narcissism. Facebook, Snapchat, Twitter and Instagram surface the problem of belonging and relationship, but they don't solve it. They may in fact take us farther afield. In *Reclaiming Conversation*, MIT sociologist and media psychologist Sherry Turkle highlights the damage our devices and apps are doing to conversation. But the ultimate aim of conversation is relationship; and the highest aim of relationship is love. Narcissism is the opposite of belonging. Belonging is the opposite of suffering. Ironically, the "tool" that is supposed to help us belong might be taking us away from belonging, and towards isolation and suffering.

Perhaps social media is sometimes a tool – but as I wrote earlier, you wouldn't use a screwdriver to change a light bulb. By distracting ourselves in the narcissist's garden, by losing ourselves in the bardo of self-promotion, we may be risking empathy, communion, relationship and love.

All that being said, most people on social media are not narcissists. They are working out their identities and finding their way to some form of connection. But there are dangers in working out identity online. My firm belief is that many of us are in some form of identity crisis. We are still in the early stages of understanding ourselves and who we are to each other, online and off. Can we learn to trust each other, or even to love? Do we need to be self-centered, to survive? Or is survival found in transcendence of self-centeredness?

I vote for transcendence. Let's Hanoi narcissism with compassion and wisdom. Let's heal the mistrust of our nations' traumas with commitment to warm relationship in the real world. Along the way, we have to learn, teach and experience empathy and compassion, the opposites of narcissism.

Unfortunately, social media seems best at broadcasting evidence of empathic failure and narcissism. We are often submerged by the needs of a troubled world. Those hurt by empathic failures can find it hard to repair those wounds online. Only real world relationships can provide compassion, build trust, and heal wounds in divisive times. And those seem harder to come by. The social media solution worsens the problem.

Relationships, including therapy, can work because they can set off an empathic chain reaction. The friend or therapist's empathic concern helps us feel understood and cared about, and helps us understand ourselves, healing the empathic failures of the past. With the practices of self-compassion and compassion cultivation, our inner world moves towards healing as well. We can become more compassionate to ourselves and others. Compassion is a learnable – and desirable – trait. When your mind is healed, it heals two minds. And when they're healed, they heal two minds. And so on, and so on, and so on…

The buck stops here, in your heart. Love is the only thing that's changed me, held me in difficult days. Sometimes I feel wounded by the world, injured and looking for the nearest rock to crawl under. When the world seems difficult, when I'm beset by the self-centered, when ghosts of the past trigger anger, resentment, fear and mistrust, I return to my meditation cushion, and repeat the metta phrases, over and over, trying to connect my mind and heart.

May I be filled with lovingkindness,
May I be well.
May I be peaceful and at ease,
May I be happy.

It's a journey. But it gets better.

Social Media and the American Identity Crisis

S ocial Media is Identity Media. We assert ourselves online, create and express our identities and personalities, and worry about acceptance. We worry about how we're viewed by others, and we become both curious about others and – let's face it – annoyed by them. The more time college-aged sample groups spent on social media, the more they developed depressive symptoms and became dissatisfied with themselves and others.

Social media is a new culture, and I believe we go through culture shock when we migrate online. Traditionally, the culture shock of migration has these five stages:

1. The honeymoon stage
2. The judgment/frustration/disillusionment stage
3. Transition/Adjustment stage
4. Acceptance stage
5. Repeat stages 2-4 as needed

Social media culture shock has similar stages.

1. Curiosity, exploration, experimentation, exuberance
2. Ambivalence, dissatisfaction
3. Adjustment, adaptation, and resignation to the limitations of the environment
4. Exit/deactivation or logout
5. Repeat stages 1-4 as needed

It's like this with all ideas, isn't it? Love and curiosity, obsession, love/hate, dissatisfaction, understanding the idea's full effects, then deciding what to do with it? Technology is our current fascinoma. But instead of making conscious decisions about it, we seem to have been overrun by it, and we are running away with ourselves in pursuit of this ultimate prophet of the "gospel of stuff." But we are still early in understanding what technology means for human consciousness, and who we are or can be in relation to it.

The life cycle of Facebook engagement for me went from curiosity to exuberant engagement, to ambivalence and frustration, to brief periods of abstinence, to my final adaptation: deactivation and exit. I still allow myself Facebook pages for my writing, but I have no personal page. I still lightly engage with Twitter – I appreciate being able to search the much broader range of people with a hashtag query. But I still generally avoid scrolling through the Twitter home feed. Too distracting and random. But at least on Twitter, the illusion of relationship, the bardo of presumed relationship, is not as cloying and frustrating as Facebook. Facebook is the biggest social network precisely because it offers a simulation of belonging that works for some. Facebook works well enough (or is addictive enough) to keep 1.2 billion users coming back to the site every day as of this writing. My subjective sense is that many of these people are also ambivalent. Facebook holds some utility, so they shrug off their dissatisfactions and keep scrolling. Or they've found some adaptation, such as hiding some or all of their "friends," to keep their newsfeed as low stress as possible. A teenager told me "no one I know scrolls through the newsfeed." Wise, perhaps. But those adaptations were never satisfactory to me. If I choose to friend you, I thought, I have some obligation to hear you out, even if it dissatisfies me. I only hid one person; she used the status box to live-update her life, almost moment-by-moment. I still feel badly about that.

But eventually Facebook became too much, and I had to quit. Only now do I realize that my difficulty with Facebook could be understood as an identity crisis. I have high ideals, and put a premium on inclusive, positive, productive dialogue. Facebook exposed me to the "undertow," both within myself and between us, in the online relational sphere. My own undertow involved the garden-variety narcissism of our daily lives. We all have narcissistic elements. As world-renowned psychoanalyst Glen Gabbard (author of the upcoming book *Narcissism and Its Discontents: Diagnostic and Treatment Dilemmas with Narcissistic Patients*, due out in April, 2018) said at the 2017 American Psychiatric Association Annual Meeting, the distinction between healthy and pathological narcissism is poorly defined and understood. I reassured myself by scoring a "5" on Dr. Craig Malkin's Narcissism Test (found in his 2016 book *Rethinking Narcissism: The Secret to Recognizing and Coping with Narcissists)*, putting me smack dab in the middle of healthy narcissism – but I know these traits are malleable. Situations, such as the Facebook experience, can push narcissistic scores up. In retrospect, this was a frustrating part of my time on Facebook. I just didn't like what my mind was doing when it was there. The bardo amplified the ego, without enough connection, validation or support. Facebook doesn't have the elements of the real world that can work to deconstruct and ameliorate narcissism. Specifically, relationships grounded in embodied, physical presence.

Social media is too much "you" and not enough glue.

I was also frustrated on a subtler level. My inherent wish to be on good terms with people, return their attention with my own, was blocked. I am a bit of an amoeba, taking up whatever I come in contact with. I absorbed something of every person's update, and part of me set to wrestling with it. If I scrolled past, I felt deflated. If I couldn't find a way to soothe their distress, I was frustrated. If they were angry, I had the growing sense that I could do nothing to help them across a screen. I cared, perhaps too much, about helping people, connecting, and belonging. Perhaps I didn't have enough acceptance, detachment or the right kind of empathy for the medium. For me, the medium led to erosion of my social senses and my social being.

I also felt envy, which was deeply distressing. I guess I have to thank Facebook for making me aware of my envy, which was largely hidden from my view until I spent time in the bardo. I felt depressed, submerged and overwhelmed by the world's problems: every explosion (sometimes literal) of the strange picture show in which we live. I got tangled in and attached to my opinions, and frustrated by the opinions of others, as they came buckshot, frequently irate and inaccurate. Personally, I needed space from that, just to feel a little more sane. Social media can be crazy-making.

I am "two spirited," like most of us. (Apologies to the Native American and transgender communities for borrowing this term – more on the evolution of this model in Appendix 2.) There is a part of me, the narcissistic, little "s" self spirit, concerned with self-protection, narrow identity, and meeting my own personal needs that is in conflict and dialogue with a transcendent spirit, that is selfless, altruistic, all-inclusive and more deeply loving. Or maybe just beyond it all altogether. My psychiatry residency mentor, Seymour Boorstein, once asked me what my purpose was in life. I thought about it for some time, until it came, during meditation. *"To love more deeply and see more clearly."* That came from my transcendent spirit. The rest is, ultimately, just chatter.

But important chatter. Identity is meaningful and necessary. To deny identity would be to not recognize my own skin or history. It would feel like giving up to the forces that have marginalized me and tried to make me invisible. It would be an empathic failure to myself. Identity is nature, nurture and an act of will based on our personal situation and goals. And still, there is something beyond all those things. Fuller identity comes in dialogue between transcendence and self-centeredness. We all have to work that out ourselves, in whatever way seems best.

My identity was in crisis on social media. In a similar way, the country (and even the world) as a whole is having an identity crisis right now. We haven't worked out the connection between our transcendent ideals as citizens of our nation and world and our personal interests. We haven't worked out who we are in relation to each other. We are in culture shock between self-centered and transcendent cultures, within and between us all. I'll use race as an example.

Many people of color in the U.S., especially my Black brothers and sisters, have developed powerful and resilient responses to racism. Very often, these responses take us to a place beyond self-centeredness, as we have to navigate varied terrains of race and culture in our daily lives. Sometimes, we even develop identities, perspectives and willpower that are powerful antidotes to the systemic and interpersonal problems we see.

I'm not suggesting that all people of color are selfless altruists, but at the very least, many do have a group identity and consciousness that is bigger than self. Those that do are #Woke. What takes white people out of their self-centeredness? Thankfully, many whites do strive to overcome narrow racial interest. But if all human beings have the potential for self-centeredness, what happens when a white person develops in a self-centered way? In subtle and significant ways, their self-centeredness gets validated by society, the media, and their local communities. Some of them find it harder to rise above their narrow self-interest or group affiliation to reach towards transcendence. They feel threatened and angered by any threats to their position. They begin to think in ways and hold opinions that support their need for dominance. When you're in the majority, that causes problems for minorities. For example, how else can we explain the rise in white resentment and racist and anti-government groups during Barack Obama's presidency, documented by the Southern Poverty Law Center? This was the first time that these whites felt particularly invalidated by "the system." They fought back, and others jumped on the bandwagon as well. Not to say that all Trump voters resented President Obama – some of them voted for him, not once but twice. But certainly candidate Trump stoked the anti-government, anti-media, anti-Muslim, anti-minority, anti-immigrant feelings that were latent and not fully articulated in much of the population before he took the stage. He validated a particular kind of white voter, and made them feel they were under siege, that they needed to "take the country back." Is that self-centered or identity driven? Those voters will have to judge their own minds and hearts. I could be wrong. I haven't spoken to many of them personally. I mean, come on, I live in one of the bluest (most Democratic) cities in the nation. The few I have spoken with are not "racists" outright, they may have voted their economic or foreign policy interests, or against Secretary Clinton, but they were certainly willing to give a pass to some very...*unusual* behavior and language by Mr. Trump. And I certainly was witness to white voter rage on the campaign trail. "Fake news" on social media only solidified their concepts of being under siege, especially by Hillary Clinton and her team. Candidate Trump was their "hero," and she was their "villain." For those in the other camp, it was the reverse. The amplification of anger online seems to have eroded and overwhelmed our collective reasoning capacity. Social media became "push button media," pushing all our buttons, but not soothing us or bringing us together. Identity under siege is identity in crisis.

But now that Donald Trump is president, can he be plied into becoming the president of all the people? Can he transcend the siege of self-centeredness? It's a tough sell, with a lot of evidence to the contrary. But perhaps he's Saul on the road to Damascus, after all. I'm just not sure if his conversion will happen in this lifetime or in a future life, though.

Sometimes love picks the toughest nuts to crack.

There, I said it. We all have to be love's nutcrackers. The best way to do that is to be yourself, I think. Work out your own two spirited solution. So there can be a solution. If we stay completely stuck in self-centeredness, and forget to listen, if we forget to empathize with and have compassion for each other and ourselves, our transcendent ideals will be lost. Social media can end up feeding narrow identity and self-centeredness. Transcendence gets lost. We lose ourselves, we can be lost at sea in the sea change.

The sea change and siege of identity is part of our accelerated, amped up relational intensity. Here we find the battle between belonging and disconnection. Those feeling disconnected, on either side of the political spectrum, invariably seem bound by a rejection complex. (There's another RC for you. See Appendix 3 for more details.) They feel rejected, invalidated, disempowered and even ostracized by the other side, and thus reject in turn. We're left with a hysteria of dueling accusations, with each side marshaling evidence and grievances. What's lost is not only a sense of transcendence, but the possibility of belonging, empathy and connection. When we're stuck in the rejection complex, our mirror neurons are undoubtedly suppressed; we can't empathize with the ones we perceive as rejecting or even oppressing us. We reject them, and the vicious circle is complete. Social media amplifies the rejection complex. Our identities become consumed with the rejected, pinioned and opinionated self-spirit, and transcendence is harder to conceive. When will our transcendent ideals of connection, belonging and character be amplified? I doubt we'll connect to them online, where our identities stay superficial, and we are only superficially related.

The self is contingent and contextual. What we do changes us. Creates us. Where and how we live changes us. Who we commune with changes us. Using technology and social media changes us. What we think about, how we think about ourselves, changes us. Anyone sensitive to these changes, anyone who questions who they are in relation to technology, apps and other people in this world we share is by definition in some form of identity crisis. (Anyone who isn't sensitive or doesn't question has the opposite problem: an insanity of certainty.) Sometimes these crises are barely perceptible. We feel ambivalence about our posts or the posts of others. We feel uncertain – or worse, frustrated, angry or in despair – about the state of humanity or human relations as presented on the evening news or our newsfeed. The identity crisis is both communal and personal. Mason, in Richard Linklater's *Boyhood* (2014), put it this way.

> I finally figured it out. It's like when they realized it was gonna be too expensive to actually build cyborgs and robots. I mean, the costs of that were impossible. They decided to just let humans turn themselves into robots. That's what's going on right

now. I mean, why not? They're billions of us just laying around, not really doing anything. We don't cost anything. We're even pretty good at self-maintenance and reproducing constantly. And as it turns out, we're already biologically programmed for our little cyborg upgrades. I read this thing the other day about how when you hear that ding on your inbox, you get like a dopamine rush in your brain. It's like we're being chemically rewarded for allowing ourselves to be brainwashed. How evil is that? We're fucked.

Mason has a somewhat paranoid insight into the ways the self is being altered. He expresses a modern identity crisis by telling a story about how devices and apps will change the essence of being human, and not in the hopeful direction that Alexander Bard and other cyberevangelists claim. Right now it seems like Mason's brand of dissent and skepticism is a minority viewpoint. Perhaps cyberevangelism is also a hyperoxygenated minority viewpoint as well. Perhaps most of us are just kind of swimming along in the sea change, using what seems cool, until it becomes a pain. The danger is that we accept the sea change for our new normal, and lose our human story in the rising tide. It is telling that some early enthusiasts and experts, like Jaron Lanier and Sherry Turkle, have come full circle to ambivalence and even critique of the technologies that they helped pioneer and chart. If it takes the rest of us 30 years of intense study and thoughtfulness to come around, what happens to society in the meantime?

We are creating an incredibly connected world in which we can hear many stories and express many possibilities. Nearly a third of the world's population has taken to Facebook and other social networks. Social networks have become an almost *de facto* condition of modern life in short order. It's important that we ask questions. We have to learn to choose our stories, and not get lost. I would argue that our world seems deeply connected in material ways, but psychologically and spiritually, we are still connected only superficially. What results from superficial connection, from superficial relationship, is intense reaction and polarization, as factions try to dominate and even decimate each other through the use of power, online and off, in a struggle not just to be heard, but to "win." What results is our current crisis in connection, which is at heart an identity crisis. Who are we in relation to each other? Who would we like to be? Who can we be, given the limitations of our environment? How can we transform our environments to allow us to become the people we'd like to be, and have the society we'd like to have? What kind of society *would* we like to have? Given what we know of the human need for relationship, and the necessity of relationship for happiness, what will relating through screens bring us? These are major, unresolved questions in the American and global psyche.

The Buddha was an incredible teacher, and his transcendent teachings have stood the test of time. But the Buddha himself was contingent and contextual. His life depended on the circumstances of his birth, his family, his surroundings, his history and his times. He embodied a powerful response to the conditions that faced him. He worked out a transcendent solution to his human predicament. He shed self-centeredness completely. He used his agency, discipline, self-awareness and compassionate intentions to transform his life and mind and become awakened, and then help others. He chose his story.

What stories will we choose?

If we are all in culture shock, if we are having personal, national and global identity crises, we have to fight self-centered culture with our integrated two spirits. And in the process, *create culture*. Nietzsche wrote "Buddhism is a religion for the end and fatigue of civilizations." Our culture shock and identity crises are certainly markers of civilization fatigue. We have need for deconstructing our suffering, renewing ourselves and starting again.

The American story, the human story, the story of our values and our spirit of transcendence, are just getting started. We've only just begun.

Happy Birthday. You Are Nothing.

I got my birthday present a couple of days late in May, 2017. Two days after my 50th, 10 years after that five-month odyssey across Asia, I collapsed in tears while meditating, or trying to meditate, terrified and alone.

My mind had been wandering, across the past, present, and hoped for future. I was noticing myself wander, getting caught up in some reaction or story, and then telling myself I was just reacting. What was the problem? What was under my skin? Why couldn't I sit still? Was I triggered? Was it this person or that, who had given me a hard ride in the past? Was it white supremacy, keeping me from my goals, putting a kink in my soul? Was this all a test, pressure to keep me working harder and achieving more? Was there a taskmaster, many taskmasters, many projects, many projectors?

Then it hit me.

I was just reacting to the world.

And the world, or my neck of the woods at least, was reacting to me.

I was nothing but a reaction.

I'd never felt more empty, alone and desperate in my life. Again and again I collapsed in tears and pain, lying on the floor to ease my physical and mental anguish.

If I am nothing but a reaction, have I done anything at all? Did I even write this book? My hands were on the keyboard, but where was the typist?

What was the sound of one man chatting?

I was nothing. I am nothing. I have nothing. There's nothing in me. I'm a shell with nothing inside.

Anybody, anything, anywhere, could do anything to me.

But wait, if I was nothing, was everyone else nothing as well?

I had no idea.

Maybe some people or beings have selves, and it's just me that's this weird reaction to all of them.

But wait – if I was just reacting – my reactions have changed over the years to my circumstances. I've gotten more mature and more helpful, I'm hopefully a better friend…so who exactly has gotten better, if I'm just a reaction? All those other beings who were actual people? All those unseen souls who have selves and surround me, beyond the visible world?

But then again, what if everything is compounded – just like the Buddha said? I mean, it always made sense to me, that whole interdependence thing. I could logically see how everything was made of parts, dependent on other parts. But it never struck me how terrifying this actually was. If everything was made of parts, and the parts were made of parts, and those parts were made of parts, and all the parts just react to the other parts, and everything just kind of leans on everything else…[108]

It meant that whatever "I" was, total emptiness, total reaction, or some process that gradually modulated my reactions to have some passing semblance at maturity…whatever "I" was… I was on the hook. Oh boy. I really had to master those reactions, or put a spin on them, or something, or else…well, something bad could happen.

What, you mean we all have responsibility? Maybe even to shape each other, whatever we are? Or that we could somehow be harming somebody else, if we're not "right" by them in some way?

Oh yeah, the Golden Rule. Relationship. Friendship. I'm soooo smart.

I got nothing.

Maybe I should just hide. Maybe everybody else knew this, and they were just putting on an act until I got it. Maybe no one's really suffering, it's just a strange movie or virtual reality that "I" am in.

I was in a new country again. I'd immigrated from India when I was a baby, I'd lived on Facebook for a while, and now I was here.

What were those stages of culture shock? In this case:

1. Being reduced to a reactionary point, shattered to tears.
2. Trying to make sense of it.
3. Keep saying to myself "How does this change anything?" and "You're so stupid."
4. Wait – my job is to help people with their reactions – so maybe "I" can help me with my own.
5. Adaptation
6. Survival.
7. Realizing I may have to repeat steps 1-5 again and again, and #6 was just temporary. I did just turn 50 after all.
8. Reconstruction of my mind, in the direction of enlightenment. According to Buddhists, the ultimate goal is the cessation of suffering through complete enlightenment, extinguishing rebirths in this world of suffering. Enlightenment is transcendence of all traces of self-centeredness.

"One who achieves the way
Will be freed from the duality of birth and death."

That pearl is 2500 years old, the Metta Sutra given earlier in this book. Makes you think about how stupid most of what we considered "advanced" really is. Facebook isn't even the half of it.

This experience could either break me or make me. If I told anyone, they could think I was just a "nut job" after all. They might think "well, if he thinks he's nothing, then I can do anything I want to him or to anyone else, because I'm somebody." This knowledge made me feel more responsible. Maybe it would drive some to sociopathy and irresponsibility.

And that was different from the world as it is…how exactly?

I mean, any idea that you put your will behind could cause problems.

Then there was that Twilight Zone episode where people just kept whispering some "secret" to each other, and each time a new person heard it, they went cuckoo. Or maybe not being aware of this knowledge makes you really cuckoo. To paraphrase Buddhist teacher Jack Kornfield, "unless we're perfectly enlightened, we're all at least a little mentally ill."

I am not sure what "perfect enlightenment" looks like. All I could believe in was my will at this moment. If there was free will at all….well even if there isn't, it seems like a good thing to believe in.

Here's to responsibility for a better world, in whatever small way I might contribute. I could put my will behind that, even more solidly than before. Maybe help people with their reactions, even more solidly than before.

Gotta really work that Eightfold Path, man…

Is this book even that important? Probably not, only time would tell.

Maybe the book isn't important, but the experiences were. So thanks, whoever you are, if anyone's out there or in here, anyway.

I remembered the words of Nisargadatta Maharaj, posted in a small hut at Spirit Rock Meditation Center in Marin. "Wisdom says I am nothing. Love says I am everything. Between these two, my life flows."

Maybe this was the first really wise experience I'd ever had. I'd had some experiences of deep and powerful love and oneness. Now perhaps my life and mind could flow between these experiences, still reaching for transcendence.

It's good when you're validated by someone who seems pretty advanced, just for being just a floating bubble of consciousness, an event, not an entity at all. At least the event of life was currently alright for me. It wasn't for a lot of other people. All that I needed to do was to help them with their events, as they were happening. Maybe even participate in their event, so we could all have an event together. That sounded fun.

Consciousness is an event, not an entity. Does the event have an event planner, or does the event plan itself?

In any event, pun intended, I was pretty sure I wouldn't be sending out invites for this particular "I am nothing" event on Facebook, though. I mean, who would come?

The place would be totally empty.

A grin. It was 9:42 am. I had to go work out. Then I had to talk to my mom. Then I wanted to go to some movies this weekend. *Colossal,* followed by *Risk.*

Whatever this event was, it had a sense of humor. And a bit of neurosis. Just like me. The guy with the Buddha face, but not quite Buddha through and through.

Reality is Compounded. Reality is Co-created. RC.

Colossally Risky, everything just leaning on everything else, like a house of cards. Or maybe Colossally Resistant, each mind just clinging to itself, at the bottom of it all, afraid of being alone, afraid of what it meant to be alone in one's head, reacting to other minds out of fear and insecurity, self-centered out of strategy and delusion, but longing for something better. No wonder Facebook is so popular. Our minds long to solidify the self, and also to go beyond it.

But wait…what is a mind anyway?

Mind Creation, the Selfless Amygdala, and the United, Nondual Mind

Between stimulus and response there is a space. In that space is the freedom to choose our response. In our response lies our growth and our freedom.

— Victor Frankl

After a movie, dinner, a couple of beers, and a nice deep sleep, I came back to my usual self, but perhaps a bit more settled. As I lay awake in bed, the Sunday of Memorial Day weekend, 2017, I felt a kind of small pop, somewhere near the base of my brain. My first thought was, "Oh, another neuron in my amygdala just let go."

I don't know if it was my amygdala, a chakra or my imagination, but it made sense.

We are, at our best, more than just an knee-jerk reaction to the world. We are at our worst when we are just reacting to each other, and when we fortify our reactions, snap judgments and knee-jerk reflexes into beliefs, convictions and ideologies that serve to protect our selfish ego and devalue others. Our reactions can come from a sense of separateness and fear-based adversariality, instead of the knowledge and experience of interdependence and connection. We are at our best when understanding and helping each other and ourselves with caring responses, when we are letting go of selfishness and cultivating love. At the very least, when our responses are guided by relationship, we can move towards peace.

At the core of our being, somewhere within that supersensitive, highly reactive primitive survival brain of the limbic system located deep within our temporal lobes, is sensation and reaction. Whatever we sense, within or without, drives our reactions. What we do with our sensations is our mind. Therefore, our inner life is key to our maturity and transformation. Our inner life is key to our response, as opposed to reaction. We can move from jittery *sensation and reaction* towards *perception and response*, by strengthening our inner life. Our inner life is the basis for our mind. The mind and the self are contingent, contextual, changing and an act of continuous co-creation. Our inner life is our most precious co-creation. Some might call it *soul*.

Inner life is how you experience, make sense of, and relate to yourself, other beings, and all that you perceive. Maturity is basically how you hold that experience. People with no inner life, a distressing inner life or a self-centered inner life might externalize instead, and can take it out on themselves or others, or get attached to superficial external ego comforts like money, status, power or possessions. Our inner life goes hand-in-glove with the creation and expression of identity, which affects our relationships and behavior in the world. The danger of modern life, then, lies in the loss or erosion of inner life, and the creation of an inner world that devalues other people, beings and the natural world. From acts of terror committed by people with a distressing, adversarial perception of the world and themselves as actors in that world, to those of us who outsource our inner life to gadgets and apps – from the quantified self movement to social media to artificial intelligence – there are many ways we can lose inner life to ideology and superficial externalization. Of course, technology and apps can be an adjunct and stimulus for inner life as well, but only if we process and think about them. Writing this book about social media and my life has certainly helped me develop a much richer inner life, come to terms with many of the seeds of my consciousness, relate to myself and others on a deeper level, and feel more at peace in this world of suffering.

Logan (@plaguelovers) said it best in a tweet.

Logan
@PlagueLovers

When you don't need to interface with your illuminated rectangle on your commute because of your rich inner life

RETWEETS   LIKES
4,397   10,146

I believe the essence of mind creation comes down to making more synaptic connections. The more cortical relationships you have (meaning synaptic connections in your cerebral cortex – especially, for purposes of spiritual growth, in the areas responsible for mindfulness and compassion), the less the limbic system can grab control and send us into greed, hatred or self-centeredness, the three poisons of Buddhism. How do you make more cortical relationships? Here's my sense of it.

1. Notice other people; relate to them, think about them and their needs, as well as your own.
2. Care for yourself and others.
3. Cultivate love.
4. Keep creating yourself, while letting go of self-centeredness, greed and hatred.

Our inner life, of heart and mind, is our most important technology. I often meet tech workers in San Francisco. After they tell me what they do, I tap my head and say, "I work with the original software and hardware." It's good for a laugh. But what's in our noggins is infinitely more complex and powerful than technology. I feel like I've barely scratched the surface of heart/mind power, in this writing and in my life. After all this, I'm still a beginner. Transforming our noodle is the most important work we have before us. Who knows, maybe even the limbic system itself can be transformed. Maybe a selfless limbic system is at the center of true altruism, of Buddhahood. Besides, the duality of "limbic system and cortex" is another duality to be transcended. They work in concert and conflict, after all, each putting some pressure on the other, until they are fully united. An early goal might be to harmonize them. The most goal directed, creative and talented people (such as jazz musicians) have, I think, extraordinarily well worked-out relationships between impulse generation and cortical modulation, at least in the direction of their talent.

The problem of goal direction might become excessive attachment to those goals. It goes without saying, we must choose our goals wisely. Reflecting over the years on my 50th birthday, I think I have followed my goal of being of service to others while earning a living, and my purpose of "loving more deeply and seeing more clearly." But most importantly, life is about having feels, and then deciding what to do with them. I hope I can continue doing my best to follow the tugs of my heart, and not all the tugs on my attention, or those pesky and sometimes petty subtle reactions of moment-to-moment awareness. As the Third Noble Truth states, "there is a goal, the cessation of suffering."

Maybe the greatest potential of artificial intelligence and virtual reality systems will be to assist human beings in the creation of heart/mind, and the generation of the selfless amygdala, unified with a selfless cortex. Maybe that's the next generation of therapy aimed at relieving the suffering of self-centeredness. If so, the best psychiatrists, psychologists, neuroscientists, sociologists, technologists, Buddhists, other spiritual leaders, other observers of human character, artists –

and comedians, just because – could join efforts. If reality doesn't make us all Buddhas, and take us beyond suffering, maybe technology joined with human effort can. Perhaps technology could increase compassion and wisdom, or at least help us interact better. For example, augmented reality assist-glasses for kids with autism help them better interpret facial emotions. But virtual reality could be a technological form of spiritual bypass, or bypassing emotional difficulties with a patch that takes us farther from their real resolution. And VR leaves out the most important aspect of reality – actual relationships with real people. No matter how you slice it, when you put on the headset, you're tuning out the world. How will that change you, your experience and the experience of those whom you're tuning out? VR environments have as much or more potential to corrupt the essence of being human as positively transform it.

For myself, I would rather meet more people, learn from them, and make more relationships than get involved with that possibility. (Not that anyone's asking.) I would rather help people with their suffering. My psychiatrist's office is where I feel most like myself. My patients come first. Helping them understand themselves and helping them get to where they want to be in life have been the most powerful and transformative influences on my life, in addition to Buddhism, my own therapy, my own relationships, writing, traveling, taking photos, going to film festivals, and being a member of the Asian American and other communities. Translating my knowledge and experience into the compassion and wisdom required to help other people, and learning from them along the way – well, it doesn't get any better than that. My patients, my mother, my friends, all the people who have ever taught me anything, and are still teaching me – create and true me. People become people through other people, indeed. The world is doing a pretty good job all by itself at nudging me towards kindness and compassion, and overcoming self-centeredness. I don't need to sign up for the virtual version of reality anytime soon, thank you very much.

In Appendix 4 is a work-in-progress diagram of the mind. At the center is "sensation and reaction." Everything else is what I can think of as important in the inner life and mind, derived from psychiatry and my own personal experience. On the outer rim are some diagnostic categories and the possibility of transcendence. Depending on one's inner world and the world one faces, one could end up experiencing those symptoms, or possibly moving towards transcendence, or beyond self-centeredness, greed and hatred. Sometimes, I view psychiatric symptoms as the expression of spiritual struggle: our transcendent spirit challenged by the demands of our difficult world, and our self spirit challenged by the demands of transcendence. I am sure I've missed things, so check back on my websites facebuddha.co and ravichandramd.com (or bit.ly/messydiagram) for updated or simplified versions as they come up. If you have suggestions, leave a comment on my guestbook. I'm sure this is not a finished product. Just something to think about.

The diagram is a bit of a forest, so I'll reduce it to a few important leaves. I think the most important parts of this mess of a figure are the circles "Understanding oneself and others; caring," "Being understood," and "Belonging," in bold. Perceive and respond to those, and you'll do fine.

As the days and weeks rolled on, a deeper peace flowed into my life. Every conversation and interaction defused the reactive, isolated, fearful core and brought me deeper into relationship. I was not simply "nothing but a reaction," I existed in the interplay between my inner world and others, perceiving and responding with intention. Mindfulness and compassion stabilized the experience. My will carried me. Emotions, sometimes intense emotions arose. They would take me by surprise and take me out for a spin. But I returned to my meditation cushion, and did my best not to turn the micro-emotions into a story about the world and other people, but used them to understand myself and my internal world better. I rested in awareness and analysis of reactions, defusing but also "making love" to them, trying to sing them into the fold of love, acceptance and ease. This precious mix of holding on and letting go, ambition and contentedness, activating anxiety and soothing it, making demands and making space for the demands of others, will find its own way, in its own time.

I close this writing with a bow of appreciation to the Buddha, Dharma and Sangha. I bow to that three rupee Buddha on my humble cluttered altar, the Buddha my mother bought 65 years ago as she was starting medical school, attracted to and soothed by his gentle radiance. She's carried that spirit, the Buddha spirit, with her throughout her life. I texted her that I followed her, and we both followed the Buddha. She texted back, simply, "follow your heart." I couldn't ask for a better teacher.

Follow your heart. Strive on diligently. Stay humble and stay related. Be a lamp unto yourselves. Ask for help when you need it. Offer help. Never give up.

Post www.facebuddha.co, and go.

Sorry, Thank You, I Love You

Dear Friends, Brothers and Sisters, Mothers and Fathers in all directions:

I think in a previous life, or even in this life not too long ago, I had some good qualities, but possibly less of an inner life. I may have caused harm to you by acting in a self-centered way, or by not understanding your needs well enough. Thank you for being patient with me, if you were. I was probably doing the best I could in those circumstances, but I can understand if you didn't see it that way. In my defense, I can only say that my soul was always striving for a goal. Ultimately, I think that goal includes all of us.

Please accept my apologies, and I'll try to do better. Thank you for teaching me. May love prevail in all the worlds. May all beings be free from suffering and the causes of suffering.

Striving on diligently,

Ravi

Coda: A Special Blessing from the Very God of Hot Air, and the Great Gaslight

There's a wise Buddhist saying. Never get attached to your experiences, good or bad. A few nights after my experience of being "nothing," a few nights after finishing almost all of this book, I awoke in the middle of a deep sleep. My consciousness was again tight, like I'd again evoked ire or jealousy somewhere, somehow. When I'm dealing with someone who's very self-centered, it can jam up my thinking, block my thoughts. This has been described by other therapists as well. I think of it as some kind of conflict between us, catching me in my mind. Is it me or them? Did I do something wrong? Maybe someone's still angry at me.

The air rippled hot and furious around me, pulsing against every inch of my skin. A man's voice said "you have no idea. You have no idea, Ravi."

I acquiesced for a moment, feeling guilt, remembering the long hard path behind me, and the difficulties along the way.

Then, I spoke back, calm but sure. "You're still blaming me. I'm still your scapegoat. That's your reaction. That's your reaction. Not my problem."

"I am a deity," he said, after a pause.

"So *you* think…" I replied, in my mind.

"Jealousy," the voice said, acknowledging my point.

I was sure it would go on like this for some time.

Consciousness has more than two spirits. They jostle like wrestlers sometimes. Sometimes they are adversaries. Sometimes they dance like

Sufi saints, in divine love with all creation. This particular spirit has been with me for many years. He plays god…and then a teacher. But he clearly has never read *Power in the Helping Professions*, in which Adolf Guggenbühl-Craig writes, "members of the 'ministering professions' can also do the greatest damage – harm caused directly by their very desire to help." Damage is done when the wish to maintain power or the wish to control overrides relationship built on humility, curiosity, love, mutual respect and kindness. I once heard this spirit in human form advise a friend to "never say you're sorry. It's a sign of weakness." This runs so counter to my values, and yet seems to still hold sway in some corner of my psyche. I'm not sure why yet.

I think it's because this spirit and others like him are Wizards of the Great Gaslight.* Together, they create a world that deceives us into believing that the way of the heart is foolish, weak or impractical. The same Great Gaslight pushes some into relationships of power and bias instead of empathy for people they don't want to understand. The Great Gaslight lures us away from transcendence and unity with its self-centered siren song of power, control, money, fame and possessions. We are being gaslighted into division, into devaluing living beings, the natural world and each other. Fake news is an obvious example of the Great Gaslight, a disinformation campaign designed to create an alternate reality, break down bonds of trust and fortify rage and power in human relationship.† Social media gaslights us into believing our story of relationship is only made better by online interaction.

---

*   *Gas Light* was a play and then a 1944 movie in which a husband tries to convince his wife and others into thinking she's insane by manipulating her environment and then insisting she's mistaken when she notices. The term gaslighting has been used since the 1960s to describe the ways an abuser can try to create a "reality distortion bubble" around his or her victim by forcefully insisting on their own facts and ways of thinking.

†   Filed under "You can't make this stuff up," as this book was going to press, Qatar accused the United Arab Emirates of hacking their social media and news websites to spread rumors of affection for Israel and Iran. This apparently played a role in Qatar's being cast as a pariah by its neighbors and the U.S. "It wasn't me, honest – my Facebook was hacked!" The truth is still murky, but how far are we from tweets – or fake tweets – leading to actual bombs?

Trust has eroded, despite or perhaps even because of social media and the internet. The Pew Center reports[109] that only 19% of millennials agree that "generally speaking, people can be trusted." This compares with 31-40% in older generations. Gen Xers started out high, with 36% answering affirmatively in 1990, but dipping to 20% by 1997 before rising again to 31% by 2012. The Baby Boomers, 20 years older, have been relatively stable during that time period, at around 40%. The Silent Generation, born between the first and second World Wars, have generally been in the mid-40% range and higher, with a dip below 40% in the late 80s rebounding by the mid-90s and another dip recently in 2012. Trust is a minority viewpoint no matter the generation, though the degree of mistrust varies. The motto of the 1960s was "don't trust anyone over 30." We have become an even less trusting and perhaps less trustworthy society since then. I believe we Americans are so untrusting precisely because we tend to emphasize individualism, competitiveness, socioeconomic status and power relations over other values.

But why are millennials so untrusting? There are clues here for our overall decline in trust. The Pew Center reports that "sociologists have theorized that people who feel vulnerable or disadvantaged for whatever reason find it riskier to trust because they're less well-fortified to deal with the consequences of misplaced trust."[110] When we feel vulnerable and unsafe, we feel mistrustful. Minorities and low-income adults have lower levels of social trust, because of all the problems they encounter from marginalization, stigmatization and devaluation, and there are more minorities amongst the millennials. Racial diversity and financial burdens including college debt have increased. Also, millennials have been exposed to more evidence of untrustworthiness at an age when they are prone to making generalizations about others. They've come of age post 9-11, in a time of terrorism, and the backlash to terrorism including racial profiling and hate crimes. Two unpopular wars have likely added to mistrust of politicians and institutions. Economic inequity and the 2008 Great Recession are certainly more cause for mistrust and vulnerability. There has also been a trend towards increasing self-centeredness among college-age students, as laid out by Jean Twenge and W. Keith Campbell in their research and in 2009's *The Narcissism Epidemic*. An environment of self-centeredness, enhanced by the rise of social media, likely degrades trust. The barrage of traumatic events spread virally through social media has been cataclysmic, underscoring vulnerability and heightening fear and mistrust. Correspondingly, in an environment of low trust, self-centeredness rises, as your "safety and survival" depend on advancing yourself over others, which only makes the situation worse. In her 2017 book *iGen*, Twenge reports that narcissism scores have fallen back to 1980s levels in the generation following the millennials, based on data from 2014, but along with a rise in depression and anxiety.

I think this is because college age students today are digital natives. They have been through all the early stages of "culture shock," and are now in identity crisis, about themselves and the world. Self-consciousness is up. Social comparison is up. They've seen enough of narcissism online and in the world to know it's not a virtue. Their narcissistic scores are down. But they still haven't worked out how to match their ideals (of equality and inclusion) with a world that still seems so opposed to those ideals. They are excited about technology, yet have mixed feelings about technology's Gaslight of money, power, fame and success. They feel unable to keep up or make it. The idea that you have to be a Mark Zuckerberg or Elon Musk to be successful in life is rather hard to square with being an ordinary human being, especially at 20. (Problems happen when we forget we are all ordinary.) If you didn't found your own startup in Junior High School, you're already behind, according to the Great Gaslight.

The internet is equal doses inspiration, information, entertainment, waste of time, traumatization, toxicity and displacement of real world interactions. The iGen has been given the full course of treatment. No wonder they're more depressed, anxious, lonely and suicidal, as detailed in Jean Twenge's *iGen*. If I were 18, I might feel at times submerged and overwhelmed by real and online worlds, my heart and soul at risk, unable to see a way through. The iGen may be digital natives, but they, and in fact all of us "living" online, are refugees, lured to flee the homeland of real world relationships that have always provided solace, warmth and personal growth, lured away by technological sirens that leave us adrift and longing, homeless and unmoored. Suffering. What heartens me is the optimism of the young people I interview for college admission. They want to find a way. Some of them are learning how to talk through differences. Perhaps they are growing wiser about social networks in a way that we don't understand or haven't yet studied, setting norms and creating culture. Perhaps social networks can evolve to solve the problems they created in the first place. But I remain a skeptic of the idea that online connection can help us really listen to each other, or deliver the compassion and relationship required to heal human suffering.

Trust is a minority viewpoint in the U.S., I think, because this country is as self-centered as it is. Living in it, we defend ourselves against the self-centeredness of others. On top of that, many among us are being gaslighted to believe that self-centered values are somehow "right," and that empathy and inclusion are unrealistic pipe dreams.

If social media and technology are tools, they are a double-edged sword. We must be wary of being gaslighted by the idea that the power they offer is greater than the power of the human heart. We have not yet invented a machine that loves, if that is even possible. Dr. George Vaillant was the longtime director of the Grant Study, one of the longest running studies of human development. Those who reported warmer, closer relationships were happiest in later life. In an interview with *The Atlantic*,[111] he reported his conclusion: "Happiness is love. Full Stop." In a world where relationships have become more superficial, and love harder to find, it's almost a foregone conclusion that we will find ourselves unhappy, lost, lonely, defensively self-centered, and suffering.

We will be more antagonistic, apathetic and mistrustful with one other, because antagonism, apathy and mistrust increase in the absence of love and relationship.

I'm sure that machines and artificial intelligence can strategize better, or at least more quickly, than many human minds. A quick thinking strategizer, though, is no more than a glorified limbic system, reacting rapidly to attain its goal. The machine world is powerful, but also limited. All its goals lie in the concrete material world. It's useful to have tools to address our human and global problems. But we risk being trapped in the concrete, no longer able to sense and attain the spiritual and transcendent. As I wrote in an earlier chapter, "the internet? Neti, neti."

We have designed social networks to help us connect, but obviously, that connection is only as good as the human hearts that use them. We must be wary of being boxed in by the technical ability to declare our opinions and identities and defame others, allowing ideology to trump relationship, as we send our avatars to battle each other in disembodied, disinhibited cyberspace. Cyberspace is far from being a "safe space." We may get better at taking down and blocking anti-social elements of society, but we must understand that their very existence is proof of our disconnectedness and the profound lack of the feeling of society itself for many citizens of our world. Including some of its current leaders. Any feeling of society obtained on the social network is by definition more superficial than our real world relationships. Perhaps the deficiencies of real world relationships, combined with our craving for connection drives us to social networks; but we can never truly "belong" online.

The race is on for artificial intelligence, self-driving cars, and autonomous systems. Our race to transform the human heart must outpace the race for outsourcing power to machines, of surrendering to the machine values of power and control. Or else we will gaslight ourselves out of our own transcendent potential. We will gaslight each other out of relationships built on love, respect and trust. We will gaslight ourselves out of being human.

Riff: Monk's Dream

June 30, 2017. I awake in the early night, abiding with calm. My mind is clear, and words appear. "I am mu…I am mu…" Mu, the lack of inherent independent existence, the quality of interdependence. I exist between all my relations, co-created by them all, and acting on them in turn. Nothing in and of myself, just this funny character who is somehow between everyone else. Yet also co-creating a space for himself and others, out of mind and heart, out of thin air and soul.

As the Heart Sutra says, "form is emptiness, and emptiness is form." I understand. I am empty of independent existence. We are empty of independent existence. We lean on each other. We make each other. We are made of each other. We are who happens to us, and what we make of that happening. People become people through other people. People become people through the earth and planets and stars; through all things, all other living beings. We make things, too, apps and phones and cars and guns. And then those things make us. What will we become, together, us and things, things and us? We must tend these possibilities, or they will upend us. Whatever our work in the world, we are working on ourselves, and on each other.

I am mu. We are mu. Shaman-artist-warriors of mu, shaman-artist-warriors of nonduality and love, connecting heaven and earth through our tree of life. Each of us connects the transcendent and earthly, transcendent and self spirits co-creating the tree of our lives. Mu, the lack of separate, independent existence, seems like love, to me. Between us, connecting us, within us, creating us. Togetherness. All love, all love, all love. Ananda. Bliss.

Thelonious Monk has been on my mind. 2017 is the centennial of his birth. *Monk's Dream* riffs in my mind, and I riff with the Monk.

What is the self? What is it not?
What is the self? What is it not?
The self is everything and nothing.
I am mu. (You too.)

What is the self? What is it not?
What is the self? What is it not?
The self is everything and nothing.
We are mu.

Holy cow. Holy cow. Holy cow, I see it now.
Emptiness is form. Emptiness is form.
Form is emptiness too.

What is the Self? Created.
What is the Self? Creating.
The Self is changing and it's change -
We are mu...

Good morning, world.

Thanks again, dear reader. If you remember one thing from this book, remember how important, precious, difficult, fragile, rewarding and necessary relationships are, and how easily and quickly we can devalue them and each other. Relatedness is the key to a good society, good world, and healthy inner life and mind. Let's help each other with all of the above.

Appendix 1:
Deactivate Facebook to Become Human Again

First published as an Op-Ed in the New York Daily News, *March 28, 2015*

Two months after deactivating my Facebook account, I feel human again. My mind isn't lassoed by the shares, opinions and ephemera of the crowd or needlessly distracted by an endless newsfeed.

Instead of checking my smartphone for notifications, I am paying more attention to the world around me. Instead of trying to create a facsimile of relatedness online, I am actively forging real relationships in conversation and shared presence. I feel more at ease and restful now, more appreciative of day-to-day life, and as I said, more human in the silences and spaces that have returned to fill the cluttered field where social media apps once held sway.

Selfhood requires a boundary, porous but manageable, and a physical and mental "room of one's own." Social media leaves us without this room by pressing the thoughts and personalities of others directly upon our synapses.

While it seems to bring together people who are distant, relying on it furthers our physical separation and the true communion of embodied, face-to-face relationship. Simultaneously, even when we are physically with each other, social media in the background shaves away our ability to be truly present.

For years, I had reveled in the ability to communicate with friends around the world, enjoyed the spread of happy events, and was hopeful about the power of social media to create positive social change. Hashtag rendezvous and Facebook post-abouts seemed to be effective ways for my geographically disparate and politically conscious community to gather force and spread ideas.

That lofty ideal came crashing down when I found myself disagreeing with my online friends. The false sense of cohesion that Facebook offered disappeared, and I felt that in cyberspace, people would much rather be "right" than related.

In person, we could share opinions and come away influenced by others. Online, we became entrenched in our own perspectives. Face-to-face, we almost automatically acknowledge and validate each other, though this is a skill we develop in maturity. Online, there is no chance to develop this ability, or even communal maturity.

No one "likes" a statement they disagree with on Facebook, though in person we will often at least find a way to accept the person making the statement. They have a point; they have a perspective; they are a person.

Online, we dismiss statements we don't like. And therefore, we dismiss the person. We deny them their humanity. This is an uncorrectable fault of the medium itself. Social media becomes a wedge between us, and a force that degrades our better selves.

Anonymity makes the situation worse. Apps like Yik Yak and even Twitter, and the anonymous comments section of many online publications encourage disinhibited banter, bullying and trolling that dehumanizes the victims as well as the ones commenting.

Without physical presence, the neural feedback loops for kindness and empathy are not fully engaged, and our sadistic shadows can come to the fore, eager to produce their harmful effects. Even simply ignoring someone and their perspective is equivalent to shunning them. The act of not "liking" an update or opinion is the same as turning your back – and yet the medium requires us to ignore each other most of the time, and thus is inherently dehumanizing.

Social media has become ubiquitous because we are vibrantly social animals. We enjoy each other's company, and we are even desperate for it. But I'm reminded of the Ubuntu proverb: "people become people through other people." By narrowing our experience of people to text and image, opinion and "likes," we endanger our ability to fully become people.

While there are exceptions, and there are substantive stories of on-line connections making a heartwarming difference, the social media experience provides a false sense of relationship. It takes us away from our real world encounter, our face-to-face encounter, the only way to develop our compassion and appreciation for one another as complete human beings. Indeed, our time on Facebook may take us away from our humanity.

Science fiction movies have long pitted man against machine. In the "Terminator" and "Matrix" franchises and the Borg attacks of "Star Trek," we find our nemesis in cold, metallic others. But the real war may be more intimate and subtle than the movies. The fight for humanity may lie in the battle to turn off our apps, tune into our own minds, and turn on to each other.

Appendix 2:
The Evolution of the Two Spirit Model

During my psychiatry residency training at the University of California, San Francisco, I was fortunate to have Seymour Boorstein as my mentor. Every Tuesday for two years, I left the skyscrapers and academic institutions of San Francisco, traversed the Golden Gate Bridge, and ranged over the Marin hills to meet with him. There was something elemental and magical about the trip; San Francisco clouds and fog would part and disappear as I crossed the ocean, and then the sun would smile on me, a harbinger of enlightenment. My personal fog over the care of my patients would similarly evaporate as I met with him, at his house atop a wooded hill.

It was like a weekly pilgrimage to the mountaintop to receive teachings from my guru. Seymour would probably be the last person to think of himself as a guru, though. He was sage-like, but absolutely humble. He was one of the kindest people I'd ever met, filled with gentle wisdom wrapped in warmth and caring. One of his favorite sayings was "don't add insight to injury," a complement to "don't give them an insight, give them a piece of bread." Nurturing your patients was far more important than blinding them with your "intellect." I ate this approach up, as it was a welcome relief from traditional analytic theory, which demanded a golden interpretation at precisely 20 minutes into the 50-minute therapy hour. The analyst's words, like a knife, could be sharp and unhelpful, even if true.

Seymour stood at the opposite end of the spectrum from that approach, which led other supervisors to snort derisively at "errors" made by their charges as they struggled to care for their patients. His approach was to remove the obstacles to love and kindness. "I used to be so stiff—even stiffer than you were when you started with me," he'd say. "Now I'm loosey-goosey!" Seymour was trained as a psychoanalyst, but really found himself through his explorations in the human potential movement. His wife is Sylvia Boorstein, noted Buddhist teacher and author, whom I'm also proud to call a teacher and friend of mine. Seymour still sees patients in Marin—over 80 years old and going strong!

Seymour says "a light bulb went on" in 1992 when he heard Daniel Goleman speak about the "two brains": the primitive limbic system and more evolved cortical and neo-cortical systems. "He said that the limbic system impulses travel many times faster than the neocortical impulses. The result is that the limbic system hijacks the thought process because it initiates action based on its agenda before the neocortical system has a chance to respond wisely. I realized that many couples find themselves in destructive exchanges without really knowing how they got there because it all happens so quickly. I recognized that couples become confused when the limbic system's speed and lack of insight takes priority over the slower reasoning of the more mature cortical system."

To make these systems easily understandable, he represented them as animals. The "crocodile" of the limbic brain vied with the "owl" of the slower-thinking neocortex. The destructive elements in our relationships—anger, contempt, resentment, hostility, stonewalling—all come from the self-centered crocodile, when it is threatened and pushed into "fight, flight, or freeze" survival mode. Typically, the crocodile is linked to a "supersensitive neural network" forged in early childhood experiences. Those of us with difficult childhood experiences carry the memories of how our parents treated us as deep and open wounds that cause us to react disproportionately and defensively to anything that even vaguely reminds us of those early experiences. We feel we are being abandoned, engulfed, criticized, controlled, not seen, and so on.

This model was very helpful to me personally and professionally. Patients found the model easy to understand and helpful.

All but one. And she made all the difference.

A traumatized young woman I worked with found the model disturbing. It made her more tense and fearful to think of herself as having a "crocodile" in her brain. I adjusted the model, calling the limbic system the "vulnerable child" and the cortex the "inner nurturer." This was more helpful to her, and allowed her to work at becoming her own ally.

But I think this was still too dualistic and hierarchical for my own limbic system. My limbic system wanted to be heard and respected, not simply as a vulnerable child but as a valuable perspective-holding consciousness that was not in denial or spiritual bypass about the difficulties of being human. At the 2017 Annual Meeting of the American Psychiatric Association in San Diego, while listening to a panel discussion on personality disorders, I had my own light bulb moment. I'd naturally been thinking a lot about transcendence and identity in the course of writing this book and doing therapy. The idea of a "transcendent and altruistic spirit" in dialogue with a more personal, sometimes reactive, always provocative "self-spirit" clicked. Identity flowed from this dialogue. The dialogue occurs in connection and disconnection, union and isolation, selfless and selfish behaviors and mentalities.

Another way of looking at it is thinking of the limbic system and self spirit as fast acting, very sensitive, precocious, impulsive, humorous and short fused, with a long memory of slights dating back to historical and traumas and injuries suffered in this life and in past lives by one's ancestors, and perhaps even cultural traumas. The self spirit suffers tremendously, and can cause a great deal of suffering as well. The transcendent spirit and cortex are slow to react, yet responsible for long term planning, forgiveness, letting go, deeper empathy and compassion, and healing. The dialogue of these spirits produces identity, vision, deep cultural awareness and creativity, and true transcendence.

I certainly have patients who suffer tremendously because their ideals are threatened or crushed by reality. Perhaps one way to view their dilemma is to consider that the self-spirit feels disconnected and alienated from transcendence. We must have fruitful connections between our transcendent spirit and our limbic system and other regions of our brain responsible for "self" for our identities to become clearer and more stable over time. It's not a matter of transcendence or the cortex simply overpowering or defusing the limbic system. Our ideals must heal our personhood; our personhood must inform our ideals.

Since we are all connected through the "open limbic loop," sensitive to each other's emotions and moods, I think there could well be a selfless limbic system, intimately aware of a bigger picture and reactive to the bigger threats facing all beings. The selfless limbic system might hold fast to principles and react to threats. The cortex has to turn these demands into long term plans and wisdom.

The two spirit model and the selfless amygdala/limbic system are intuitive leaps, and could well be modified over time. Certainly, internal family systems therapy recognizes that we all have many "voices," spirits or personalities within us. Jungian analysis recognizes the importance of myriad archetypes and symbols in our collective unconscious. Psychodynamic therapy recognizes object relations, transference and attachment as the foundations of our inner experience. There are parallels between all these models. Creating inner harmony requires listening to all these parts of ourselves, our inner family, and bringing them into harmony. In some sense, we are all spirits to each other. We all influence each other in subtle and powerful ways. This creates some kind of inner dialogue based on relationships in the real world. Our inner world is a representation of the outer world of relationships. Making peace within, therefore, has some effect on our world and how we interact with it.

Through the dialogue of self and transcendent spirits I believe we reach a deeper sense of identity, wholeness and freedom from suffering. The transcendent spirit is forged in deep, mutually caring relationships with others and connecting to transcendence, oneness, or selflessness through meditative or other spiritual practices such as those described in this book. In all these ways, we can transform the inner life, and approach freedom from suffering. The goal, of course, is a unified, whole mind beyond even the duality of self and transcendent spirits. Perhaps this is another way to view enlightenment.

I hope the two spirit model can be helpful to you.

(A portion of this appendix, related to the Owl and Crocodile model, was published as a blog on Psychology Today on February 9, 2012. You can read more about Seymour's model and very helpful approach to couples therapy in his book, *Who's Talking Now? The Owl or the Crocodile*, Authorhouse, 2011. It's filled with fun illustrations by his daughter Elizabeth Boorstein.)

Appendix 3:
Loneliness, Belonging and
the Rejection Complex

Dealing with isolation and loneliness is one of four essential existential tasks of life. (Classically, the others are dealing with death, meaning and freedom, per Dr. Irvin Yalom's *Existential Psychotherapy*.) We are all ultimately alone in our skins. That can be terrifying at times. At other times, we might revel in solitude. Most of us want to feel some kind of belonging in our lives. This quest is part of what leads us to online social networks in the first place. Questions of meaning, freedom and mortality also migrate with us when we try to live online. *New Yorker* satirist Andy Borowitz nicely sums up all the existential questions on his Twitter profile: "There is a fine line between social networking and wasting your fucking life."

Here's a table that lays out my sense of the spectrum of belonging, from the highest, most desirable state of transcendent belonging to experiences and perceptions of ostracism. We may each feel at different points with different people, and at another point with ourselves and our inner lives. We may feel differently at different times, because the self is always changing and contextual. All points of contact need some kind of attention and awareness. Perhaps true belonging can only be experienced with a relatively small number of people. Transcendent belonging is possible, with the right cognitions, emotions, experiences and relationships to allow one to feel safe and welcome in the world, despite experiences of rejection and even ostracism. I think of transcendent belonging as being compassionate in relationships, but not excessively dependent on them to provide a sense of self. In other words, equanimity married with belonging.

Racism, sexism, homophobia and other forms of bias rooted in self-centeredness can activate a Rejection Complex both in the recipients of bias and those biased against them. Once a Rejection Complex is triggered, a person or group might reject, blame, scapegoat or bully those who they feel are rejecting them. To complete the cycle, those emotions, thoughts and behaviors make it more likely that they actually will be rejected by their targets. In the duality of "victim and oppressor," each side can feel rejected or even persecuted by the other. As night follows day, each side of the duality can fall into rejecting the other side, in order to assert themselves and gain or retain power. When the bonds of affection are weak and aversion is strong, empathy and compassion are sacrificed, and power tactics advance. Each side rejects or even sadistically persecutes the other, and the vicious cycle of rejection continues. Resistance to oppression can turn into bullying, scapegoating, blaming and shaming the perceived oppressor. When those in the majority return the "favor," they do in fact become oppressive. Fears, angers, sorrows and traumas gain ground. The blame game has no winners. By contrast, in the responsibility game, we can all be winners. Experiences of rejection and subordination are commonplace in this world, as people exert power in human relationships. How to respond? The essential problem in human relationships is empathic failure, a failure of love. We can't solve love problems with power. It never works.

There are alternatives to the Rejection Complex, such as compassion for, pride in, and assertion of, one's own identity; cultivating compassion, appreciation, acceptance and forgiveness for those who knowingly or unknowingly caused one harm; and taking responsibility for creating belonging for self and other. Instead of blaming and calling out, we can *call in* with compassion.

How can we generate genuine compassion for others, as individuals and as a group? How do we communicate in ways that respect all individuals? To my eye, that's hard enough in the real world (particularly when we act as groups and not individuals), and nearly impossible online, but it can be done. Buddhist techniques outlined in this book can be helpful and transformative.

It seems the cycles will continue until all biases are resolved in equity, or each side can learn to *perceive and respond* to actual bias productively, rather than *sense and react* to perceived bias mindlessly. We would all have to agree that bias is something we want to do something about, that it is a necessary step towards belonging. We might start by asking ourselves "am I creating belonging or rejection for this person or group?" instead of "is this person or group a friend or foe?" It's possible to create belonging for others while also questioning objectionable tactics and worldviews. Kindness and respect go a long way in establishing and maintaining relationships.

Worse than those who only react to perceived bias are those who use their biases to hold power over others and specifically reject and harm vulnerable individuals or groups. In my humble opinion, that's the kind of power we should all fight against, within and without, because ultimately, we are all vulnerable. But some are more vulnerable than others; attention must be paid.

Related to the Rejection Complex is what I call the Subordination Complex, which can be activated when one feels submerged by another person or group. In this world, transcendence is often submerged, swamped and criticized by the primitive. Our light is often covered by darkness. When we deny our shadows or attempt "spiritual bypasses" around our unresolved issues, they come back to haunt us. They are drawn to us like a moth to a flame. This can feel like an oppressive onslaught to our transcendent spirit. But it may also be a challenge for our transcendent spirit to become fully and truly transcendent, by being inclusive and responsive to the unresolved. In any event, this process brings us into deeper contact with ourselves and others, and simultaneously shows the need for boundaries. We are all connected. We are all in this together, like it or not. We are rarely aware of our shadows until someone brings them to our attention. May we all find belonging, and not try to solve our problems of love and disconnection through power, control and calumny.

Transcendent Belonging	Selfless compassion for self and others; internalized feelings of security, safety and trust
Belonging	Feeling accepted, valued, welcomed, loved and supported as an individual, and accepting, valuing, welcoming, loving and supporting others in turn.
Marriage, love partners **Friendship** **Companionship**	All three are desirable outcomes of mutual relationship.
Group acceptance	Acceptance for conforming to group, and taking responsibility for being part of group.
Solitude	Private happiness and joy in being alone.
Loneliness	Ordinary loneliness; may cycle through feelings of being unloved and unlovable, and excessive personalization of the problem.
Being ignored **Isolation** **Rejection, Exclusion, Alienation, Abandonment** **Experiences or perceptions of being shamed, blamed, demeaningly criticized, scapegoated, humiliated, bullied, persecuted and subordinated** **Experiences or perceptions of ostracism or being shunned**	These five lower rungs have a lot in common. Most problematic is a developed "Rejection Complex," which leads to emotions, thoughts and behaviors that interfere with relationship, such as anger, self-righteousness, black-and-white thinking, adversariality, fear, grudges, resentments, hostility, feelings of superiority, inferiority or grandiosity, or avoidance and emotional withdrawal.

Appendix 4:
A Very Messy Diagram

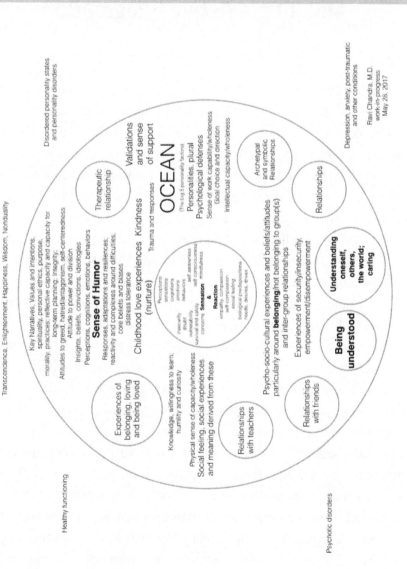

Appendix 5:
Transformative Meditative Experiences
and Jung's Active Imagination

Some readers may be taken aback by the closing chapters of this book, which include a meditation-induced deepening of awareness, and a seeming encounter with a spirit being. I mean, you didn't sign up for this! You thought you were reading a book about social media, then it turns into a memoir, then…this?! I'm sure I triggered some eyerolls and gasps. "You've gotta be kidding me, right?"

The list of people who've had these kinds of experiences is beyond the scope of this book. I wasn't taught anything about them during my residency training. Psychiatrists and psychologists do now discuss similar hallucinogen- or other drug-induced episodes, both recreational and therapeutic to treat certain mental health conditions such as depression. The experiences of oneness, bliss and transcending everyday neuroses and obsessions are powerful and life-altering.

Oneness can be reached in meditative practice as well. And cultivating awareness of one's patterns of thoughts and emotions is the very definition of mindfulness. Moreover, some individuals reach profound awareness suddenly and without the use of drugs or regular meditative practice. Spiritual teachers Eckhart Tolle and Byron Katie both describe their story-making egos dropping away while they were very depressed, transforming their consciousnesses into present-centered awareness and joy. As a child, Yongey Mingyur Rinpoche suffered great anxiety. After what he calls a "nervous breakthrough" during meditation, his anxiety was gone.

So these experiences of kensho, satori or enlightenment are part of the possibility of human experience itself. Gee, just like the Buddha said. Who knew?

My own experience came after years of mindfulness and lovingkindness practice, and was totally unexpected or unheralded. I'd certainly noted my mental reactions in meditation before, and theorized on how reactivity worsened suffering, but this didn't result in completely transcending the reactions altogether. I'd touched oneness and bliss many times, so I knew there were states beyond reactivity. I think what happened on May 27, 2017 was that my awareness made a conceptual leap, and I was able to simultaneously observe and experience my "self-ing" reactivity as not inherently existing in and of itself, but that it was dependent on causes and conditions. The realization of the insubstantiality of the reactivity was painfully upsetting to me in the moment. But as the days rolled on, those micro-reactions did subside, and my sense of myself as an agent with freedom to choose my response instead of only reacting to immediate circumstance grew. I don't know that my actions are noticeably any different from before, but the experience of being "nothing" is certainly a touchstone in my consciousness. I feel less identified with any reaction, and more free to cultivate and express my intentions and purpose in life. I am more acutely aware of my reactions, and feel more able to marshal my intentions to remedy them. I also feel more deeply compassionate to my patients' suffering. I continue to ask myself where their reactions come from and how those reactions help or harm them.

And what of talking to a "spirit being"?

Carl Jung wrote about his own experiments with "active imagination." These were times when he allowed himself to go into a waking dream state, and his imagination ran free. He saw visions, interacted with various spirits and other elements of his subconscious, and emerged with wisdom that still guides therapists today. There's more to mind and psyche than a wiring diagram of the brain.

Eastern philosophies often speak of life as a dream. Zhuangzi famously wrote of dreaming himself as a butterfly, then waking to wonder if he was a butterfly dreaming he was a man. If we are all in a life dream, are we all co-dreamers? Or are we being dreamt, by one or many? This may be fanciful and useless speculation. Even if we're in a dream, how do we live our lives? My life has included experiences with spirit beings, such as the one described. Perhaps they are dream beings of the life bardo.

Generally, I pay them little heed, as my day-to-day life and real relationships are far more important. But as I work through this material, I will probably find that the spirits, perhaps elements of my own deconstructed consciousness, must be related to and thus integrated into my own sense of self. Since they impinge on and interact with my own mind, I am interdependent with them. So on that level at least, I know I'm not separate from them. And I know as my own inner peace has grown over the years, they've also become more settled. Months go by without any "visitation." Only when there's some trouble – my back goes out, or I'm emotionally stressed in some other way – do they suddenly reappear. Thanks, I guess.

I don't know if these experiences are similar or dissimilar from, or parallel to, the auditory hallucinations and psychoses of schizophrenia. But I don't think they're a disorder at all, but rather stem from a heightened state of awareness of my own inner being.

Since I'm writing about social media, the only question left is: "why share at all?" I think the time has come to open up this area of my life. There's a lot of shame, stigma and confusion around spiritual, transpersonal and meditative experiences. Silence is deadly. Secrets kill. I can only say I'm trying to deepen interdependence, not bypass it by saying I'm unique in some way. I'm also trying to force some kind of accountability with my own superego and unconscious. If there's some part of me (or the world in which I live) that still criticizes me mercilessly for my errors, despite all my self-examination, conscious self-critique and therapy, despite all my lovingkindness and compassion practice and despite whatever good I hope I've done in the world, it needs to be understood, tempered and brought into alignment with my own transcendent spirit. Only then can I truly be at peace. Only then will my work in the world be fully effective.

Thank you, dear reader, for bearing with me.

Acknowledgements

Even if I were to upload all the contacts from my iPhone into this acknowledgements section, I would still come up short. Every person I've met has been influential in some way on the development of my ideas on the importance of relationships and in my experience of them. Beyond that, we're all connected somehow. So many writers, artists, musicians and other members of our local, national and global communities put their efforts into creating the world we share. Thank you for being you. Members of the Asian American arts community deserve a special thanks from my tiny outpost in the Asian American world. At the top of the list is my favorite musician, Goh Nakamura. Everyone buy his music, dammit! Goh's gotten some good attention, but why is it that some of the best work barely registers on our national consciousness? Or even the Asian American consciousness? I feel privileged to have been a witness to Goh's work and the work of so many other sometimes unsung heroes (Dan Lee and Scrabbel, Jon Jang, Francis Wong and the Asian American jazz establishment, and the incomparable Vienna Teng – who's hardly unsung, but still – to name a few).

So many teachers inspired me to think critically, but also to be a better person. I've forgotten many of their names – why does that happen? At Frost, Mrs. Morgan, Ms. Hardwidge and Mr. Brown were the rock stars of my adolescence. At Cranbrook Kingswood, Howard Berkowitz, Richard Lamb, Fred Roth, Scribner Jelliffe, Jeff Welch and Nelson Lebo among many others were outstanding guides to the human spirit. At Brown, Paul Knopf, Ken Miller, the Rotmans, Elizabeth Leduc, Jean

Wu, Marjorie Thompson, Pammi Suri, Hon Fong Mark, Lenny, Harriet Sheridan, President Vartan Gregorian and so many more inspired with their intellectual curiosity, humanity, kindness and vision. At Stanford, Ellie Segal, Elliot Wolfe, Ann Bolger, Charlotte Jacobs, Kelly Skeff, President Donald Kennedy, Rick Yuen, Floyd Thompkins and others made medical school a humane and humanizing experience. At UCSF, the SFGH and the San Francisco VAMC I learned from more amazing psychiatrists and health care professionals than I can count, including Kenny Gee, Nang Du, Paul Yang, Anna Spielvogel, Albert Gaw, Descartes Li, Alla Spivak, Fred Hiatt, Keith Armstrong and Rob Daroff. In addition, the Committee of Asian American Psychiatrists of the Northern California Psychiatric Society have been friends, supporters and teachers since 2002, particularly Jacquelyn Chang, Francis Lu, Rona Hu, and Robert Lee. A special thanks to the organizers, speakers and attendees of the American Psychiatric Association Annual Meetings. I've learned so much from your wisdom and compassion, and benefited from your generous inclusion in the program twice so far. A special thanks to Glen Gabbard and Jean Twenge with whom I presented in 2017. I've grown closer to and benefited from my psychiatric friends and colleagues Fred Huang, Mari Ormiston, and Naomi Lam over the last decade and more, particularly since adopting a more bohemian schedule allowing me time for precious lunch dates with them all. Priceless. The 2536 Clay gang (Nancy Haugen, Tom Singer, Richard Stein, David Richman, Alan Maloney, Jim Bae and especially David Tresan, who passed away in 2016, and Neil Russack, who passed in 2011), Seymour Boorstein, Allan Chinen, Steve Walsh and Justin Hecht have all been incredible examples of knowledge and camaraderie. A great thanks is due to all the researchers whose work informed this writing. I doubt any of these friends or researchers have much of a Twitter, Facebook or even web presence, underscoring how much wisdom there is beyond the online social network, wisdom that's – surprise, surprise – only contained in real world relationships and minds. Things that make you go hmmm.

Several friends read early drafts of *Facebuddha*, and gave encouraging feedback. Particular thanks to Sylvia Boorstein and Deann

Borshay Liem who were enthusiastic, kind, generous and thoughtful early readers. Fred Huang, David and Mayany Brody, Rania Ho, Alina Hua and Christine Kim-O'Connor also provided important feedback. Jenn Fang read a version of "The Internet? Neti, Neti" and gave her thoughtful comments. I spoke with all my friends and many a new acquaintance about these ideas, and all of them might find traces of our conversations in these pages, particularly Tony Nguyen, Betty Chan, Rik Isensee, Barbara Koh, Ruth Nott, Nicole Hsiang, Sara MacPherson, Lucy Bhisitkul, Kelly Huang, Isabelle Thuy Pelaud, Evelyn Lee, Rafael Gray, Linda Tuggle Zhang, Sita Bhaumik, Marta Belcher, and Atsuko and Warren Miller, who also read the early draft. Warren, my dear friend, passed away in May, 2016. I was honored to know him, and miss him deeply. He was always intellectually curious, kind, deeply compassionate and concerned about society and the planet. I am sure he's in some Pure Land, continuing his good deeds. We need all the help we can get. I will forever remain humbled by his spirit.

Tenzing Rigdol generously allowed the use of "Hollywood Buddha" for this book. I am grateful to Việt Lê (vietle.net) for designing the cover. Valerie Mih (seeherestudios.com) did an incredible job with the animation and music for *Facebuddha*'s book trailer. Deann Borshay Liem, Debbie Lum, Stephen Gong, Rick Steele, Tony Nguyen and Momo Chang all gave helpful feedback on the trailer. Thanks to Bob Hsiang for my author photo. Rick Hanson provided teachings that helped me understand the meditative "opening" experience I describe near the end of the book. Of course, I have to thank all those who appear as "characters" in the book: my relatives in India, Yasue, Tony Nguyen, Nguyen Qui Duc, Bao Phi and others whose pseudonyms are scattered throughout. My uncle "Vishnu", aunt "Deepa" and cousin "Ram" passed away before publication of this book. I'm so grateful to have seen them again in 2012. Sam Fleishman was an impeccable early steward and supporter of this work. I'll remember our conversations at the Algonquin and Fairway fondly. Susan Lee Cohen was also gracious in her early encouragement and advice.

I must also acknowledge my friends in the community who have supported me as a writer and human being for many years. Including: Pireeni Sundaralingam, Neelanjana Banerjee, and Summi Kaipa, editors of *Indivisible: A South Asian American Poetry Anthology*; Melody Takata of GenRyu Arts; T.J. Basa and Jason Bayani (previously and currently of Kearny Street Workshop); Deborah Clearwaters, Allison Wyckoff and Coral Reiff, all of the Asian Art Museum in San Francisco; Vinay Patel, Melanie Elvena and Laura Priscilla Paule of the API Cultural Center; Stephen Gong, Eddie Wong, Jennifer Chu, Shelly Kim, Momo Chang, Ashlyn Perri, Masashi Niwano, Lin Kung, Chi-hui Yang, Christine Kwon, Claudia Leung, Michael Kwan, Michella Rivera-Gravage, Ben Armington, Mitch Vaughn and so many more currently and previously at the Center for Asian American Media; Karen Larsen, Vince Johnson and Corey Tong; Gaetano Kazuo Maida and Ayelete Maida of the Buddhist Film Foundation; Rick Shiomi, David Mura, Bao Phi, Alex Lubet, Iris Shiraishi, David Furumoto, Kenny Endo, Zoli Hall, the late and very much missed Yali Peng, and many others who befriended me in Minneapolis/St. Paul through Mu Performing Arts and Asian American Renaissance; friends united in the Asian Pacific Islander American Spoken Word community; Jane Kim, Annie Koh, Samantha Chanse and Julia Kim of Locus Arts, the Locus Coeruleus and Beyond; Sunny Angulo, Viva Mogi, Sheila Chung Hagen and Paul Hagen; Louise Nayer, Zoe Carter, Justine Gubar, Jenny Bitner, David Munro, Mark Decena and other friends at the S.F. Writers' Grotto; Francis Wong, Jon Jang, Tatsu Aoki and Lenora Lee of AsianImprovArts; Rania Ho, Wang Wei, Darryl Chiang, Kathy Lu, Pearl Wong, Greg Watanabe, Todd Nakagawa, Kim Kajihara, Michael Hornbuckle, Rhoda Gravador, Harold Byun, Pamela Wu-Kochiyama and the late Valiant Chow of 18 Mighty Mountain Warriors and friends; Katherine Eng, Cress Forester, Mai McGuire-Tran, Kristina Bang and my other friends from community mental health; Derek Chung, Nisma Zaman, Tamlyn Tomita, Pam Matsuoka, Nancy Hom, Shizue Seigel and Benjamin Pease, Peter Yamamoto, Truong Tran, Melissa Hung, Abigail Licad, Christina Fa Mark, Gloria Jan, Eileen Adamian, Bophany Huot, Chun Yu, Dawn

Kang, Kristina Wong, Emily Chang, Sin Yen Ling, Yi Yi Yin, Anida Yoeu Ali, Irene Leung, Elizabeth Ren, Annabel Park, Davy Chou, Rithy Panh, Socheata Poeuv, Charles Vogl, Greg Pak, Karin Chien, Karen Lin, Naomi Onaga, Eric Byler, Jacqueline Kim and Genny Lim; Mary Taylor, Rosemary and Jack Wardell, Rena Jardine and the rest of my Palo Alto-ish friends, including Sam Wu and Ellen Licking, Midori Nishimura and Hitoshi Takahashi, Belinda and Otak Jump, Pancho Chang, Leslie Kim and Joel, Nick, Sam, and Jonathan Wu; all my friends from Frost, Cranbrook Kingswood, Brown, Stanford, Hennepin County Medical Center, UCSF and everywhere else I've been welcomed; the Hunter families, especially Roberta, Lee, Theresa and Vicki, and in memory of Donna and Lee; Steven Silletti, Roderick Kim, the late Naveed Kashaf and families; the Whidby family; Shantum Seth of Buddhapath Tours; Soren Gordhamer and the Wisdom 2.0 organizers of 2014; and Kaja Perina, Lybi Ma, Hara Estroff Marano and everyone at *Psychology Today*. Mitayuke oyasin. Every meeting counts. Another time, soon. A special thanks to Tsering Wangmo Dhompa for friendship and literary camaraderie. Everyone buy and read *Coming Home to Tibet*, a necessary and poetic companion in the world (much like Tsering)! And of course a big shoutout to all the filmmakers, musicians and actors who inspire me with their visions at CAAMFest, year after year.

I don't have a single sangha, but rather many, each of them providing home, friendship and teachings over the years. Spirit Rock Meditation Center in Marin, particularly Jack Kornfield and Sylvia Boorstein; San Francisco Buddhist Center, especially Viradhamma and Viveka Chan; San Francisco Zen Center, especially the late Lee Lipp and Blanche Hartman, and Tova Green; and East Bay Meditation Center, especially my friend John Mifsud. Shambhala, and friendship with Brian Spielmann, was an important starting point for my Buddhist journey, and other sanghas have provided important teachings along the way, including San Francisco Insight, Mission Dharma, Nagara Dhamma, Soka Gakkai International, the Buddhist Churches in Berkeley and San Francisco as well as Tibetan Buddhist communities and friends in Minneapolis and the Bay Area, particularly Tsewang Ngodup and family. The Buddhists of Color Yahoo group has been a continuous thread of connection for many years. Much gratitude to my root teachers, His Holiness the Dalai Lama and the Venerable Thich Nhat Hanh. Thich Nhat Hanh's *Old Path, White Clouds* was an indispensable inspiration for my high-tech take on Buddha's life, different from the legend usually told, and likely much more accurate.

This book is primarily dedicated to my mother, B.V. Amrutha. Without her, I really would be "nothing." Finally, my heartfelt appreciation goes to Rick Steele. Your affection, warmth, insight and support over our years of conversation are a precious gift. It doesn't get any better than talking to someone who cares, and caring about them in turn. How else does the world get rich?

I dedicate any merit that comes from this work to the benefit of all beings. May my work especially benefit my patients, particularly those in the Cambodian group I've co-led since 2010. Every moment with patients and friends brings meaning and depth. Thanks for teaching me about your lives, and helping me to "see more clearly and love more deeply."

It's been said we're all at least a little mentally ill until we're enlightened. To me, that means we're all at least a little mentally ill until we're related. Let's get well soon.

There is no Facebuddha.
Buddha appears in the face-to-face.
Let's meet.
Let's make Buddha.

Endnotes

1. Kim SY, Wang Y, Orozco-Lapray D, Shen Y, Murtuza M. Does "tiger parenting" exist? Parenting profiles of Chinese Americans and adolescent developmental outcomes. Asian American J Psych 2013, Mar 4(1): 7-18

2. Seppälä E. Top ten scientific benefits of compassion. http://www.emmaseppala.com/top-10-scientific-benefits-of-compassion-infographic/#.WUW4-sbMxE4 accessed 6/17/17

3. Slater, Dan. Love in the Time of Algorithms. New York: Current, 2013

4. Hu X, Kim A, Siwek N, Wilder D. The Facebook paradox: effects of Facebooking on individuals' social relationships and psychological well-being. Front Psychol. 2017 Jan 31;8:87. http://journal.frontiersin.org/article/10.3389/fpsyg.2017.00087/full accessed 5/8/17

5. Fullwood C, James BM, Chen-Wilson CJ. Self-concept clarity and online self-presentation in adolescents. Cyberpsychol Behav Soc Netw. 2016 Dec; 19)2) 716-720

6. Gil-Or O, Levi-Belz Y, Turel O. The "Facebook-self": characteristics and psychological predictors of false self-presentation on Facebook. Front Psychol. 2015 Feb 17; 6:99

7. Muise A, Christofides E, Desmarais S. More information than you ever wanted: Does Facebook bring out the green-eyed monster of jealousy? Cyberpsychology & Behavior 2009; 4:441-444

8. Muise A, Christofides E, Desmarais S. "Creeping" or just information seeking? Gender differences in partner monitoring in response to jealousy on Facebook. Pers Relationships 2013 http://dx.doi.org/10.1111/pere.12014 (obtained by personal communication with author)

9. Hand MM, Thomas D, Buboltz WC, Deemer ED, Buyanjargal M. Facebook and romantic relationships: intimacy and couple satisfaction associated with online social network use. Cyberpsychol Behav Soc Netw. 2013 Jan; 16(1):8-13

10. Muscanell NL, Guadagno RE, Rice L, Murphy S. Don't it make my brown eyes green? An analysis of Facebook use and romantic jealousy. Cyberpsychol Behav Soc Netw. 2013 Apr; 16(4):237-42

11. Clayton RB, Nagurney A, Smith JR. Cheating, breakup, and divorce: is Facebook use to blame? Cyberpsychol Behav Soc Netw. 2013 Oct; 16(10): 717-20

12. Lyndon A, Bonds-Raccke J, Cratty AD. College students' Facebook stalking of ex-partners. Cyberpsychology, Behavior and Social Networking 2011; 14:711-716

13. Marshall TC. Facebook surveillance of former romantic partners: associations with postbreakup recovery and personal growth. Cyberpsychol Behav Soc Netw. 2012 Oct; 15(10):521-6

14. Sheets VL, Fredendall LL, Claypool HM. Jealousy evocation, partner reassurance, and relationship stability: An exploration of the potential benefits of jealousy. Evolution & Human Behavior. 1997; 18:387-402

15. Elphinston RA, Noller P. Time to face it! Facebook intrusion and the implications for romantic jealousy and relationship satisfaction. Cyberpsychol Behav Soc Netw 2011 Nov; 14(11): 631-5

16. Carter JM, Wilson FL. Cyberbullying: a 21st century health care phenomenon. Pediatr Nurs. 2015 May-Jun; 41(3): 115-25 and Rice E, Petering R, Rhoades H, Winetrobe H, Goldbach J, Plant A, Montoya J, Kordic T. Cyberbullying perpetration and victimization among middle-school students. Am J Public Health. 2015 Mar; 105(3): e66-72

17. Buckels EE, Trapnell PD, Paulhus DL. Trolls just want to have fun. Pers and Indiv Diff. 2014 Sept; 67: 97-102 doi.org/10.1016/j.paid.2014.01.016

18. Mooney C. Internet trolls really are horrible people. Slate. Feb 14, 2014. http://www.slate.com/articles/health_and_science/climate_desk/2014/02/internet_troll_personality_study_machiavellianism_narcissism_psychopathy.html accessed 4/10/17

19. Homayoun A. The secret social media lives of teenagers. The New York Times June 7, 2017 https://www.nytimes.com/2017/06/07/well/family/the-secret-social-media-lives-of-teenagers.html accessed 6/8/17

20. Mickes L, Darby RS, Hwe V, Bajic D, Warker JA, Harris CR, Christenfeld NJ. Major memory for microblogs. Mem Cognit. 2013 May; 41(4):481-9

21. Campisi J, Bynog P, McGehee H, Oakland JC, Quirk S, Taga C, Taylor M. Facebook, stress, and incidence of upper respiratory infection in undergraduate college students. Cyberpsychol Behav Soc Netw. 2012 Dec; 15(12):675-81

22. D'Amato G, Cecchi L, Liccardi G, Pellegrino F, D'Amato M, Sofia M. Social Networks: a new source of psychological stress or a way to enhance self-esteem? Negative and positive implications in bronchial asthma. J Investig Allergol Clin Immunol. 2012;22(6):402-5 and Wright KB, Rosenberg J, Egbert N, Ploeger NA, Bernard DR, King S. Communication competence, social support, and depression among college students: a model of Facebook and face-to-face support network influence. J Health Commun. 2013;18(1):41-57

23. Bazarova NN, Choi YH, Whitlock J, Cosley D, Sosik V. Psychological distress and emotional expression on Facebook. Cyberpsychol Behav Soc Netw. 20(3): 157-163

24. Clerkin EM, Smith AR, Hames JL. The interpersonal effects of Facebook reassurance seeking. J Affect Disord. 2013 Nov; 151(2): 525-30

25. Kross E, Verduyn P, Demiralp E, Park J, Lee DS, et al. Facebook use predicts declines in subjective well-being in young adults. PLoS ONE 8(8): e69841. doi:10:1371/journal.pone.0069841

26. Chen W, Lee KH. Sharing, liking, commenting, and distressed? The pathway between Facebook interaction and psychological distress. Cyberpsychol Behav Soc Netw. 2013 Oct; 16(10): 728-34

27. Neubaum G, Kramer NC. My friends right next to me: a laboratory investigation on predictors and consequences of experiencing social closeness on social networking sites. Cyberpsychol Behav Soc Netw. 2015 Aug;18(8): 443-9

28. Verduyn P, Lee DS, Park J, Shablack H, Orvell A, Bayer J, Ybarra O, Jonides J, Kross E. Passive Facebook usage undermines affective well-

being: experimental and longitudinal evidence. J Exp Psychol Gen. 2015 Apr; 144(2): 480-8

29. Veretilo P, Billick SB. Psychiatric illness and Facebook: a case report. Psychiatr Q 2012 Sep; 83(3): 385-9

30. Gajaria A, Yeung E, Goodale T, Charach A. Beliefs about attention-deficit/hyperactivity disorder and response to stereotypes: youth postings in Facebook groups. J Adolesc Health 2011 Jul; 49(1) 15-20

31. Litt DM, Stock ML. Adolescent alcohol-related risk cognitions: the roles of social norms and social networking sites. Psychol Addict Behav 2011 Dec; 25(4): 708-13

32. Ridout B, Campbell A, Ellis L. 'Off your Face(book)': alcohol in online social identity construction and its relation to problem drinking in university students. Drug Alcohol Rev 2012 Jan; 31(1): 20-6

33. Moreno MA, Jelenchiak LA, Egan KG, Cox E, Young H, Gannon KE, Becker T. Feeling bad on Facebook: depression disclosures by college students on a social networking site. Depress Anxiety 2011 Jun; 28(6): 447-55

34. Egan KG, Moreno MA. Prevalence of stress references on college freshman Facebook profiles. Comput Inform Nurs 2011 Oct; 29(10): 586-92

35. Myhre JW, Mehl MR, Glisky EL. Cognitive benefits of online social networking for healthy older adults. J Gerontol B Psychol Sci Soc Sci 2016 Mar 16: 1-9

36. Orr ES, Sisic M, Ross C, Simmering MG, Arseneault JM, Orr RR. The influence of shyness on the use of Facebook in an undergraduate sample. Cyberpsychol Behav 2009 Jun; 12(3): 337-40

37. Lee-Won RJ, Herzog L, Park SG. Hooked on Facebook: The role of social anxiety and need for social assurance in problematic use of Facebook. Cyberpsychol Behav Soc Netw. 2015 Oct; 18(10): 567-74

38. Lin JH. The role of attachment style in Facebook use and social capital: evidence from university students and a national sample. Cyberpsychol Behav Soc Netw. 2015 Mar; 18(3): 173-180

39. Manago AM, Taylor T, Greenfield PM. Me and my 400 friends: the anatomy of college students' Facebook networks, their communication patterns, and well-being. Dev Psychol 2012 Mar; 48(2):369-80

40. Sophos. Facebook ID probe shows 41% of users happy to reveal all to potential identity thieves. http://www.sophos.com/en-us/press-office/press-releases/2007/08/facebook.aspx. Accessed 7/27/13. And Lemieux R. Fictional privacy among Facebook users. Psychol Rep. 2012 Aug;111(1):289-92

41. Greitemyer T, Kunz I. Name-valence and physical attractiveness in Facebook: their compensatory effects on friendship acceptance. J Soc Psychol 2013 May-Jun; 153(3):257-60

42. Kittinger R, Correia CJ, Irons JG. Relationship between Facebook use and problematic internet use among college students. Cyberpsychol Behav Soc Netw 2012 Jun; 15(6):324-7

43. Turel O, He Q, Xue G, Xiao L, Bechara A. Examination of neural systems sub-serving Facebook "addiction". Psychol Rep. 2014 Dec; 115(3): 675-95

44. Rouis S. Impact of cognitive absorption on Facebook on students' achievement. Cyberpsychol Behav Soc Netw 2012 Jun; 15(6):296-303

45. Sheldon KM, Abad N, Hinsch C. A two-process view of Facebook use and relatedness need-satisfaction: disconnection drives use, and connection rewards it. J Pers Soc Psychol 2011 Apr; 100(4): 766-75

46. Pantic I, Damjanovic A, Todorovic J, Topalovic D, Bojovic-Jovic D, Ristic S, Pantic S. Association between online social networking and depression in high school students: behavioral physiology viewpoint. Psychiatr Danub 2012 Mar; 24(1):90-3

47. Tiggeman M, Slater A. Netgirls: The internet, Facebook, and body image concern in adolescent girls. Int J Eat Disord 2013, May 25 doi: 10.1002/eat.22141

48. Smith AR, Hames JL, Joiner TE Jr. Status Update: maladaptive Facebook usage predicts increases in body dissatisfaction and bulimic symptoms. J Affect Disord 2013 Jul; 149(1-3):235-40

49. Qiu L, Lin H, Leung AK, Tov W. Putting their best foot forward: emotional disclosure on Facebook. Cyberpsychol Behav Soc Netw 2012 Oct; 15(10):569-72

50. Schumann S, van der Linden N, Klein O. Bridging the gap on Facebook: assessing intergroup contact and its effects for intergroup relations. Cyberpsychol Behav Soc Netw 2012 Aug;15(8):411-6

51. Qiu L, Lin H, Leung A.K-y. How Does Facebook Browsing Affect Self-awareness and Social Well-being: the Role of Narcissism. 2010 Proceedings of the International Conference on Advances in Computer Entertainment Technology, Taiwan

52. Gonzales AL, Hancock JT. Mirror, Mirror on my Facebook wall: effects of exposure to Facebook on self-esteem. Cyberpsychol Behav Soc Netw 2011 Jan-Feb; 14(1-2): 79-83

53. Kalpidou M, Costin D, Morris J. The relationship between Facebook and the well-being of undergraduate college students. Cyberpsychol Behav Soc Netw 2011 Apr; 14(4) 183-9

54. Gosling SD, Augustine AA, Vazire S, Holtzman N, Gaddis S. Manifestations of personality in Online Social Networks: self-reported Facebook-related behaviors and observable profile information. Cyberpsychol Behav Soc Netw 2011 Sep; 14(9): 483-8

55. Moreno MA, Swanson MJ, Royer H, Roberts LJ. Sexpectations: male college students' view about displayed sexual references on females' social networking web sites. J Pediatr Adolesc Gynecol 2011 Apr; 24(2): 85-9

56. Mehdizadeh S. Self-presentation 2.0: narcissism and self-esteem on Facebook. Cyberpsychol Behav Soc Netw 2010 Aug; 13(4): 357-64

57. Buffardi LE, Campbell WK. Narcissism and social networking web sites. Pers Soc Psychol Bull 2008 Oct; 34(10): 1303-14

58. Zaki J. What, me care? Young are less empathetic. 2011. http://www.scientificamerican.com/article.cfm?id=what-me-care. Accessed 7/29/13

59. Lee E, Lee JA, Moon JH, Sung Y. Pictures speak louder than words: motivations for using Instagram. Cyberpsychol Behav Soc New. 2015 Sep; 18(9):552-6

60. Utz S, Muscanell N, Khalid C. Snapchat elicits more jealousy than Facebook: a comparison of Snapchat and Facebook use. Cyberpsychol Behav Soc Netw. 2015 Mar;18(3):141-6

61. Stapleton P, Luiz G, Chatwin H. Generation Validation: The role of social comparison in use of Instagram among emerging adults. Cyberpsychol Behav Soc Netw. 2017 Mar;20(3):142-149

62. Yang CC. Instagram use, loneliness and social comparison orientation: Interact and browse on social media, but don't compare. Cyberpsychol Behav Soc Netw. 2016 Dec;19(12)703-708

63. Lup K, Trub L, Rosenthal L. Instagram #instasad?: exploring associations among Instagram use, depressive symptoms, negative social comparison, and strangers followed. Cyberpsychol Behav Soc Netw. 2015 May;18(5):247-52

64. Tiggemann M, Zaccardo M. "Exercise to be fit, not skinny": The effect of fitspiration imagery on women's body image. Body Image. 2015 Sep;15:61-7

65. Brown Z, Tiggemann M. Attractive celebrity and peer images on Instagram: Effect on women's mood and mody image. Body Image. 2016 Dec;19:37-43

66. Turner PG, Lefevre CE. Instagram use is linked to increased symptoms of orthorexia nervosa. Eat Weight Disord. 2017 Mar 1 doi: 10.1007/s40519-017-0364-2.

67. Tromholt M. The Facebook experiment: quitting Facebook leads to higher levels of well-being. Cyberpsychol Behav Soc Netw. 2016 Nov;19(11) 661-666

68. Shakya HB, Christakis NA. A new, more rigorous study confirms: the more you use Facebook, the worse you feel. Harvard Business Review. April 10, 2017. https://hbr.org/2017/04/a-new-more-rigorous-study-confirms-the-more-you-use-facebook-the-worse-you-feel accessed 8/9/17

69. Sleigh MJ, Smith AW, Laboe J. Professors' Facebook content affects students' perceptions and expectations. Cyberpsychol Behav Soc Netw. 2013 Jul;16(7):489-96 dio: 10.1089/cyber.2012.0561 Epub 2013 Apr 24

70. Cain J, Scott DR, Akers P. Pharmacy students' Facebook activity and opinions regarding accountability and e-professionalism. Am J Pharm Educ 2009 Oct 1; 73(6): 104

71. Chretien KC, Goldman EF, Beckman L, Kind T. It's your own risk: medical students' perspectives on online professionalism. Acad Med 2010 Oct; 85(10 Suppl): S68-71

72. Finn G, Farner J, Sawdon M. 'You're judged all the time!' Students' views on professionalism: a multicentre study. Med Educ 2010 Aug; 44(8): 814-25

73. Coe JB, Weijs CA, Muise A, Christofides E, Desmarais S. Understanding veterinary students' use of and attitudes toward the social networking site, Facebook, to assist in developing curricula to address online professionalism. J Vet Med Educ 2012 Fall;39(3):297-303

74. Coe JB, Weijs CA, Muise A, Christofides E, Desmarais S. Teaching veterinary professionalism in the Face(book) of change. J Vet Med Educ 2011 Winter; 38(4): 353-9

75. Osman A, Wardle A, Caesar R. Online professionalism and Facebook - falling through the generation gap. Med Teach 2012;34(8)e549-56

76. Appelbaum P. Social media and the internet: new challenges to boundaries in psychiatry. 2013. Annual Meeting of the American Psychiatric Association.

77. Goel V. Facebook tinkers with users' emotions in news feed experiment, stirring outcry. The New York Times. 6/29/14 https://www.nytimes.com/2014/06/30/technology/facebook-tinkers-with-users-emotions-in-news-feed-experiment-stirring-outcry.html accessed 6/16/17

78. Sherman LE, Payton AA, Hernandez LM, Greenfield PM, Dapretto M. The power of the like in adolescence: effects of peer influence on neural and behavioral responses to social media. Psychol Sci 2016 Jul; 27(7):1027-35 doi: 10.1177/0956797616645673

79. Aldridge G, Harden K. Selfie addict took 200 a day - and tried to kill himself when he couldn't take a perfect photo. Mirror, March 23, 2014. http://www.mirror.co.uk/news/real-life-stories/selfie-addict-took-two-hundred-3273819 accessed 5/17/17

80. Twenge J, Campbell WK. The Narcissism Epidemic. New York:Free Press, 2009

81. Quoted in Susan Sontag's On Photography. New York:Anchor Books, 1977

82. Fan R., Zhao J. Chen Y., Xu K. Anger is more influential than joy: sentiment correlation in Weibo. 2013, accessed at http://arxiv.org/pdf/1309.2402v1.pdf

83. Seneca. Anger, Mercy, Revenge. Trans. Kaster RA and Nussbaum MC. University of Chicago Press, 2012

84. Quoted in Epstein, M. The Trauma of Everyday Life. New York: Penguin, 2013 p. 135

85. Williams A. Friends of a certain age: why is it hard to make friends over 30? New York Times July 13, 2012 http://www.nytimes.com/2012/07/15/fashion/the-challenge-of-making-friends-as-an-adult.html?pagewanted=all accessed 8/10/13

86. O'Connor L. San Francisco train passengers too distracted by phones to notice shooter's gun in plain sight. Huffington Post, 10/8/13 http://www.huffingtonpost.com/2013/10/08/san-francisco-train-shooting_n_4066930.html accessed 10/30/13

87. Lanier, J. Who owns the future? New York: Simon and Schuster, 2013 (p. 140)

88. Piesing M. Is the internet God? Alexander Bard's Syntheism paves the way for a new elite. The Guardian, October 7, 2014. https://www.theguardian.com/technology/2014/oct/07/god-internet-alexander-bard-syntheism-new-elite accessed 4/27/17

89. Notes on religion derived from Smith H. The World's Religions. New York: HarperCollins, 1991

90. Nadkarni A, Hofmann SG. Why Do People Use Facebook? Pers Individ Dif. 2012 Feb 1;52(3):243-249. Epub 2011 Nov 26. doi: 10.1016/j.paid.2011.11.007

91. Kim J, Lee JE. The Facebook paths to happiness: effects of the number of Facebook friends and self-presentation on subjective well-being. Cyberpsychology, Behavior and Social Networking. 2011; 6:359–364.

92. Gnambs T, Appel M. Narcissism and social networking behavior: a meta-analysis. J Pers. 2017 Feb 7. doi: 10.1111/jopy.12305

93. Walters NT, Horton R. A diary study of the influence of Facebook use on narcissism among male college students. Computers in Human Behavior 2015 52, 326-330. doi:10.1016/j.chb.2015.05.054

94. Gentile B., Twenge JM, Freeman EC, Campbell WK. The effect of social networking websites on positive self-views: An experimental investigation. Computers in Human Behavior September, 2012;28(5): 1929-1933. doi:10.1016/j.chb.2012.05.012

95. Mehdizadeh S. Self-presentation 2.0: narcissism and self-esteem on Facebook. Cyberpsychol Behav Soc Netw. 2010 Aug;13(4):357-64. doi: 10.1089/cyber.2009.0257

96. Buffardi LE, Campbell WK. Narcissism and social networking web sites. Pers Soc Psychol Bull. 2008 Oct;34(10):1303-14. doi: 10.1177/0146167208320061

97. Malik S, Khan M. Impact of Facebook addiction on narcissistic behavior and self-esteem among students. J Pak Med Assoc. 2015 Mar;65(3):260-3.

98. Brailovskaia J, Margraf J. Comparing Facebook users and Facebook non-users: relationship between personality traits and mental health variables - an exploratory study. PLoS One. 2016 Dec 1;11(12):e0166999. doi: 10.1371/journal.pone.0166999

99. Rouis S. Impact of cognitive absorption on Facebook on students' achievement. Cyberpsychol Behav Soc Netw 2012 Jun; 15(6):296-303

100. Pantic I, Damjanovic A, Todorovic J, Topalovic D, Bojovic-Jovic D, Ristic S, et al. Association between online social networking and depression in high school students: behavioral physiology viewpoint. Psychiatr Danub. 2012; 24(1): 90–3.

101. Glum J. Millennials selfies: young adults will take more than 25,000 pictures of themselves during their lifetimes. Int Bus Times 9/22/15 http://www.ibtimes.com/millennials-selfies-young-adults-will-take-more-25000-pictures-themselves-during-2108417 accessed 6/3/17

102. Brandt R. Google divulges numbers at I/O: 20 billion texts, 93 million selfies and more Silicon Valley Business Journal 6/25/14 http://www.

bizjournals.com/sanjose/news/2014/06/25/google-divulges-numbers-at-i-o-20-billion-texts-93.html accessed 6/3/17

103. Krämer NC, Feurstein M, Kluck JP, Meier Y, Rother M, Winter S. (2017) Beware of selfies: the impact of photo type on impression formation based on social networking profiles. *Front Psychol.* 2017 Feb 16;8:188. doi: 10.3389/fpsyg.2017.00188

104. Wang SS, Moon S-I, Kwon KH, Evans CA, Stefanone MA. Face off: implications of visual cues on initiating friendship on Facebook. Computers in Human Behavior. 2010; 26:226–234

105. Kapidzic S. Narcissism as a predictor of motivations behind Facebook profile picture selection. Cyberpsychol Behav Soc Netw. 2013 Jan;16(1):14-9. doi: 10.1089/cyber.2012.0143.

106. Fan R, Zhao J, Chen Y, Xu K. Anger is more influential than joy: sentiment correlation in Weibo. 2013, accessed at http://arxiv.org/pdf/1309.2402v1.pdf

107. https://xkcd.com/386/ accessed 5/25/16

108. As I think Wes "Scoop" Nisker put it in *The Big Bang, the Buddha and the Baby Boom: The Spiritual Experiments of My Generation.* San Francisco: HarperSanFrancisco, 2003

109. Trust trends graph available at http://www.pewsocialtrends. org/2014/03/07/millennials-in-adulthood/sdt-next-america-03-07-2014-0-05/ accessed 9/14/16

110. The Pew Center. Millennials in Adulthood. http://www.pewsocial-trends.org/2014/03/07/millennials-in-adulthood/ accessed 9/14/16

111. Stossel S. What makes us happy, revisited. The Atlantic, May, 2013. https://www.theatlantic.com/magazine/archive/2013/05/thanks-mom/309287/ accessed incessantly since that date!

About the Author

Ravi Chandra is a psychiatrist and writer in San Francisco, California. He graduated from Brown University with Honors in Biology, and got his M.D. at Stanford University School of Medicine before completing a psychiatry residency at the University of California, San Francisco. He is a Distinguished Fellow of the American Psychiatric Association. He has a fondness for poetry and puns, resulting in occasional side gigs in slam, performance poetry and the indulgent groans of friends. The editors of the award-winning South Asian American Poetry anthology *Indivisible* created a monster when they decided to include his work. This poetry beast caught the eye of other scheming dreamers, and together they birthed the 2011 jazz and poetry collaboration *Fox and Jewel*, taking aim at redevelopment concerns in Japantown, San Francisco. This led to the publication of his first book of poetry, *a fox peeks out: poems*, which actually won an Honorable Mention at the San Francisco Book Festival. He's happy that some folks enjoy his writing and humor, and sends a big shout-out to poets and artists everywhere. His collection of essays on Asian American relational anger, misogyny and domestic violence is available for free download. His blogs for Psychology Today (The Pacific Heart) and the Center for Asian American Media (Memoirs of a Superfan) are available along with other writings at www. RaviChandraMD.com. *Facebuddha: Transcendence in the Age of Social Networks* is his first full-length nonfiction work, and is his attempt to turn the zig-zag of consciousness into a cha-cha-chá. To support the possibility of future writing projects, please sign up for an occasional newsletter at www.facebuddha.co.

Twitter: @going2peace
And yes, there are pages for this book and
Ravi Chandra's other writing on Facebook!

CPSIA information can be obtained
at www.ICGtesting.com
Printed in the USA
BVOW08*1601101017
497186BV00001B/1/P